RAISING HELL

BACKSTAGE TALES FROM THE LIVES OF METAL LEGENDS

Into the Fiery Pits of Chaos . . .

JON WIEDERHORN

DIVERSION
BOOKS

For more information, email info@diversionbooks.com

Diversion Books
A division of Diversion Publishing Corp.
443 Park Avenue South, suite 1004
New York, NY 10016
www.diversionbooks.com

Book design by Neuwirth & Associates

First Diversion Books edition January 2020
Hardcover ISBN: 978-1-63576-649-3
eBook ISBN: 978-1-63576-648-6

Printed in The United States of America

1 3 5 7 9 10 8 6 4 2

Library of Congress cataloging-in-publication data is available on file.

In memory of Nancy Irene Wiederhorn, Jean Cecile Wiederhorn, and Jeremy Kaplan.

Also, farewell to all the metal crusaders who passed while *Raising Hell* was being written: Lemmy Kilmister (Motörhead), "Fast" Eddie Clarke (Motörhead), "Philthy Animal" Taylor (Motörhead), Larry Wallis (Motörhead), Vinnie Paul (Pantera, Hellyeah), Chester Bennington (Linkin Park), Chris Cornell (Soundgarden), Malcolm Young (AC/DC), Scott "Daisy Berkowitz" Putesky (Marilyn Manson), Terry Marostega (Razor), Bruce Corbitt (Rigor Mortis), Warrel Dane (Nevermore), Martin E. Ain (Celtic Frost), Chuck Mosley (Faith No More), Matt Holt (Nothingface), Paul O'Neill (Trans-Siberian Orchestra), Jill Janus (Huntress), Oli Herbert (All That Remains), Todd Youth (Agnostic Front), Morten Stützer (Artillery), Aaron Zimpel (Anvil Chorus,), Perry McAuley (Graveyard Rodeo), Richard Brunelle (Morbid Angel), Shaun Boilanger (Terror), Jeff Martinek (Sacred Reich), Nigel Benjamin (London), Lizzie Grey (London), Ralph Santolla (Deicide), Joey Alves (Y&T), Josh Martin (Anal Cunt), Caleb Scofield (Cave In), Frank "Killjoy" Pucci (Necrophagia), Dave Holland (Judas Priest), Nature Ganganbaigal (Tengger Cavalry), Paul Kosanovich (Surgical Steel), Carsten Otterbach (Morgoth), Bernie Tormé (Ozzy Osbourne), Richard Bateman (Nasty Savage), Carlos Denogean (Weedeater), Kyle Pavone (We Came as Romans), Paul Whaley (Blue Cheer), Dave Castillo (Deceased), Willy "Lange" Langenhuizen (Lååz Rockit), Randy Rampage (Annihilator), Glen Telford (Skinlab), Scott Willey (Vital Remains), Eric Eycke (Corrosion of Conformity), Mark Shelton (Manilla Road), Brett Hoffmann (Malevolent Creation), Bill Tolley (Internal Bleeding), Mick Burke (Mortal Sin), Paul Raymond (UFO), Jason Luttrell (Primer 55), Nic Ritter (Warbringer), Guillermo Calero (Wormed), Pat Torpey (Mr. Big), Gabriel "Negru" Mafa (Negură Bunget), Ted McKenna (Michael Schenker), Johnny Hansen (Vulcano), Geoff Nicholls (Black Sabbath), and Trish Doan (Kittie).

Raising Hell also raises the metal flag to anyone we accidentally overlooked. Rock in peace.

This product could cause drowsiness, dizziness, nausea, or agitation and may increase the effects of drugs and alcohol. If affected, do not drive or operate heavy machinery. If symptoms persist, proceed directly to the nearest mosh pit.

CONTENTS

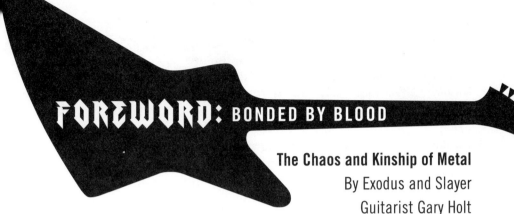

FOREWORD: BONDED BY BLOOD

The Chaos and Kinship of Metal
By Exodus and Slayer
Guitarist Gary Holt

I was Kirk Hammett's roadie, but not for Metallica. Before Kirk joined what would become one of the world's most popular metal bands, he was part of the Bay Area thrash band Exodus. Back then, I didn't even play guitar. Then, Kirk showed me some simple chords, and from there I took to the instrument like a duck to water.

The guitar just made sense to me—how it's structured, how the scales work, how the notes repeat themselves in different octaves, how harmonies went . . . I just got it. Six months after I picked up the instrument, Exodus's second guitarist, Tim Agnello, was gone and I was in the band. Within a year, I was shredding, and within 18 months I was playing really good solos. By the time Kirk left in 1983, I had been in the band for nearly two years and I was ready to take over as the main songwriter.

My first time ever playing with Exodus was for about 300 fans at the Montara Bay Community Center on a New Year's Eve when I was seventeen-and-a-half. Five minutes before showtime, the place was packed, and I was nervous as shit. But seconds after stepping on stage, I felt like I'd found my calling. From that day forward, I knew that's what I had to do with my life—not what I wanted to do, what I *had* to do.

There's no question that vocalist Paul Baloff was a crucial part of Exodus in the beginning. He was a fucking animal, a maniac—the very definition of a thrash metal lunatic. Kirk was the first one to meet him and invited him to band rehearsal at my parents' garage. For some reason, the rest of Exodus canceled but no one got in touch with Paul to tell him we weren't getting together, so he showed up.

"Sorry dude, there's nothing happening," I said.

So we went to his car and parked in a lot at the end of the street next to mine and did some cocaine, smoked a bunch of weed, and listened to metal for two or three hours. It was fuckin' killer. That was the first of many memorable times with Paul.

After Kirk joined Metallica, I started writing most of Exodus's new songs, which were way faster, heavier, and more violent than the earlier stuff. Paul Baloff was the perfect frontman for songs like "A Lesson in Violence," "Bonded by Blood," and "Strike of the Beast." He walked it like he screamed it. When Paul said, "Posers must die!" he meant it. Posers at the show got nervous because he would eyeball them, and we'd be thinking: "That's who Paul's talking about. Let's get him!"

He was the real deal, and he bled for this shit—literally—and always did until the day he died. Paul had a penchant for destruction. A lot of guys in the past would destroy shit, but it was usually rock stars smashing something because they knew someone would pay for it. Paul smashed shit because he liked it.

In high school, I was a stoner outcast. With Exodus, I was part of a little comedy troupe of merry pranksters. Along with our friends, we went by the name The Slay Team, and when we were drinking and doing drugs—which was all the time—we were out of control. Nothing was sacred, and no one that got in our way was spared. We spoke our own language. The funniest shit to us, which had us laughing our asses off, made no sense to other people whatsoever. We didn't care if anyone else thought we were humorous. We didn't care if anyone wanted to hang out with us or run away in fear.

Some of the shit we pulled was nuts. The destruction was massive. We broke everything we could get away with, and once at a party I dropped a plugged-in curling iron into a big fish tank to try to kill the fish. It didn't work, so Andy "Airborne" Anderson, another Slay Team member, handed me a sharpened pencil.

"Kill a fish, Gary!" he said.

A fish came up to the top of the water like it wanted to commit suicide. I stabbed it in the head. That didn't kill it. However, the ammonia I poured into the tank did the job on that fish and all his friends.

If you look at the back of our first album, *Bonded by Blood*, we thank "Dartboard Dan and knives, scissors and deadly-hot pokers" because we used all those tools against poor Dan, who, for some reason, was just one of our targets. We'd have this kid cowering in the corner of the room, and we'd wave a heated-up fireplace poker at him. Baloff would throw steak knives at the dude. We had a blast.

Of course, it was all fun and games unless you were the person being targeted. I can look back now, feel bad for Dan, and think, "No, it's not funny killing a fish," but it sure seemed funny then. And, obviously, it's not cool or fun to be helplessly addicted to meth, something that also happened.

Actually, there's a misconception that Exodus was heavily into meth from the start. We'd get a quarter gram, but that would be for all five guys in the band and it was fuel for the alcohol that allowed us to drink longer and harder. It put some extra legs under our feet. But meth became a big problem much later in our career. In 1986, five years after he joined, we had to fire Paul for being too much of a maniac. I'm glad we brought him back in 1997, but by that point, most of us were as methed up as he ever was and we had no business passing judgment on anyone.

I don't regret anything, but you know what? I'm lucky to have survived my wildest years. Unfortunately, overdoses, fatal accidents, and fluke misfortunes are all part of the story for a lot of metalheads that fully lived the lifestyle. I buried Paul in 2002, and I've lost more friends than almost anybody I know.

About two years after Paul died I got clean. Now, I'm vegan and totally conscious of what I put in my body. But even though I'm no longer a crazed party animal, I still like to reminisce over the outrageous, crazed antics of my youth. Some of my favorites are captured in the pages of this book. But while I've got a bunch of totally metal tales, I'm just one fuckin' dude. All the band guys and girls I've ever met also have great stories. In *Raising Hell*, Jon Wiederhorn captures the energy, excitement, and lunacy of metal culture, not just from thrash musicians, but also from a wide variety of artists in other genres, including classic metal, melodic metal, death metal, and even those crazy church-burning fucks that play black metal.

Nowadays, when I wake up after playing a wild show with Exodus or Slayer, I'm never hungover. I'm clear-headed, and I have lucid memories of what happened the evening before—and I'm not jonesing for anything. I'm happy to have passed the "crazy" torch to the younger generation of metal musicians, and now it's just fun for me to read about how a lot of them try to live in the cloven hooves of their heroes. I wish them nothing but the best.

PREFACE: WHY RAISE HELL?

There are plenty of good, nearly academic books about the history of metal. *Raising Hell* is not one of them.

Within its 17 chapters are tons of anecdotes, observations, and laments that are hellishly metal in content and spirit. Over the years spent creating *Raising Hell*, dozens of artists were interviewed exclusively for the book, including members of historically significant bands such as Black Sabbath, Judas Priest, Twisted Sister, Quiet Riot, Warrant, King Diamond, Slaughter, Slayer, Exodus, Megadeth, Anthrax, Testament, Death Angel, Pantera, Sepultura, Prong, Helmet, Morbid Angel, Entombed, Watain, Saint Vitus, Deicide, Dethklok, Cradle of Filth, Behemoth, Slipknot, The Sword, DevilDriver, Disturbed, Monster Magnet, Trivium, Limp Bizkit, Fear Factory, Biohazard, Kittie, Stryper, Ministry, Halestorm, Avenged Sevenfold, and Lamb of God.

In addition, *Raising Hell* includes an abundance of voices from the underground. Members of Charred Walls of the Damned, Pentagram, Deceased, Raven, Eyehategod, Misery Index, Profanatica, Gorgoroth, Goatwhore, The Dillinger Escape Plan, Crowbar, Possessed, Atheist, Municipal Waste, Every Time I Die, Throwdown, and others play as much of a role as the more commercially successful bands in exposing the sights, sounds, and smells—to paraphrase the film *This Is Spinal Tap*—of metal. And while the marquee acts vividly recount some bizarre, terrifying, and hysterical experiences they have had navigating the turbulent oceans of sex, drugs, and rock n' roll, in many cases, the lesser-known artists are the ones that spin the more visceral and insightful tales about touring in a barely running van with no heat in the middle of winter, living on gas money, stealing instruments to form a band, banging frightening groupies, puking in a sleeping bag by the side of the road, throwing down against small-town rednecks, getting harassed by the police, finding solace in the grip of everything from alcohol to heroin, fighting the most adversarial audience, and sometimes losing hard to the whims of nature and society.

In its entirety—or even in chunks no longer than a death metal chorus—this book explores the metal subculture and lifestyle and, in its best moments, conjures the uncertainty, instability, excitement, and mind-altering mania of being on the road with the same people week after week, month after month, and thriving on the thrill of creative expression and the ecstasy of performing. On that level, *Raising Hell* could be considered a bit of a sociological and philosophical treatise about a microcosm of music that's as denigrated by critics as it is celebrated by its fans. It is a subgenre colored by thievery, vandalism, hedonism, the occult, stage mishaps, mosh pit atrocities, and general insanity.

But wait! Before anyone starts to think that this book is gonna be all intellectual and shit, take note: *Raising Hell: Backstage Tales from the Lives of Metal Legends* is no *Sapiens: A Brief History of Humankind*.

It's more like a gripping encyclopedia of true crime that's even messier but contains far fewer violent offenses and practically nothing about serial killers.

Like the book I co-authored in 2013, *Louder Than Hell: The Definitive Oral History of Metal*, this tome we're calling *Raising Hell* (which may sound like a sequel to *LTH*, but was crafted from entirely different cuts of spandex and leather) is structured as an oral history and, this introduction aside, consists almost solely of quotes from musicians from across a wide range of metal subgenres. Instead of being constructed chronologically and unraveling in a mostly linear path that starts with Black Sabbath and ends with, maybe, Full of Hell, *Raising Hell* focuses almost entirely on different outrageous aspects of the metal lifestyle.

Every chapter, save Chapter 11, "That Was Spiñal Tap," is named after a recognizable metal song or album (anyone smell a Spotify playlist?) and, following with a couple factoids about the tune, the material within addresses ideas implied by the song titles: "Trashed" consists of wild drinking stories, "Welcome to Hell" is about all things demonic and paranormal, "Raining Blood" contains tales of performance injuries and other bloodshed, "Fighting the World" illustrates the endless physical and psychological battles fought by musicians both impoverished and obscenely wealthy, "Metal on Metal" features musicians talking about their greatest inspirations. And the list goes on . . .

I took this approach mostly to keep the book light and entertaining, but also 'cause chapters about stuff like promotional appearances, recording techniques, soundchecks, and playing videogames in a tour bus would make *Raising Hell* about as easy to get through as *Moby Dick* (spoiler alert: the whale wins). My aim was not to demonize anyone or condemn certain life decisions. At the same time, I didn't want to glorify irresponsible, illegal, or dangerous behavior. Many of the more captivating stories are best viewed as cautionary tales. If there were a slogan for the book it would be: "Don't try this at home."

Along with the hundreds of amazing and amusing stories that could only happen in—to quote Spīnal Tap again, the "topsy-turvy world of heavy rock" (For more Tap, check out the chapter "That Was Spīnal Tap," which features the most Tap-like moments metal acts have experienced over the years)—there are numerous harrowing and horrific tales. No one could laugh at Baroness frontman John Baizley's recollection of the bus crash that nearly took his life, Megadeth bassist Dave Ellefson's incapacitating heroin addiction, or stabbings in Biohazard mosh pits. For better or worse, pain, dependency, depression, violence, and misfortune are often byproducts of the metal lifestyle which, itself, is rooted in the counter-culture and dedicated toward extremism and destroying conventional notions of what is acceptable when it comes to material that is thematically frightening, lyrically offensive, and musically valid. Many of the most fascinating figures in the genre—including Gary Holt (Exodus, Slayer), Philip Anselmo (Pantera, Down, Superjoint Ritual), Corey Taylor (Slipknot), and Al Jourgensen (Ministry)—have stories riddled with tragedy and triumph. And each has a gripping tale or two about escaping unstable and frustrating environments and becoming rebellious, self-destructive, and celebrated metal heroes who eventually got clean and sober and are now, in general, less menacing to society. Some might say I'm making excuses for a metal book that isn't really about metal music. I fully expect a certain amount of backlash from critics and naysayers that think *Raising Hell* is salacious, exploitative, and a glorification of dangerous, self-destructive behavior. To them I say, "Yeah?? And?"

But that's not my purpose here.

If readers piss themselves with laughter, shake their heads in disbelief, or gasp with horror at some of the unbelievable stories in *Raising Hell*, I will have achieved my goal.

Since I was a young teenager reading great rock biographies including *Hammer of the Gods* by Stephen Davis and *No One Here Gets Out Alive* by Jerry Hopkins and Danny Sugerman, and enjoying movies such as *The Kids Are Alright, The Song Remains the Same, Pink Floyd—The Wall,* and *AC/DC: Let There Be Rock,* I was entranced by rock and roll antics, the wilder, the better. At the time, I was too young to party and in college, my hedonistic revelry was pretty tame compared to that or my metal peers. Although I did get kicked off my college radio station for drunkenly calling random students and giving away concert tickets to metal shows when I wasn't even on the air. It didn't help my case that I told the gleeful ticket winners that I was the program director of the station. Then, I got even drunker, called the radio station program director and told him I was him and he had just won concert tickets . . . and he recognized my voice. Oops. Now, I'm a semi-responsible adult with a wife, two kids, and a house in the suburbs of New fuckin' Jersey. My home even has a white picket fence and there's a feisty little Shi Tzu ruling the roost, making the Norman Rockwell portrait of The American Dream complete. Call me a poseur, I can take it. I still fuckin' love metal and I thrive on the extremism of the genre. I'm the only person in the neighborhood that can be regularly spotted in an Entombed, Coffinworm, or equally "metal" shirt, and that includes pimply-faced teenagers my kids' age that appear to look through me as if I'm one of the apparitions in the "Welcome to Hell" chapter—just another "dad" floating around the periphery of a sea of adolescent angst. If they harbor a hidden love for metal, I stand corrected and I hope—with their parents' permission (if they're under 15)—they'll pick up *Raising Hell* and enjoy it as the roller coaster ride through the metal carnival it was meant to be.

In the decades I have followed metal (which was widely called "heavy metal" when I was a young-un), I have watched the genre transform from one that showcases steady, crunchy guitar riffs, flailing solos, and near-operatic vocals to a music form that largely values speed and aggression above even hooks. The vocals are mostly growled or shrieked and are best enjoyed with online lyrics (and to think, metal fans used to hope they were lucky enough that bands would include lyrics in their CD booklets and album sleeves). I'm not strictly old-school; I enjoy listening to Goatpenis as well as Iron Maiden. But there's a definite divide between '80s metal and the stuff newer bands are churning out today. As a result, thrash groups that were considered insanely fast and brutal in the '80s (Metallica, Slayer, Exodus) now sound almost tame next to many death and black metal bands. And while a lot of traditional metal of the '70s and early '80s, including Black Sabbath and Judas Priest, has aged well musically, most of it has been stripped of the rage and rebellion that once heightened its appeal. There was a time in 1982 when Iron Maiden's "Number of the Beast" caused cautious listeners to brand the band as Satanists and burn their records. Four years later, the far more nefarious-sounding Slayer were denounced for writing "Angel of Death," a song about Nazi butcher Josef Mengele and were promptly abandoned by their distributor, Columbia Records (Geffen picked up the album, which came out on Def Jam). Today, practically no one east or west of the

Bible Belt is afraid of Iron Maiden, or even Slayer, for that matter. And songs by the once-dreaded Black Sabbath and their "Prince of Darkness" vocalist Ozzy Osbourne can regularly be heard on classic rock radio. Who says the more things change, the more they stay the same?

With *Raising Hell*, I have tried to address some of the changes from the routines of musicians from decade to decade. For example, traveling artists once lacked cell phones and had to rely on torn, beer-stained maps, and later, crinkled MapQuest printouts to get from venue to venue. Back then, musicians didn't get hassled at the border as much, but sometimes went to jail for getting busted with even the smallest amounts of weed. When I was weeding out which anecdotes to include and which to scrap, I decided not to write about most of the time-tested metal lore. There's nothing in *Raising Hell* about Ozzy Osbourne removing the heads of small creatures with his teeth, pissing on the Alamo, or attempting to strangle his wife. You won't find details about the Metallica bus crash that killed bassist Cliff Burton or Mötley Crüe frontman Vince Neil's beer run that turned into a manslaughter charge. No one praises Judas Priest frontman Rob Halford for being the first major metal figure to come out as a gay man, and there's no discussion about the tragic murder of Pantera guitarist Dimebag Darrell or the death of Ronnie James Dio. Also, stories about Lamb of God frontman Randy Blythe's arrest and trial in Prague and the Norwegian black metal community's propensity for burning churches and killing one another have been left out in favor of newer, lesser-known metal tales. Those who would rather read details and quotes about the above can seek out the first book I dedicated years of my life to, *Louder Than Hell: The Definitive Oral History of Metal*; they're all in there. But I encourage you to continue this book here with the knowledge that you won't have to read stories you've already heard or hear from artists that have done so many interviews over the past forty years that they've become restrained and reserved when it comes to the more decadent elements of metal. Besides, many of them have already written their own books, so why not focus on the newer guys?

Over the four decades I have followed metal, I have become somewhat of a historian on the subject. I have learned about how a million bands formed, and I've gained insight into the correlation between metal and various schools of academic thought—including philosophy, sociology, and theology. I have observed the gradual emergence of a multitude of metal subgenres and recognized the key players in each. I have been exposed to production and playing techniques, learned about gear, and taken a toe-dip into contracts, the difference between mechanical and performance royalties, and the way metal acts are acquired, marketed, and promoted. I've also discovered how hard it is to survive as a musician and how many bands get screwed over by managers, agents, promoters, and labels. But aside from the music itself, what remains most exciting to me is the irresponsible, insane, and endlessly entertaining behavior of headbangers from one generation to the next, which is why *Raising Hell* contains so many war stories about danger, volatility, and jaw-dropping chaos.

If that seems exploitative, consider this: There's a reason why the Mötley Crüe biography *The Dirt* was a bestseller and was eventually turned into a full-length motion picture even though it barely addressed the band's albums or their process of making music. The same can be said for many metal memoirs, magazine articles, and Website posts. Today's readers still hunger for lists about the most dangerous bands, the most violent incidents, the most drugged-up artists, and the most controversial exploits. And web traffic for such pieces proves that more than 50 years after The Who's Keith Moon drove a Rolls Royce into a swimming pool and members of Led Zeppelin allegedly used a mud shark as a sex toy, metal fans still want to know about wild musicians that got far too drunk, sometimes overdosed, broke laws, smashed jaws, engaged in wild sex romps, and blew shit up.

A final word: Nothing in *Raising Hell* endorses racism, homophobia, misogyny, or prejudice of any kind. Even the most bizarre sexual shenanigans included are testified as having been consensual. And what's more, the ultimate lessons from the abundant tales of addiction are that excessive partying can break up bands and, in the end, lead down one of two paths: either the user gets clean or he or she doesn't and dies.

If this sprawling preface seems heavy-handed or overly academic, feel free to skip directly to the chapter of your choice and read about drunken antics, vomiting, paranormal experiences, fights, pranks, horrible stage accidents, hostile crowds, gangbangs, bus crashes, and more. And if some of you are still concerned that addressing some of the wildest activity in metal is irresponsible, lighten the fuck up. This is a book about metal, not neuroscience.

Dig in, and enjoy the sights, sounds, and smells of some of the wittiest and wildest musicians who ever played a stage. Or to loosely paraphrase Kiss: "You wanted the best; you got the best. The hottest book in the land, *Raising Hell!*"

Horns up!

CHAPTER 1: BREAKING THE LAW

Cops, Border Patrol & Pesky Airline Stewardesses

One of Judas Priest's most enduring songs, "Breaking the Law" reached #12 on the British singles chart and remains a staple of the band's live set. Priest included the tune on their 1980 record *British Steel*, and, along with the radio single "Living After Midnight" (which also hit #12), "Breaking the Law" helped catapult Judas Priest from a club act to arena rockers.

Considering their reputation for rebellious acts and inebriated antics, a surprising number of metal musicians have never done any time behind bars. A far greater percentage, however, have spent at least a day or so in the pokey for a variety of offenses, including being drunk and disorderly, assault, and drug possession. Then, there are all the long hairs that have been harassed by cops or interrogated and searched at the border—all of which makes for some pretty entertaining stories, and all at their expense.

COREY TAYLOR
Slipknot, Stone Sour

I had been throwing shot glasses at people all night at The Rainbow. They were on the verge of banning me from the club and I had no idea I was so fucking out of it.

So we left, and I was running down the street with my friend. We get to the corner of Sunset and Larrabee, right across the street from the fucking Viper Room. And we see a big window of this beeper shop, and he goes, "Man, I bet you could put your foot right through that."

So I said, "Yeah?" and then I kicked it to pieces.

I swear to god, dude, it was slo-mo.

I turned around. There was a cop sitting at the stoplight. And I just wandered over and put my hands on the fucking hood. I am not trying to run from L.A. cops, no fucking way. And I'm out of my mind. I've got black makeup running down me, my hair's fucked up. I'm barely dressed. I am fucking 200 pounds and I'm not giving a shit about anybody. So they cuff me and sit me in front of the Viper Room and all these Hollywood people are coming up and laughing at me, so I started spitting at them 'cause I don't give a fuck.

They took me to the station, and I was so out of it, all I wanted to do was piss. So I kept making them take me to the bathroom, which was delaying my fingerprinting process. In that time, my buddy manages to work out a deal with the owners of the shop that if I could pay for the window, they won't press charges.

So, I'm just about to be processed. I'm on the verge of LA County fucking jail and they get the call, help me put my clothes back on—because I was getting in the orange suit. I was going. They take me back down, uncuff me. I stumble across Sunset with a fistful of gnarly money and I drunkenly slur an apology. I go back home and pass out and I wake up and go, "Oh my god, what the fuck just happened."

RANDY BLYTHE
Lamb of God

The first time I ever went to prison in Richmond I had bright blue hair because I had gone to an Eyehategod concert and had to take a leak, so I ducked out back of the club and took a piss. And [there was] an undercover peepee patrol cop.

The guy was a cop the other cops didn't like. So they made him cruise around in this stupid Honda 250 motorcycle pretending he was a fucking Hells Angel or something and he was on piss patrol. So I'm taking a leak in this alley, and this cop was a complete fucking idiot. I'm standing there in shorts and a short sleeve t-shirt. It's summertime. He asks my name; I give it to him. Then he goes, "Do you have any tattoos?"

They're on my arms. You can see them.

I'm like, "No."

And he goes, "Okay."

So I figure, okay, I gotta go to court but it'll be no big deal. I'll pay fifty dollars or something. So I go to court and I wind up going before this motherfucker of a judge. May he rot in hell.

I didn't dress up for court because I figured it's a fifty-dollar fine. So I walk in there and he took one look at me and was not pleased. And he said, "Sixty-five community service hours for taking a leak."

"Can't I just pay a fine?" I asked.

"Nope, I think you need to learn a lesson, son," he said.

I wound up not doing them and a cop arrested me during a Critical Mass, it's a bicycle ride thing. So I went to jail for not doing community service and I still had blue hair. I walked into jail and all the dudes sitting there were like, "Holy fuck."

I remember this one big dude looking at me and he was like, "You're one of those motherfuckers who killed the native's neighbors, aren't you? You crazy looking."

And I was like, "Yeah, that's right." Nobody bothered me. I was there for a couple evenings.

MAX CAVALERA
Soulfly, Cavalera Conspiracy, ex-Sepultura

My wife and I went to see a Rage Against the Machine concert in Phoenix between the time Sepultura did *Chaos A.D.* and *Roots*. As we were leaving the show to go home, a jeep full of jocks started to give us shit. I screamed, "Fuck you!" and they came back with guns and shot at us.

I got really freaked out because my wife was pregnant, so I was trying to protect her. The police heard the shots and showed up. They grabbed my passport, which was Brazilian, and they said, "We're gonna deport you, motherfucker."

I explained that these guys had shot at us, but it was like talking to a wall. The cops ignored me and came up with their own story. They blamed us and let these asshole jocks go. We spent eighteen hours in jail and the whole time I was thinking, "When I get out of here, I'm going to write so much hateful shit!"

GARY HOLT
Exodus, Slayer

After some of the guys in Exodus stole this gear from another band, our former guitarist Tim Agnello—who I replaced—ratted them out because he was so mad he was out of the band. There was bitter hatred there. The heist happened between the time Tim left in a rage and I got hired. So, I wasn't a member yet at the time of theft. Back then, I let them rehearse in my garage, so they stored the stolen equipment there. After they got caught, I got dragged out of a local show at Alvarado Park. My father showed up with a policeman, and my first thought was that someone in the family died. The cop says, "You gotta come with me."

He took me down to the Richmond Police Department. They asked if I helped steal from this band and I said I didn't know anything about any stolen equipment, and I convinced them I was an innocent pawn in this whole chess game—until I got home and transported the remaining gear out of the garage and went and hid it. Someone saw me doing that, which cemented my guilt.

I was a juvenile and so was [Exodus drummer] Tom Hunting so we had to do work detail. They had us shoveling roads to help clear these giant floods and mudslides. It was heavy fuckin' labor and it fucking sucked. I was seventeen.

[Our lead guitarist] Kirk [Hammett] (who later joined Metallica), [bassist] Geoff Andrews, and our friend Mark were all adults, so they had to spend a lot of money to get off, but they didn't do a day of time. I missed a day of work duty, and if you miss a day you have to go straight to Juvenile Hall. I had to do a night in there. That was the only night in my life that I spent behind bars, but that was enough for me. It sucked. Being behind a locked door is no fun. I've just never liked being confined in any way. And by the time I was locked up, I *was* in the band. We were playing a party the very next day, so I got picked up from Juvenile Hall and went straight to the party and partied very hard. So I guess the story sort of had a happy ending.

BILLY GRAZIADEI
Biohazard

I was in Montreal and I was with this punk rock girl I was friends with. Suddenly, some cops pulled us over and started talking to us in French. I said, "I'm American. I only speak English."

They wouldn't speak English to me.

I said, "Dude, ask me in English. If you got a beef with me speak to me in my language. I know you speak English. I don't know French."

They refused. So I walked away.

They pulled up on the curb and arrested me and my homegirl. I had no idea what they were arresting us for. My friend knew a little French and she said, "Billy, I heard the word battery."

I thought, "Fuck, maybe I got in a fight at a show here once and something happened."

The police brought us into the station. They wouldn't let us talk. They took all my shit. I emptied my pockets. They took my belt and my shoelaces out of my Docs. I remember thinking, "That's weird. That's what they do to people on suicide watch."

They put me in a cell by myself. No one else was there and I sat there for an hour. I was hoping for the best and I thought, "Okay, I'll have a story to tell my homeboys."

Finally, some of our crew guys came in and they asked me, "Do you know what you're arrested for?"

"The dude said something about assault and battery," I said,

"Yeah, but it's worse than that," he said.

"What do you mean it's worse than that?"

"You've been arrested for attempted murder."

I was like, "What the fuck? This is a case of mistaken identity!"

The police asked me all these questions and interrogated me while I was in the cell. They asked me where I was the night in question.

"I was back in New York," I said.

"Can you prove you were there?"

"Yeah, call my job."

The thing is, back then, once or so a week I would leave early or come in late and ask my buddy to punch me out or punch me in. So I was sitting there in this cell praying, "Please let this not be one of those times when I forgot to punch in or punch out." I was shitting my pants for two or three hours and then they came back and let me go. They said I checked out.

Then they told me [that this was about an] attempted murder and my friend and I fit the description of this couple who abducted a young girl and kidnapped her and raped her and cut her throat. The girl lived, but man, that shook my soul. I'm a dad so what that little girl went through hit me right in the heart.

DINO CAZARES
Fear Factory, Divine Heresy, Brujeria, Asesino

In 2008, during the Divine Heresy tour, we had just played Portland, Oregon, and we were going to play Beaverton, Oregon. We had to change a tire, so we pulled into this tire place. And on the way out, I realized, "Oh my God, we forgot the receipt."

So I had to jump out of the van, go back into the tire place, and ask the lady, "Can I get a receipt?"

She gasped and looked at me and I could tell she was totally terrified. I was like, "What the fuck? I'm a Mexican guy in Oregon, but I'm not that scary."

She wouldn't give me a receipt. She said something to another guy and then she ran into one of the offices. The guy came over and brought me the receipt and I went back into the van kind of annoyed. But I was like, "Whatever."

About two miles down the road we got pulled over. The cops spoke over a megaphone and told the driver, who was a friend of mine, to get out of the van and walk backward. Then they said, "Get on your hands and knees." He got down. They handcuffed him and put him in the back of the cop car and asked him, "Who is that Mexican guy in the van?"

"That's Dino Cazares. He's in a band and they're on tour," my friend said.

"Has he ever been in prison? Is he a gang member? Does he have any weapons on him?"

Then the cop got back on the loudspeaker: "Dino Cazares, get out of the van and keep your hands in the air!"

I got out and they made me get on my hands and knees. They searched me, patted me down, and asked me all these questions. I kept saying, "Why are you asking me these questions? What's going on?"

"There's a Mexican guy that fits your description that has killed four people in Oregon," said one cop. "You fit that description and the woman at the tire shop thought you were the guy so she called us."

They took my wallet and my ID and realized I wasn't the guy. We got let go, but it was pretty scary.

HEIDI SHEPHERD
Butcher Babies

We were on tour with Otep in 2016 and we woke up one morning in Lexington, Kentucky, to find the transmission had gone out in our bus. We were trying to rent a van to get to the next show in Knoxville, Tennessee, and nothing was available anywhere. It was Labor Day weekend and the only thing available was a U-Haul truck. So we rented a U-Haul to put all of our gear in and our sleeping stuff and we camped out in the back of a U-Haul truck, in the box of the truck, for four days.

It was the heat of summer in the South. We were in Alabama and [vocalist] Carla [Harvey] and I were sleeping in the back and we both woke up and had to pee. So we called to the guys in the front to pull over. We jumped out, peed by the side of the road, got back in, and started driving. A couple miles down the road a bunch of cops pulled us over. A cop walked up to Jason [Klein], our old bass player who was driving the U-Haul, and said, "So, what you got back there?"

"Equipment, a couple things," Jason said.

"Anything else?" asked the cop.

"Nope," lied Jason.

"Well, why don't I go back there and take a look," the cop said.

I thought we were definitely going to jail.

The back popped up and the cop goes, "Aha, equipment, huh?"

Five or six cop cars came up out of nowhere and surrounded us. As it turned out, someone from down the freeway [had seen me and Carla peeing] and called the police and said Carla and I were two little girls that had been kidnapped and were in the back of this U-Haul. They threatened to take Jason to jail because he lied. We told them we were a band and we were on tour, which was the truth.

"Sure you are," said one of the cops. "You've already lied once."

We figured, "Okay, we're fucked," but it was right in the middle of Hurricane Sandy and all of a sudden there was a flash flood rainstorm. We were about four miles from the venue. And they said, "You know what, we have better things to do. Get in your truck and just go."

AL JOURGENSEN
Ministry, Revolting Cocks

I got arrested for having two kilos of coke. That was creepy. I was dealing coke to pay my tuition and I had this dealer in Florida. So, I met these people that said they wanted to do a twenty-kilo deal. Twenty kilos of coke! I was like, that's above my head. I have to get permission for this.

So the guy I was dealing with flew up from Florida. That was the guy that was sending me the coke at my college, and I would distribute it to fraternities an eight ball at a time. I had eight fraternities that immediately buy this shit. So I had a pretty good deal but then I got greedy, and this sounded good. They were going to pay me 20k just to introduce them, the two parties, and to count the money. 20k for, like, a couple days of work.

But the one guy was a DEA agent. My lawyer claimed that this was a clear case of entrapment, so I got lucky. I only got probation. These days you could still be in jail for two kilos of coke but I got probation for that. The caveat was that I had to finish college. That was part of the probation. I figured I'd graduate and teach music.

But then in my third year of college, Arista signed me. Clive Davis. And offered me a bunch of money so they waved my graduation requirement and I got to go be a rock star and it got me away from my teaching career.

MIKE IX WILLIAMS
Eyehategod

I've been arrested too many times to count. I've been arrested for shoplifting, being drunk and disorderly, and a lot of stuff I don't even remember. The biggest one was probably after Hurricane Katrina happened, and I looted a pharmacy. I didn't get busted until three days later. But that one was bad, and I think it was my only real drug-related arrest, surprisingly.

JERRY DIXON
Warrant

One time we got in a band fight in Alabama. Some rednecks were calling us names while we were onstage playing. They were going, "Fuck you! You Suck!" They were flipping us off and we could see them in the crowd.

After the show, they were outside waiting for us. We were like, "You guys are crazy. We got a band and crew and a couple security guys."

There were only three or four of them, but they wouldn't back down, so we tore them up. They had the chance to walk away but they didn't and they definitely got a beat down.

The cops pulled up and grabbed those guys and arrested me and our tattoo artist and put us in the cop car in the parking lot. We took a little trip to the jailhouse for a few hours.

Alabama jails are pretty scary for teenagers with long hair. Fortunately, the tour bus followed the police cars to the jail. We had people with us so the cops knew not to throw us in the tank with all the furious freaks. Our tour manager got us out later that evening and we were on our way.

MARK MORTON
Lamb of God

I lived in a really small town in southeast Virginia and the cops knew my car. They just did. There was nothing going on and we were long-haired party kids. But they never caught me doing anything. They pulled me over an inordinate amount of times but they never busted me.

ETHAN MCCARTHY
Primitive Man

I've been thrown in cop cars more than five times for nothing other than having black skin. That's always pretty fucking scary because you can totally listen to the cops and do everything they say and you can still end up getting shot.

When I was a kid, in about 2004, I was in a park with a white girl and the cops rolled up on us in their cars. We were just sitting there talking. We weren't even doing anything. They came up and handcuffed me, threw me to the ground and searched me. And they asked her if she was there willingly or if I had coerced her or threatened her somehow. She said, "Yes, I'm here by my own choice, so why are you handcuffing him?"

And then she said some things that made me worry the cops would get mad and take it out on me. She said, "Are you just asking me these questions and putting him in handcuffs because he's black?"

They said, "Well, maybe we are."

That was pretty fucking terrifying. Fortunately, they uncuffed me and let me go without any further incident.

WILLIE ADLER
Lamb of God

Back when Burn the Priest changed their name to Lamb of God, they were supposed to play a warehouse squat in Philly called Stalag 13. Some dude brought a pit bull into the crowd and just unleashed it on dudes. Other guys had baseball bats and they were swinging them around. The show turned into a total riot. It was utter chaos. Then the cops showed up and emptied everyone out of the club before Lamb even got a chance to play.

KING FOWLEY
Deceased, October 31

Me, [guitarist] Mark [Adams], and [guitarist] Doug [Souther] used to like to smoke PCP. One day in 1986, we did a bunch of it, went and practiced and when we were done, we stayed up all night and walked the streets.

At some point in the morning, we decided to go to the high school and shake the doors and we set off the silent alarm. A second later this policeman comes walking down the street. We've got a glass Steamroller bong and we're like, "Pitch the fucking shit!"

We were really wasted on PCP and we didn't want him to catch us with any evidence, so we threw the bong down the sewer. The cop asked us if we just threw something in the sewer 'cause he heard something break and we said, "No, officer."

He couldn't prove anything because he couldn't see it and it was gone. But he figured something was up. He said to each of us, "Give me your goddamn addresses."

I gave him my shit. Mark gave him his shit. When it came to Doug the cop said, "Okay, you're Doug Souther. What's your birthday?"

And Doug said, "2941 John Marshall Drive."

The cop goes, "Your birthday, son!"

"2941 John Marshall Drive!"

This happened five, six, seven times. Doug, in his PCP haze, was just screaming his address at the cop.

"Aw, shit, we're going to fuckin' jail," I thought.

And then the cop suddenly goes, "Get your fucking asses home. Go on, get the fuck out of here."

None of us could believe we had escaped that one.

JIMMY BOWER
Eyehategod, Superjoint Ritual, Down, ex-Crowbar

The first time I drank Mad Dog I was thirteen or fourteen years old. I was with a friend and two cops walked up. We were at an outside mall, we were hanging out, and my friend was wasted. I said, "Dude, be cool, be cool."

"What time is it?" my friend asked the cop.

As the cop looked at his watch my friend threw up purple shit all over him. The other cop was just cracking up.

That was my first encounter with the law.

They called my mom at the bowling alley. I grew up in a really small town, so they knew where she was and she came over to get me.

RICHARD CHRISTY
Charred Walls of the Damned, ex-Death, ex-Iced Earth, ex-Public Assassin

Death toured with a band from England called Benediction, and those guys are drinkers. I got so blitzed with those guys. I almost got arrested one night because I put on a pair of ballet tights with no underwear. You could see all my junk. I went out dancing in the middle of the street. And from what I remember, I think I got spotted by the cops, but I ran past them and back to the shelter of the bus.

The only time I've ever been busted for drinking was for drinking on the subway in New York on the way to a Yankees game. As soon as I got to the stadium, I threw my empty beer in the trash and a policeman said, "Come on over here."

And that was a fifty-dollar fine I would have rather not paid.

MICHAEL SWEET
Stryper

I was a bit of a troublemaker growing up from the age of ten to thirteen. I had a buddy in crime and we used to do basically everything. I was arrested a couple times for stupid, silly things.

I was in my brother's Roadrunner muscle car and we were cruising Whittier Boulevard, which was the thing to do at the time. We're honking the horn and I'm sticking my bare butt out the window. A cop came by and happened to get a face full of butt. They pulled us over and arrested me. I was twelve years old. And my dad wanted to kill me. They told him I could be charged with indecent exposure. But, internally, I think my dad laughed a bit.

I was also arrested for cutting school with my buddies and being locked up in a house with our pellet guns and shooting at cars. We blasted the windshield out of a Cadillac, and they got out of the car and called the cops. They came and took us away. I had just gone into my freshman year of high school, so I was fourteen and that was it, man. I decided I don't want to live like this anymore.

SAM RIVERS
Limp Bizkit

We were [at] Ozzfest in the middle of nowhere on a day off. We were in a hotel. All you could see in every direction were fields and then way in the distance there was a Walmart. We were bored so we went out and bought a bunch of pellet guns and we were shooting them right around the bus, target practicing. Some woman called the cops and they received the report that shots have been fired.

Next thing you know, we were on our tour bus chilling. We were done shooting. Then we looked out the window and went, "Oh dude, there's a cop over there."

And somebody on the other side of the bus said, "Dude, there's a cop over here. Oh, shit."

"Oh, there's a cop on top of that roof with a rifle pointed at us."

"Oh, there's another cop on *that* roof."

The whole police station was there. Suddenly we heard them talking to us through a megaphone: "Don't move! Everybody get on the floor!"

We didn't know what the hell was going on. One of our crew guys walked up from the hotel and the cops yelled at him to clear the area. He asked one of the cops, "What happened to our bus? What's going on in there."

And the cop said, "Shots were fired."

"We just went to Walmart and bought air shock guns. That's it," the crew guy said. "They're not real guns!" "It better not be just frickin' pellet guns!" another cop screamed.

They had us all get out of the bus walking backwards with our hands on our heads. They raided the bus and found the guns. They realized our crew guy was telling the truth and they confiscated them for whatever reason. We were about to go on our way and then right at the end, the cops decided to check us all for weapons. And [our drummer] John [Otto] had a small knife. It wasn't a full switchblade, but they said it was illegal. They figured after all the commotion somebody had to go to jail that day, so picked him. And we had to play the next day.

We were trying to get him out and Ozzfest was going on. By that time everyone on the festival knew what had happened so everyone made their own shirts that said, "Free John Otto."

During a break in one of their songs, System of a Down burst into a really fast hardcore part and they all did gang vocals: "Free John Otto! Free John Otto!"

It became a full-on day of Free John Otto. And right before the show, he pulled up and we all got on stage and played.

VINNIE PAUL
Pantera, Hellyeah

In Pantera, one of our favorite things to do at the studio was this game called Twist and Hurl. You'd drink one of these little bottles of beer and guzzle it until you finished it and then you had to spin and throw it at this stop sign and if you hit it you won. We did that just about every night. We'd drink tons of these little beers, so we had ammunition.

And then one night in 1991, we did it and these flashlights popped up through the trees and there were, like, five cops there ready to arrest us. I don't know how we talked our way out of it.

PHILIP ANSELMO
Pantera, Down, Superjoint Ritual, Scour

[Guitarist] Dimebag [Darrell] and [producer] Terry [Date] were playing it cool. But I was always a paranoid cop kid 'cause I was really the only one that smoked weed daily.

We had just come home from doing a huge show in Russia with AC/DC, Metallica, and believe it or not, the Black Crowes. It was the first open-air concert in Moscow and 500,000 people showed up. And I think I said something like, "Man, we just got back from Russia where we played a show for the Russian citizens. We're the good guys."

And Terry and Dimebag were just like, "Dude, shut *up*."

I don't even know what I was trying to get across and I think even the cops started laughing.

DAVE WYNDORF
Monster Magnet

I got arrested in the Midwest in Minnesota for having totally naked strippers onstage. I had put out the word during the *Powertrip* era when we were doing almost a burlesque, full-on sex, drugs, and rock and roll thing just because it was fun. We would solicit four strippers in every town we went: "Calling all strippers. If you want to dance during a Monster Magnet show, you're certainly welcome to."

So a lot of strippers came out.

It got boring after a while so I started saying, "Could you please do it totally naked? Fuck this burlesque shit. Let's go all-out sleaze. The crowd demands nudity. They wanna see rock, naked women, fire . . ." I was crossing the checklist items off.

I had a bucket list of stereotypes: Drugs "check." Booze "check." Naked women "check." Fire "check." And everyone loved it. Nobody was hurting anybody. It was just a big show.

We finally ran into a couple girls who took the challenge. They went on and there were cops there. They yanked the girls offstage, shut down the show for five minutes and arrested the girls. I said, "No, I'm responsible for this. Arrest me!"

I didn't think they would—but they did! They arrested me and released the girls. I went before a judge the next day and he was like, "Get the fuck out of here. Just go be responsible." And that was the end of the whole thing. He was really cool about it.

JEFF BECERRA
Possessed

I was a drug user in the early '80s during the first wave of Possessed, but after we broke up [in 1987], I became more of a profiteer. Usually, members of our band were doing a quarter of a gram of hash tops. Me and some other guys were selling six pounds a month, so we were dealing with real criminals.

I used to feel naked if I didn't have a pistol on me, but I never shot anybody. I've had guns pointed at me lots of times. Sometimes you stay calm and the situation works itself out. Other times people would pull guns and we'd clock them in the head with a baseball bat, take their guns, hold them upside-down, and shake them out of a second-story window. Then we'd make them apologize and go and fuck their girlfriend—not against her will, but chicks dig that kind of power.

KING FOWLEY

We went downtown one night in 1986 to buy some PCP. It was me, Mark, and another guy down in the Waterfront in Washington, D.C., which was a really, really bad area. We had some friends who sold PCP, but when we got down there nobody had any. Then a guy with a spider web tattoo on his face came over and said he could hook us up. Mark said, "I'm gonna go with this guy."

"Dude, you don't want to go with him," I said. "That shit's bullshit."

"It's cool. I'm gonna go get some shit." Mark said.

He went into this apartment complex. More than twenty minutes passed. Nothing from Mark. I was thinking, "This motherfucker's been shot and killed."

All of a sudden, here comes Mark running. He's got a big knot on his head. He yelled, "Oh man, this guy's got a gun. He just robbed me! Let's go!"

We got in the fucking car but the distributor cap was wet so the car wouldn't start at first. Thankfully, the gang dudes didn't see where Mark went and they ran the other way. They didn't finish the job.

I found out later, Mark ran down into a laundromat on the bottom floor and he shimmied through the window before these dudes gave chase. They had definitely planned to kill him.

KELLY SHAEFER
Atheist, ex-Neurotica

There weren't that many clubs to play in so when we were booked in regular rock n' roll clubs that were used to booking bands like Mötley Crüe, we'd play and they were like, "What the fuck?!"

On two occasions the clubs called the police to come drag us out. They actually put our stuff out in the alley, and we weren't allowed to be in the club. We didn't do anything other than play music that sounded crazy. They just didn't know how to take it.

I remember the guy giving us the cutting of the neck sign like "Stop, stop." We thought it was great. It was a notch in our belt to be kicked out and have police carting our cabinets out the door.

WILL CARROLL
Death Angel, ex-Machine Head

When I was seventeen years old, I went to see Sacred Reich playing The Stone in San Francisco on the *American Way* tour. Before the show, we used to go down the street to drink beer at an alley a couple blocks from the club. We were drinking beer, no big deal, and all of a sudden two foot-patrol officers crept up on us out of nowhere. I had no idea where they came from. They said, "Empty your beers and show us some ID."

Unfortunately, I didn't have an ID on me, so they took me in to the police station in the North Beach district of San Francisco, so I wasn't too far from The Stone. They held me there, but they didn't know what to do with me because I was sixteen. They said, "Okay, we're going to call your parents and have them pick you up."

I started laughing to myself. I lived a whole town over, and it was already 9 p.m. There was no way my parents were going to come and pick me up. A few minutes later the cop came back and said, "We talked to your parents. They refuse to pick you up and we can't hold you. So we told your parents that you promised to catch a train and take it right back home. And don't even think about going back to The Stone because we're going to stop by and take a look and see if you're in there. And if you are, you're in a lot of trouble."

"Okay, I'll go right back home.," I said.

I already knew I was in trouble with my parents and when I got home, I was going to be grounded for the rest of my life. So I was like, "Fuck that. I'm gonna go see Sacred Reich!"

I went straight to The Stone and my friends were psyched to see me. They couldn't believe I was there.

Sure as shit, forty-five minutes later someone comes up to me and goes, "Dude, the cops are in the lobby. They're looking for you."

I ran upstairs and hid in the bathroom. The two cops walked into this sold-out show and saw eight hundred people with long hair and leather jackets. And they went, "Fuck this!" and walked out.

Everyone in there looked like me!

So I stayed out all night partying and then I went home and was grounded for the next five months.

KEN SUSI
Unearth

I once got arrested for battery. It was at my ex-girlfriend's twenty-second birthday party at some pool hall, and some douchebags thought it would be cool to hit on her cousin and get grabby with her. I came out of the bathroom where I saw two guys getting mouthy with my ex and she shot back at them. I guess since they couldn't hit her, they picked the closest dude to her, which was me.

When the guy took a running charge at me, I ducked his punch and hit him back, breaking both of his eye sockets out of his face. Even though it was self-defense, the officer told me that since someone went to the hospital, someone had to go to jail.

I spent thirteen hours in a maximum prison cell, without my one free phone call, next to two angry dudes in a single cell. I made some new friends at that jail and I still haven't gotten my one phone call. But $3,000 in court fees later, I was a free man. Going to jail is expensive and it totally sucks.

CHRIS GARZA
Suicide Silence

The first time I was arrested was when I was a sophomore in high school. That year was a fuckin' mess. I went to this girl's house and she said you can trash my house if you want to. So I took a bat and golf clubs and destroyed the house. I broke all the windows. I broke everything. And then her mom came home, and she wasn't so down with us trashing everything. So, the cops came and I got arrested. I guess the girl was mad or something and wanted to piss off her mom.

TONY FORESTA
Municipal Waste

Our guitarist [Nick Poulos] got arrested for prowling while we were on tour in Pittsburgh in 2008. We were staying at a friend's house across the street from this bar, which is where we always go, and he got confused and went to the wrong house. He was wasted and passed out on the porch. The people who lived there saw this weird looking dude sleeping on their porch, so they called the cops.

The police came and Nick was explaining that he accidentally went to the wrong house. And the owners didn't want to press charges, but the police were being dicks, so they charged him with prowling and he had to spend a night in jail.

The owner dropped the charges, but now, every once in a while, we call Nick "The Prowler" as a joke.

KING FOWLEY

In 1989, we played a local show and I brought in Ripping Corpse and Revenant down from New Jersey. The show was an afternoon matinee on a Saturday and a friend of mine said, "We're going to stay the night, man. Let's get fucked up. Let's get some bitches. Let's get some beer. Let's freak out."

He charged everything on his American Express card. There were all these fucking rooms for everybody. It wasn't a high-end hotel, but it was really high-end for us because there were no bugs in the hotel.

As the day went on, we ran out of beer. That night we walked over to the 7-Eleven and the guy said, "Hey man, what are y'all doing?"

"Well, I'm trying to buy some beer," I said.

"I can't sell it to you," he said.

"Well then, I'm gonna have to take it, man," I said. "Here's the money, dude. I know it's after hours. But we got to have it."

We ran out with eight cases of beer, but we gave him the money, so I figured we were cool. The 7-Eleven was in the parking lot of the hotel so obviously, the guy figured, "Oh, they're going to the hotel."

We were in our rooms with all this beer. And we were laughing about it, thinking it's hysterical. Fifteen minutes later the phone rang. The guy who called us said, "There's fucking ten cop cars outside the hotel."

"What?"

"Yeah, they're all coming up here."

We started running through the halls. We tried to break in people's rooms to hide out because we were just trashed. I tried to change clothes hoping they wouldn't recognize me. I'm a big boy, and I was trying to put on someone else's little size 26 jeans, which just wasn't happening. The cops burst in and they busted us all.

They said, "You motherfuckers. C'mon, we're all going to 7-Eleven to talk to the manager you stole from."

We went over there and saw the guy who was behind the counter. I was sitting there giving him this hard as shit look that was like, "Look, I'll kill you if you fuckin' narc us out!"

And all of a sudden, the guy goes, "These aren't the guys. No, it's not them."

We were like, "Holy shit."

We got to keep the beer. We walked outside and the cops started laughing. They knew we were guilty. But one of them said, "Well, if the guy doesn't want to single you out, I guess it's your beer."

Unfortunately, we didn't get to stay in the hotel because by then we had beaten the walls with fire axes and shut off the fire alarm. In the end, we got a bill for $1,500.

DANI FILTH
Cradle of Filth

We were doing a photo shoot at the Vatican in Rome, and one of us had an "I love Satan" shirt on. Another one of us had a "Jesus is a Cunt" shirt, and our keyboardist was dressed as a priest, which is illegal in Italy. Also, you're not allowed to do photo shoots in there. All these armed guards surrounded us with Uzis. The Vatican extols its own law, so they could have done anything to us. And the only thing that kept us from having a really good kicking in the cells for an indeterminate length of time was the fact that at the other end of town, twenty-five hundred people were gonna riot if we didn't show up at that evening's concert. So they sort of weighed the pros and cons and let us go.

DALLAS TOLER-WADE
ex-Nile, Narcotic Wasteland

My wife was in the back watching television and I was in the living room playing video games. The phone rang and she answered it. I couldn't hear anything 'cause I had the sound up. My wife came in and said she got a call from one of our neighbors who told her that another neighbor named Tom had crashed his car into the garage door of the house. The neighbor was out on the street trying to help the guy out of his car and he was breaking out and trying to start a fight. The guy was just trying to help him.

Needless to say, Tom lost the fight.

During that time, someone called the cops. My wife and I went outside to see what was going on. Tom had both his arms stretched out like he was on a crucifix and he was stumbling around the front yard yelling, "I love you, Jesus."

All of a sudden, the cops rolled up all smooth and quick without their lights on. They got out of their car and yelled, "Get on the fucking ground, now!" and Tom just walked toward them, thinking he was Jesus.

He's lucky they didn't shoot him. Instead, they hit him with a Taser. He tried to get up and they hit him again. Once they subdued him a pair of medics took him away. As they dragged Tom off, he waved goodbye to everyone and told them how much Jesus loved them.

A little while later his roommate, who had been out of town on business, got back to the house. I talked to him about what happened, and he just started laughing and said, "Yeah for the past couple weeks Tom hasn't been eating and hasn't been sleeping. He'd just been smoking pot and taking Adderall and writing poems about the clouds and talking about how he's figured out the whole Bible."

I can't say for sure the prescription drugs make him crazy, but sometimes it's not the heavier drugs that cause the most damage.

PHIL FASCIANA
Malevolent Creation

We've been cursed with Johnny Law since before the band even fuckin' started. In 1999 we got pulled over at 8 a.m. by six cop cars in Little Rock, Arkansas. They searched the bus and found three ounces of weed, and we went to jail for four days. They charged us with drug trafficking and took all our merch money, saying it was drug money.

Our bail was twelve grand and we couldn't pay it. The cops called us "bikers" and when they put us in holding cell with a bunch of huge black guys, they said, "We got a bunch of bikers coming in here and they hate niggers." I thought that our lives were over.

BEN WEINMAN
The Dillinger Escape Plan

I broke the law, but I didn't get busted. I mean, I got busted for spray-painting the Slayer logo on the back of people's sheds. The neighbors told my parents and they got pretty mad but no one pressed charges. My parents took my Slayer albums away from me. They thought the artwork was gross and obviously it was the band that inspired me to vandalize the sheds.

But all I cared about back then was music. I was fourteen or fifteen and it was the soundtrack to my life. I was obsessed with it and it was my culture. I drew the logos on my books at school. So I was also drawing the thing that meant the most to me on this shed. It was like an early version of tagging. I was making a symbol that was transformative for me.

MORGAN LANDER
Kittie

[Bassist] Jennifer Arroyo and [guitarist] Jeff Phillips were playing with the band in the later *Oracle* cycle in 2002 or 2003 and we had a bus driver who wasn't the brightest. We were in Texas and I was up at the front of the bus and I saw signs to Mexico. I said, "Are you gonna turn or whatever?" and he said, "No, no, we can turn up here."

And then there was a covering overhead and there was nowhere to turn. So we made a wrong turn into Mexico. Obviously, we had no business being in Mexico. On the side going into Mexico they were like, "Come on in, have a great time."

But the way out was a different story because we were literally in Mexico for thirty seconds so we could turn around and they thought that was suspicious. They ripped our bus apart and interrogated us pretty bad. They fingerprinted us and took a couple guys into the room and touched their butts and stuff. They pulled out all of our suitcases and laid them out on the tarmac. They pulled our underwear out, throwing it all over the place—probably smelling them. They tossed around our dirty stage clothes.

It was so absolutely fucked up. We were there for hours and hours and then we had to pick up all of our clothes and our stuff that they had spread all over the place.

One guard asked me where we were going and what our itinerary was. I didn't have that shit memorized. I get ready to tour, get on the bus and I know what our next few shows are, but I can't tell you what the next thirty-two dates look like. He said, "If you can't tell me exactly where you're going every single day, we're going to throw you in jail."

I started crying. I did that please-feel-bad-for-me cry. And I don't know if he felt sorry for me, but they let us back in the country and we made the show. I found out later that we actually had weed on the bus hidden under a seat in the back lounge. They had dogs there and everything. I don't know how they didn't find it. We got very, very fuckin' lucky there. If they found it, we probably would have been in jail—probably still.

JOHN GALLAGHER
Raven

In 1984, we had Anthrax out with us. Neil Turbin, who sang on their first album, was an interesting character. He had all these vitamins individually wrapped in aluminum foil. When we crossed into Canada the customs guys saw all these foil packages and they had a field day. We were pulled over for five hours as they made us open our suitcases and pull out our dirty socks one at a time.

By the time we got to the gig, we were super late and the conditions were horrible. There was a pillar right in the middle of the stage. The drum riser was totally unusable so we couldn't fit on the stage. The guy didn't want to give us food or water. He just wanted us to play so we said, "Fuck off" and blew the gig off.

That was the first time we'd ever missed a show. He complained to the promoter and the promoter had us stopped at the border.

We had legal problems for years after that. Anthrax had all their gear taken off them the following year. It was impounded. We had our stuff impounded the year after that. Our bands were labeled with a "harass at will" stamp until the whole godawful thing was financially sorted out.

KYLE SHUTT
The Sword

Being in a band, you're a target for cops and some of them aren't the most cultured people. Some of them are like, "How come y'all are in a van?"

Or they'll look at your IDs and go, "Why is one of you from Chicago, three guys from Texas and a dude from Florida? Is there something yer not telling me? Y'all gotta be up to no good."

It's like their brains can't comprehend people in a band living in different places. We learned how to deal with cops and border patrol people and eventually we got really good at it. A trick that works is you just ask them, "Have you heard the word of Jesus Christ today?"

They're like, "Go on through. You're good."

They don't want to hear about it.

GLEN BENTON
Deicide

In the early days of Deicide we really wanted to be different and extreme. So I would go to the butcher's before the show and buy all sorts of animal organs and innards and throw them into the crowd. When we were up in New York, the club owner said, "If you bring any guts or shit in, you're out of here."

I had to bury a whole 30-pound beef liver in the backyard of the place we were staying. It was a shallow grave and it attracted a million blowflies. So when someone saw all these flies swarming around this spot, they thought there was a dead body buried there. They called the cops and all these police cars swarmed in and dug out this giant beef liver.

WILL CARROLL

I went to The Stone five nights a week. This one night I was on Broadway Street right outside the club. I was seventeen. I was with a friend and we saw this stack of orange pylon cones. So we started picking them up and throwing them in the middle of the street and chucking them at cars. We were total hoodlums.

One of the cars skidded and almost caused an accident. We were high-fiving each other.

All of a sudden, the cops rolled up on us and said, "Stop right there."

They handcuffed us and took us to the police station. We were sitting on a bench. My friend has long, black curly hair and he has a darker complexion. And I was sitting next to him I've got long blondish-reddish hair. This big fat cop wanted to heckle us, so he said, "What do we have here? We have Mötley Crüe—Axl and Slash!"

I thought, "No, you got it wrong you fucking idiot. You're trying to make fun of us, and you mix up your bands!"

My friend knows how I am. They call me "Heavy Metal Judge" or "Cathy Correction." I correct people all the time, especially if it involves heavy metal if they get their facts wrong. I took a breath and I was about to say something and my friend elbowed me in the gut and said, "Don't you fuckin' say a thing."

It was killing me not to correct the cop. In the end they let us go because we weren't eighteen yet.

KEITH BUCKLEY
Every Time I Die, The Damned Things

We were in South Carolina around 1999 and we were just trying to kill time. This was before we had a trailer, so we were all packed into this shitty van we had borrowed from a friend.

We went to this plaza that had a grocery store and a dollar store. I had literally zero money on me so I stole a rubber snake from the dollar store because I had to have it.

The person working the dollar store had seen me come in and thought I was sketchy. I didn't go in with the intent to steal anything. But they clocked me and kept an eye on me and saw me grab this and called the cops as soon as I left.

I saw the cops coming into the plaza and had a bad feeling it was for me. So I ran into the grocery store and it was like a mobster movie. I tore through all the aisles and went into the back where all the employees were stocking food. I went out the back of the store and ran down to a gas station behind the street, keeping to the field behind the buildings.

I called the promoter and said if the band leaves, they have to come back and get me. I remember hiding and watching the cops looking for me. And then the van pulled up alongside where I was and I fuckin' jumped out and got in the van. That's the closest I got to being arrested and it was for stealing a toy snake.

I'll never understand how I got away with it and how they knew to pick me up where they did. They found me walking in the woods, coming out of the fields behind the gas station. That might have been purely coincidence, but the universe works in mysterious ways. I'm still probably wanted in South Carolina.

JIMMY BOWER

We were in Slidell, Louisiana, back when [drummer] Joey [LaCaze] was still alive. We had to stop at Home Depot to get a lock for the trailer. I was walking around and I heard on the announcement speaker, "Jimmy Bower please come to the back of the store."

I thought, "Oh man, what the fuck?"

I went to the back of the store and the manager had Joey detained because he tried to steal a battery. I said, "Dude! What the fuck!"

We were [still] in Slidell. We weren't even out of town yet, so I was really pissed. And I guess since I was really pissed Home Depot said, "Well, we're gonna let him go with you. We're not gonna press charges."

And it was all over a fucking battery.

KEITH BUCKLEY

Jimmy Bower frzom Eyehategod was in town in Omaha, Nebraska, the same night Every Time I Die was playing. His manager called us and said he wanted to go to the show.

We said, "Of course," but I had never met him.

He and I went out drinking after the show and I really tied one on. I was still pretty young, twenty-seven or twenty-eight, so I could definitely keep up. We went to a bar and it got pretty messy. I guess I was trying to impress him and prove that I could hold my own.

He ended up getting so drunk that he bumped into a girl and her boyfriend started trying to fight him. He was talking back and the two of them started arguing. Out of nowhere, the girl's boyfriend smacked Jimmy across the face and his false teeth flew out. I didn't know he had dentures. They flew out and everyone stood there stunned and looked at each other.

And then she fuckin' stomped on them and ground them under her foot.

That set him off. He lunged at the guy and this fight broke out. Next thing I knew, there were cops everywhere and me and Jimmy Bower are sitting out on the curb in handcuffs.

I was arrested in 2013 in my hometown for trespassing in an old shut-down mental institution. It was a place called Greystone and it had a reputation for being the creepiest, most fucked up place. It was built in the 1800s and the town was going to be knocking it down and I just really wanted to see it before it got demolished.

I went there with a friend and we got stuck in there. We couldn't get out. We were there for hours and it was really horrifying because the place was huge. Until the Pentagon was built, it was the biggest building in the United States. And it was so creepy. There were files everywhere and all this medical equipment.

When we finally found a way out there was a cop waiting for us who had seen us on the video footage from inside the place.

SCOTT "WINO" WEINRICH
The Obsessed, ex-Saint Vitus

Being the singer in Saint Vitus and being the band that Saint Vitus was I had to get really loaded to get into it. That was just sort of what I needed to do to get my head in the right place for the band, so that's what I did.

On any given day I would go from drinking ten or twenty beers, half a fifth of whiskey, and putting as much shit as I could cram in my nose. When I got busted [in Norway], we were already through the border. So I climbed out of my bunk and I was sitting there doing some music on my computer when we pulled into what I thought was a toll.

Our driver told us it wasn't a toll and that we were actually being pulled over. I wasn't too worried, but then the police brought the dog and it sniffed out my drugs. The cops threw me in a cell and gave me bread and water for a couple days. That was pretty rough since I was so used to being ripped.

I petitioned hard for them to let me finish the tour. I wasn't there to sell or deal. What they found was just my personal stash—the same way as people who drink coffee in the morning to get them going have their equipment. Same deal. The only thing I regret is the fact that I wasn't able to finish the last leg of the tour and the hardship I caused the guys in my band.

So after a couple days of bread and water, shitty coffee, and a piece of bread with some funky luncheon meat on it I started to hear that word "deported." They asked me where I lived and I said, "L.A." So they arranged to have me flown to New York City accompanied by two plain-clothed officers. After I cleared customs they were going to fly me the rest of the way to L.A.

I had no intention of going back to LA. I was going to see my girl-friend in New York City.

I was on the plane with one young male and one young female officer escorting me the whole way. All I wanted was a fuckin' beer. They wouldn't let me, so I was miserable the entire flight. I asked the Norwegian cop, "What's going to happen when we get back to New York?"

I thought we were gonna meet the New York cops and they were gonna drag my ass back to Rikers Island. We landed and I went through customs. I was fast-tracked right through. One Norwegian cop had his badge and he went with me, but they wouldn't let the second cop through. So the Norwegian cop told me, "Don't worry. I'm gonna tell them you're a nice guy."

We got to the American customs desk and there was a black dude sitting there. The Norwegian cop said, "I'm from the Norwegian police and this is the deportee."

"Deportee? What'd you get deported for?" said the cop.

"Oh, I had a gram of speed," I told him.

He pulled out his stamp. BLAM! Welcome back to the U.S. I just walked on through and left the Norwegian cop behind.

ROB CAVESTANY
Death Angel, ex-The Organization

We were already going on tour when we were seventeen. At that point, you're definitely going crazy and you don't know shit except that you want to have fun and the world's revolving around you. After a show, we were at a hotel and everyone was getting back to the hotel pretty wasted after partying. I was sharing a room with our drummer, Andy [Galeon] at the time and we wanted to keep the party going. There were a couple of crew guys next door. They got one of those adjoining doors, so we were knocking on the door and trying to get them up to party.

We were totally lit so pretty soon we were trying to break the door down. We slammed into the door, using ourselves as battering rams. At one point our phone started ringing. It was an old woman's voice. She sounded terrified: "Please stop! What are you doing?"

I thought it was a joke or something. So we tried even harder to break the door down. Little did we know that our crew had already checked out and was on their way to the next show ahead of us and now there was an old couple staying in the room next door to us.

This old man was trying to hold the door from smashing open and he and his wife were terrified. They called the police and wanted to have us arrested. Our tour manager had to stop them from pressing charges.

ADAM JARVIS
Misery Index, Pig Destroyer, Scour

In 2007 in Belgium, Misery Index played with Necrophagist and Origin. We had a matinee show, but me and Mark [Kloeppel], the guitar player for Misery Index, went out and had some fine Belgian beers before the gig. We were going to go back and pass out before the show.

Then we came back for the show and our tour manager said, "Where the fuck have you been? You're on in twenty minutes."

We were still drunk so we were like, "What the fuck?"

We played the show and it went pretty well.

Afterward, everyone was drinking a lot and arm wrestling. Then things got really wild. The last thing I remember before I went down was people throwing bottles against the wall and pieces of broken glass flying everywhere. At some point in the night, a couple of the guys on the tour decided that they wanted more beer after the club had kicked everyone out. The club was in a residential area, smashed between some houses, so, in their drunken stupor, they haggardly walked up to what they thought was the door of the venue and started pounding on it. "Let us in!!! We want more beer!! Give us beer!"

After a little while, the door opened and there was this grey-haired old man standing there looking up at these two long-haired metalhead dudes screaming about beer in a different language. The guy was so scared he had a heart attack. Cops and paramedics came. Fortunately, the guy lived.

Fast forward to the next morning. We were in the Netherlands and I stumbled off the bus at 10 a.m. There was a circle of people talking and then I heard, "Adam! Come here!"

It was our tour manager, Thomas.

"What time did you go to bed last night?" he asked me.

"Honestly, I think it was the earliest I went to bed on this whole tour. I know it was before anyone else went to bed," I said.

"Are you just saying that?"

"No, dude. That's the truth."

"Did you realize the cops were on the bus this morning and you wouldn't wake up?"

I was like, "What?"

I was fucked up the night before and I guess I slept through this police raid on our bus. They asked all kinds of questions about what happened to the old man and if any of us had anything to do with it. No one fessed up to it and no one from any of our bands was arrested. I don't think we were really banned from Belgium, but the story got around and we weren't booked in Belgium for a while.

WILL CARROLL

Back when I was touring with Machine Head, we were on the last night of this one tour. We had a driver for about two weeks and he hated us. He was this cowboy guy and we didn't like him either. So, this night we were in Hollywood at the Troubadour there was a big party on the bus after the show. Everyone was smoking weed and there were tons of people from Coal Chamber and Brujeria and everyone was partying.

The bus driver showed up and saw all the smoke coming out of the bus so he called the cops on Machine Head. I was getting ready to leave. I was going to stay in L.A. for an extra two weeks with a friend in Malibu. I took off just in time. I got off the bus, threw all my bags in the trunk of my friend's car. We were about to leave when the police showed up. They stormed the bus everybody on the bus got arrested for smoking weed.

ROSS THE BOSS
ex-Manowar, Ross the Boss, The Dictators

I got arrested when I was in the Dictators. We had just formed and we were living in upstate New York away from people to try to learn how to play. We lived outside of New Paltz and the girl we were living with, Karen, had a car.

One night me and [Dictators co-founder] Andy Shernoff were in New Paltz and we were all sorts of drunk. We had to get home and we saw Karen's car so we just took it and she reported it stolen. The next day we found ourselves in jail. We got locked up for auto theft. We took the car and Karen didn't know it. We were even in the New Paltz paper.

It sucked being in jail. You're in jail. They close the door on you, man. You're there. You ain't getting out. You ain't goin' nowhere.

DANI FILTH

In France, I was thrown into jail for the night. I was with my wife and we went to an award ceremony and then we went back to the hotel and had a bit of an argument. It escalated into a joke. We had a pillow fight and the pillow went and smashed something. We were screaming with laughter, but it was quite late at night and someone next door thought I was physically attacking her and called the police.

Before I knew it, what seemed like the entire police force burst into the room and arrested me.

ROB CAVESTANY

We did a show at Centennial Hall in Hayward, California, back in the day and during the first song the pit broke out so crazy and people were thrashing insane. The security panicked and, all of a sudden, cops came out in riot gear. We didn't want to stop playing so we kept going and the people kept moshing. The cops literally came up to us at gunpoint and made us stop.

When that happened, the people got fucking pissed and the crowd destroyed the entire place. They threw the tables and chairs through the windows and completely destroyed the hall, which got us permanently banned from the city.

DAVE PETERS
Throwdown, ex-Eighteen Visions, ex-Bleeding Through

When I was playing with Eighteen Visions, we played one show in Salt Lake City because a bunch of guys knew the straight-edged Salt Lake guys. It was the first show I ever played out of California and we were all excited. At the time, the Salt Lake City straight-edge scene had this wave of violence every couple years. They were under scrutiny by local police.

We got out there to play this warehouse show and security did full pat-downs and had everyone take their shoes off. It was like airport security the year after 9/11. We were scheduled to play second to last. The first band played and we saw a couple cops in the venue. A minute later, the whole Salt Lake City gang task force/S.W.A.T. response unit showed up.

We were sixteen and seventeen years old at the time and inside the whole venue surrounding the whole crowd in the middle are the cops with riot gear and masks all standing shoulder to shoulder. We were freaked out and wondering how this was gonna end. They arrested a few people and shut down the show.

We got out of there unscathed, but we didn't get to play and neither did some of the other bands. So someone moved the whole show over to a practice space a couple miles away and we did the whole concert in someone's basement, which was an insane first tour experience.

TONY FORESTA

We were driving to Memphis, like, twelve years ago to start a tour for *The Art of Partying*. On the way, we stayed at this run-down punk rock party house in Asheville, North Carolina. We drove six or seven hours and got there really late. And of course, everyone there was thinking, "Municipal Waste is staying here! Let's party with them 'cause they're a party band!"

And we were just like, "We've been driving so fuckin' long, we just wanna sleep."

A couple of us slept in the van and some of us were on the floor in the dining room while the party raged all night. At like 6 or 7 a.m. this lady was screaming bloody murder and freaking out. She shouted, "Shame on you. It got on the book and everything."

"What the fuck is this crazy woman talking about?" I thought.

Apparently, she went outside to read a story to her granddaughter at a picnic table right when some drunk, fuckin' punk kid started pissing off the balcony and didn't bother to look down and see he was peeing onto the grandmother, the daughter, and the book she was reading. We had to get the fuck out of there as fast as possible.

As we left, the cops were pulling up. They saw me and [bassist Land] Phil sprinting to the van and us storming off. So they pulled us over. One cop said, "What are you doing? Why are you getting out of there so fast?"

I was frazzled, so I said, "I don't know, man. We just stayed at this fucking house and we were just sleeping and the peepee . . . We don't even know these people. You gotta believe us!"

The cop laughed and said, "Yeah, all right. Just get the fuck out of here."

BURTON C. BELL
Fear Factory, Ascension of the Watchers

We were driving through Texas in 1993. We had Jägermeister in the van and our keyboard player Reynor [Diego] was smoking weed in the back.

Suddenly this cop pulled us over for speeding on Interstate 40 outside of Amarillo. Reynor hid the weed and thank god the cop didn't check the van or we would have gotten busted.

A year later, we were in an RV. I was driving. Our tour manager, Hatter, was in the passenger's seat and he had a bag of horrible dirt weed that he was constantly smoking. I was going down Interstate 40 outside Amarillo doing 75 in a 65. I saw a cop but I got busted. I pulled over and the policeman came up to the window to tell me I was speeding. Then he said, "You guys got anything illegal in your car?"

"No," I said.

"Do you mind if I come in?" he asked.

"Yeah, I do mind," I said.

"Hey, you look familiar," he said.

"You look familiar, too."

"Didn't I stop you guys last year?"

"Yup."

I was hoping he'd see the humor in it and give us a break. Then he said, "Yup, I'm gonna bring the dogs out."

We waited an hour. I had to sit in the cop car while he searched everything. He found Hatter's stash and Hatter actually copped to it, thank goodness. So they took him to jail and because they took him to jail they didn't give me a speeding ticket. So we left our tour manager in Amarillo and kept on going.

JOHN GALLAGHER

We were at the airport in Oslo, Norway, and when we went through customs we were trying to do the right thing and declare our items. So the customs agent pulls us aside and interrogated us. He said, "Did you know you're only allowed to bring items valued at 6,000 Kroner [without paying tax]?"

And I said, "No, how much is that in pounds?"

He said he didn't know. So they kept us in this room, patted us down, checked out our IDs, and asked us all these questions. And then we found out later that the customs agents were using us as guinea pigs to demonstrate what an interrogation looks like. I couldn't fuckin' believe we got detained and questioned and all because we tried to do the right thing and declare some things.

BEN FALGOUST
Goatwhore, ex-Soilent Green

When we're on tour we usually sleep in the van at rest areas and truck stops. One time we were parked at a rest area and all of a sudden we felt the van rock. We looked up and a car had run into the front of the van. The way he hit us, his bumper got hooked to us.

Then he was trying to back the vehicle up to get it out but that wasn't working. So then he went back to his car and got a crowbar and came back.

I said, "What are you doing?"

He started mumbling something and we immediately knew he was drunk. So we grabbed the crowbar from him and he jumped into his vehicle and throttled it in reverse then pulled away and he took off down a little strip and ran into the side of an eighteen-wheeler that was parked as well. We realized later that when he came into the rest area he was going down the interstate the wrong way. That's when he hit us. One of us ran over and called the police.

Meanwhile, the guy that was in the car was stuck to the eighteen-wheeler. The guy in the eighteen-wheeler got out, but before he could do anything the drunk guy finally broke free, drove out of the rest area, and took off down the interstate the wrong way again.

Finally, the cops showed up. We explained the story and all of a sudden it turned into an interrogation of us! We told them, "We just parked here and we were sleeping . . ."

"You got any drugs? Have y'all been drinking?"

"No, but hey, this guy was going down the interstate the wrong way and he rammed into us and then into this eighteen-wheeler."

The police interrogated us for about an hour.

"Well, maybe we need to search your vehicle," a cop said.

We were trying to do the right thing and call the police and it ended up working against us. The cops gave us the third degree. We had nothing to hide. But we were still questioned and patted down.

PHILIP ANSELMO

When you're in your twenties and you're on the streets and you're Philip from Pantera, there's gonna be some prick who wants to test the guy who did some good with his life. I'd end up going to a bar and there'd be some drunk fuckin' guy in there. And either his old lady's eyeing me up or he's just a fuckin' loser and he wants to fuck with me. These dudes would always say something stupid like, "Hey, you think you're fucking big shit?"

I tried to ignore these idiots. Lord knows I fuckin' did, but some dude would always provoke me and egg me on until I fucking bashed his fucking teeth through the back of his fuckin' head. And sure enough, when the cops got there they'd see a dude there asleep in a pool of fucking blood and everybody pointing the finger at me. I was always the dude that went to fuckin' jail.

And they all knew who I was, so then right after jail, here comes the lawsuit and the assault charge. It wasn't worth it at all. And that's the main reason why I eventually went into solitude—to get away from the assholes and the idiots and the ambulance chasers

ADAM JARVIS

On a trip coming back from Europe, our guitar player Darin [Morris] was in the bathroom when the alarm went off. A stewardess came in and unlocked the door and pretty much attacked him.

It was the final hour of an eight-hour flight from Germany to Montreal. Darrin was in there smoking one of those little Juul vapes. I was standing there in the aisle stretching.

"What are you doing in there? Are you smoking?" shouted a stewardess.

I've never seen them unlock the lavatory door from the outside. They had this tool and they opened the door. Darrin was standing there wide-eyed, like they were shining a light on an owl. They escorted him off the plane to talk to Air Canada's transportation security. He was extremely cooperative. He gave them his vape and apologized.

They said, "Okay, you've been agreeable and you weren't actually smoking. It was a vape."

We had a connecting flight from Montreal to BWI. I was sitting at the gate when they call my name over the intercom. I went over to the ticket counter and the person there said, "Yeah, we just wanted to make sure you wanted to continue on with your travel today since your travel partner will no longer be on this flight."

Darrin was banned from Air Canada. He had to take a different airline.

I used to have a Juul vape and I've definitely used it in an airplane bathroom before. I couldn't even imagine it setting off the smoke alarm.

CHAPTER 2: TRASHED

Happy Drunks vs. Uninhibited Idiots

"Trashed" was an obvious title for a song by Black Sabbath, which, along with being the most important metal band, were once one of the most wasted and dysfunctional. What's surprising is that the song was on Black Sabbath's 1983 album *Born Again*, which was released long after Ozzy Osbourne left the band and launched a successful solo career, and a year after Ronnie James Dio quit following two records with Sabbath. Also, *Born Again* is the only Sabbath album to feature Deep Purple vocalist Ian Gillan and was largely considered a disappointment for the short-lived lineup.

The prevalence of booze in most bands' careers is a chicken and egg scenario. Why do so many rockers wind up becoming heavy drinkers? Are the kinds of people that become musicians predisposed to drowning in booze or is it the cutthroat nature of the music business that drives them to drink? It certainly doesn't help that every touring band has a rider that guarantees them enough beer and liquor to keep most house parties rollin' until the wee hours. Of course, for those that relish liquid courage before they take the stage, that's not necessarily a bad thing. It's all about moderation and learning one's limits—and keeping car keys far from anyone that's already slurring and suffering from balance issues.

OZZY OSBOURNE
Black Sabbath, Ozzy Osbourne

When you drink you become a different person. You become like Dr. Jekyll and Mr. Hyde. I honestly didn't know what I was doing when I drank. And that was the biggest fear I had at the end of the day. I'd become what they call a blackout drinker. I didn't know what I was doing and it was fucking horrendous. Waking up and thinking, "What the fuck have I done now?" You wake up covered in blood and you don't know where the blood's come from. So, you just drink more to forget about it. I used to be that wild man onstage and offstage.

ROB HALFORD
Judas Priest, ex-Halford, ex-Fight

In the very early days, my favorite concoction was a drink called Barleywine, which is like a small bottle of very, very strong beer. The thing is, in those days, when you had so little money, the goal was to spend the least amount of money to get totally fucked up in the shortest space of time. So, if you had two Barleywines and a pill called a Mogadon, which was a downer—you mix those two together and you were flying within fifteen minutes. You were having the time of your life. And after doing God knows what, I would wake up the next day and somehow I was able to stagger back from town into my own part of the world and get back into bed. That lasted for many years with alcohol and cocaine and pills. I'm just glad I was able to finally see the light at the end of the darkness before it completely sucked me in.

GLENN TIPTON
Judas Priest

I lived close to Ozzy. I lived in a little village in Staffordshire and Ozzy moved into a cottage close to the same village so we ended up sharing the same pub; it was a place called Ecclestone, if I remember rightly. There are seven pubs in the main street and you know, Ozzy very often and myself we used to drink in all of them in a pub crawl and that's how I got to know Ozzy personally. There were so many funny stories from that era. He used to knock about with a guy named Charlie Clapp who was a vegetable dealer in a market. They were always up to no good. One time Ozzy was shooting [a gun] through the thatched roof over the porch of the cottage where Ozzy lived.

Charlie said, "What you doing that for?"

Ozzy said, "It's my porch."

So Charlie said, "Oh, okay. Why not shoot at the church clock?", which he did next and the police came. There were always things going on in the village and most of them involved Ozzy.

OZZY OSBOURNE

I've done a lot of stupid things in my life, but there's one thing I've learned: A stupid thing has, and always will have, a stupid result. You cannot do a stupid thing and expect a different result. That's impossible. Sometimes I've jumped and said, "That is stupid," and it's too late. I'm already falling. I've got to crash and burn before I realize that a stupid action has happened. And usually, it's involved alcohol.

FRANKIE BANALI
Quiet Riot, ex-W.A.S.P.

The first show we opened for Judas Priest in 1983 was in Newcastle, England. We went over a day early before the show and [Judas Priest guitarist] K.K. Downing was at the pub at the Holiday Inn hotel. He was the one that introduced me to Newcastle Brown. Now, the Newcastle Brown in Newcastle is completely different from the Newcastle Brown you'll get anywhere else. It's my understanding that there is an actual ward for people who abuse Newcastle Brown and let me tell you, that stuff was evil in a good way. One time I drank so much Newcastle Brown that when I went to the bathroom to take a piss I wound up standing in front of the urinal with my pants zipped up and I peed through my own pants. That stuff was evil and I had quite a fascination with it for quite a bit of time.

JERRY DIXON
Warrant

We drank our weight in alcohol every night, that's for sure. Imagine being a teenager. You start a band and then the next thing you know you're touring in this big giant bus, driving around the country, and having everything handed to you—alcohol, drugs, girls. It was awesome. When we got bigger, the arenas were so stale and informal that a lot of times we would pick out a local club and invite the whole arena to the club and we would play another show after our arena show and then drink all night. We definitely partook and killed a lot of brain cells along the way.

ZAKK WYLDE
Black Label Society, Ozzy Osbourne

I saw a psychiatrist once and he said, "Why do you think you drink? Is it because you're depressed, maybe?" I said, "Nooo, Doc. Put it this way. When my immortal beloved is pleasuring my manhood and fisting my prostate to make sure I'm regular, I don't usually analyze it. I just go, 'Man, her fist feels great up my ass.' Drinking's kind of like that. Now people ask me, "Zakk, when was the last time you had a drink?" I go, "About eight years ago. But I'm fine. Now I just sniff glue and eat paint chips and the results are remarkably the same. I wake up and my pants are around my ankles and all the fellows go, 'We had a great time last night!'"

SAM RIVERS
Limp Bizkit

We were really young when we started touring. On the first big tour we did, one of the members of the band that took us out came up to us with a bunch of cases of beer and he said, "If you all don't drink this all tonight, you're off the tour." And me and John literally took that for real. He probably meant it, I don't know. But we took that as, "Okay, sir." And from then on, we were on it.

MAX CAVALERA
Soulfly, Cavalera Conspiracy, ex-Sepultura

At The Omni in San Francisco, someone was making mudslides before Sepultura did a show there in 1991. I drank a lot of those and I went onstage plastered. But I was really excited because the Metallica guys came to watch us. Faith No More were there. The whole Bay Area scene: Exodus, Sadus, Machine Head were there, too. The show was going pretty good. During the set, we played a cover of Black Sabbath's "Symptom of the Universe." That was good, too. We played two more Sepultura songs, and I was so out of my mind that I announced the Black Sabbath song again and I started playing it. My brother [and drummer Igor] would not play the song. He threw the drum sticks at me. "Fucking idiot, asshole! We already played that!" I was confused for a second, so I turned around. And just at that moment, [Machine Head's frontman] Robb Flynn, who was drunk, too, fell over and knocked down my stacks of Marshall amplifiers. My whole rack was all over the ground and Robb was lying on the stage. And everyone forgot I tried to play the Sabbath song twice.

RANDY BLYTHE
Lamb of God

I didn't think I was a problem drinker because my pattern would be to come home and sober up and then go on tour and get crazy. I was kidding myself and it was really self-destructive. I had some scary experiences waking up all bloody from fucking myself up falling on the stage barricade. That happened a lot and it started to get really fucked up. By just drinking non-stop, I was killing myself. The guy who signed us once looked at me onstage and said, "You know, either that guy's gonna be a star or he's gonna be dead." And that was the way it was going. I never would have made it to dying of Cirrhosis of the liver. I would have been the guy who died because I was drunk and I watched *Lethal Weapon IV* and decided I could jump between two buildings. I got idiotic ideas when I was intoxicated. After a while, I got sober, but it took a long time for me to get to that place

ZAKK WYLDE

You know you've got a good drinking story when piss and shit start happening. That's when you know you're drinking and having a good time—when you're drinking so much and you actually think you're in the bathroom and you piss all over the place. Once, I was with my old lady in the middle of the night and I just started pissing up her back. She said, "What the fuck do you think you're doing!?!" When I realized what had happened and I wasn't in the bathroom I said, "What's the matter? You don't like that kind of stuff?" Seriously, when you're passed out and you either shit the bed or you wake up and there's shit everywhere and you can't remember how it got there, you're like, "Wow, what a great party!"

KEITH BUCKLEY
Every Time I Die, The Damned Things

Being on Ozzfest in 2004 was pretty much like an Alcoholics Anonymous preparation class without the anonymity. We were from the hardcore world and we liked our drink, but suddenly we were out there with these *real* metal bands and these fucking guys absolutely loved to party. I had always been skeptical about crazy rock-and-roll road tales and I was made aware that these stories I had heard were very much real and were not fabricated in any way, shape, or form. I felt like a visitor but I was really drawn to it and I liked it and participated as best I could. I wanted to observe it and see what it was about. Some of these people were such characters it was amazing. Zakk Wylde got so drunk that he pissed in his hand and rubbed it in his beard.

MICHAEL SWEET
Stryper

When I was 16 and 17 years old I was going every weekend to Holly-wood and drinking, smoking, and womanizing and doing all that stuff that all the other bands did. We'd go to Gazarri's and drink with Stephen Pearcy from Ratt and our peers. And then we'd walk the streets to go from Gazarri's down to the Troubadour on Santa Monica and then see someone passed out in the bushes and recognize them. I'd think, "Man, that was the dude that just played two hours ago on the stage at Gazarri's."

FRANKIE BANALI

Drinking was a big part of the early '80s for me. If drinking was an Olympic sport, I would have gotten a gold medal every single year. But I was a happy drunk. I was never the guy that got morose and got into fights when I was drunk unless somebody started one with me, and I can't remember most of those. But there's still evidence of my drinking days. In my archives, I have a pair of salmon-red leather pants and a pair of red leather boots with stacked heels that I had bought at Kensington Market in London. Those were my favorite. And if you look at the front of those pants, both legs are completely and totally stained. And if you look at the top part of the boots, most of the red leather is gone. All that's left is raw leather. The reason I kept them and the reason they got that way, and the reason the pants are stained, came from me throwing up on myself all the time. The leather came off from the top of my shoes because I was always dragged from the hotel and onto the tour bus. I keep those things to remind me of my past.

ALEX HELLID
Entombed

I was 15 when we did our first album. Our first shows were in youth centers that didn't serve alcohol and then we played a punk club called the Ultra House, but sadly there was no alcohol there either. The guy that ran it was making cinnamon rolls and milk for the bands. When we started getting outside of Sweden that's when the real rock-and-roll world hit us. Instead of getting soda pop, we got beer. So the first 10 years of Entombed we drank a lot. I got a lot of shit from being too drunk early on. In between every song I thought I was Slash from Guns N' Roses, so I started playing "Sweet Child O' Mine" to piss the other guys off. It's not really what you should do between death metal songs and they didn't think it was funny after a while so I eventually stopped.

DINO CAZARES
Fear Factory, Divine Heresy, Brujeria, Asesino

When I was 16, I went to a house party and it was one of those things you see in the movies. My friend's parents were out of town and his parents had a huge mini-mansion. We had a few kegs in the backyard and there was music playing. I was hanging out with my buddies in the kitchen and they challenged me to do shots. It happened to be eight shots in a row—four tequila and four vodkas. I did them all and then blacked out. I woke up in my buddies' parents' bed wearing just boxers, which were not mine.

"You motherfucker!" my buddy said to me the next morning.

"What happened?" I asked.

"What happened? You blacked out. You were running around the party naked. You ran into my parents' closet and you took a shit and wiped your ass on my mom's dress."

I was so freaked out that everybody was going to make fun of me at school, but some girls actually took some interest in me after they saw me naked. I guess I had a good time because I don't remember it. But that's one of the only times I've ever been drunk.

SCOTT IAN
Anthrax, S.O.D., The Damned Things

In late '85 or so, [Anthrax vocalist] Joey [Belladonna], Jonny Z, who signed us to Megaforce, and I went over to Europe to do promotion for our second album *Spreading the Disease*. We went to London first, did press all day, and played a show. After the show, Joey and I got invited out by some of the *Kerrang!* writers to go see The Sweet at the old Marquee Club. I wasn't drinking much at the time, but I was in London where the beer is good. Joey was drinking then, too, so we were drinking beer and I was pretty drunk already by the end of the show. Then some of these guys who were there went across the street to a bar called the St. Moritz. The *Kerrang!* guys were like, "Oh, that's where all the guys in all the bands go to hang out." I was expecting some cool, fancy place, and we went across the street and it was this shitty basement with chairs and tables and a bar at one end of it, The first thing I see in there is my hero, Lemmy [Kilmister from Motörhead] standing there at the bar, and I'm in a Motörhead sweatshirt under my leather jacket. I was 21 years old. I hadn't done anything significant or met anyone famous and the guy I think is the coolest motherfucker on earth was ten feet away from me.

I thought, "Holy crap, Lemmy's here, what do I do?" Someone had already handed me a pint, so I downed the pint pretty quick to get a little bit more courage, and I said to myself, "I have to go up to him, I have to say hi, here's my chance."

So I walked up to the bar, "Excuse me, Lemmy. Hi, my name's Scott, I play in a band called Anthrax, and we're over here doing press for our second album. I'm just a huge fan. I wanted to say hi, and can I buy you a drink?"

Then I repeated, "I'm a huge fan." He looked at me, saw my shirt, and said, "I can tell." Then he said, "You're in my town. I'll buy *you* a drink. What are you having?"

I didn't really know what to say, because I wasn't a drinker, so I just said, "I'll have what you're having."

Lemmy asked the bartender for two whiskey and Cokes. I had never had a whiskey, ever. All that was going through my head was, "You cannot fuck this up. You're gonna down this drink like you're Clint Fuckin' Eastwood."

Lemmy said, "Cheers." I took a manly gulp. And I think I pulled it off without making a face. I thought he thought I was cool now because I drank my drink, which is his drink. I caught a buzz right away and it loosened me up a little bit. So we just started shooting the shit, I told him that I saw Motörhead open for Ozzy in 1980 at the Palladium on the *Ace of Spades* record when Randy Rhoads was still in the band. And Lemmy was talking to *me* and asking me about my band.

He kept ordering us drinks because he was Lemmy. At the time I was the happiest dude on earth.

The next day I wasn't so happy.

MAX CAVALERA

We were on tour with Ministry and I was really hammered one night when I was on Al Jourgensen's bus. I was getting a little wild, and the tour manager said, "Man, this guy's got to go to sleep. Goddammit, he's a fucking terrorizer."

He tried to take the bottle away from me. That's one thing you don't do to a guy who's drinking. Nobody does that shit.

So I grabbed the bottle and broke it on his head. After that, Al was like, "Okay, enough." So, he came over to me with three Valiums. He put them in my hand and said, "Take those things right now. You have to take them."

When Al Jourgensen is freaking out on you that you need to calm down, that's when things are just bad. So I took the Valiums and finally passed out. I missed the bus call from Sepultura, so I rolled with Ministry to the next show. I woke up in the back of Al's bus and had no idea what happened. All I knew was that I wasn't on my bus. Everything else was a blur.

I saw Al's passport and I went, "Okay, I'm in the Ministry bus."

I started walking to the front of the bus and saw this guy with a big bandage on his head.

"Whoa, what happened to you?" I said.

"You happened to me, Godammit!" he said. "You don't remember hitting me in the head with a bottle last night?"

"No, man. I kind of had flashes, but I didn't remember that."

WILLIE ADLER
Lamb of God

There was a night we were in Chile and Paul Wagoner had filled in for [guitarist] Mark [Morton]. He had a family emergency and had to go home. Me and [vocalist] Randy [Blythe] decided to get shitfaced before the show. We were both pretty hammered. I was able to hold my own, but I can't really say the same thing about Randy. After the first song, he went back to Paul and he was just standing there. And he said, "Paul, how many songs are left in the set?!?"

And Paul goes, "The whole set, dude. You've played one song."

Randy was just like, "Ohhhhhhhhhhh!"

There's footage of that show where Randy comes out and he had forgotten his microphone. You can just see the utter frustration when he throws his hands up in disgust.

KEITH BUCKLEY

Randy Blythe and I hung out quite a bit on Ozzfest. One night we were up until about 3 or 4 in the morning drinking. I couldn't keep up and had to go to bed. We had to wake up at 9 a.m. and Randy was still there drinking, but now he had a beer in one hand and a coffee in the other and he was going back and forth between the two to keep himself going.

KING FOWLEY
Deceased, October 31

We had no more beer one night and I was already hammered so I said fuck it, and I picked up a quart of motor oil and drank the whole fucking thing . . . and I felt fine. I didn't even throw up. Years later, I told someone and he said, "I don't believe you. You're full of shit. You'd've been sick."

"Produce it again," I said.

No one had motor oil. But a girl at the apartment took out Wesson cooking oil. I drank the whole thing and *that* made me deathly ill, but not the motor oil. Dan Lilker (Brutal Truth, S.O.D., ex-Anthrax) was there when I did it. He caught the tail end of it. And then he grabbed the empty container and put his mouth over the pour spout and got a ring of black oil on his lips. To this day, he might say he drank it, but I'm the one that downed the whole quart. People always ask me what happened afterward and I tell them I ran great for 3,000 miles.

KYLE SHUTT
The Sword

When we were on tour with Metallica we did our own one-off show at the Viper Room in Los Angeles, and Dave Grohl [Foo Fighters, Nirvana] came out. Whenever Dave Grohl goes somewhere with his friends, he rents a party bus so nobody has to drive and everyone can get loaded and have a good time. He calls it the Grohlercoaster. [Our drummer] Trivett [Wingo] had been talking with Dave—they're both drummers—so after the show, he ended up on the Grohlercoaster. Trivett got so wasted and in the process invented a drink called the Champaeger, which was two parts Jägermeister, one part champagne. He was pounding these all night and becoming the entertainment of the evening. Him, [Metallica guitarist] Lars [Ulrich], and Dave Grohl were like the Three Stooges. Eventually, Trivett got so fucked up and felt so shitty he plopped down under the bar and passed out. Dave Grohl picked him up, lay him down on a couch and sat with him for a little bit, trying to comfort him. In the end, they took him off the Grohlercoaster and sent him back to the hotel to sleep off his alcoholic haze. The next morning, he woke up and he had these huge black stains all over his pants and he was all pissed. "Oh, God, who the hell spilled shit all over me!?!" he asked. I said, "You did, buddy. You spilled Champaeger all over yourself all night long. You were awesome." He didn't remember a thing.

REX BROWN
Pantera, ex-Down, ex-Crowbar, Kill Devil Hill

You know what's funny? Everyone always talks about how Pantera were born drinkers. They were straight edge as fuck when I got into the band.

I walked into practice with a cigarette dangling from my mouth and a six-pack of Lowenbrau in one hand and my bass in the other. I went down into the studio, which was Dime and Vinnie's dad's place and I laid down three tracks without knowing them that well. And they said, "Well dude, you can't smoke or drink in our band." I went, "This is a fucking rock and roll band and you don't want me to drink or smoke? Are you kidding me?" The rest is history. I got Dime drunk for the first time when he was 16. And pretty soon we were all trying to out-drink one another.

JIMMY BOWER
Eyehategod, Superjoint Ritual, Down, ex-Crowbar

We were on tour with White Zombie and Pantera and we were in Miami. I hung out with [Pantera guitarist] Dimebag [Darrell] and [tour manager] Big Val. We all went to a couple bars and I got fuckin' wasted with Dime. When we got back, we were outside of the club banging the backs of our heads against the wall super-hard. We weren't gonna stop. And Big Val had to pick us up and drag us away. Another time, I was playing drums with Corrosion of Conformity and we were in Australia with Pantera on one of their last tours ever. Me and Dimebag were in the lobby drinking margaritas getting wasted. Next thing I knew we were dancing with these old ladies in the fuckin' lobby. And I'm looking over at him with this expression that says, "Dude, what the fuck?" And he goes, "Roll with it. Roll with it, son." Not ten minutes later we were cursing these old ladies out. I have no idea what happened that got us upset. But no more than five minutes later, I fell down and cut my hand open on a margarita glass and needed a bunch of stitches. And after that night in Australia, we both woke up in the same bed together in his room. I woke up and said, "Dude, what the fuck happened, bro?" and he went, "Dude, I don't know." We were just dumbfounded. That dude was fun to get drunk with.

JERRY DIXON

Man, I loved Dimebag. He was so cool. I don't know if people know this, but he was a huge fan of '80s metal. And he loved Warrant! Him and I used to get pretty hammered. You know those big one-gallon bottles of Jack Daniels? One time, he was trying to give me one and he threw it down to me. I didn't even have my hands up. It hit the top of my foot and almost broke it. But again, we drank that pain away.

BILLY GRAZIADEI
Biohazard

We were in Japan in winter of 2002 and it was the last Pantera show of the tour. I was with Dime and a couple girls from Kittie and we went to a local bar. I bought drinks for everybody. When we got the bill I was like, "What the fuck?" It was insane. We had been oblivious to the cost of everything.

When we left, they had a giant wall full of Jack Daniels. I grabbed a giant bottle on the way out and I was like, "You know what? For the fuckin' money I spent here, this is my fuckin' trophy!"

We all went out and I started chugging the Jack. We went to a club. I don't remember the name. I was wasted. Someone started talking shit with me about something, so I walked across tables to go after this kid. I dove across the dancefloor to fight him. I'm a crazy, wild, fighting kind of dude when I'm drunk. The club owner decided to throw me out. As I was being escorted out of the club, I saw Biohazard drummer Danny [Schuler] and my tech Nick coming in. They were coming in as I was being kicked out, but I didn't want to leave and I was fighting against it 'cause it was early and I wanted to stay. I was ripping the walls apart, pulling down pictures of the owner of the club with Ozzy and Mötley Crüe and Van Halen. Then, this kid was trying to get by and he said something to me. Later, I found out what he really said, but in my drunken state I heard, "kick your fuckin' ass." So I clocked him and ripped his shirt to try to get more of him. They finally get me outside. Then I saw the rest of the guys in Biohazard, who asked me what the fuck was going on. And I said, "I dunno, they just threw me out for no reason."

So they tried to help me squash the beef and get me back in the club and get everyone to calm down. With respect being such a big thing in Japanese culture, I went up to the security guard and shook his hand and apologized. I asked him if I could go back in with my friends. And he said, "Yeah, you can go back in." I said, "Thank you, man." And then I grabbed his face, put both hands on his cheeks and I licked him from his chin to his forehead. Then I put my hands up and said, "C'mon, mother-fucker!" I wanted to fight this dude. The guy was furious. I waited with my fists up and the guy wouldn't fight me. My bandmates said, "You fucking asshole. What are you doing?" So I said, "I'm sorry, I'm sorry." And I went up to the security guard again and said, "Man, I'm just wasted. I put my hand out to him again to shake and I said, "I'm just gonna go home. I just want to say I'm sorry." As he reached for my hand, I pushed his hand out of the way and licked his face from his chin to his forehead again and then I turned around and fuckin' hightailed it out of there.

They arrested me and put me in lockdown in the hotel. I wasn't allowed to leave for the rest of the weekend. I had to pay a lot of money for damages and write a letter of apology to the owner and promoter. I felt like a little kid being scolded by my father. I had to write a letter of apology to this kid. I had to go face to face and apologize to him and pay for his shirt, which his mother bought him for his birthday.

And then I found out what he had said wasn't "kick your fucking ass," it was, "Hey man, be careful because these bouncers will kick your ass."

SCOTT IAN

I had been in London hosting the *Kerrang!* Awards while the rest of the band took a day off in Sweden. Then, I had to meet them in Copenhagen, Denmark, at a festival, so I was on the same flight as Lemmy [Kilmister] from Motörhead, who was also playing the festival. Since we took the same flight, the promoters arranged for a van to pick both of us up at the airport. We all got in the van to ride there and Motörhead's tour manager told the driver we needed to make a stop as soon as we could at a convenience store that sold liquor. So, the driver stopped at this place 30 minutes away and at about noon, Lemmy went in and bought a quart of Jim Beam, a liter of Coca-Cola, and a bunch of *Hustler*s. We were about to get back in the van when Lemmy poured out three-quarters of the liter of Coke onto the ground and then filled the bottle with Jim Beam. We got back in the van and started driving again. He was just sitting there with his giant Jim Beam and Coke reading *Hustler*. I was there with a donut and coffee. A few minutes in, Lemmy looked at me and leaned the bottle toward me to offer me a drink.

"No, I'm good. Thanks," I said.

"Are you hungover? 'Cause this will cure it," he rasped.

"No, actually I didn't drink last night," I replied.

"Are you sure because I know you like whiskey. I know Maker's Mark is your drink and this tastes pretty good right now."

I assured him I was good. He wasn't taunting me or anything. He was really trying to be a good guy and offer me something nice. Over the next 90 minutes in the van, he finished the bottle and read the magazines and he looked as sober as the driver. Next thing you know, he's onstage: "Hey, Sweden Rock. How's it going?" And he's playing great and singing great in the middle of the afternoon. If it had been me, I would have been passed out and they'd have had to drag me out of the van. I'd never have made it to the stage. But Lemmy rocked the crowd for ninety minutes and didn't even blink.

MICHAEL SWEET

I'd wake up in different people's apartments every weekend and not know where I was. I used to hang out with guitarist Doug Aldrich (ex-Whitesnake, ex-Dio). He came out from Philly and we were best buds for a while. We used to do a lot of drinking and partying together. I met [Poison guitarist] C.C. DeVille when he came out of New York. He actually auditioned for Stryper and he was going to join the band but the thing that caused him to say no was the yellow and black look we had. He wanted to do the pink and purple thing, so he did. But we partied with him and Stephen Pearcy from Ratt, whether it was drinking at Gazarri's or wherever. I lived that lifestyle for a while and eventually it got too crazy for me, so I got out. When I hit twenty I went, "You know what? I don't want to do this anymore. I want to take what I do serious." Getting drunk every night and wondering where I'm gonna wake up the next morning—that's not taking music serious[ly].

JESSE JAMES DUPREE
Jackyl

I was partying so hard one night I could hardly stand up. We got through the show and at the end of the night I looked across to the other side of the stage and I said, "Brother, I'm done." I wound up in the dressing room and there was a party of about fifty people there. I was laying on the floor. I was so out of it and everyone was stepping around me. I knew what was going on, but I couldn't move. I woke up the next morning in that same dressing room and a DJ buddy of mine was sitting up against the wall. He had kept an eye on me overnight because he thought I might choke on my own vomit and die.

"Where's everybody at?" I asked him when I woke up.

"They went on to California," he said.

They loaded me up in a van and drove me to the airport and I paid $1,000 for a last-minute ticket to California. I was so sick on the plane. I was puking. I got to California and I was in a cab going to the arena we were playing in and I was laying over in the backseat.

"You sick?" asked the cab driver.

"Yeah," I muttered.

He pulled the pillow out from underneath his ass that he had been sittin' on and fartin' on all night.

"Here, you want this pillow?"

"No thank you," I moaned.

I was green for two days.

BRENDON SMALL
Dethklok, Galaktikon

We toured with Mastodon and got pretty drunk together. They were up for the party all the time and every night turned into a report about their guitarist Brent [Hinds]. "Did you hear about Brent?" "Yeah, he slipped on some ice and he's not sure if he broke his back. I guess we'll find out tomorrow." He was always fun to be with and his heart was always in the right place. But he would come on our bus and it would be like that scene in the animated Robert Zemeckis [movie] *Beowulf,* where the Grendel creature would come in screaming and saying all kinds of crazy stuff.

BRENT HINDS
Mastodon, Giraffe Tongue Orchestra, Legend of the Seagullmen

I have a lot of friends who are just as crazy as I am. We'll get drunk and go, "Hey man, let's fight!" And we'll beat the shit out of each other for fun! Before that whole fuckin' "Jackass" show started, I was going down hills in a golf cart beating the shit out of my friends. When I saw that movie I was like, "I've already been there, done that between the ages of 18 and 23."

WILLIE ADLER

We were loose cannons for years. We all sat in the chair of being the fuck up. And in hindsight, looking back, it was a huge asset. But in the moment and at the time we just wanted to party and drink everything we could find. I was a huge rager, too. I can look back at myself and [vocalist] Randy [Blythe] and think, "Golly, we could have just wrecked the ship at any point." But I think that whole unpredictable factor was part of the appeal of the band. People would look at Randy and think, "What the fuck is he going to do tonight?" That really made him an asset to what we were doing.

ALEX HELLID

We were on tour with Napalm Death and we had just stopped to rest for a minute. Then the driver started the bus up again and our tour manager came running down from upstairs yelling, "You have to stop the bus!"

"What? Why?" said the driver.

"[Guitarist] Uffe Cederlund's on the roof!" our manager yelled.

He had been drinking and he thought he was a vampire and could fly. So there he was on the roof of the bus. Fortunately, he didn't fall off. The driver slowed down and stopped at the side of the road and we were able to get Uffe back in the bus, where he kept drinking.

WILL CARROLL
Death Angel, ex-Machine Head

In the early '90s, I was at The Stone and we were watching The Mentors. They were this crazy, foul-mouthed band that used to wear hoods onstage, so I brought a hood with me to the show. We got backstage because me and Ted used to play there all the time so we knew the security. We're hanging out backstage and we're in The Mentors' dressing room. There's this woman who's coming back there and constantly bringing drinks to everyone. I'm not sure if she was their wench or if she worked at the club. But eventually, we said, "Where's our drinks?" She said, "You're not in the band, are you?" And I pulled the hood out of my pocket. And she went, "Oh, I guess you are in the band, too!" So she started getting me and three people I was with drinks, too. This was all going on The Mentors' tab. She gave us drinks for hours just 'cause I had a hood in my pocket. Then, the show was about to start, so we left the dressing room and went into the crowd. We were in the front row watching The Mentors play and she still hadn't put two and two together that we're not in the band. She was still running over and handing us drinks! Finally, their back-up singer yelled at her, "Stop giving them drinks! They're not in the band!" We went, "Oh shit," and walked to the back of the club.

SCOTT IAN

After a Pantera show at Roseland in New York in the mid-'90s, we headed down to some bar on Avenue A and [Pantera guitarist] Dimebag Darrell got down there before anyone else and lined up two hundred Black Tooth Grin shots on the bar for whoever was coming down. I walked in and there were only ten people there at this point. Me, [Pantera bassist Rex Brown] and Dime immediately downed three shots, bang, bang, bang. And in the course of the next thirty minutes, I probably did another ten very quickly—a really stupid amount because they just go down so easily, and it was so ridiculous there were so many shots sitting there. The next thing I knew, I was being dragged out. I had literally dropped. I was standing there and I dropped face-first and passed out. A couple people carried me outside and I woke up and went, "What the fuck happened?" That was the end of the night for me. I went home. And that was one of the 400 times things like that happened with Darrell.

TOMMY VICTOR
Prong, Danzig, ex-Ministry

When Ministry went to the Czech Republic, I did some absinthe. [Ministry frontman] Al [Jourgensen] was always trying to hide it from his wife. In Prague, he got somebody to go to the merch booth and get cash and we bought thirty or forty bottles of absinthe. I drank a whole shitload of it and next thing I knew I was writing my memoirs on hotel stationery all night long. I wrote, like, fifty pages and I have no idea what happened to it. I left the hotel without even looking for it. The way I was writing I could have kept going for two more days and had a book. I was like, "Fuck, I could have sold it."

M. SHADOWS
Avenged Sevenfold

We went snowboarding all day in upstate New York in zero-degree weather. There was a lodge and we got drunk all morning. It's funny because I suck at snowboarding, but when I was totally hammered, I was way better. I started out on the bunny slopes and by the end of the day, I was going down the expert slopes. I wiped out like crazy, but I didn't feel it. But the next day I was all black and blue. My ribs felt like they were broken and I had the flu, so I was sick as fuck and it was hell on earth.

RANDY BLYTHE

I spent an inordinate amount of time drinking, thinking about drinking, recovering from drinking, feeling guilty about drinking, getting mad about the fact that I couldn't drink when I wasn't drinking. There were certain things I got from alcohol when I was writing. Certain parts of my psyche became unlocked. And some good things came out of that. Unfortunately, after a while it locked the rest of my psyche and it became an all-consuming obsession. The longer I'm sober the more I realize exactly how much time I spent fixating on getting fucked up. So many times when I was drinking I would be thinking about writing and think-ing about creating, but never doing anything.

PAGE HAMILTON
Helmet

When Helmet came back in 2004, and [Interscope Records co-founder] Jimmy Iovine asked me to make a Helmet record, I had a phase when I was drinking way too much. I kinda got into a bad habit of drinking whis-key before I went onstage. And during a show in Melbourne, Australia, I went on this long, long drunken rant about alternative music. I called it "Indier than thou." When we started out, indie rock was made up of all these bands that were on independent labels. And then it turned into this fashion thing. So I went on this twenty-minute drunken tirade: "Metal's way cooler than indie rock will ever be." And I meant it. I really appreciate the purity and passion of metal even though a lot of metal guys probably don't accept us because we don't look the part. But I love the commitment to the music that metal fans have. I've always said I don't like labels, but that particular night in my drunken state I felt com-pelled to rail on the hipster ethos because there still is something pure and amazing about metal.

MATT HEAFY
Trivium

One of the first tours we did, we were staying in someone's basement. We were drinking Jäger and I did a front flip into a glass table and it smashed to pieces. Surprisingly, I didn't get hurt. But actually, one of my favorite stories dealing with broken glass and myself and drinking was kind of recent. It was on the *In Waves* cycle [in 2011]. We had several days off so I decided to stay in Warsaw, Poland, with some friends. We kept going back and forth to vodka pickle bars, where you do a shot of vodka and it pairs with pickled herring or pickled vegetable. And you keep hopping from place to place. Finally, we ended up in a beer bar. I have this nervous tick. When I drink on tour it's usually out of a plastic cup and I chew on the edge of the cup a little bit. I was doing that, but it didn't cross my mind that this was a glass. So the glass shattered in my mouth and I had to take the pieces out of this lake of beer in my lower mouth. Somehow, I didn't slash my mouth to bits. The bartender was so impressed he bought us shots and rounds for the rest of the night.

PAUL LEDNEY
Profanatica, Havohej

We drove from New York to Rhode Island to play a Relapse fest in 1993. I was really wasted on the way there and we stopped to go into a Dunkin' Donuts. I was only wearing underwear and we got kicked out. Then when we got to Rhode Island all of the rooms in the hotels had been booked by people who were going to this huge Jehovah's Witness conference. We got kicked out of a couple hotels because I was yelling at the people at the front desk for letting these scumbags book all the rooms. We went to three different hotels and we finally got a really divey motel—the kind most people pay for by the hour. We got a couple of rooms. I was still drunk from the night before and in my underwear. There were piles of shit in one of the rooms. I was too drunk to care.

WILL CARROLL

The only time I blew it onstage with Death Angel was on the second 70,000 Tons of Metal cruise. We were one of the first bands to play when the ship set sail. It was an amazing set. Then we had the next two days off and we played again the last night. But those two days I raged hard. When the boat docked in Tahiti, me and [vocalist] Mark [Osegueda] went to a tequila beach where you pay $30 and it's all the tequila, beer, and tacos you can eat for two or three hours. We were with Burton [C. Bell] from Fear Factory and the guys from Symphony X. I stayed up 'til 9 a.m. the day of our show and we were playing at 3 p.m. I had a horrible gig. I dropped the drumstick and completely fucked up parts. That's the only time I've ever completely blown it. But Death Angel were cool with me. They were like, "Okay, this isn't a recurring problem, but don't ever do that again."

PAGE HAMILTON

We were in Tokyo, Japan, on the *Betty* cycle in 1995. We were there during the harvest celebration and we went to a sushi place. It was our bassist Henry Bogdan's birthday, so we were just getting hammered. The people in the place started throwing soybeans as part of a ritual and they were wearing masks. So we were like, "Hey, food fight!" and we started a food fight in this restaurant. I take it you're not supposed to throw bowls of seaweed and sushi for the harvest celebration like we did, but it was hilarious.

DEVIN TOWNSEND

Strapping Young Lad, ex-Steve Vai, ex-Wildhearts, Devin Townsend Band

When I was singing with Steve Vai, we were playing in Barcelona and I was really sick. So the doctor went and got me a bunch of cough medicine. It wasn't like the standard Dimetapp, it was this crazy codeine cough medicine that I wasn't familiar with. I drank the whole bottle. For the first song, I was supposed to walk dramatically up to the microphone and start singing. I walked right past it and fell into the audience. But I got back up and started the show.

SAM RIVERS

I know I had a blast being in the band. I don't remember *any* horrible times. But I was so wasted all of the time that I really don't remember *anything*. I can't recall many super-funny things that happened or even a lot of horrible stuff. I was drinking way more than any of the other guys—way more. A lot of people say things about themselves like, "Man, if I didn't stop drinking, I would have died." I *definitely* would have died. I had to leave Limp Bizkit in 2015 because I felt so horrible, and a few months after that I realized I had to change everything because I had really bad liver disease. I quit drinking and did everything the doctors told me. I got treatment for the alcohol and got a liver transplant, which was a perfect match. Since then, I haven't stopped looking forward. I'm finally back with the band and I'm feeling one hundred percent. I'm actually healthier now than I was before.

DAVE WYNDORF

Monster Magnet

Once, in 1995, I decided to go on a diet of vodka and bananas. I felt like all the food I was eating was getting in the way of the vodka. But I had to exist, so I figured bananas were a benign food that could give me energy. They were on our rider, so I would take a handful of bananas and a bottle of vodka, and that was my night.

I did a European tour that way, and things got sloppier and sloppier. I got a cold, and it turned into pneumonia. After Europe, we did another three weeks in Canada, and by the end of the tour I was pretty much a zombie stomping around. I had plenty of potassium but very little vitamins in my body. I had to go to the emergency room in Canada. I think they brought in a priest to read my last rites. I was on all kinds of IV fluids, and they put me on a hospital plane to get me home.

After that episode, I figured out that I'm just not cut out for this drinking thing anymore. It's too good. I got too used to it and drank too much. But about three months after that episode in Canada, I tried to take a drink and I was like, "Yuckkk!" It was totally unpleasant. It just didn't do it.

And that was it. I haven't drank since.

RANDY BLYTHE

I was sitting on a balcony and looking at these empty beer bottles from the night before. I was just sitting there hungover as fuck and I was like, "Y'know, I don't feel like doing anything but drinking, and I don't even feel like drinking." I was in this weird fugue state. All I cared about at the time was altering my consciousness and I decided that was no way to live. I had to break the pattern of being sober at home and then getting fucked up on tour. I had to be sober on the road as well.

It was a beautiful day and I realized there was a park down the street. It was about 1 p.m. and there was a bookstore nearby. I love going for a walk in the park and then checking out the local bookstore because I'm a big fucking nerd. And I'm gonna spend too much fucking money on books and read and maybe write. That was good because at that point I was going onstage almost every night, but I might as well have been going to clock in at Seven-11 for the amount of enjoyment I was getting out of it. That's fucked up. I always loved playing shows and being in Lamb of God and I was taking that away from myself. I realized I wasn't living. So I got sober. I couldn't really think clearly and realize where I was until I was about six months sober. The first few months sober were incredible. I had a great time.

And then at four months sober I felt terrible. I was depressed. I felt like the world was collapsing on me and that's because I put so many substances in my that physiologically the pathways to my brain were fucked up and now that I was sober they were rewiring themselves and it was causing my psyche to go completely haywire. You ride that out. You push through.

I firmly believe I was going to die if I kept going the way I was. I had to find things to do to substitute for the time I used to spend drinking. My coffee intake has increased. I have always loved record stores and bookstores. It's a very sad fact for me that very few record stores exist. But I can still spend a lot of time at the bookstore.

MIKE IX WILLIAMS
Eyehategod

There have been so many times when we would get drunk and destroy a club. We'd smash our shit and throw beer bottles at the walls. That was kind of typical for us. It wasn't something that only happened on occasion. A lot of times, I would even forget I was on a stage or I'd end up passed out behind the drums while the rest of the band finished the show. That's happened more than once. It was a long time ago, and it's nothing I'm proud of. When things like that happened, I'd wake up the next day and see that everybody was pissed at me and I had no idea why.

And one thing that woke me up a little was when I'd ask the other guys what the money situation was like for the gig we played, and they'd say: "You're not getting any money. You were passed out behind the drum riser for half the show. Forget it!"

That was bad, and at that point, I felt like I had to get control of this thing a little bit somehow.

IVAN MOODY
Five Finger Death Punch

I basically almost drank myself into oblivion. I lost all contact with my kids and my family. I got to a point where I wouldn't wake up in the day at all. I'd just sleep through it and then wake up and go to the bar and then go back to bed. It got to be such a pattern. I felt gross. I felt like a junkie. When you lose all of that, everything you love, it's pretty hard. My own band members wouldn't return my calls for a while. They were tired of dealing with it. I lost multiple tour managers, crew members. I can't tell you how many friends stopped talking to me. It's really sad sometimes that you have to go to that extreme to find your way back up, but it somehow felt necessary for me.

"Cold," one of the songs I wrote [for 2013's *The Wrong Side of Heaven and the Righteous Side of Hell, Volume 2*], was a suicide note. I had been up drinking for 36 hours in a row. I drunk dialed everybody I knew and went off on just about everybody I knew. I had burned about twenty bridges. I had management, my band, everybody, screaming down my throat that it had to stop. The poison was festering, obviously, and it had to end. I could have killed myself but that would have been too easy and I've always been a fighter. That's when I looked backwards and figured out where my need to drink was rooted. It started with something very personal that I was trying to escape. So I said, "Okay, let's go back there and work our way up to now to find some clarity." When you find yourself in a house all by yourself and no one to answer your phone calls, that's when you resort to what you do best. Fortunately, it wasn't drinking, it was mostly writing. I locked myself at home and dried out. I can't tell you how many nights I was shaking and had cold sweats and tried to get some kind of clarity. I was in tears half the time I worked. There were sleepless nights, but it was necessary and I knew it and I felt it in my heart. I believe that there was some higher power pulling me away from it. That's where the title of the album comes from. *The Wrong Side of Heaven, Righteous Side of Hell* is like being in purgatory. I felt like I was lingering between the two and I had no purpose. I'm really proud that I pulled my head out of my ass and got back on course and it was a hard thing to do. I had the guys send me a few tracks and "Cold" is one that really fueled me. I was in tears half the time I worked on it but it was a starting point to a very therapeutic process.

CHAPTER 3: TAKE AS NEEDED FOR PAIN

From Weed Warriors to Smack Addicts

One of the pioneers of the New Orleans sludge metal scene of the late '80s, Eyehategod, wrote grime-coated songs about drugs, addiction, desperation, and pain that drew from doom metal, southern rock, and even the blues. "Take as Needed for Pain" is the title track of their second album.

Drugs, including meth, cocaine, mushrooms, and, of course, weed, have been catalysts for creativity as well as the poison that ruined and even killed great musicians. Heroin is excluded from this list since, aside from some suicidal doom bands and grunge outfits that might have benefited from its sedative effects, as is revealed in this chapter, those who have turned to smack for pain relief have often found themselves in a pit of despair that was agonizing to escape. That said, just as the Beatles relied on uppers to keep them hyped up to play multiple sets a night in Germany in the early stages of their career, meth-inspired musicians including Motörhead's Lemmy Kilmister and top thrash bands such as Exodus and Death Angel tweaked their balls off to maintain the hyperactivity to play intense songs that required frantic beats and speedy riffs. As with many music scenes, however, drugs have often led to aggressiveness, fuzzy thinking, compromised musicianship, and worse. Still, some of the most self-immolating drug users have the craziest, most alluring stories to tell.

GARY HOLT
Exodus, Slayer

When I was still pretty young, before I played in a band, I started getting into some serious drug experimentation. Me and my friends used to listen to Black Sabbath's *Master of Reality* at night with the windows all blacked out, in pitch blackness, just high as fuck on tons of LSD. It was a life-changing experience. If you turned the lights on you expected Satan to be two inches from your face. It felt like the end of the world and I loved it.

DAVE ELLEFSON
Megadeth

[Megadeth frontman] Dave [Mustaine] and I basically met over a case of Heineken. We lived in the same apartment complex. I was 18 and he was 21. I knocked on his door and told him I had beer, so he let me in. We drank the beer and he played me some songs and I was floored. I told him I played bass and it went from there. We started with beer and we got into deeper, darker stuff. You know, pills, cocaine. I don't regret it. They were fun days. It was kind of the status quo back in the day: sex, drugs and rock and roll. Megadeth just got deeper and darker into the stuff than most other bands. And heroin became our drug of choice.

DEZ FAFARA
DevilDriver, ex-Coal Chamber

Half the people in the band were going crazy on speed and coke and bringing in porn stars. The other half of the band were taking the completely opposite kind of drugs. I suffer from ADHD, so if you give me speed, it doesn't speed me up, it mellows me the fuck out to the point where I don't even recognize people. I just sit there like a zombie. So I never went in that direction. I was always like, "Just give me something that takes me down. Give me mushrooms, acid, marijuana. I'll take Valium or Xanax."

In the early days of Coal Chamber, I had days where I would binge on drugs for a week straight. I would call it "the quickening." I was either on acid or ecstasy for six or seven days straight. Of course, I would sleep. But as soon as I got up, I'd start up again. And those shows were some of the best and the worst we ever played. I can actually see why people in the '60s used to trip before a show and why Jimi Hendrix put acid in the headband he wore onstage so when he'd sweat the acid would seep into his pores.

BRENT HINDS
Mastodon, Giraffe Tongue Orchestra, Legend of the Seagullmen

I have to take Xanax because I'm very high strung. I'm a very anxious, vivacious person. I'm very talkative and outgoing. So I need a quarter of Xanax to rein that in so I'm not bothering people, basically. I've been doing it for years, ever since I realized I was way too thought process active. I'm kind of like Gary Busey in a way. I'll say shit off the cuff and people will go, "What are you talking about?" It'll make total sense to me and I'm just like, already on to the next subject that's not even at hand yet in my mind. I think that's good writing music because I come up with way more ideas than I need and I can plan for everyone and see if everyone likes the ideas by presenting them with a lot of different options. I usually trail off into many different directions. If you ask me a question, I'll end up talking about sandwiches.

GARY HOLT

Some of the craziest moments happened when we were barely a band and Kirk Hammett was still playing with us. He hadn't been asked to join Metallica yet. We had one whole summer we called our Summer of Love, where we'd go down to Berkeley to Telegraph Avenue with some of Kirk's dad's classical albums. We'd go to Rasputin's record store, sell 'em and go buy acid at People's Park. Then we'd buy some beer and we'd get completely fucked up. We did that shit for a whole summer. And we ate a lot of magic mushrooms. I kinda learned to play guitar on that stuff. It opened up and bent my mind a little and broadened my horizons. I really think it made me more creative.

SCOTT IAN
Anthrax, S.O.D., The Damned Things

I took mushrooms one time in 1994 in New York City. I was hanging out with some real peripheral people I knew. Some girl that [ex-Anthrax vocalist] John Bush (ex-Anthrax, Armored Saint) was dating and her sister ended up in the West Village one night at a second-story apartment on Bleeker Street with a crew of people that I knew but didn't really know. Someone had a bag of mushrooms, and I'd never done any psychedelics before. I knew about mushrooms. I asked, "What does it do? What is it going to be like?" And one of the girls said, "It's fun and it's usually mellow, depending on how much you eat."

I took a couple of pieces and chewed them up. That was fucking disgusting. I washed it down with beer and waited. Thirty minutes passed and I didn't feel anything. I took another two little pieces and ate them. About fifteen minutes later, I was sitting there watching everyone else. Some people were already tripping and I started to feel something, I was like, "Wow, this is kind of weird, but good."

All of a sudden, I turned into Albert Einstein, only more all-knowing. My brain was a sponge and I started absorbing every drop of information that had ever rained down from the heavens and been absorbed by the ground. Everything made perfect sense. I thought I should immediately write down all this information that was being transmitted to me so I could solve everyone's problems afterward. But I was probably too high to remember how to use a pencil. So instead of writing the answers to the greatest mysteries, I wandered out onto the fire escape and looked down at the people in the street. Suddenly, I just knew that I could fly like a superhero. I was yelling at people on the street and in the party that I was going to fly down to the street like the Human Torch and take them for a ride. Naturally, this kind of worried some of the people at the party and a few of them ran out and got me and dragged me back inside before I jumped. If they hadn't done that, I think I really would have tried to fly off the fire escape.

DAVE WYNDORF
Monster Magnet

The worst experience I had and the most paranoid and bizarre one happened in the early '90s in Holland. I jumped into the crowd and someone stuffed a giant wad of paper in my mouth. He really got it in there, and I couldn't get my hands to my mouth. I rolled back on the stage and pulled it out, and it was rolled-up hits of blotter acid.

I started getting off right away.

I hadn't done LSD in ten years at that point, and within two songs I was completely tripping my ass off. It was like an episode of *The Twilight Zone* or *Batman* where the walls were tilted and askew. The horizon line was crooked. Everything took on this oversaturated color, and it seemed like I was looking through a fish-eye lens. I couldn't hear what I was singing, so I was trying to fake it and it was fucking horrible.

In hindsight, it sounded pretty cool. My guitarist's rig sounded amazing, and for a while that's all I could hear. My sensory input would only accept the guitar—no drums.

It took me about a day and a half to come down from that. I learned to keep my mouth shut when I went in the audience from then on.

CHRIS URENNA
ex-Nine Inch Nails, ex-Marilyn Manson

We were in Miami, Florida, working on the *Natural Born Killers* soundtrack and us and Marilyn Manson went up to go to this show north of the city.

We were all high as a kite. I don't know if it was mushrooms or what, but it was intense. And then we got in this massive food fight in the van on the way back. Our poor tour manager was driving all of Nine Inch Nails and most of Marilyn Manson in this van and we were tripping so hard. We were giggling and we were trying to eat McDonald's. We trashed the van pretty bad with McDonald's breakfast food. There were pieces of food in the air vent, the glove compartment and all through the passenger area. The next day our tour manager was so mad at us and none of us remembered a single thing.

DAVE ELLEFSON

Where other bands were into girls and beer and maybe some cocaine, Megadeth went all the way down into the dark roads of heroin addiction and some really, really heavy stuff. Every day was a nightmare story that people wouldn't believe. We'd drive down from East L.A. to L.A. to score bags of heroin before we could get to rehearsal and then we'd rehearse in Hollywood at Mars studio, which is over in East Hollywood. We were strung out on the road, too, and that was difficult. Alcohol is everywhere. Cocaine was pretty easy to find but heroin was a refined taste. And once you got the flavor of it, you were hooked.

JIMMY BOWER
Eyehategod, Superjoint Ritual, Down, ex-Crowbar

A lot of the people in the New Orleans metal scene did heroin and other narcotics. I did all that. I'm not proud of it. There's nothing to glorify about it. I lost my girlfriend to that shit. And I buried a lot of friends.

MIKE IX WILLIAMS
Eyehategod

It's pretty well known that we've all had our little drug problems. I've missed shows. I was totally addicted, and I was dope sick because I couldn't get any drugs for whatever reason. That's all in the past, but man, there are so many different stories, and there were so many times the band was just a huge felony rolling down the highway. We were always in danger of getting pulled over with the stuff we had on us. Guys were shooting up and doing coke. There was paraphernalia and drugs and methadone and Xanax and pretty much everything you can imagine going through the van. We knew that it was terrible, but we felt like it was a necessity. That's how we wanted to do it. It was a stupid ideal that some young bands have. I look back and cringe at all the things we did that were illegal or dangerous, and I thank somebody—knock on wood—that nothing ever happened.

DAVID VINCENT

ex-Morbid Angel, Vltimas

We were on tour in South America, and oftentimes everything is quick but you're not on a tour bus. You have to fly every day. You fly into a city, hurry up and race to the city, hurry up and do soundcheck, then do press and finally the show. By the time you're done with the show at night and you get back to the hotel it's 3 a.m. and there's a 6 a.m. lobby call so everyone can assemble in the lobby and make the next flight. After several of these days, it starts taking its toll. No sleep, no time to zone out. We got to Argentina and as soon as we got out of the plane, we're informed we had to go straight to the venue and do press and then soundcheck. I was like, "Ugh, I don't care if I soundcheck today." I'm not gonna sound like anything if I don't get some sleep. The people at the venue said, "Hey, can we get you anything?" I thought, "Well, we're in South America." So I said, "Yeah man, a gram of coke sure would be nice." Somehow or another, the word gram wasn't interpreted and a guy came back with a big solid rock of coke larger than a golf ball. It was very potent, being that it was from the region. So I took a little shave off that and I was good, ready to go. We played the show. No hitches. All was good.

So we get back to the hotel room. TI was in the hotel room looking at this thing and even after everybody had partaken in it, it didn't look like the rock had gotten any smaller. I said, "Gosh, we can't really waste this, guys. No one's ever given us this kind of a gift before." So I was like, "Well, we might as well see if we can't put a hurtin' on this." So, me and other unnamed individuals did our best to try to put a dent in this rock of cocaine. We stayed up all night carving up lines, one after another. I definitely realized how high you can get—what the ceiling is. There was a point where I was bleeding down the front of my shirt and it wasn't possible for me to get any higher. We were sitting on a plane going back home and I was still high as fuck, but I was trying to remain as calm as I could. I had my shades on. But behind the shades, my eyes were completely bugging out. That was after three days of no sleep, but we were so jacked up it didn't matter. And I think that's the last time I ever used cocaine because when you find out what that limit is you don't ever need to do it again. And that's hard because usually, you do a little bit and then you always run out and go, "Well, let's do a little more." But there is no more, so there's always a level of moderation. Up to that point, I had never had so much where there was this extra quantity that we literally had to throw away.

BILLY GRAZIADEI
Biohazard

The name of our band was born out of smoking crack. My pop was a scientist, and as a kid I helped him clean up the lab and I would see that sticker with the biohazard logo everywhere. Fast-forward years later. [Vocalist] Evan [Seinfeld] and I were sitting with our first drummer and a bunch of friends. Somebody handed me a crack stem. While I lit it, Evan said, "So what are we gonna go with as a name?" I sucked in the crack and exhaled it, feeling that rush wash over my whole body. "Let's go with Biohazard," I said. I figured it was a cool, dangerous-sounding name and we could use that biohazard logo I always saw as a kid. Everyone thought it was a cool name. Eventually, we cleaned ourselves up and kicked all our shit because we were more interested in making good music together than getting high. We had a period where we fell off a little bit, but we never got as bad as we were at the beginning of the band.

AL JOURGENSEN
Ministry, Revolting Cocks

The first time I met Motörhead's Lemmy Kilmister was backstage and I turned him on to his first Rohypnol. He didn't know what they were. Knowing that he was full well on speed and coke and this damn speed over in Europe was so potent, he was spun out and I wanted to help. He was bitching about how he hadn't slept in days, so I said, "Well, here, do some of these." He said, "What are these, man?" And I explained to him that it was the perfect way to take the edge off. I didn't even get into the date rape aspect of it. I didn't tell him to slip it into the drinks of underage girls or anything and then have sex with them, which is, eventually, what they become useful for in some circles. I said, "Hey, if you need some sleep, pop a couple of these." So then we played another festival with him a few days later and he was all about it. He wanted me to get him some more. It was all about one friend helping another with a medical condition.

KYLE SHUTT
The Sword

The Sword was basically a fifteen-year weed-smoking contest between four dudes. We tried to calculate how much weed we actually smoked during our career. If you bring it down to a quarter a day for 1,500 shows plus off days, it had to be upwards of forty pounds, at least. The thing about being a stoner is you have to have weed all the time and you have some pretty strange priorities when you're hooked on the reefer. It gets sticky when you get to Europe. There's a border crossing every day and they take that shit really seriously.

SCOTT IAN

I used to steal pin joints from my parents and we'd smoke them, but they never really did anything to me. I figured I was probably immune to pot. But I always liked the smell of it. One time some guys were smoking it in our bus so I decided to smoke some figuring it wouldn't do anything to me. My friend Artie took a hit and passed the joint to me. I took a big hit and held it in for a while. Just as I thought, it didn't affect me. Whatever. We still had beer. Then, about twenty-five minutes later I felt really weird. I thought, "Okay, I did it. I'm high!" But I didn't like the way it felt. I've said this before, and it's really nerdy, but the best way I can describe what went on in my head was to reference that scene from *Star Wars* where Luke Skywalker, Princess Leia, and Han Solo go down the garbage chute and the walls start closing in and there's a monster called The Dianoga who grabs Luke with one of his tentacles and drags him into the sewage. It felt like a wall in the back of my skull was moving forward towards my forehead. I passed out before it got to the front of my head. I woke up about a minute later, but I was shaking and freaked out. "What happened?" I asked my friend. "You passed out," he said. The same thing happened later in my life and that's how I discovered I'm allergic to weed.

BRENDON SMALL
Dethklok, Galaktikon

I like smoking pot now, but I never used to enjoy it.

[Bassist] Bryan Beller was the same way. One night we decided we were going to smoke some pot, so we tried to create an environment for ourselves that was calm and Niceville. We figured we'd rent a Disney movie and get pizza and ice cream. We'd have all these comforts to make it the nicest thing in the world. We were in Lawrence, Kansas, on a Tuesday night. There was no good pizza place that was open and we were in a shitty hotel room. So we smoked it anyway and it was really strong pot and I didn't know how much I should smoke, anyway. So I smoked way too fucking much and I started having a panic attack. I felt all our little safety nets were going away. Someone who's really loud showed up and started talking and talking and totally killed our chilled-out mood. Then, somebody took off the nice, pleasant music we were playing and put on something that was the heaviest, scariest music possible. I really felt like I was dying inside. And then our bus driver came in and started screaming at us because we didn't get "mom and pop" pizza and we ended up giving our money to Domino's or some shitty chain that doesn't stand for all the right political issues. I was about to start crying in front of people. I looked over at Bryan and he had the exact same look as me, paralyzed with fear. We went down to the hotel bar to try to get as drunk as possible to make this feeling go away. And we did. We ordered all these fruity balloon drinks with orange slices and cherries in them just to make the bad effects of the pot stop happening, anything to fucking stop it from happening. Looking back, it's really funny because I never freak out from pot anymore. I get high to go out to dinner or go to an IMAX movie. Now, it's just fun.

BUZZ OSBORNE
Melvins

I was in high school in 1980 or 1981 and me and our old drummer went to Judas Priest's *Screaming for Vengeance* tour on two hits of acid each, because one hit of acid wasn't working. And then we went in and realized it *was* working. We were completely arsed on acid. One hit's pretty good, but two hits, depending on the acid, can be a little bit more than you want to deal with. All we could do was walk around. We couldn't stop. And at one point we looked at each other and I said, "Where is everybody going?" because people were all going to their seats. And then Priest played, and it was fuckin' amazing. I was completely blown away. It would have been great not on acid, probably, but tripping like I was, it was incredible. And then we got outside and realized that we couldn't drive. We had to wait until we were sober enough to drive back where we lived.

KING FOWLEY
Deceased, October 31

My first and only acid trip was insane. A guy who worked for the Grateful Dead gave me five hits of LSD. I had no idea one would have done the trick so I did all five at once and then me and my friend went out to Bull Run Park in Virginia. Some friends were out there at a campsite. They had been living there for a little while. I was sitting in this tent and one of the guys said, "We're gonna watch *Apocalypse Now*, man."

We started watching it and all I saw was blood and limbs blown off. I started crying and I said, "Oh my God. War is hell. It's fucking hell!"

"Dude, you're losing your mind," someone said. "You're losing your fucking mind."

'I am," I said, "I am, man. I am!"

"Hey, chill out," said my friend Marcel. "I know. Let's go get some more acid."

For some reason, I thought that was a good idea. We went back to Arlington, got some more LSD and I did five more hits and went back to Bull Run. Now I was on 10 hits of acid and they were trying to get me to watch *2001: A Space Odyssey* with them. They were like, "Isn't this great?"

They were tripping on, probably, one hit each. I thought the movie was boring so I started looking around and I looked at myself and I thought I was breaking out in pimples all over the place. I freaked out and said, "I want some milk and some fuckin' pickles!"

They got me milk and pickles.

"Fuck man, this shit sucks!" I screamed. "I'm getting the fuck out of here!"

I opened up the tent with the zipper and as soon as I went outside the world turned black. The tent was glowing so I closed the zipper and all of a sudden it was gone and I was out there alone. I walked around freaking out at around two in the morning. I thought, "I need some food or I'm gonna die!" That's all I remember. They found me the next morning at about 9 a.m. I was sitting in the shower with hot water blasting on me. I was holding a pan I stole from someone's tent and a cup of Oodles of Noodles. I guess I tried to boil the noodles with the shower water. I was burned from the hot water and it took me a long time before I stopped tripping and was kind of able to think straight. That's when I said to myself, "You know what? I ain't fuckin' with this shit no more."

CORITY TAYLOR
Slipknot, Stone Sour

There was a lot of addiction in my life that I had nothing to do with, but it certainly led to my going down those roads. When you grow up the way I did you tend to try to push the limits really quick. I'm glad that I went through all that shit when I was younger because if I'd gone through it when I was older I might not have gotten out of it. Everyone knows the stories about all the drugs and alcohol in Slipknot. They've been well-documented.

I started really young and then I got it out of my system—but not drinking. That lasted a while. The funniest drug experience I can remember is when I was about fifteen I went through a period of huffing paint. It was such an odd high. Then some friends of mine turned me on to huffing Scotchgard, and after doing that I was convinced for a while that by huffing Scotchgard I could see the future and I could have these déjà vu moments. I felt like everything I saw was something I previously saw in a dream, so I just kept inhaling Scotchgard thinking that I could see the future. Fortunately, that was a short-lived phase.

DEVIN TOWNSEND
Strapping Young Lad, ex-Steve Vai, ex-Wildhearts, Devin Townsend Band

For about ten years, I did acid, mushrooms and psychedelic things, and smoked a bunch of weed, but it became clear rather quickly that if I was to keep my relationships it would be best to reexamine those things. Strangely, the most dramatic way I ever killed brain cells was by doing whippets for a couple weeks straight. I put my $CO2$ cartridges into a whip cream container and sucked on that. It felt like someone put a railroad spike in the back of my head and everything sounded like it was going through a flanger [effect pedal]. It was fun and it's a short-lived high so you could just do some more and when you were done you were fine. But those things kill tons and tons of brain cells.

One day I was doing that with a bunch of buddies for an afternoon and I suddenly thought to myself, "Wow, I just got ten percent dumber than I was when I woke up this morning."

DAVE NAVARRO
Jane's Addiction

Those were the days, man. We didn't make music on a computer. We did it together. It was four guys spun out on speed, hashing out riffs for a week in a single room, and we wouldn't sleep until it sounded good. And then we went and recorded it live and did it in one take.

ROB CAVESTANY
Death Angel, ex-The Organization

Thrash metal was born out of heavy metal, punk rock, coke, and meth. Everyone was on fucking meth back then and everyone was speeded out of their minds. That's how we all played so fucking fast. These days, I play fast at practice without meth and I'm chill. But it's not the same. To play fast like that goes against the grain of being chill. The thing is, as you get older you can't keep going like that. So it was great for a while, but some people didn't know when to stop. Crew dudes were losing their fucking minds 'cause of that shit. We've had multiple people we've had to part ways with because they went full-on paranoid.

One dude thought people were watching him through mirrors in his hotel. He had a nice Nikon camera and next thing we know he'd completely taken it apart. He thought "they" were spying on him. One night we played a show at The River Theater in Guerneville, California, and afterwards the dude who thought people were watching him through mirrors climbed the rafters in this venue, went upstairs into this attic, and had a panic attack in there because he thought everyone was after him. We tried to calm him down but he didn't recognize anyone. To make matters worse, there was a weak spot in the ground and he fell through the floor and onto the next level. He was in hysterics and he ended up going to the ambulance to the psych ward. That was it for him.

GARY HOLT

Throughout Exodus's career until 2002, after [vocalist] Paul Baloff's death, chemicals were a problem. I had eras where I didn't use. But in the early days, a lot of us did speed so we could drink longer. And then as the years went by all of a sudden we're doing tons of it, completely spun out.

In the beginning, I think the speed contributed to the energy and aggression of the music. But that went for a lot of bands. Would you have had Motörhead if Lemmy didn't do lots of speed? I don't know. And I don't know if we would have done *Bonded by Blood* the way we did if that hadn't come into play.

I always used to say that we started out as a band of musicians that dabbled in drugs and then we became drug addicts who dabbled in music.

Somehow, I came out of it with all those brain cells intact, which is the amazing, fortunate thing. After all the years of trying to fuck my brain up, I failed. And I'm a guy who does not like failure, but in that circumstance, I'll take it.

DAVE ELLEFSON

The first risk is the taboo of drinking because if you drink, you might turn into a drunk. And then you drink once, and go, "God that was fun." It's no longer taboo. And it went like that for everything I did: pot, pills, blow, heroin, everything. Once I did it and didn't die or get arrested or go to jail—basically no consequences—it was like, "Cool, that was good. I think I'll do more of that."

With each drug, there's a social circle, and every time you move on to the next substance you kind of go down into the underground another notch or two lower until you're strung out on dope. And then all of a sudden you think, "God, I'm so fucking cool." You're hanging out in an apartment bathroom smoking crack and doing heroin with people, and you're thinking "How did I get with these people? I hate these people."

And then there's the fear of trying to stop that because once you've done it for so long, that becomes your only reality. It becomes normal. So, stopping it makes it seem like, "God, the people who don't do this are square. I don't wanna be like them."

But the reality is, once you've been there, you're never square again. It has laid its fingerprint on you forever.

DAVE MUSTAINE
Megadeth, ex-Metallica

It's funny how you start off and you're doing a certain level of drugs, and as the level of your friends go lower, the drugs get harder. And you realize that the people you're hanging around with are frightening. If you're lucky, you get a wake-up call, but for me it took putting my hand on the hot stove a lot of times before it finally sunk in that, "Oh yeah, that fuckin' burns."

MARK MORTON
Lamb of God

I spent such a huge part of my life drinking and drugging. And sometimes it was fun. And it was fun until it wasn't. Really, it's all fun and games and then some of your friends start dying and you find yourself looking back at situations where you could have very easily gotten hurt or worse. So it's something that's real close to me. It progresses and it gets to the point where it's not a sustainable lifestyle. It wasn't for me and it wasn't for some of the people I was friends with. And some of them made it to the other side and some of them didn't.

There are definitely funny stories, but for me, in particular, it got so bad at the end of it that it was hard to see any of it as funny. I just got tired of feeling like shit all the time. And I was tired of relying on other substances to keep me well and to keep me going. And then they weren't working anymore. It had become a priority above all else. There were things I needed to function. And I knew that there were people that were close to me that had found a way to not live like that anymore. And I was so exhausted by the lifestyle that I decided to do what they were doing and see if it worked for me. And it did. The craziest thing that happened to me from drugs was that I survived.

DAVE WYNDORF

After years of getting away with murder, I finally met my match with ben-zodiazepines. I was taking heavy, heavy doses of Temazepam. I started taking this stuff to make me sleep. I used it as a tool. I wasn't getting high on it. I just couldn't sleep at night. My mind was too wound up.

I took it for years, and it built up in my system. So over time, you have to keep upping the dose. I went to a doctor, who, it turned out, had been investigated by the DEA for overprescribing pills. They yanked him, so he yanked me. He took me off the stuff. I was taking ten Xanax before I went to sleep. And the stuff affects your neuroreceptors, and when you're yanked off it completely your neuroreceptors go totally out of whack. All this worry and all this anxiety that was shunted away sud-denly came out all at once.

Basically, six years of accrued anxiety all came out at the same time, and I went nuts. I wanted more pills, and I got them. And then I ODed on them because I couldn't stop taking them. They just didn't work the same way. All of a sudden, my body demanded more. It was like a switch went off. I had complete control over this thing. I had never considered it an addiction. It never even crossed my mind. And then I almost ODed. It was horrible.

My girlfriend found me passed out on the floor. I wouldn't wake up, and they rushed me to the emergency room. I did a Judy Garland thing. I woke up, took a pill, went back to sleep. It didn't work. Woke up, took another one. Didn't work. And at one point, I think I just downed the bottle like a shot glass. Maybe some inner demon said, "Just end it!" Whatever. I can't remember it.

But I wound up in the hospital.

Coming out of that, I totally looked at my life differently. It was a complete reassessment. I was like: "Well, you almost died and now your mind's mush. Why? Was it worth it? Did you get anything out of it just because you wanted to work harder?"

As I came out of that, I started appreciating things more like when I was younger. In a way, I learned a lot from it. I was a lot more humble, for sure. I read a lot to get better. I didn't realize at the time, but I think my mind wanted to be stimulated with more than I was getting so I started reading books more and more. I was reading like I did when I was sixteen.

And now I'm still doing it. It really saved me—reading and writing. So, now I'm this boring guy who reads all the time. In a way, I feel lucky. A lot of people get really crazy when they suddenly stop taking benzodiazepines and do shit like jump in front of trains. The high rate of suicide and just absolute manic behavior is astounding. You don't want to go off the stuff cold turkey.

SAM RIVERS
Limp Bizkit

I dabbled with things here and there, but nothing got to me. I did blow for a while, but it wasn't a thing to me. I just stopped because it wasn't fun. The hangovers were too bad. I liked me some MDMA and a little bit of acid.

I kind of remember at the end of Ozzfest when we were playing before Tool. Me and [bassist Justin] Chancellor hooked up and we were gonna party. He took me to his bus and we were chatting for a minute. He said, "Hey, you want a drink?"

I was like, "Sure."

He had whiskey and he poured it into these big ass glasses. It was one ice cube and the rest of the thing was full. Then he made one for himself. We were drinking straight whiskey and then he went, "Hey, you want some MDMA?"

I said, "Dude, it's the last night. Sure."

Next thing you know, we were tripping and drunk as crap. We got off the bus and went our separate ways. I was so fucked up I got lost. I wandered around for a while completely unsure where I was. I could have been in the middle of another country.

Finally, somehow, I stumbled back to our bus. Later somebody came and got me and took me to a different place for a little bit. We hung out and did some stuff and then I met Justin again as we were both walking back to our buses. And we both looked at each other smiled and then one of us said, "Whoa, man. I'm fucked up."

KING FOWLEY

One time, we went in this car and we all did a bunch of cocaine. We were driving and the guy we were driving with would always buy all the drugs for us 'cause he had money. He usually just liked to do a couple dumb coke hits on his lips. He'd get a little euphoria from it, enough to make him think he was cool.

One night we were driving around the Great Falls area in Virginia, which has all these winding roads. It was me and two other guys and this guy that was in the front seat started getting real high. I was like, "Dude, settle down. Settle down."

But he wouldn't settle down and he wrecked the fucking car. And this fucking tree limb came right into the car through the fucking window. I literally jumped out of the way just in time. If I didn't do that it would have gone right into me because it was right where I was sitting.

DAVE WYNDORF

I did a lot of coke when I was in the band Shrapnel on the Lower East Side of Manhattan in the late '70s and early '80s. We had a friend who was a little hippie girl in New Jersey, and she had an almost unlimited supply of it and I think she was stealing it from somewhere.

For about two years, I had almost all the coke I could handle. There were five of us that ran around in New Jersey and Manhattan in cars constantly with these giant pill vials completely packed with coke. It was nonstop. We probably gave as much away as we did ourselves.

Did we sell any of it? No.

Could we have been millionaires? Yes.

By the end of that scenario, my girlfriend contracted epilepsy since she did so much blow. One of my friends was diagnosed as a diabetic and went into seizures because of the coke. And there were two hangers-on of the band they went out of their minds with cocaine psychosis and never came back. I only survived by sleeping every couple of days while everyone else just kept going and going until they broke.

MATT HEAFY
Trivium

The band used to party a lot. I drank too much and was doing drugs and I'm glad it happened early in our career and we got it out of our systems because now we can just focus on the music and not worry about acting like rock stars.

A career-changing moment for us happened when we played the Download festival. I was doing a lot of a substance that made me feel very up. I guess I was using pretty seriously because we'd get to the border somewhere and we didn't want to throw it away so we'd consume everything we had left before we got to the border. I was using this stuff before the Download show, that very first show that got us tons of press and really put us on the map. Right before we went onstage, my nose was still bleeding and my voice sounded like crap. I could hardly utter a note. We walked out on the stage at 11 a.m. and 40,000 people showed up and they were screaming. For some reason, everything kicked in and everything worked. I mean I sounded a little crappy but I guess the vibe of the show and the crowd really made us shine.

But after that show, I said to myself, "I can't do this anymore. I can't risk this." So that's the big moment I decided to stop using and start taking what I wanted to do really seriously.

GARY HOLT

[Exodus drummer] Tom Hunting and I quit doing meth around the same time. Before Tom got clean, he couldn't get through a rehearsal without feeling like his heart was going to explode. He was having trouble playing his drums and he was struggling with his foot speed. After he got clean, he started getting really bad anxiety attacks. So he quit and moved up to the mountains and found some peace for a little while before he came back to the band.

I also tried to help [guitarist] Rick [Hunolt] get clean. I spent two full years after I got clean from meth trying to get him off the stuff. He'd get through a tour without using and by the time we got home he was right back at it again. He was missing practices, playing sloppy and being unproductive—times ten. He wasn't fired. I love the guy. He's the only guitar player other than Kirk Hammett that I had ever played with. I want nothing more for him than for him to straighten up his life and realize that's a dead-end street, that shit. When you're smoking that shit it's a whole different ballgame. I'd try to impress upon him how good I feel, how productive I am now, but sometimes as hard as you try you can't get through to someone. Upon completion of [2004's *Tempo of the Damned*], there was certainly going to be a rehabilitation ultimatum.

After I quit doing meth, I cut off all ties from my past life except one. And that's one of your dearest friends and the guy you play in a band with. And I couldn't sever that tie, at least I never wanted to. But Rick's solos had gotten so bad that steps were taken to get through to him and he chose to quit the band rather than do anything about it. [Since his departure, Hunolt has remained an Exodus fan and reunited with the surviving members at a San Francisco show on April 20, 2019, to play several songs at the Metal Allegiance concert, a metal supergroup with a rotating lineup.]

REX BROWN
Pantera, ex-Down, ex-Crowbar, Kill Devil Hill

Everything changed after Pantera did *Far Beyond Driven*. We all got more extreme, then we go on the road and Philip fucking OD's [on heroin] and puts out a press release saying he didn't see any light while he was out.

Why put anything out like that? You cover that shit up!

It was the dumbest thing he could have ever done. He said he only did it once. No. For ten years I'd be picking his head out of a first-class fucking meal [when he nodded off]. That got a little tiring to say the least. I just wanted to make everything work, but I was more pissed at the fact that he would even go and do something like that when we were at the peak of what we all achieved or wanted to achieve. I had just gotten married and I was looking at a brighter future on the road. And then here comes my best buddy OD'ing. It was really rough for everyone.

But that's rock and roll. Shit, it's amazing I'm fucking alive. There is no moderation. It's not a healthy thing to go on the road 250 dates a year and the temptation alone will kill you even if you are sober. It's amazing that somebody didn't leave the band in a body bag. Poor [Dimebag] Darrell did after Pantera split up, but not by his own devices. [And, tragically, drummer Vinnie Paul died of a heart attack in 2018].

PHILIP ANSELMO
Pantera, Down, Superjoint Ritual, Scour

Some prick, Nikki Sixx, who has been nothing but nice to me, put out a book, *The Heroin Diaries,* that was the biggest joke I ever saw because Nikki's full of shit. I'm calling you out right now. If you're on dope—look—yeah, you can function. Shit, I functioned. You can sleepwalk through anything. But you're not going to scribble down coherent notes while you're dopesick. The last thing you want is a pen in your fucking hand. I would know. Shit, I've been through some wars, man, so your average fucking prick junkie is not going to fool me with the same old, '*I'm fine*' story. I used that same line about a thousand times.

I was in so much fuckin' pain in the '90s and the doctors wouldn't operate on my back because technology had not advanced to the point yet where they could do so without causing irreparable damage. So I felt cornered. I took painkillers, muscle relaxers, anything I could get my fucking hands on. As long as it numbed out the fucking knife that I felt in my fucking spine in the center of my body before I had to go out there and go ape shit for the kids. Then I was doing heroin and I wasn't keeping a fuckin' diary, Nikki. There's no denying it and no hiding it. I was fucking annihilated. I couldn't do shit.

Then you get on the heroin calendar where you try to keep your shit together so you don't say no to anybody and you're obligated to be in eight places at one time because you done forgot how many people you said yes to. Then you let them all down. That's how they get lost. That's how all the friends have gone, how the parents disappear. Then they're all alone. There ain't no such thing as a great junkie story unless you come out of it alive. That's the only way you can even dream of having a happy ending.

MIKE IX WILLIAMS

We took efforts to try to make sure we were always hooked up. Back in the day, you'd go to a show and there'd be people with stuff. Or you would call up your drug connections days ahead. It seemed like a lot more people would have it back then, and it wasn't such a stigma the way it seems to be now. If that didn't work, you'd get somewhere and look for a bad neighborhood. If you saw some people just hanging around, you could usually buy drugs from them.

So we were pretty okay in the U.S., but when we went to Europe it was a lot harder to get stuff. It was there, but there was always a language barrier, which was a problem. So you'd end up going to Europe, and after three days of being sick, you'd be done. You felt better, and you'd just go through the rest of the tour.

AL JOURGENSEN

There was this movie *Fix* that I never wanted to come out, and it was shot when I was in the depths of heroin addiction. And it's not fuckin' pretty. The first time I did heroin was when I was eighteen or nineteen. I was a weekend warrior for a few years. I liked it, but then it became a problem after four to five years. I didn't realize I'd become a full-blown heroin addict until I was about twenty-eight. I knew, "Oh shit, this is a problem" because if I didn't get it that day or my dealer was late, I'd be freaking out and I'd literally be sick and in withdrawal. That went on until I was forty-four. From twenty-eight to forty-four—my heroin years—that's pretty long, like sixteen years. I've died two times by 44 from heroin overdoses. So there's really no plausible reason why I'm here. I should be gone. I should be long gone. But I'm here.

TOMMY VICTOR
Prong, Danzig, ex-Ministry

I tried to stay clean and sober but being in Ministry got me back into smoking cigarettes and then drinking and doing drugs. That's the way it was with them. People were popping out cocaine all the time and there was nothing else to do. I was on the bus and everyone was doing it and it was like, "Okay, fuck it." Then it got really bad. I started drinking and I'm a bad drunk. Every time I'd drink, I'd get pissed off and wind up in a really angry, horrible mood, time and time again.

DAVE NAVARRO

Back in the late '80s, Jane's Addiction played Madison Square Garden. It was the biggest show of our lives. It was crazy. People were like, "Really? Jane's Addiction? That little, weird band from L.A. that no one gave the time of day to, that didn't know who they were or what their music sounded like and they couldn't agree on anything? Those junkies? They're playing Madison Square Garden?"

It was a fuckin' big deal because bands like us didn't fill places like that back then. So, of course, [bassist] Eric [Avery] and I needed to get good and high before the show. We took a cab to Alphabet City, which, at that time, was really dangerous. That's where you would score heroin or get street drugs. You had to get out of the car, you had to walk around, you had to look for somebody, and maybe he knew somebody. You'd end up getting instructions like, "Yeah man, go up to the fourth floor and it's

4E and knock twice." Dudes opened the door with guns and they'd point them at your head and ask, "What do you want?" That night I was standing there dressed in full stage gear, like a Raggedy Anne with dreadlocks. We scored the dope and did it and nodded out for a little while. I came to and shook Eric, who was nodded out.

"Bro, we got a show to do tonight!" I said.

It was twenty minutes until start time and we were still high in Alphabet City. There were no cell phones, no computers. We couldn't find a landline. Management didn't know where we were. [Jane's Addiction frontman] Perry [Farrell] and [drummer] Stephen [Perkins] didn't know where we were. And, frankly, we didn't know where we were. All we knew was that in twenty minutes the biggest show of our lives was scheduled to start.

We found a cab, raced to Madison Square Garden. Back then, we just looked like punks. We tried to get backstage. Nobody would let us in.

"No, no, no. You don't understand. We're playing here tonight!"

"Yeah, not without a wrist band you're not," said a security guard.

"C'mon dude! You gotta let us in. Everybody's in there waiting for us. You're holding up the show."

"Well, you gotta go talk to the guy at the gate in the back," he said, seemingly unconcerned.

So we went around and talked our way into this gate entrance. We were still fuckin' loaded and the circus was in town at Madison Square Garden, but when they have concerts or other events they put all the circus shit down below. We ran around down underneath Madison Square Garden to find the stage entrance. At this point, we were already fifteen minutes late and we were still so high and nobody knew where we were. Then we realized we were running by cages full of tigers and elephants. All the animals from the circus were down there. Our hearts were pounding, we were almost nodding out as we were running. There was blood dripping down our arms from where we shot up. And there were wild animals growling and clawing at their cages. We saw giant clawed arms swinging at us, which was terrifying. They probably smelled blood and we really thought we were going to die. It was the most surreal thing to go from street level, gutter-hype life to being surrounded by wild animals— and, at the time, we couldn't even figure out why they were there because we didn't know there was a circus there. We figured that out later. We wound up making the show. We were late and I don't remember a thing about the performance. I don't think Eric does either, but we made it.

KYLE SHUTT

We were in the Netherlands and were gifted with this pillow sack full of weed and two bricks of hash. We got a quarter-pound of weed from this one guy and eighty grams of hash. That's a shit-ton of really good shit. There was no way we were getting rid of it. We were like, "We can't possibly give this away or throw it out. This is incredible. It's enough weed for the rest of the tour."

It got decadent.

The hash was 40-gram bricks and I would just fluff a whole bowl full of it and torch it. We had to sneak it around all over the place. We stuffed it in the back of Bryan [Richie's] bass head and shipped it on ferries and across borders. We took that thing in and out of so many countries. By the time we got to the end of the tour we had smoked all of it except four joints worth and we were so green-faced. We couldn't do anymore. So we left the four joints on the bus for the next band that was gonna be on there and then we hopped off in Germany and got on a plane home.

Over three weeks we went through a quarter pound of weed and 80 grams of hash.

BURTON C. BELL
Fear Factory, Ascension of the Watchers

[Guitarist] Dino [Cazares] and I were still living together at the end of '93 before we went on our first tour to Australia. We had a party before we left. A friend of ours had this amazing meth so we were doing it and I forgot that I had put it in my pocket. The next day we went to the airport to fly to Australia and halfway through the flight I dug into my pocket and I go, "Oh my God, I've still got this meth on me. What am I gonna do?"

Instead of throwing it away I tried to do it all. I cut up some lines and did a little meth in the bathroom. I tried to think of some way to get it over the border instead of throwing it away, 'cause I'm an idiot. I put it in a place that's very dark and safe and I went through customs that way sweating like crazy and tweaking my balls off. But we got through.

The first night we're there it's a day off and the guy who picked us up took us out to dinner. He had some friends with him. And they said, "Hey, do you do speed?"

I said, "Yeah, sure. I'd do some."

I tried a little bit of theirs and I was like, "Oh my God, don't even bother. Here, try this."

I had the speed back in my pocket in a different container. They tried that and they lost their minds. At the end of the night, I gave it to them. I said, "I'm done. That's the last time."

KING FOWLEY

We decided to sneak into the outdoor pool in the middle of the night. We got in and started smoking PCP. I decided to swim laps. I tried to swim the whole fucking pool underwater at 2 a.m. It was pitch black and I was swimming and suddenly I was thinking to myself, "Where's the fucking wall at the end of the pool? I can't do this. I can't do this!"

I came up to get air and when I got above the water, I was so high that I felt like I was still in the water and I couldn't get air. All of a sudden, I thought the whole world was made of petroleum jelly. I needed to escape it so I got out of the pool and took off into the night. I still thought I couldn't breathe.

About ten hours later my friends found me and I was still out of my mind. They said, "Breathe, man." I tried to explain to them that the petroleum jelly in the pool was in my lungs and I couldn't breathe. Finally, they convinced me I could actually breathe normally, but I was still fucked up.

JIMMY BOWER

Crowbar played in Jacksonville, Florida, at the Freebird Lounge, which is Ronnie Van Zant's wife's bar. I was doing coke behind an amp cabinet and playing Crowbar songs slow as tar. I wanted to play faster 'cause I was jacked up on fuckin' coke and it was so hard to keep the tempo of the songs. Also, it's hard to play drums on coke just in general. Your heart's pounding and you feel like you're gonna die the whole time. And then afterwards I felt like shit. Coke's not a big winner with me.

KIRK WINDSTEIN
Crowbar, ex-Down

I was always afraid of needles, so I never touched one, but I had a pretty bad problem with coke for a long period of time. The funny thing is I never really enjoyed weed so that sure wasn't a gateway drug for me. As I got older, it went from beer to whatever the strongest thing I could do a shot of was.

So, I was a drinker. I didn't really start having an issue with cocaine until I was about thirty. It was like something clicked and my brain went, "Alcohol's just not enough."

That lasted for a long while, man. It became a regular part of my diet for twelve or thirteen years. I couldn't drink a beer without coke. My rule was, "Well, I'm not gonna do any coke if I'm not drinking." It was kind of a rock and roll diet for me. God knows how many brain cells I killed that way. I'm not proud of it and I'm glad I was able to kick before it was too late.

You know, snorting a line of coke off the back of some filthy toilet in Europe somewhere is not the healthiest thing in the world. And when you're God knows where and you're riding around at three or four in the morning trying to score stuff in the seediest places, that's not too good. I did that for many years. I would wake up from a blackout and I'd be on my couch I'd make sure I had my wallet and, on many occasions there would be two or three bags of blow in my pocket and I had no idea how it got there.

That was my excuse. I was just at home, doing nothing, so I'd go, "Well, I got all this cocaine. I gotta do it." And I had to drink in order to do it so I'd go straight to the corner store and get a case of beer and come back. I'd guzzle a few beers, chop up some lines, put on some music, and that was that.

PAGE HAMILTON
Helmet

I grew up in Oregon at the end of the baby boom and I idolized Jack Kerouac and Tim Leary and Ken Kesey. In Eugene, Oregon, drugs were everywhere. We were open to anything and everything. We didn't even think about the dangers or how shitty cocaine is.

But I went through phases. The heroin thing was really, really short-lived. The first time I tried it was at the bar Max Fish in New York and I tried it in Portland twice with some buddies of mine. I smoked it and snorted it. I never shot it. I just knew if I kept doing it, I'd get hooked and I didn't want to do anything that would interfere with my music. I never did it on the road, and in fact, I banned drugs on the road when we were in Helmet because we had a crew guy that used to be addicted to heroin and he had gotten clean and sober. I hired him on the condition that there would be no hard drugs on the bus.

And then he ended up overdosing on the bus. He didn't die, but it was incredibly nerve-racking. I explained to everyone that this is my career and my life and should something happen and we can't get into Canada or somewhere else ever again, it would be disastrous.

Being at home was another story. There were periods after we had done a couple of hundred shows in an album cycle and I would just tear it up and be an idiot. One time, I did some cocaine with a couple of friends from other bands. I offered some to Henry [Bogdan], our bass player and he said, "Nope, I'm good." Henry and [drummer] John [Stanier], to their credit, never, ever did that shit. I really admired them for that.

CHRIS SPENCER
Unsane

I went through a lot of shit with massive amounts of drugs and drinking all the time when I was idle while [drummer] Vinnie Signorelli (ex-Swans, ex-Foetus) was recovering from a really bad, life-threatening infection and the band couldn't do anything. I was smoking crack and just drunk nonstop every day. I was doing whatever drugs I could get my hands on and I was pretty much in the worst place you can possibly be. I was really disappointed in myself and I hated myself. I really wished I could just die. My friends lost faith in me and I was doing shit that was totally out of character.

For me, being a drunk is worse than being a junkie. Think about it, man. When do you see a junkie fighting people or causing trouble like a drunk? Well, I was both. I hit rock bottom after months and months of fucking nastiness. And then I cleaned up. Honestly, I did it by myself without going to any sort of rehab program. I just knew I had to get my shit together and become myself again. And when I was better I started working again. And then we did our 2017 album *Sterilize*.

DAVE NAVARRO

I don't want to glamorize heroin in any way. It's something I did and somehow I survived it, but I don't recommend it to anyone else. But this one time I was in England, and I was hanging out with these street junkies. We had a squat. It was an abandoned building and we were running power from the building next to us so we could light a lamp. There were homeless junkies shooting up there. It basically looked like a crack house. Apparently, I did a shot of dope and said, "Give me another one." And I did it and then I died. They tried to revive me. They tried to put me in a bathtub. It didn't work. So they dragged me down four flights of stairs and left me on the curb and called for an ambulance. And then they scattered like roaches because they were afraid of getting arrested.

One guy was running away and he had second thoughts so he came back and tried one more time to compress my chest. I started coughing and spitting up and he brought me back. He hauled me back up four flights of stairs and kept ice on me until I came to.

I woke up in daylight. A whole day had gone by. He said to me, "Dude, you were dead last night."

And the first thing I said was, "Uhhhhhhh. Do you have any dope?" The first thing I wanted to do was get high! So I actually did.

I had a show that night in London that I was afraid I wasn't going to make. But I made it and during the show I actually nodded out and fell asleep onstage holding my guitar. I honestly don't remember what happened next—if they propped me up and I finished the show or if they dragged me offstage and that was the end of the gig.

There have been plenty of shows where we were so fucked up we couldn't finish a show. So many times either [frontman] Perry [Farrell], [bassist] Eric [Avery] or I couldn't make it through the show. It was never [drummer] Stephen [Perkins]. But we would get halfway through the set and the house lights would go on. That was the life and I'm glad I lived it. But yeah, there were a lot of OD's on tour and horrible stuff. We were all really far gone.

DAVE ELLEFSON

As this whirlwind ride of heroin abuse got darker, we didn't see any need to stop until we were stuck in the pitch-dark blackness. And then it was really hard to dig back out. It superseded any other aspiration or dream, and that was the biggest problem. It's a dark, artistic drug. But it's one that certainly handcuffs you to your home because it's such an insidious, cunning drug that you come to rely on it like food or air.

We eventually got away from it and that lifestyle. And thank God we escaped it because not everyone from our band did; most people aren't so lucky.

PHILIP ANSELMO

I promised my girl I was gonna leave the church of the hypodermic and I did. I made that choice to stay with her. Except I fucked up and ran right into the waiting arms of methadone. There was excruciating physical back pain involved with my condition and methadone is also a painkiller. I ran into a crooked doctor who was prescribing me enough methadone in one month to kill about five people. Plus, he was giving me about four other prescriptions for other things that, mixed with methadone, should have killed me. It was a suicide cocktail.

The methadone alone is debilitating. It's like falling off a fifty fucking story building every five minutes you're awake. And in-between that five minutes, you're getting pushed to the ledge. You're inside a hotel room and the world is coming to an end right there. You feel like the most significant motherfucker on the face of the earth and your horror comes before anything. And, it's unfounded horror. Anxiety, depression, war, war, constant war, man.

Yeah. I've been there.

BOBBY LIEBLING
Pentagram

I was addicted to heroin for forty years and methadone for thirty years. I was a full-blown addict, all fucked up on dope and crack. I was on methadone and shooting heroin on top of it seven days a week and smoking $500 to $1,000 of crack every single day around the clock. I did way too much a lot of times but I always came back. Then, I tried to kick with just the methadone. People don't realize that methadone withdrawal lasts six to eighteen months. It's a living hell. I was kicking my legs up and down and I was constantly throwing up. I felt weak, anxious, dizzy. I was crawling around the floor then lying down and rolling up in a ball. And then I'd start the process all over again until I was finally clean.

CHAPTER 4: REVELATION NAUSEA

Technicolor Rainbows & "Yuck Malts" for All

One of the many melodic death metal bands to emerge from Sweden in the aughts, Vomitory was the natural choice for a chapter about vomiting. "Revelation Nausea" is the title track from their third album, which was regurgitated in 2001 and included the tasteful cuts "The Corpsegrinder Experience," and "Under Clouds of Blood."

No one but the straightest of straight-edge bands has escaped a career of touring without puking at least a few dozen times. On its own, barfing is kinda gross but hardly spectacular. It's only when one examines the cause of the nausea, the circumstances in which it occurred, and the details about the experience that stories from metal musicians develop shape and texture—kinda like puked up shrimp. From barfing on rock stars, to being vomited on during sex, "Revelation Nausea" is not for the weak of stomach, but anyone who thinks a good, gross story is worth its weight in vomit will surely be amused by these disgusting tales.

AL JOURGENSEN
Ministry, Revolting Cocks

After *The Last Sucker* [in 2007], I was like a spent shell casing from a rifle. I was puking up blood every day. I didn't know why. That had been going on for the last four or five tours, though, and I didn't see a doctor because I just thought that was part of what happens when you're my age on a rock tour. I didn't know there was a condition attached to it.

I would puke blood and get off tour and it would go away. But this time I got off tour and it was worse. Blood was coming out of my nose, my dick, my mouth. I'd stand up and fall over. I lost so much blood, I couldn't even walk. Instead of calling the doctor, I put on this medieval helmet that I had made in the Czech Republic, and I would quit hitting my head on the tiles if I put on the helmet. I wore the helmet around for a couple days.

I was a tired, run-down, bloated drunk – just a mess.

And then I exploded on March 27, 2010, and they had to take me to the emergency room.

RANDY BLYTHE
Lamb of God

I puked on a girl at the side of the stage once. I was trying to get off the stage because I didn't want to fall and slip on my own vomit. So I'm heading toward her and she's looking at me and I'm trying to say, "Move," but right as I said it the technicolor yawn exploded all over her and she was horrified and left and I didn't see her anymore. I think that was on Ozzfest. I stopped drinking since then, it just took a while.

MAX CAVALERA
Soulfly, Cavalera Conspiracy, ex-Sepultura

I once puked on Eddie Vedder. I was hanging out with the Ministry guys on the Ministry bus. We were touring with them and Eddie came to the show in Seattle. He's friends with them so was hanging out on the bus. While Ministry was sitting in the back of the bus, Al and some of them were all shooting up and drinking. I had a bottle of rum. I was drinking it nonstop. I took one more chug and everything went black. I looked to my left side and I knew I didn't want to puke on Ministry. And Eddie Vedder was to my right, so I turned to him and threw up all over his pants and all over him.

It was a whole cascade.

I was so apologetic.

Not long before that, my sister said, "If you ever meet Eddie Vedder, I want an autograph." So right after I puked on the guy I asked for his autograph for my sister. I grabbed a little piece of napkin from the table and he actually signed it.

WILL CARROLL
Death Angel, ex-Machine Head

Until about seven years ago, I used to puke while I played or after I played. I just used to throw up all the time. My old band, Old Grandad, played a show in the late '90s in San Francisco at a club called the Cocotree. It was with Suffocation and Impaled. I was pretty surprised I got through the set without throwing up.

I'm loading my drums off the stage and when I bent over to pick up my bass drum I was like, "Oh no, I spoke too soon!" And I threw up all over the stage.

There was no time to clean it up because Impaled had to set up. I don't know if they even noticed I had puked on the stage, but as soon as they started playing they were slipping and sliding on my vomit. It was funny to watch them standing there playing and see their legs slowly sliding and spreading wider and wider. Fortunately, no one fell in my puke.

JOHN GALLAGHER
Raven

Our first drummer Rob ["Wacko" Hunter] wore a hockey goalie helmet onstage and he'd smash it into things. I know he threw up inside of that once or twice from going so crazy and being constricted by the thing. But when T.T. Quick was opening for us, Rob was hanging out with their drummer, who got Rob into Southern Comfort. We didn't know how much Rob was drinking until his drumming would get slower and slower during the shows.

"What the fuck's going on?" we wondered.

Well, he had Southern Comfort in his water bottle and it was throwing off his timing and running down his motor, which caused a few arguments. That's one time we caught him throwing up in the helmet and the alcohol was definitely to blame for that one. The road case didn't smell too good after that.

ROBERT MEADOWS
Left to Vanish, ex-A Life Once Lost

On the first Sounds of the Underground tour, we were in Denver and I spent pretty much the whole day puking my brains out up until the time that we played, and then I was still puking onstage. I don't remember raging that hard the night before, but I do remember waking up outside in the middle of the night underneath a tent that I had pulled out when I was drunk. I woke up to the sound of trucks moving. And then I just started puking and didn't stop.

SCOTT IAN
Anthrax, S.O.D., The Damned Things

I was having a great time that first time I got drunk with Lemmy. We drank whiskey all night and the next thing I know, I was getting woken up by Megaforce Records owner Jonny Z in my bed in a hotel because we had to catch a plane to Munich for the next stop on the promo tour. I was still in all my clothes and Jonny was kicking me to wake me up. He yelled at me and he wasn't nice about it.

"Get up motherfucker because I am not calling the label and telling them that you fucking drank with Lemmy and now we're canceling the promo tour. You're not gonna blow this shit the first fuckin' day!" he shouted.

I sat up and immediately waves of nausea washed through my whole body. I threw up. Then I started feeling this pain I've never experienced. It felt like a cop beat the fuck out of me with a baton. Every part of my body was in pain. I rolled over and puked on the bed. I wiped off my mouth with the back of my hand, but I was in a cold sweat and then I felt the nauseous again.

I couldn't stop throwing up. Jonny sat there waiting for me, pissed. I was trying to get my shit together.

Finally, I got out of the hotel. We were already late for the plane, and by the time we got to Heathrow, I couldn't even walk under my own strength. Johnny was literally carrying me over his shoulder through the airport and I was throwing up over his back. It was disgusting. I hadn't even found out what happened or why my whole body ached. I was literally just a puddle.

Somehow, we made it to the plane. I went straight to the airplane bathroom and started puking again. The stewardess made me get out for takeoff so I went back in my seat and I sat there shaking with a barf bag on my lap. I was dry heaving and spitting out stomach acid, but there was nothing of substance left in me.

By the time we got to Munich I wasn't throwing up anymore, but I was shivering and felt feverish. I was lying in bed shaking. This didn't feel like any hangover I'd ever had. At some point, I asked Jonny, "What happened to me last night?"

"You were talking to Lemmy for about an hour and drinking a lot," he began.

I started doing the mental math. A normal person would drink four drinks in that time and a Lemmy would down, maybe, 15 drinks. Suddenly I was beginning to understand what had happened. Jonny kept talking: "The next thing we knew, you were out of the bar and running up and down the street. I followed you outside because I wanted to make sure you were okay. You started running zigzags down Waterloo Street.

Your arms were over your head like a gorilla and you were screaming incoherently. I couldn't understand a word you were saying. And you were jumping and diving into piles of garbage on the street, big garbage bags that were out for pickup."

I was like, "Whaaaat?" I had no memory of any of this. No wonder I fucking stunk so bad.

"Why didn't you try to stop me?" I asked.

"We tried to stop you but you were pulling moves like an NFL running back evading tacklers and then you dashed the other way and dove into another pile of trash," he said. "Finally, you just lay down and passed out."

"Okay, I got it. Well, let's go to the record company office and do the rest of these interviews."

"We can't. Your pants are filled with shit," he said.

I went into the bathroom and when I dropped my pants it was so disgusting I almost puked again. My underwear was seventy percent brown and my pants were a mix of half-dried and thick, wet poop. Before I could shower, Jonny handed me a piece of paper with a lifetime management contract written on it.

"Fuck you, motherfucker," he said. "You're gonna make me deal with this shit? This is what I want. Sign it!"

I took his bullshit contract to the bathroom with me and wiped my shit-smeared ass with it. Then I took a shower and got all cleaned up and when I came out I tossed this stinking contract on the table where he was sitting and said, "Oh, Jonny, by the way, here's that deal you wanted."

That's actually the least messy way I've ever gotten out of a contract.

LEMMY KILMISTER
Motörhead

I've been drinking a long time. I meet all these musicians that want to drink with me. I'm all for that. But a lot of them try to keep up with me. That's madness and a lot of them end up getting sick. It's nothing I aspire to. I never pressure them but maybe they feel pressured, I don't know. All I know is I don't drink with them so they'll be sick. I don't take any pleasure in that.

DAVE WYNDORF
Monster Magnet

I was 17 or 18 and just getting into the rock business, playing CBGB whenever possible. We had a manager who was trying to get us more exposure, and they took us to a restaurant downtown where all the punk rock elite were gathered. Debbie Harry, Meat Loaf, and Elvis Costello were all there. We sat around, and our manager said: "Maybe if you behave yourself we'll introduce you to Blondie. If they like you, they can help you out."

That was back when they were completely huge. I was waiting and drinking, waiting and drinking. It was free booze, which was fucking awesome. I never got free booze in New Jersey.

I drank so much that I got completely fucked up and went outside to get a little air. I saw my guitarist's car, and for some reason, I thought it would be a good idea to climb on top of it and lay down for a while. I was on my back, and I got sick just at the time the party was over.

Out came Debbie Harry and her manager, and I projectile vomited straight up from a prone position. It was like a geyser of puke just shooting up. She looked over at me with this, "So, you want to be my latex salesman" expression. I totally ruined the whole thing. My band hated me.

COREY BEAULIEU
Trivium

I was hanging out with [Pantera guitarist] Dimebag Darrell's girlfriend Rita [Haney] and [Pantera drummer] Vinnie Paul and Vinnie's covers band, Gasoline, was playing this club. They invited me to come onstage with them and play "Cowboys from Hell." I was totally loaded by the time I got up there.

After the set, Vinnie and I got into this in-depth conversation, and the next thing you know, I was like, "Dude, I'm really sorry, but I have to throw up."

I just tilted my head and puked, and Vinnie was just dying laughing at me. Then we got in a limo and headed off to the next bar.

ERIK TURNER
Warrant

[Our Singer] Jani [Lane] was the king of peer pressure. He would not take no for an answer. When we were on tour, our goal was to make as many people puke as possible—any band or anyone from another band or anybody's friend that came out to visit. We made them drink tequila with us all night until they puked. Pretty much anybody and everybody that rode with us puked at least once, except maybe bassist P.J. [Farley] from Trixter. Jani was a legendary drinker so he really prided himself on the puke thing.

FRANKIE BANALI
Quiet Riot, ex-W.A.S.P.

We made sure that everyone we toured with got excessively drunk, puked and passed out. And then, they might wake up with their pants down and a mustard bottle hanging out their ass and we would take pictures and put them up backstage. Or someone might hold a big fake penis next to someone's face and take pictures.

ALEX HELLID
Entombed

Wild nights of drinking are kind of weird because you're usually not happy until everyone is passing out and puking. That's when it's supposed to be a good time, but really, the whole experience is kind of miserable and embarrassing. You don't feel too proud when people take you in and let you sleep in their apartment with freshly painted walls and you repay them by destroying their bathroom because there's puke everywhere. It's nothing to be happy about, it's just that we were kids in a candy store. We had as much free booze as we wanted and no one was there to tell us when to stop.

RICHARD CHRISTY
Charred Walls of the Damned, ex-Death, ex-Iced Earth, ex-Public Assassin

At the Dynamo Festival in Holland in 1998, I was on tour with Death. It was only our fourth show and we were playing in front of 40,000 people right before Pantera. And I am a huge fan here and it was just amazing that we got to play in front of that many people right before one of my favorite bands.

After the show, I was walking back to our bus party and I saw Dimebag Darrell hanging out there. I was pretty buzzed at the time and I don't remember exactly what I said to get invited onto their bus. But it worked, and a few minutes later I was drinking Seagram's 7 with Dimebag and The Rock and a couple of their roadies. It was so surreal.

And as it turned out, one of their roadies was from Kansas, which is where I'm from. So I was hanging out with a fellow Kansan and partying with Dimebag and The Rock. It was so crazy that I didn't even know if it was real or not. Of course, the next morning I barely remembered what happened. I knew I partied with those guys. And then somebody banged on the door of the Death bus and we opened it up and they walked to the front of the bus and pointed down and started laughing. There was a huge pile of my vomit there.

And I suddenly remembered that after I partied with those guys I stumbled back to our bus and puked up all of my internal organs before I passed out on the bus. I even have a picture of it to prove I had a good time.

TOM ARAYA
Slayer

The last time I got out of control and puked everywhere was in Japan in the late '80s. I was in my hotel room. It was a scary thought because I woke up with a pizza pie of puke around my bed, and I thought damn, I did that in my sleep. I just didn't like the thought of doing that. People die that way. Before I realized what I had done, I rolled around and I was like, "Man, who the fuck stinks?"

STEPHEN CARPENTER
Deftones

I hardly ever puke. But the day the Alanis Morissette record went number one, our label Maverick threw a big ass party and we basically drank all the drinks. By 10:30 that evening I was one-eyed and staggering. I came into the hotel room we were staying at, and I just threw up a pancake, like, three feet big. Then I passed out in it. [Vocalist] Chino [Moreno] tried to wake me up and I think I lifted my head but then I fell right back down in my vomit.

MIKE IX WILLIAMS
Eyehategod

We played Ground Zero in Spartanburg, South Carolina. I had been drinking Jägermeister all night, and for some reason after the show we all went to Waffle House and I ordered a glass of milk.

We slept inside the club that night because we had no money. Sometime in the middle of the night, I woke up and started to vomit. It was the Jägermeister mixed with the milk, and it was so much and so loud that our drummer, Joey [LaCaze], was pouring buckets of mop water out to try to water it all down.

Another time, we were somewhere in Texas and I was upstairs in the dressing room. I was all fucked up and started vomiting profusely. The club was old and worn down, so the vomit leaked through the ceiling and was dripping down on the people downstairs by the front door.

CHRIS VRENNA
ex-Nine Inch Nails, ex-Marilyn Manson

One night, Marilyn Manson was in L.A. working on *Portrait of an American Family*. We had tickets to see U2 down in Anaheim for the Zoo TV tour. Me, Trent [Reznor], Manson, and some guys in his band decided to go.

We had this old beat up '70s-ish van with blue shag carpeting on the inside. There were no seats in it at all. We used it to haul stuff around.

We had backstage passes, so we were herded into this area and at one table way across the room was Axl Rose, at another table was Winona Ryder. There were lots of other celebrities there and I was really nervous because it was my first time being around so many famous people. They had white wine backstage and I just drank and drank to calm my nerves.

Then Bono came and I was like, "Holy shit!" I was that wide-eyed fanboy.

When we were on the way home in the van, we had beer in the back. I kept drinking and I got really, really sick. All we had in there were empty Bud Light cans and I was trying to puke into the opening of the beer cans. Of course, that didn't work out too well and I had puke running down my clothes. I was trying to be so polite about it and get it into this can and I just made a huge mess.

For years no one would ever let me forget about it. Every time I'd run into someone who was there, they'd go, "Ah, there's Vrenna! Where's your beer can to throw up in?" I'll never live it down.

DINO CAZARES
Fear Factory, Divine Heresy, Brujeria, Asesino

We were in Kansas City with Obituary. After the show, I picked up a girl and she gave me a blowjob in the back of the bus.

"Hey, that was great!" I said afterwards. "You know, I've got some buddies. Would you mind?"

"No, not at all. No problem," she said with a smile.

We had everybody from the whole tour, the crew guys, the headlining band, the opening band—everybody lined up to get a blowjob. There were at least 10 guys.

After she was done, I escorted her out of there. I said, "Thank you very much. I appreciate all that."

She walked a few feet, leaned up against the wall, and puked up all this cum.

PAGE HAMILTON
Helmet

We were in Tokyo, Japan, having the best time. It was during the *Betty* tour. We drank too much at a restaurant and we ended up with our entourage going to another place. Me and [drummer] John Stanier started fighting in the back seat. This Japanese woman who was helping to guide us was on the left side of the back seat, I was in the middle, and John was on the right. John was on top of me and this poor girl was getting squished. It was really hard to get in a punch in that confined space. John's six-foot-five and 220 pounds and I'm six-foot-three and this girl was saying, "Please stop fighting!"

It was drunken horseplay and it was hilarious.

Henry was half-passed out in the front seat. Suddenly, he vomited out the front window. [Guitarist] Peter [Mengede] was still in the band at the time and he was disgusted by our shenanigans. The cab drove across a bridge and pulled over and the driver threw us out.

ALEX WADE
Whitechapel

We did the Liquid Metal radio show. We were only supposed to be there for an hour and it ended up being three hours. Usually, they bring a bottle of Crown for every band that comes in there, and then they have all these empty bottles of Crown that bands have signed inside the studios. Well, they brought us a whole handle of Crown and by the time we did the interview everyone was absolutely obliterated. Our bassist Gabe [Crisp] was screaming over the radio while other people were trying to talk. Then, at one point, he wandered off in the corner and threw up in a box of CDs.

MORGAN LANDER
Kittie

In 2001 at Cox Coliseum in Hamilton, Ontario, Pantera played and we went down to hang out with them. We saw the show. It was awesome. We drank all night and we had a limo take us home. [My sister, drummer] Mercedes [Lander] was so wasted she was throwing up out of the window of the limo on the highway on the way back home. She was puking down the side of the limo. We had to stop a bunch of times so she could puke some more. It was hilarious but it was also tragic.

KYLE SHUTT
The Sword

Our bassist Bryan's not a drinker. He can only have one drink at a time without getting sick. His body just rejects alcohol. But every once in a while he cut loose and tried to have a bunch of drinks and he always paid for it.

The first time The Sword played in New York at the Mercury Lounge was in 2005. It was one of those classic nights where Bryan decided he was gonna drink three vodka tonics. To a normal person it's not that big a deal but to Bryan it's world ending. He got real loose. He had his bass on him and he couldn't get it open. He was pushing [the clasps] instead of pulling them. So he started kicking it as hard as he could and he broke his toe.

It was a freezing night in New York City and we had to walk ten blocks to our hotel. He dragged his bass behind him with a broken toe, screaming into the night. Then he proceeded to scromit—which is a combination of screaming and vomiting—all night. We were in the same room and he was going on and on for eight hours.

TREVOR STRNAD
The Black Dahlia Murder

The first time we went on a full national tour to the West Coast was 2004. We were with Every Time I Die and As I Lay Dying and we were second on the bill. When we got to Rock Island in Denver, Colorado, I was having some Jägermeister at the bar. I didn't have any clue about the altitude difference and what happens to you when you drink up there and it makes your blood thinner and so much more susceptible to drunkenness. So I got trashed and by the time we played, I was blackout drunk.

I went onstage with the guys and during our set, I stage dived no less than seventeen times in twenty minutes. I was rambling incoherently between the songs and they had to shut me up. And at one point I thought it would be a good idea to dump water all over our drummer while he was playing. He didn't like that too much.

After the show, I vomited in pretty much every inch of the club. The next morning I was throwing up in a truck stop bathroom, standing in an inch of water. That was a low point in my life. I learned at least not to go that hard in Denver. Know the limits when you're exposed to altitude.

BILLY GRAZIADEI
Biohazard

We were in Brookling and we spent a whole day filming a video for our third record. We had a show that night with Overkill and Misfits. We didn't eat all day. We went right from the shoot to the show and they were going to film the show. We got there an hour before we were supposed to go on.

Being a Guinea from Brooklyn, I'm a sucker for pasta. And they had this giant tub of pasta on the catering table. I put together a huge plate and I wolfed it down in two seconds. I found through the years I always had to have two hours between eating and stage time so I could play without stomach cramps.

Obviously, I ignored that rule and jumped onstage five minutes later. The video cameras were on, and with the fire of Thor burning in my gut I ran onstage and went crazy. Midway through the first song, I puked all that pasta onto all the kids in the front row. They were just covered in puke and they looked at me like, "Yeaaaaaahhhh!!!"

KING FOWLEY
Deceased, October 31

This girl who I was fuckin' came to the house, but she was fucked up. She took off her clothes but she threw up and passed out before she could be bad. I lay her down and she didn't wake up. She was still was unconscious when my girlfriend was about to come home. I was trying to get this girl home so my girlfriend wouldn't see her.

I kept trying to put her fucking clothes on her, and then I got them halfway on and figured that was enough. Her panties were on but her pants were at her knees. I got her in the car. She was barely conscious.

"Where do you live?" I yelled so I could drive her home.

She opened her mouth and I thought she was gonna tell me and instead she just puked this fountain of cherry Kool-Aid liquor. She lay there in her puke, which looked kinda like blood. I didn't want her to overdose or choke on her vomit. I eventually had to roll her out in the middle of the street, right there with her tits hanging out of her shirt. She eventually sobered up and found her way home. And then she came back to my house later for more.

KERRY KING
Slayer

All this great shit can happen on tour and then when something fucked up happens, that's what everyone talks about. I hurled all over our manager's car, and I said, "Man, come the end of the tour, this is the only thing you're gonna fucking remember." And I was right.

IVAN MOODY
Five Finger Death Punch

I was acting in a friend's movie—*Bled*—and I had to play a monster. The outfit I had to wear was so hot I could only wear it for two or three minutes at a time and even so, I puked inside of the mask because of the intense heat, which was gross.

ANDERS COLSEFNI
ex-Slipknot

Shawn ["Clown" Crahan] found a dead crow and put it in a jar until it liquefied. It was just disgusting. I can't remember how long he kept that thing in there, but he brought it to every show and we were all scared the thing was going to get broken onstage and there was going to be a puke fest, which probably would have been its own rock and roll moment. It's even hard to growl and scream when you've been puking. Shawn definitely inhaled the bottle of liquefied crow once and threw up before a show.

SHAWN "CLOWN" CRAHAN
Slipknot, ex-To My Surprise, ex-Dirty Little Rabbits

We've all thrown up in our masks during shows. That's a given. When you're already overexerting yourself and then you push yourself that much more, which is what Slipknot is all about, your body is bound to rebel against you and you're gonna puke. It's like a rite of passage or a badge of courage. Usually, it happens the most on these outdoor festivals where it's 105 degrees and we're under these hot stage lights, wearing tight masks and jumping all over the place. We've practically killed ourselves in those conditions. There have been so many injuries. They're battle scars. A little puke ain't shit.

JOEY JORDISON
ex-Slipknot, Murderdolls, Sinsaenum, Vimic

Back in Slipknot, I used to puke almost every night due to heat exhaustion, overexertion, and lack of air. I have really long hair and I had a slit in my mask for breathing. My hair would get caught in the slit a lot and it would go down my throat and gag me while I'm playing.

Whenever I puked while I was playing I had to lift my mask up and pour the puke all down through my drum riser. It really sucked for my tech and the wardrobe person but I never missed a beat.

ANDERS COLSEFNI

When I was in the band, Joey's specialty was the yuck malt. He would take a blender and go through the house and see what he could throw in there—raw hamburger, cereal, ice cream. And then he'd dare somebody to drink it and they would do it. That would be a good laugh for the rest of us that weren't so eager to puke.

COREY BEAULIEU

Travis and I came up with this pretty cool thing in Quebec the night before the first show of the Children of Bodom tour. It's called the Zakk Wylde drinking game. You put on a Black Label Society CD and every time Zakk does a pinch harmonic, you have to drink.

It's pretty fun because once you start having to drink for a pinch harmonic, you realize how many pinch harmonics are in one fuckin' song. We went through a whole twelve-pack in two songs. And after ten minutes of the game, [ex-drummer] Travis [Smith] threw up and came back out and then we started again.

MORGAN LANDER

We were in a hotel in Tennessee in 2000 and somehow we went out and got a bottle of vodka and orange juice. We were drinking and drinking at the hotel. I ended up so drunk.

We were excited to get up in the morning and go to Graceland and see Elvis' house. But I was throwing up all night and I was so sick the next day that I couldn't go and I never got to see Graceland.

We have so many puke stories.

In New Mexico, [late bassist] Trish [Doan] puked after going to a strip club. Mercedes puked over her shoes at Ozzfest after partying with Pantera. There was lots of barfing.

WILL CARROLL

A long time before I joined Death Angel, me and some friends went to see them at The Stone in San Francisco on the *Frolic in the Park* tour. I was with [current Death Angel guitarist] Ted Aguilar 'cause him and I went to high school together. We went to 7-Eleven and I stole a big Vincent Gallo jug of wine. Then we went back to a friend's house and I drank the whole thing myself.

A little while later, I had to go home for dinner, and after dinner I was going to go to the show. Ted and our friend Gil drove me home. I was totally wasted and slurring my words. I've always wondered why those guys didn't just stop me from going home.

When they pulled up outside of my house I got out of the car and my pants had slipped down below my knees.

"He ain't going to the show," Gil said.

I walked into my house and my mom immediately knew I was smashed. She yelled, "Go to your room."

I went to my room. I had a huge wall poster of Gene Simmons from Kiss spitting blood. I looked right at that picture and I threw up all this wine on the wall. Needless to say, I didn't go see Death Angel that night. I had to take down all my posters and wash my walls.

AL JOURGENSEN

I went to the bathroom to do some coke to clear my head. While I was cleaning up in the bathroom, this guy asked me who I was and I told him. Then he said he was with the FBI so I put away my coke, punched him in the face, and ran out.

It turns out he was one of the Copeland Brothers, who runs FBI Booking agency. I thought he was with the actual FBI and was trying to arrest me!

As I was running out a big entourage came in with Robert Williams, the artist, who did the first Guns N' Roses album cover. I was so freaked out about the whole FBI thing I puked all over his brand-new blue suede shoes. He had just bought them that day and there's vomit everywhere. He was cool about it, though.

He wiped up the vomit, autographed some napkins with vomit on them and handed them back to me. I thought that was classy.

ROB CAVESTANY
Death Angel, ex-The Organization

After Death Angel broke up for a little while in 1991, we formed the group The Organization and did a couple albums. We were in Europe and I puked pretty good in Madrid, Spain on my 22nd birthday. It was a bad scene afterwards. We were driving on these windy roads around Costa Brava in the Mediterranean Coast of Spain. We were on these amazing, beautiful cliffs. But the roads were so twisty the driving was making me feel so sick. I began this epic marathon of constant puking. I don't know how many hours I was in the bathroom of the bus puking. We stopped at one point so the driver could take a minute. I ran off the bus and as soon as I stepped off, puke was flying out of my mouth. Someone took a photo of me doing that, which I still have. But I felt better for a while because I threw up so much.

And then we partied again to the point where we all took off our shirts and blasted thrash and had a pit on the bus, jumping all over each other and smashing everything and laughing. And then I got sick again because of that. I went from shirtless thrashing back to puking and puking. I was laying on the floor of the bathroom and my guitar tech dragged me out of there and threw my halfway into my bunk.

When I woke up, I had fuckin' puke all over me and my bunk—everywhere.

ADAM JARVIS
Misery Index, Pig Destroyer, Scour

Back in 2006 we did a seven-week tour with Fear Factory all through Europe. We changed drivers once we got closer to Scandinavia. This guy Tomas came along as a tour manager. He's now a longtime friend, but he hated me after that tour.

We took this overnight booze cruise. We went to the duty-free shop and bought the biggest bottle of Jägermeister possible and 170 beers. Then, we went back to the tiny little cabin we were sleeping in for the night and started pounding beers and playing drinking games.

Me and [guitarist John] Sparky [Voyles] went out to the nightclub and the last thing I remember was sitting down at a table with a bunch of people that didn't speak hardly any English. I was having the time of my life conversing with these people and nobody knew what anybody else was saying, but we were shooting the shit forever.

I stumbled back to the cabin and Sparky said he found me with my head against the door trying to punch the key into the door. I was so drunk I couldn't even figure out how it worked.

There were bunk beds on both sides and I was sleeping up top above our new guy, Tomas. At some point in the middle of the night, I woke up and projectile vomited off the side of my bed all over Tomas' clothes and personal stuff. Everything was covered in puke.

Mind you, he's a straight edge vegetarian and I ate a kebab with lamb meat in it and I threw that up with Jägermeister all over his stuff. Tomas was ready to leave the tour.

I crawled out of the cabin the next day and I kind of knew I did something fucked up, but I was so hungover I just wanted to die. I got out of my bunk and thought, "Oh gross! There's vomit all over the place. Who the fuck did that?"

I came out of the cabin and Jason [Netherton], the bassist in Misery Index, said, "Dude, you fucked up."

And I had that gut feeling that maybe the vomit was mine. He told me what happened and said Tomas was so mad he was bailing on the tour and was gonna leave us stranded. He didn't even want to take us to the venue we were playing that night.

Tomas is a big guy. His calves are just massive. I went up to him and apologized: "I'm sorry, man. I didn't mean to puke all over your stuff. I never usually drink like that. I know you don't drink so this must really freak you out. I'm such a stupid fucking asshole."

I tried every way possible to apologize to the guy. He ended up staying with us. And he's driven us a bunch of times since then.

Now, it's a funny story, but he wanted to murder me at the time. Tomas is a super cool guy who has worked with a lot of great bands like Isis, Russian Circles, and Converge. And a lot of people know that story. They see us and ask, "So, which one of you is the one that threw up all over Tomas?"

"Uh, yeah. That would be me."

BEN FALGOUST
Goatwhore, ex-Soilent Green

Goatwhore played a show in New Orleans in around 2003 on the *Funeral Dirge for the Rotting Sun* tour, and the next show was in Little Rock, Arkansas. This was back when we had a van that didn't have any seats in it. We took all the benches out and just had two front seats and we put mattresses in the back.

So, since we were playing our hometown the guys got really wasted. I was driving. At one point, I had to get off the main interstate and take state highways. We had seven people lined up in a row—two in the front, five in the back—wrapped up in sleeping bags like little burritos. The ones in the back were right against the doors. The guy all the way in the back was our old drummer, Zak Nolan. At one point, he said, "I feel sick. Pass me the trashcan."

Before anyone could get it to him, he projectile vomited across three of the guys in their sleeping bags. He could have opened up the back door a little bit and we would have slowed down the van while he threw up. That's happened before, but not this time.

It was funny 'cause I was in the passenger seat and I turned around and you could see his puke all over these sleeping bags.

We stopped and pulled over and put all these sleeping bags in a big garbage bag and we just tossed it then got back on the road.

ROBERT MEADOWS

We were hanging out in North Carolina with Dave Owens, one of the old singers of Codeseven, and I was drinking can after can of Sparks. So, we went to a supermarket and I got out of the van and puked orange vomit everywhere.

Then, we drove to Dave's house and, in a semi-conscious state, I leaned my ass out of the van and took a crap.

Then [Robert Carpenter], our old guitar player, took his folding mat out of the van and threw it into my poop without realizing it.

During the night, everyone was trying to sleep and they smelled the rank scent of shit and they were like, "Dude, this guy's house is so dirty."

And then Bob turned over his things and went, "What the fuck? There's shit all over my mat!"

That's the last time I get drunk on Sparks.

ROBB FLYNN
Machine Head

After a long night of partying, I was still raging. I stumbled onto the bus like a hurricane. I was fucking laughing. I went into the bathroom. I locked myself in and I threw up and then fell asleep in there. They had to pick the lock and drag me out and throw me in my bunk.

onto all fours and threw

tech, who is a fucking

... ... best. If there's a better guitar tech out there I have not found him.

SILENOZ
Dimmu Borgir

There was a Polish fan that came up to our bus on the *Abrahadabra* tour. We were somewhere in Germany and we had a homemade moonshine chili drink that [another] guy who handed it to us on the bus called the Suicide Throat Cutter. I didn't taste it because I knew it was going to be really strong, but this fan was there to try to impress so someone handed him a shot and he just poured it down and went, "Oh yeah, this is some really cool shit."

And two minutes later we almost had to call an ambulance because he was on the ground puking his guts out and shivering. We were really worried, but after a few minutes, he became better. I guess the drink lived up to its name.

MARIA BRINK
In This Moment

One time [ex-guitarist] Blake [Bunzel] was so sick he was sitting next to me in the van puking in a bag. There was this smelly bag of puke sitting right next to me for two hours and I thought I was going to get sick as well. I kept almost gagging but I didn't puke.

Another time, my drummer was so drunk he threw up and then we couldn't wake him up so we left him in the van and just put this sticky paper on his forehead with the motel room number on it.

BRETT CAMPBELL
Pallbearer

We stopped at a gas station while driving through the night in a van. We all went in and peed and got some snacks. Our guitarist Devin [Holt] was first in line and he bought a bag of six to eight hard-boiled eggs and there's this nasty egg water juice in the bottle. Mark was second in line and he bought cookies or something and left.

Suddenly, I heard this, "Ohhhh, godddd!"

By that time, I was done buying chips so I opened the door to walk toward the van and I heard this loud retch sound.

In the three minutes it had taken for all of us to check out, Devin had gone to the van and eaten all these eggs like a fuckin' snake. And by the time Mark got out there, Devin unleashed this eight-egg burp right as Mark was crawling in the door. He smelled this egg burp and immediately vomited.

SCOTT HEDRICK
Skeletonwitch

We were at a Truck Stop in Kansas and I ordered the Captain's platter. I don't know what the fuck I was thinking ordering clam strips in the middle of Kansas. I threw up horrendously for a day or so.

MATT BACHAND
ex-Shadows Fall, Times of Grace

I had bad food poisoning in Cleveland from falafel. You'd think that would be reasonably safe. As we were loading out, I vomited more than my body weight. It was all over the street behind the trailer. The guys were trying to load the trailer and there was puke everywhere.

ERIK RUTAN
Hate Eternal, ex-Morbid Angel, ex-Ripping Corpse

On Mother's Day in 2015, Hate Eternal were playing in Lisbon, Portugal, right on the ocean. It was beautiful. So we went and ate seafood on the water. I had a medley of shrimp, crabs and fish. I talked to my mom on the phone to wish her a happy Mother's Day.

The next thing I knew I was like, "Hmm, my stomach's not feeling too good."

Then, sixty minutes before we're going to go on I was puking my guts out. I puked two or three times before the show. I told one of the crew guys, "Listen man, put a garbage can on the side of the fuckin' stage because I don't think I'm gonna make it an hour without puking."

In between songs I went over to the side of the stage to find the trash-can. It was hidden so everyone in the audience didn't see it. I puked like crazy. But I had to finish the show, so I got back onstage.

I finally finished the show. To get to the dressing room we had to walk through the crowd and it was frickin' packed. All these guys want to

talk to me. They're goin...
"Holy fuck! I've got a twe...
ing again."

I got through the crowd,
my aim was pretty good.

CLARE CUNNINGHAM
ex-Thundermother

Poor [ex-guitarist] Giorgia [Carteri] fell ill first. She got the shits and then she started vomiting. And then there was a domino effect. We were driving and we were like, "Oh no, pull over, pull over!"

All five of us ended up with diarrhea and two of us were literally vomiting on the stage. We were so ill. Georgia ran off the stage and was literally puking her guts up.

It was hard to concentrate when you're sweating on stage needing to go to the toilet. It wasn't very ladylike, I must say. But it's one of the funnier memories we have.

We were supporting Michael Monroe during a Scandinavia tour. It was mainly Sweden and Norway. We were sick for five or six days. We were popping those tablets that stop the demons from coming out but it didn't work.

CHRIS GARZA
Suicide Silence

There was one afterparty barbecue with chicken and beer and Ivan from Five Finger Death Punch kept handing me shots of Jäger. I threw up everywhere. Our drum tech had to carry me out and put me in my bed and put a trashcan next to me. I was puking for a good hour straight. People were just pointing and laughing at me.

ERIK DANIELSSON
Watain

Of course vomiting happens at our shows. When you fuck, you sweat; and if you drink rotten pig's blood, you vomit. But the important thing is what you're doing. The statistical consequences, to me, are very irrelevant. These things, when they happen, they are the clash between the energies that we are trying to evoke and the peaceful energies of this world.

That's when vomiting happens. People also vomit when they get into a very extreme situation. People can vomit out of sheer anxiety or panic. That happens with people in our audience, but it's the same thing. The physical reactions are not the important thing, they're just proof that our intentions are being met.

CHAPTER 5: GIRLS, GIRLS, GIRLS

Groupies, Strippers & Chicks that Rock

After two bluesy, blustery metal albums (1981's *Too Fast for Love* and 1983's *Shout at the Devil*), and a more commercial record of metallic hard rock (1985's *Theater of Pain*), Mötley Crüe hit commercial stride with 1987's *Girls, Girls, Girls*. Despite its arguably sexist content, songs like the title track, "Wild Side," and "You're All I Need," were embraced by metal-loving chicks and hair metal dudes alike, and Mötley Crüe quickly expanded their reputation for being the nastiest, sleaziest rockers to emerge from L.A.'s Sunset Strip. For the next five years, *Girls, Girls, Girls* would be the primal slogan for a generation of boozed-up, coke-sniffing, party-lovin' hedonists. Then the dawn of grunge and alt-rock brought with it a devastating, guilt-ridden hangover that sapped all the fun from the party even if bands like Nirvana, Mudhoney, and Jane's Addiction wrote great, heavy songs that blended aspects of punk, metal, and indie rock just as hair metal bands were running out of Aqua Net, Manic Panic, and good lighter-raising ballads.

From the moment teenage girls started swooning when Elvis Presley shook his hips, even dudes that weren't aware that the term "rock and roll" was slang for getting it on realized that chicks dig musicians with guitars. The fervor grew. Girls were even more fanatical about singers, no matter how ugly they looked. The Beatles and the Stones were widely viewed (thanks to press and promotional teams) as polar opposites of the good guy/bad boy chick magnet continuum. And when the flower power generation brought together an eclectic array of sexually liberated freaks in bands like The Who, Cream, The Jimi Hendrix Experience, Led Zeppelin, Grateful Dead, and Jefferson Airplane, dudes flocked to cities like San Francisco and London to get in on the action and musicians showed up in droves, drawn by the promise of hot, promiscuous chicks who loved rock and roll. As it has done with much of the pop culture it usurped, metal took sexual expression to a new plateau of deviance.

Black Sabbath were dark, mysterious and curious girls attracted to their colorful occult imagery took the bait and strived to tame the beast. By the time the Sunset Strip scene had started, metal was no longer an underground art form and young girls swarmed long-haired, denim-and-leather bedecked rockers like bees to pollen. Even thrash metal, alt-metal, and death metal acts discovered women who wanted to give back to the musicians that touched them so, both literally and figuratively. Some female metal performers saw the abundance of horny dudes in the crowds as an opportunity for carefree sex with no strings attached. But most sat and watched in bemusement as girl fans stalked the male members (no pun intended) in their bands. Still, others united in solidarity, regarding their male admirers with contempt, especially when guys thought they had the right to grab and grope, which sometimes earned them a kick to the head.

DAVE MUSTAINE
Megadeth, ex-Metallica

I enjoy getting a nut just like the next guy, but there was a time where at the end, before I got married, I couldn't fuck just one girl. I had to have two chicks fucking each other for me to even get excited. And that's when I started to think, "Man, I'm losing my perspective on things because pretty soon it's gonna be like I have to have a whole naked college cheerleading squad in there for me to get an erection."

KING FOWLEY
Deceased, October 31

One night I had this girl over. She said, "You wanna do it in my ass? I've never done that."

"Fuck yeah!" I said.

We were fucking in my kid's baby pool in the middle of the night. Then we got on top of my car. I put it in her ass and she was screaming. My neighbor heard the noise and came out.

"What the fuck is going on?" he asked.

"Dude, this girl's never had it in her ass before," I told him.

"All right!" he shouted, and he came over and high fived me!

The next day he knocked on my door and woke me up. I answered the door.

"Hey man, is that chick you were with last night—that naked girl passed out in the back of your yard—still *with* you?" he asked with a hint of caution.

"What girl passed out?" I asked somewhat confused.

"That one," he said and pointed at her.

"Oh, shit. I forgot about her," I said. "Man, my kid's mom is coming over. I gotta get her out of here!"

I called her a cab, went out, and woke her up, and borrowed twenty-five dollars from my neighbor to pay the driver. I'm sure I paid him back but I'm even more sure he would have rather kept the money and hooked up with the chick I fucked in the ass.

DINO CAZARES
Fear Factory, Divine Heresy, Brujeria, Asesino

We were touring with Brutal Truth in Europe in 1993 and halfway through the dates we linked up with a festival tour that featured Cannibal Corpse, Fear Factory, Brutal Truth, Cathedral, Sleep, Hypocrisy, and Desultory. We did eight or nine shows. When we were in Germany one of [vocalist] Burton [C. Bell's] friends showed up. He had relatives there. So he came over with this very beautiful, blonde hair, blue-eyed young woman. Her body was voluptuous. I thought, "Oh my God, this girl is so hot. I've gotta go up and talk to her."

I said, "Hi" and she shrugged me off. I figured she was playing hard to get, so I kept talking to her. She wasn't very warm. I thought, "Hmm, what do German women like? . . . Beer!" So I got some beer out of the refrigerator in my bus and brought it back. I gave her a beer and invited her to come to the bleachers with me so we could check out the show. She said, "Okay." Boom! She came with me.

We were in the balcony watching Cannibal Corpse and drinking beer. I told her how beautiful she was. Next thing, we're making out and I started fondling her. She said, "Let's go somewhere."

So we went back to the bus but there were too many people partying there. I looked around and all these other bands had RVs parked next to our bus. I told her to come with me. I figured most of the bands were inside the venue watching Cannibal Corpse. I went and checked one of the doors, which was open. I looked in and didn't see anybody. We started making out and things proceeded from there. We began having sex and she said, "Put it in my ass."

I put it in her ass.

"I want more!" she gasped.

"What do you mean more?" I said.

"Your hand!"

I put a couple of fingers in her ass.

"More!" she yelped. "More?!?"

So I put another finger in and then another. I had my whole hand in her ass. I was fucking her with my whole hand. That made her cum and she was happy. And then I got to do my thing, so I was good.

When we were both satisfied, I heard somebody laughing. One of the guys in Desultory was in his bunk resting and he watched the whole thing. Soon, everyone on the tour knew what had happened.

AL JOURGENSEN
Ministry, Revolting Cocks

At Lollapalooza, I did a mom and daughter tag team in Charlotte, North Carolina, which was weird. They'd done it before. Apparently, this was a routine of theirs. I had to fuck the mother before I got the daughter and let me put it this way; the daughter could have been in a beauty contest and the mother should have been in a nursing home. So being with her wasn't that pleasurable and it was really kind of creepy. While I was doing the mom the daughter was sitting there in a chair not doing anything, not helping out. At least the daughter was hot, but by the time I fucked her, I just kinda felt gross.

BILLY GRAZIADEI
Biohazard

There was a couple who reached out to us. They were both huge fans. The boyfriend wanted to be there while his girlfriend had sex with one of the members of Biohazard. That whole thing went down backstage in a production office with a tour manager present. I'll just say I wasn't involved, but it wasn't an uncommon situation. I've been offered dude's girlfriends so many times, but I've never gone there. It's not in my DNA.

LEIGH KAKATY
Pop Evil

It's amazing when you see mother/daughter duos come on and mothers will sell out their daughters to get a better position with a band member. The moms are so into it. They're usually not ugly, but they're not as hot as their daughters. And you expect them to go, "Okay, this is my daughter. She's younger. Be nice to her."

No, no, no. They get pushy. And even when their daughter's going, "Mom, it's time to roll, it's time to roll."

Oh no. They make their daughter wait. We've had times when a mom and daughter were with the same dude but I don't know if they've gotten incestual. I'm sure it's happened.

DINO CAZARES

I've never had a daughter offer me her mom, but I've fucked fans' moms. We had a huge fan who always came to the shows. We always talked to him for a few minutes and he was seventeen so his mom came to pick him up after the shows. He was still talking to us and his mom was getting annoyed, saying, "C'mon, we gotta go."

His mom gets out of the car and I thought, "Holy shit! She's fuckin' hot."

So I started talking to his mom and I convinced her to come to an after party at my friend's house and bring her son. So she came to the party, which wasn't really a party at all. There were just a few people there. My buddy has a jam room in his basement, and the kid played the drums so I told my buddy, "Hey man, take the kid down to the jam room while I hook up with the mom."

I took her into my buddy's room and banged her and at the end, I made a mess all over her. There was nothing to wipe up with so I grabbed my buddy's shirt and wiped her off. Everything was cool. We went back to the party and the kid came back downstairs. The next day my buddy was pissed off because the piece of clothing she stained was one of his favorite shirts.

BOBBY LIEBLING
Pentagram

By about 1973, there were between fifty and one hundred people at each of our practices. We'd lock ourselves in. You couldn't break the door because it was metal with metal reinforcements. So no one could get out.

We had the place full of young girls and hippies and everyone would have all kinds of sex and drugs all night.

One night when I was especially high I went to the back of the warehouse, took off all my clothes and I got on a forklift and drove it into the main room. Then I jumped off of it and grabbed a Romper Room broomstick horse and started galloping around. I jumped up on tables and did lewd things in front of all these chicks, like walking over their heads with my balls in their faces. A lot of them thought it was funny, and I had no reservations because it was all in the name of rock n' roll. It was doped out, immature fun. And we'd all be so friggin' high that we'd be like, anything goes.

DAVID VINCENT
ex-Morbid Angel, Vltimas

Thankfully, there are always ladies to help keep rock and roll going. Many moons ago we'd have a female candidate—on her own free will and of age—who would be blindfolded in the back lounge. And we played a game that we called "Whose Is It?"

You can pretty much use your imagination to figure out what happened next. A lot of times someone said something, then it was much easier for the girl to get the right answer. It was always best to be silent, but that was hard to do.

BILLY GRAZIADEI

[Vocalist] Evan Seinfeld [who later married porn star Tera Patrick for five years and acted in and directed adult movies] was always the guy in the band who was with all the groupies. He even had a scrapbook full of all these X-rated pictures he took with them. One day, I got a call from the woman who booked the *Jerry Springer Show*. She told me they were doing an episode about groupies and they wanted to have me on the program. "Me? What do you mean me? I said. "You sure you don't want Evan or [guitarist] Bobby [Hambel]?"

"No, your name keeps coming up. All the women we've been speaking to keep mentioning you," She told me.

"Oh, you got it wrong," I said. "Sometimes people mix up Billy for Bobby. And definitely, Evan should be on the show."

"No, no. It's right. All the girls talk about you and they want you on the show." She insisted.

I was flattered, but I had a girl at the time and I didn't feel good about being asked to do the show. I swore it was a mistake. I ended up not doing it.

Looking back, I wish I did it. But they got Peter Steele [from Type O Negative] to do it instead and it was fucking hilarious. I knew that if I did it, they would pull out people from the dark closets and go, "Do you know her? Do you know her?" And then I'd be put on the spot.

But Peter was proud of who he hooked up with and he was really clever so the show was really funny.

JERRY DIXON
Warrant

To promote the band, we had all these freaky fliers that were disgustingly rude. They had pictures of girls in bathroom stalls and the images were accompanied with suggestive titles like "Scratch and Sniff," "More Than a Mouthful is a Waste," and "The Quality You Can Taste." It seemed like the more disgusting and outrageous the fliers were, the more people showed up for the gigs. It was stupid as shit—anything our little sixteen-year-old brains could think of that was rude. So we stumbled on that shock value and ran with it.

MIKE IX WILLIAMS
Eyehategod

We played a show in New Orleans in 1993 at a place called RC Bridge Lounge. They had some of the wildest shows ever; they were free-for-alls. At the end of the show, the stage would be completely covered in glass. You could break bottles on the floor, and no one cared. They also had free beer some nights.

When we played there, we were all doing Rohypnols, which were pretty big at the time. People would go to Texas through Mexico and get these pills, which some people used as roofies. We just liked the high they gave us. We crushed them up and sniffed them. The whole club was drinking and on Rohypnols.

In the middle of one of the songs, these two girls got up on the stage and started eating each other out. One of them fell back off the stage and was unconscious for a minute. I'm not saying the girls were on Rohypnols because I have no idea. At one point, I looked out in the crowd and there was a dude just standing there completely naked.

KING FOWLEY

One time, this girl came up to me after a show and started talking to me. She was like, "I want to be with you." She was a pretty girl, but for what-ever reason, I wasn't in the mood to hook up with her. So I told her, "I will be with you if you fuck a chicken."

I told her it didn't have to be a real chicken, just parts of a chicken. I figured that was that and she'd be grossed out and take off. But she went and got Purdue chicken parts and then she came back and took off her clothes and started shoving a raw piece of chicken in her pussy. It was a frozen boneless chicken breast so it was slippery and she pushed it in and out of herself without any problem.

Talk about dedication. After she did that, I didn't have the heart to let her down, so I guess she got what she came for.

IVAN MOODY
Five Finger Death Punch

There was a time when I was going way overboard with partying. I was living the rock star life and there was no stopping me. I had just gotten a divorce, so I was going through women like they were water. It's something that seems like every kid's fantasy who dreams of being a rock star, but it was kicking my ass and I didn't understand why.

So, I kept going.

It really took some serious intervention from my bandmates for me to see the light. They saw what I was doing and they said, "Hey, we're gonna sit and talk to you and help you out and get you back to where you belong. That meant everything and that's when I started changing my behavior and getting back on track—getting back my self-esteem and some self-respect.

DAVID DRAIMAN
Disturbed

My first time in Paris we played a great show and after we got offstage, I found a nice little restaurant near the venue. I was sitting down to eat and these two beautiful Parisian women, who had obviously been at the show because they looked the part—were making all kinds of suggestive faces at me and laughing and joking around with each other. It looked as though I was going to have a fun evening in front of me.

I called the waiter over and I asked if he would be willing to translate a message I wanted to give to the girls. I said, "Hey *monsieur*, please forgive me. I don't speak the language and those two lovely women over there have been very, very friendly. Do you think you might be willing to translate for me?"

He took his platter and, slammed it on the table.

"No, *monsieur*," he snapped. "I will take your order. I will bring you your food. But I will not be your pimp!"

The girls were startled and they got up and left. So there I was eating in this little place alone and I missed my opportunity all because Jacques got all pissed off.

AL JOURGENSEN

Motörhead played Austin, [Texas] and Lemmy's tour manager got hold of me and asked if I wanted to come to the show. I was like, "Cool. Awesome. Great."

So I went and it was a kick-ass show, of course. I went out to the bus afterwards. I walked on and his motley crew were sitting there. I said, "Well, where's Lemmy?"

They all kind of smirked and pointed toward the back. So I walked back there and knocked on the door. I heard some spanking noises and some yelps, yips, and yaps. Then I heard, "Come in! Come in!"

I opened the door and there was Lemmy in a full SS uniform spanking this naked fat chick with a riding crop. That's the noise I was hearing. He started talking to me but he was still hitting her.

"Do you have any Quaaludes, man?" he asked.

"Uh, no, I've just got some heroin."

"Fuck that shit! I don't touch the stuff. I was really hoping you had Quaaludes. Well, fuck off, then. Leave me alone," and he went back to whipping her. That was perfect Lemmy, primal to a fault.

DAVE WYNDORF
Monster Magnet

In the early '90s I was in Europe. I was completely wide-eyed. It was like rock paradise. I was going to all these foreign countries and there were all these rockin' looking people and cool chicks. I got into this thing with two girls riding around on these bicycles. They got me a bike and we rode through Amsterdam to this weird flat they had by a canal.

"Yeah, I'm fuckin' cool!" I thought.

They knew who I was and they knew what they were doing. They were a couple years older than me and they knew they were getting me and I knew I was got! I was so excited and wanting to really make my mark. I wanted to be James Bond and John Holmes all in one. We all get into bed and it was insane. It was like a European hallucination—a slow-motion dream of eroticism. There were beautiful women with long hair and tattoos. We got into it and then—European hotels are very small and squat; there was a ceiling fan because God forbid they have air conditioning—I got up to make my move to show these girls from another world that I knew what I was doing. I stood up on the bed to make a manly lion roar and look down at these women to say, "I am here!"

I threw my hair up and it got caught in a ceiling fan.

In a second I went from conqueror to conquered. I was sitting in a half crouch position with my hair caught in the fan, which had stopped because it was so tangled in my hair. One girl pointed and laughed and the other had a horrified expression on her face. They made so much noise that all of sudden there was a knock at the door. It was their neighbors. A fat old lady and a guy came in and I was standing there completely naked. The girls had towels and sheets wrapped around them. Suddenly, everyone's discussing how to get me out. I was completely helpless. They went and got scissors.

"Don't cut the hair! I need the hair," I yelled.

Of course, they had to cut the hair, so I had a big chunk out of my head. I quickly got dressed and left on my bicycle in shame.

DINO CAZARES

We got to a certain level in 1998 when *Obsolete* came out and we had a song on the radio, [a cover of Gary Numan's "Cars"]. When you have a song on the radio it's not just a metal show anymore, it's a rock show. The average person that listens to rock doesn't go to metal shows. So we were getting radio crowds, and that meant a lot of really hot girls were showing.

When we did Ozzfest, we opened up for Rob Zombie and Iron Maiden and we saw more amazing looking girls than ever. But when "Cars" hit, we knew that the girls actually were there for *us*, not the other bands.

I got the label, [Roadrunner], to hire a friend of mine to do marketing. He toured with us to make sure all the record stores had the albums and the displays. The real reason I wanted this guy to come along with us was because he knew how to go to the crowd and pull the best-looking girls. He gave them backstage passes. Everybody else in my band was married or wasn't into that. I was and he knew what I liked.

We had walkie talkies. Every night I would go to the back of the bus and he would bring these girls onto the middle of the bus. Then he'd call me on the walkie talkie and say, "Okay, tell me which one you want first."

I had my choice!

And I would do three girls a night. There were multiple times when we had multiple girls at the same time, but when you try to be with three girls at once it's really hard to navigate all three of them so everyone gets what they need. So I usually preferred one at a time.

PAUL LEDNEY
Profanatica, Havohej

There were several times when we would be out drinking and I would be able to finagle someone into group sex.

It was actually us three plus the girl. That happened in 1991 and we did everything you can imagine, including creampies and there was a mannequin involved. And, of course, there were no condoms.

A couple months later I was incredibly wasted and I got this letter from that girl we were all with, and she was trying to pin me as being the father of her kid. We all had to get blood tests to prove that it wasn't us. She was a dancer at a strip club. We were kids at the time. I lived with my parents and my mom was like, "Who is this person?"

"I don't know? I've never heard that name before," I said.

We had to get a lawyer and the guy was cool.

"Oh, this chick's a slut. It definitely wasn't you," he said.

But I remember going into extreme detail because he wanted to hear everything that we did and my mom was in the room as we were going over the details. She was rolling her eyes huffing and puffing. But the fact that it wasn't us who fathered the girl was good. I cut my losses after that and did everything a little smarter.

ROSS THE BOSS
ex-Manowar, Ross the Boss, The Dictators

We always had plenty of female companionship to keep us busy. It was unbelievable. I couldn't even leave my hotel room. I'd open the door and they'd be lining the hall walking back and forth.

"I'll take you and you."

And then you go back into your room and go at it. We had twosomes, threesomes, foursomes, and moresomes. It was the early '80s before AIDS and no one was worried about catching anything. It was beautiful.

ADAM JARVIS
Misery Index, Pig Destroyer, Scour

Back in 2006 we toured with Fear Factory. When we were in Stockholm there was an afterparty at one of the main metal bars in the city. We had an upstairs area and it was all you could drink. I was hanging out and I saw all these guys in Mnemic, Entombed, Grave, Meshuggah, and other Swedish metal royalty. We were all drinking and after a while, I saw this pretty little blonde chick and one thing lead to another. I was all drunk and full of liquid courage and I said, "Hey, I'm going home with this chick. I'll meet you at the next show."

Before we went back to her place I said to her, "Okay, remind me to book a train so I can go to the next show in Oslo, Norway."

We went back and did our thing. I did not look up the train schedule and I woke up in the morning. The sun was blazing in my eyes and I thought, "Oh shit! What did I do? Where am I at?"

I didn't have a cell phone back then, so getting a train was out of the question. She took me to the airport and I had some euros on me from money we made on the tour. There was only one flight that would get me to Oslo in time, but it was a first-class ticket. It was a forty-minute flight so I figured it couldn't be too bad. I asked the ticket agent how much it was and it turned out to be four hundred fifty euros, which was five dollars less than everything I had. I wound up spending almost all the money I had made at that point on this ticket. I was sitting in first class at noon with all these businessmen in suits. I was wearing a Napalm Death long sleeve and I smelled like booze and pussy.

I showed up twenty minutes before the doors opened and I'll never forget Christian Olde Wolbers from Fear Factory watched me walk in from the backstage entrance and he stood up and started clapping. That was Misery Index's first show ever in Norway.

KING FOWLEY

There was a redhead stripper in Richmond, Virginia, who would come down and we'd go crazy all night dong anything you can imagine. You could fuck her for an hour and spill everything you had. Ten seconds later she'd be grabbing it to go again.

One time she said, "I'm gonna bring my friend with me."

I was like, "Sure, cool."

I told my buddy Jim and he went, "Man, I hope she's hot!"

I figured I'd be with the redhead and Jim would fuck her friend. They both showed up and my girl's friend was a nymph whore from hell. She got out of the car and she had her shorts up to her puss and she flashed us these pierced nipples.

"Yeah man! Hook me up!" Jim said.

"No, this is for me and King tonight," said the redhead, dashing Jim's fantasies.

I looked at Jim and he was so crushed. He was like, "You're a fucking asshole."

JOHN GALLAGHER
Raven

Once upon a time I was with some girl who hit on me. We went off to the bus and did what comes naturally. And everything was wonderful. Then I came back and there were a lot of sniggers. Everyone was laughing because, apparently, five minutes before she picked me up she was putting on a sex show with a mag light flashlight and being videoed. I didn't feel too clever after that.

JEREMY MCKINNON
A Day to Remember

We have a song called "All Signs Point to Lauderdale" and that's actually based on something that went down in Florida. Me and a few of my friends were hanging out with these girls in the worst area of West Palm Beach and something really disgusting happened. Let's just say one of the females had female problems and the problem ended up on someone.

So we were just like, "Ewww, this is gross. We're leaving."

We left and me and [bassist] Josh Woodard were half nude on the corner by a Drexel Road. We waited at a gas station for some of our friends to pick us up while all these really scary looking people stared at us. The friends who came and got us had been involved before we got into this situation and the song title is something one of them said to us: "I told you that you shouldn't have gone back there. All signs pointed to Lauderdale, man. All signs."

KYLE SHUTT
The Sword

I hooked up with my fair share of consensual ladies. But it was nothing super-decadent. We're in a doom metal band so, c'mon! It's mostly a lot of fat dudes at the shows. Here's my best story: "Yeah, I hooked up with this chick and we had sex!" That's the extent of my stories.

PAGE HAMILTON
Helmet

The first time I ever stepped foot in a strip club I was thirty-two years old. We were on the road and we had a good ol' boy bus driver, Bill Harway, and our tour manager, Craig Overbay—who later worked with Nirvana and Foo Fighters—was super overworked because we were so busy at the time playing so many shows.

"We're going to show Craig a good time," Bill said one night.

We went to this place in Phoenix called Bourbon Street. Bill was cracking up. He kept buying me these lap dances. I was just paralyzed. I was sitting with my hands on my knees. The girl said, "You can touch me."

"No, I'm good. I'm fine," I said.

Bill was just cracking up and kept sending over Wild Turkeys and Budweisers. Craig had a good time, too. But I don't know. Strippers are just not my thing.

BUZZ OSBORNE
Melvins

We toured with Nine Inch Nails and those guys had a lot of strippers and parties. That's a polite way to say it. I had no interest in partying at that point. Certainly, whiffing weasel dust wasn't something I wanted to do at all and that stuff was going on pretty heavily. And strippers have never had an appeal to me. Why would I want to look at the menu if I can't eat?

CHRIS VRENNA
ex-Nine Inch Nails, ex-Marilyn Manson

I've seen crazy shit on the bus and in dressing rooms. Most of it is stuff everyone's heard of before. But one time, we had a fan that was incredibly physically handicapped in a wheelchair. He was backstage with us and the dressing room happened to be full of local strippers completely decked out. So we thought, "You know what? We don't need the attention from these girls. But that guy, who's a fan, clearly he needs some love."

We got all the strippers to give him the lap dances of a lifetime in his chair and he dug it. We told ourselves, "We're doing a good thing, right?"

And then we looked back at what we had started and thought, "No, we're definitely going to Hell."

SCOTT IAN
Anthrax, S.O.D., The Damned Things

Before I married Pearl [Aday], my friends threw me a bachelor party. We were in this weird apartment complex rec room right in Huntington Beach. These friends had a tradition of always getting the groom to strip down naked and then sit down on a chair in front of the whole room of dudes, which I just did not get at all. Going into this thing I was like, "Really. I'm not into this."

And they were like, "Well this is what's happening, bro."

I was in this chair and three or four strippers came in. There was nothing actually sexual going on. They were dancing but they were only topless and there was no actual touching. I wasn't enjoying any of it. I was bummed but I was trying to go with it 'cause all my friends were totally into it. My arms were loosely tied to the chair so after about four minutes I started planning my escape. Then, Gene Simmons came in and saved the day. As soon as he arrived the whole room stopped, every head turned and the music came to a screeching halt. Gene just stood there smiling and took off his glasses.

Two of the strippers immediately made a beeline for Gene. I swear, it was almost like he choreographed the whole thing because the next thing I knew one of the strippers got into a handstand position right in front of him, with her legs over his shoulders. Her crotch was right near his face. He grabbed her legs and of course, obliged.

He didn't touch her, but he stuck his tongue out suggestively and the whole room erupted into a standing ovation and the music came back on.

By then, all of the strippers were all over Gene and no one was paying any attention to me, which was great. I was off the hook. I got out of the chair, got my clothes on, and snuck away very quietly.

HEIDI SHEPHERD
Butcher Babies

We were asked to play a spring party for *Girls N' Corpses* magazine. The party fell on my birthday so I thought it'd be fun if we played and also invited all of my friends to celebrate. I guess I should've done a little bit of research before inviting my friends because it wound up being an S&M party including fuck tents spread throughout the lawn, people being tied up and whipped, and lots and lots and lots of public sex. So, we just got wasted, played the show and had a cake fight during the set. As we finished the gig, we jumped in the pool for our grand finale. It wound up being one of my favorite birthday parties ever.

CARLA HARVEY
Butcher Babies

Early in our career, we played a swinger's party. It was surreal to look out as we played and see people walking around naked and having sex right in front of us on the lawn. We were giggling and pointing like little kids. There was even a naked grill master BBQing for us. We brought our own meat, of course.

JESSE JAMES DUPREE
Jackyl

We were doing one hundred shows in fifty days, two shows a day in different cities—to set a *Guinness Book* world's record. For the ninety-ninth we were in Jacksonville, Florida, and we went from the height of solemn tribute to sheer debauchery in an afternoon.

A morning radio station had all these people in this shopping center parking lot, so we played a show there and when we got through we signed some autographs and some fellas said, "Are you gonna see Lynyrd Skynyrd's grave while you're here?"

"We don't have time," I said.

"What'ya mean you don't have time?" he replied. "It's just right up here on the other side of those trees."

"Lynyrd Skynyrd is buried on the other side of these bushes right up against this shopping center?" I asked.

"Yes."

"Y'all wanna see Ronnie Van Zant's and Steve Gaines' graves?" I asked my guys.

We walked a hundred fifty yards across this big shopping center parking lot through these bushes and we were standing right on top of Ronnie Van Zant's grave. We spent a bit of time there paying homage and got all got choked up.

Then we went back and the road crew was already on the bus. We walked in, and they were using a big venison sausage that Ted Nugent had given us to fuck this girl that was right there in broad daylight. Her legs were pulled back and they were just giving her the once over—just throwing down.

"Go to the back of the fuckin' bus 'cause people can see in here," I said and laughed.

There's just no end to that kind of crazy stuff.

TOMMY VICTOR
Prong, Danzig, ex-Ministry

There was some big pandemonium on the Danzig bus. There were a bunch of chicks there and, apparently, I wound up with one of them.

Those were the days when everyone was partying heavily There was a champagne bottle with human waste on the top of it. Somebody fucked a chick up the ass with the champagne bottle and it was lying in a back alley by the time the night was over. And everyone said it was me who did it. I don't remember doing it and I really don't think it was me but because I'm an asshole I took credit for it.

DAN DONEGAN
Disturbed

One time, somewhere in Florida, a girl took a champagne bottle and inserted it in a couple places, not just one. It was quite entertaining to see what some of these chicks were willing to do to be able to hang out with the bands.

One time we finished a tour in Vegas, so, of course, we were going to be partying there. Somebody had set up a suite in the hotel, stocked it with beer and brought up a bunch of girls, and I just remember thinking, "Man, we are living a damn good life here."

They were definitely fun, crazy moments. We're all married now, but I'm not gonna say those things didn't happen, and our wives know that. That's definitely part of our past. We were living the dream.

DAVE WYNDORF

There's a boutique level of S&M, which is a chi-chi or phony thing that came into the rock and roll world with industrial bands like Nine Inch Nails. Some goth people were into this kind of bondage chic, too. But below that is where the real stuff goes on There is an underground in rock and beyond rock all through the world. I used to think it was preserved for some sort of '60s bondage novel or high-powered executives getting their ass beat. I never dreamed that there was a place that really existed where there were women and men that both liked S&M that much and that was the criteria for cool. It wasn't just fashion, it was serious aggro sex. There was pain and humiliation and it was really psycho shit. When I was first exposed to it, I thought, "Wow, this is interesting. Let's see what happens."

I met girls that were into that and they would yell, "Slap me! Choke me!" So, I did.

I got into it for about a year and it was insane. Eventually, I slipped out of it because it wasn't doing it for me and I kept questioning it. And the girls didn't like me too much because after we were done, I'd ask them, "So, why did you want to do that?"

I became like a therapist.

"What are we doing here? Did you have a problem with your father?"

"Shut the fuck up! You're ruining it."

I explored that stuff for a while and I just thought it was really mean. It was too mean for me. I like power, too, but the power to smack somebody around? It doesn't make any sense. I thought I could be a sadist. I was mean to my sisters. I teased them. But I discovered there's a fine line between giving somebody what they want and taking responsibility for not adding to their mental illness.

JOHN GALLAGHER

Back when Slayer were just starting out, [guitarists] Jeff [Hanneman] and Kerry [King] walked up to us looking very sheepish. We were like, "Yeaaah?"

And one of them said, "You guys seem to get a lot of girls at the show. How do you get girls to [hook up with you]?"

[Raven guitarist] Mark [Gallagher] put his hands on both their shoulders and said, "Okay guys, let me tell you how it is and he took them away for some instruction."

Apparently, they followed his advice and did pretty well after that.

MARTY FRIEDMAN
ex-Megadeth

The four of us in the band were more into sex than anything else. The conversations that went on between us were primarily things of a sexual nature. And it was just probably the main impetus for us to play music in the first place. You start off as a kid playing music because you want to get chicks. And the longer you do that, when you get all the chicks and you reach that goal, then if you still stick around in music, you eventually develop some integrity and style and purpose.

The original purpose is just to get your rocks off. And then you pursue that for as long as it takes. Anybody who tells you that's not the original reason for picking up a guitar when you're a kid, they're definitely throwing you some bullshit. The guitar is an extension of your penis, and to some extent, you're kind of naked when you're playing out there. You really are because you're giving of yourself to people whether they like it or not. It makes you really quite vulnerable. You act like you're all confident, but you're hoping everyone likes what you do.

DAVE ELLEFSON
Megadeth

We took what we could get anywhere we could get it. When I was hanging out trying to get close to girls that were posing in porno mags, I thought, yeah, this is great. These are true rock star moments. But that ended for me about 1993. It just got old.

We had just done the *Countdown to Extinction* tour. Then I moved on and left L.A. The thing is, it doesn't go away. You see the sex and alcohol and drugs going on all around you when you're in rock and roll. But I got over it. Been there, done that—twice. At that point, it was just time to move onto something else and make music my absolute main priority.

I started to realize there's a big price to be paid for sleeping around. Every time you do that you leave a little bit of your soul behind. And also, the potential for disaster is pretty great when you've got a girlfriend.

Now I'm married and have children, but it's cool because having done all that I don't have to worry about having a midlife crisis and then going off and cheating on my wife. I don't have to worry about that because I did all that shit already.

PHILIP ANSELMO
Pantera, Down, Superjoint Ritual, Scour

I ain't gonna sugarcoat it, Jack, and I'm not gonna deny it. I fucked more chicks than most people could even imagine and I had a lot of fun. It was a fantasy turned reality.

But I got to the point where I started really thinking, "What kind of self-image am I creating here by fucking anything that moves?"

It's kind of an immature type of outlook, I think. It's very shallow. There have been moments of glorious fucking sex with a beautiful woman that you never take back or deny, but to find a woman that you can talk to and relate with is something else altogether. And I feel grateful to have experienced both.

BRETT MICHAELS
Poison

Some bands may remember [Sweet] Connie [Hamzy] from Little Rock and how crazy their experience was. We've got so many of those stories, including Connie. Some girls were coked out of their brain and went all night. All of that stuff happened, but not just once. I was single and playing in front of 10,000 people a night. That increases the odds that you're gonna get laid. So, when the girls come backstage there's so much insanity that happens.

There was Florida, where four strippers started doing each other. And there was Toronto at the Skydome, where a girl started fucking another girl with a dildo onstage? No matter what you want to call it, that's a rock and roll moment.

PAUL LEDNEY

Multiple times between 1990 and 1993, the hottest chick in these East Coast clubs approached me and said, "You can have sex with me if you find a condom."

And that happened quite often back in the day. The dirtier I looked, the more that happened. It was always the hottest girl and there were a lot of times I thought I was on a hidden camera show.

BURTON C. BELL
Fear Factory, Ascension of the Watchers

I went to a party in LA. It was our first time there and we were starstruck. I don't remember who invited us but we showed up at this huge house and there was an insane party going on. I walked around feeling very out of place. I opened a door to a bathroom and there was a woman there who had an audience of men. She was inserting different sized beer bottles in different holes.

I was kind of taken aback and everybody looked at me like the record had scratched and I obviously didn't belong there. So I closed the door and left. That's all the groupie action I ever needed to have.

There were a lot of weird smells in the party that I didn't recognize and I later found out it was crack. That sort of stuff makes me very uneasy so I never wanted to encourage it or engage in it.

M. SHADOWS
Avenged Sevenfold

2006 interview
I heard last night there was this girl giving one of those motherfuckers a blowjob while the other dudes walked in and pissed on her.

SYNYSTER GATES
Avenged Sevenfold

2006 interview

Dude, we were peeing all over these girls last night. We had a couple of girls that were at our meet and greet. We were supposed to play strip poker. We play strip poker with the fans so they get to see some Avenged Sevenfold good times in action. And the strippers followed us to Atlantic City.

So, we all filled up a bucket with urine and we dumped it all over her and she was freaking out. She couldn't believe it. She was soaked head to toe in the band's piss. So [bassist] Johnny [Christ] said, "Don't worry baby. It's just alcohol."

She picks up this bottle of Patron [Tequila] and says, "I can't believe you wasted this bottle of Patron on me. Oh, my God, you guys are so stupid."

And we're just busting up because she's covered with piss.

JESSE JAMES DUPREE

One night we flew into Sturgis, South Dakota, to play The Full Throttle Saloon and there were a bunch of wrestlers there and the Dahm Triplets from *Playboy* magazine. They were there and their mom was with them and she was as good looking as they were. We planned to do a sound-check and then we were gonna go to our hotel room and crash for a while and get back to the venue in time to play. But when we got to the club for soundcheck a major storm came through and everything closed down for a couple hours. We basically got stranded in the dressing room.

Then, all these people started showing up and they had brought moonshine and all kinds of crazy shit. They wanted to take pictures of me with all these wrestlers and these beautiful girls. We were all drinking moonshine. These photographers wanted to get the right pictures with bubbles coming out in the bottles. I had a little too much to drink even before we hit the stage and each one of the girls and wrestlers kept walking out and doing shots with me. I was doing my own shot of moonshine to every one of theirs.

By the end of the night, I was blind. The band got in an argument with our road manager about whether or not they were gonna hand me the chainsaw I use onstage or not.

I told them, "I'm using the chainsaw!" and I wound up handing it to one of the Dahm Triplets that was standing there with her top off. And she was slinging it around, not realizing it was real and it could cut some-one's head off.

SAM RIVERS
Limp Bizkit

When we played arenas there would be strippers backstage. In the arenas, there were locker rooms that had showers. So a lot of these girls would go into that shower with some dude in a band and do whatever.

We happened to have huge-ass super soakers with us at the time and we had some fun with that. Girls were dancing in the back and we'd shoot them in the ass. That was fun and funny but it wasn't degrading. We really didn't do a lot of the horrible shit you read about bands doing with these girls backstage.

DEVIN TOWNSEND
Strapping Young Lad, ex-Steve Vai, ex-Wildhearts, Devin Townsend Band

I'm so not into rock and roll shenanigans. My whole thing as a musician is, I'm not here to party. I'm here to make music and perform it. I remember going backstage with some band we were touring with and there were all these girls and everybody was fucking each other and I was like, "I'm out, man. This is stupid." I went back to the van and phoned my wife.

GENE HOGLAN
Dark Angel, Testament, Dethklok, ex-Death, ex-Strapping Young Lad

It was so ridiculous. You'd be at a party and you'd be walking to the bathroom and see the bedroom door slam open and some naked, drunk drummer from whatever band would start running through the party. And in the background, the girl he had been with would be putting her clothes on. The whole thing was such a cartoon, but I saw it all at a very super-young age and that's why I have to laugh about it all.

JOHN GALLAGHER

On that tour we did with Metallica, Lars [Ulrich] was enjoying the rock and roll lifestyle. He was always chatting up the ladies. He'd always say, "Dude, do you have the keys to the white truck?" while he was holding some girl's hand.

And it was like, "Oh, no. You do realize we have to sleep in there tonight, don't you?"

It was pretty wild coming over to America from England 'cause everywhere else girls would be very reserved and maybe a little friendly, but not much. But in America, they'd literally throw themselves at you, which was very disconcerting to be honest.

LEIGH KAKATY

Our ex-drummer [Josh Marunde] once got some new drumsticks for a drumstick company. So, to help promote the drumsticks, this stripper put them up her crotch. They took a couple pictures of that and put it up on the Twitter page.

DAVE MUSTAINE

We had plenty of good times, but we never looked at girls as lesser human beings to be degraded. We liked sex and they liked sex, so it was consensual and respectful. We used to go from girl's house to girl's house to live. And when we couldn't find some chick that would feed us and hopefully have sex with us, we would sleep in the car.

PHILIP ANSELMO

When I first quit high school, I had no job, no money. There were times we had a gig to play and I had not eaten all day, but somehow I was absolutely drunk. I shouldn't have been in the club to begin with. I was probably fifteen. I had no place to stay. Usually, I'd hook up with some chick and see what she could provide in the way of sustenance and other things. That's how I lived for, like, a year and a half before I joined Pantera.

CHUCK BILLY
Testament

We were in Stuttgart, Germany, and before the show we were sitting on the bus when we saw a group full of girls coming to the show. That's always nice because there usually aren't a lot of girls at our shows. Mostly it's guys and sometimes their girlfriends.

When the show started, me and [guitarist] Alex [Skolnick] were on Alex's side jamming and we saw the group of girls that came in together before. They were dancing and going crazy. At one point, this girl's skirt got hiked up a little high and a set of testicles fell out of the skirt right in front of me and Alex. Our jaws dropped and we almost lost our place in the song because we couldn't believe our eyes.

JERRY DIXON

There were always these girls that had rich parents and they would provide for us. They would get the beer and buy the food. They were just part of the gang. There was a group of people that would all go to the Strip. It was kind of like a clique. Everybody went to the same person's house after shows and hung out and did everything together.

The weirdest thing that ever happened to me with a chick happened when we were playing with Mötley Crüe. There was a lady and she got all the way into our dressing room by telling people that she was my mother. And she got locked into the dressing room. And then someone came up to me and said, "Jerry, okay, I got your mom."

And I was like, "That's not my fuckin mom!"

And this lady was just like, "I just wanted to meet you!"

And she broke down.

Wow, that was pretty ballsy. She was as old as my mother, so there was no way I was gonna hook up with her, but that was probably the craziest fan ever.

MORGAN LANDER
Kittie

We once did a photo shoot with Ozzy, which was so bizarre. We were like, "Why are we getting to do a photo shoot with Ozzy?"

It was because when we agreed to do the Ozzfest we were the youngest people on the tour and he was the oldest. So a magazine wanted to do this fun thing where the young generation of metal meets the oldest. Ozzy was kind of weird about it. He was like, "Oh, these young girls. I don't want to do anything wrong. Oh, oh, I don't want to say the wrong thing. Am I allowed to touch them?"

He was being funny and joking around. But it was a little strange and really surreal.

CARLA HARVEY

Some people have viewed us as sex objects, but fuck them. We used to perform [topless] with electric tape across our nipples in an "X" because it was a tribute to our hero Wendy O. Williams, whose band The Plasmatics did a song called "Butcher Babies." She's a hero of ours and we did that as a tribute to her individuality and a statement that we're going to do what we want and not care about what other people think. We haven't done that in many years now. We basically got sick of it. We did that look and we evolved. But we're not ashamed of anything we've ever done in our lives. I'm very proud of what we did wearing that tape and the movement we made doing it.

But it got to the point where it became too controversial and then people weren't hearing the music. We don't want to hinder people listening to our music. That's the most important thing for us to get out there.

One woman was at one of our shows with her husband, and she dragged him out of there. But when people saw our live show, even with the tape on, they realized we didn't go up there with the intention of looking sexual. We went up there with a very defiant attitude. Our show is pretty hardcore and once they saw it, they got it.

LZZY HALE
Halestorm

I understand why guys develop an attraction to female musicians. When I was a teenager, I loved Cinderella and I was going to marry [their guitarist] Tom Keifer. That was my equivalent to the boy band phase girls go through as teenagers.

One of my mom's friends, Shelly, lived about an hour from us. She was a huge '80s girl back in the day and she gave me a VHS video of Cinderella's *Night Songs*. It was a compilation of videos from that album that played out in a story, so it was kind of like a mini-movie with a bunch of live performances. I was absolutely obsessed with that. And I thought Tom was the coolest, sexiest man alive. And it's really weird because now we're really good friends and his wife knows about my teenage crush. Obviously, I've moved past that. I'm not going to stalk him, but we have barbecues with his family all the time over the summer.

It's really strange that the whole thing has come full circle and he wound up being not only one of those people that got me into playing guitar, but he also became a really good friend. He's such a nice person and a golden soul. I always think about that whenever things get too crazy. We'll text each other. If I'm freaking out, he'll go, "No, it's all right. You got this."

WILL CARROLL

Death Angel, ex-Machine Head

About eight years ago, Death Angel toured with Soilwork, Augury, and Mutiny Within. The opening band was Swashbuckle, a pirate metal band.

There were three bands on one bus—us, Swashbuckle and Augury. All the bunks were completely packed and me and one of the guys from Swashbuckle were sleeping in the back lounge.

One night on the tour we were all partying and drinking. And there's a girl on the bus that none of us knew. She was in there for a long time. And she comes out of the bathroom and says, "Whoa, it smells like Taco Bell in there."

It was so disgusting. What kind of girl says that? What kind of person says that in front of a group of strangers? She had taken a shit. You can't take a shit on a bus. It's all liquid. Even vomit fucks up the system. She walked out and it totally reeked.

The party was immediately over and we kicked everyone off the bus. Everyone was really pissed. It costs, like, $500 to get it cleaned.

So Pat, the guitarist and singer from Augury said, "Oh, I know her. She's my friend. She didn't know you couldn't shit on the bus. I'm so sorry. I'll clean it, I'll clean it."

And he did! He told her to leave and he got down on all fours and scooped the shit out with his hands—every last little piece. And while he was doing that, he was throwing up in a waste paper basket. It was unbelievable.

CHAPTER 6[66]: WELCOME TO HELL

Playing the Devil's Advocate for Kicks or Damnation

Sure, there were satanic references in AC/DC and Black Sabbath, as well as proto and prog acts including Blue Öyster Cult, Coven, and Black Widow. And, of course, early New Wave of British Heavy Metal (NWOBHM) pioneers including Judas Priest and Angel Witch had their devilish moments. But when Newcastle trio Venom released *Welcome to Hell* in 1981, they took satanic metal to a new fiery abyss and unlocked the gates for bands like Slayer, Mercyful Fate, and Possessed to burst wide open in the years ahead. If the cover art of a goat's head in a pentagram and songs like "Sons of Satan," "Welcome to Hell," and "In League With Satan," weren't blasphemous enough, the slogan on the back of the album was enough to make Black Sabbath look like The Archies: "We drink the vomit of the priest, make love to the dying whore, we suck the blood from the beast and hold the key to death's door." Whether the heretical display was meant in sincerity or jest, Venom provided the basic blueprint for real devil worshippers including Mayhem, Marduk and Gorgoroth to surface from the netherworld.

There's an inextricable connection between metal and darkness. The music often relies on haunting textures and eerie minor key riffs, and ever since Black Sabbath wrote their titular classic, countless metal bands have relied on the once-shunned tritone—or Devil's Triad—to make their compositions sound more frightening. For many, including Sabbath, Venom, and Slayer, satanic lyrics and theatrics are more showmanship than theology. Since metal typically relies on extremism to evolve, it's only natural that occult-oriented bands went from singing about the Devil in somewhat vague terms to blatantly praising Lucifer and extolling various rituals, including human sacrifice, even if it was all for show. Other acts, including Morbid Angel, Deicide, and Acheron don't fuck around when it comes to Satan. They're as serious about their lyrics as God-praising gospel singers are about theirs.

For both dedicated Satanists and metalheads interested in the occult, two figures have been integral to the search for the palace of darkness.

In 1969, a decadent evildoer named Anton LaVey released his renowned book *The Satanic Bible*, which was filled with essays, hedonistic screeds, and actual rituals that served as a guide to his idea of the Satanic lifestyle. Formerly known by many as "The wickedest man in the world," a title that pleased him greatly, Aleister Crowley was a British writer, occultist, magician, poet, and painter who founded the Thelema sect, which ascribed to the motto, "Do what thou wilt shall be the whole of the law." He was also the subject of Ozzy Osbourne's 1980 fan favorite, "Mr. Crowley."

Even for some non-religious metallurgists, life can't be explained by the limitations of science, especially if they've seen a ghost or experienced some other sort of paranormal activity. It's unlikely that all the answers to the mysteries of the meaninglessness of human existence lie in LaVey, Crowley, or satanic metal, but a lot of those album covers depicting pentagrams, inverted crosses, horned demons, rivers of blood, and raging flames still look pretty damn cool.

OZZY OSBOURNE
Black Sabbath, Ozzy Osbourne

I'm not a crazy man, I'm not a Satanist. I'm not the antichrist. I'm not into seeing people get hurt or injured at my concerts. I suppose a sign of success is when you're the rock and roller people like to hate. People used to hate me—not my fans, but the public did. It didn't even bother me. For every ten that liked me, there were one hundred people that hated me. It was all part of the big picture.

CRONOS
Venom

Venom were a product of all the things I wasn't hearing in other bands. When I would listen to a Sabbath track and Ozzy was going off about all the fuckin' witches or the fuckin' elves and then all of a sudden he would get to the point [in the song "Black Sabbath"] where he would go, "Oh, God, please help me."

And I would think, "Oh, what the fuck? Noooo! You're supposed to be the evil bastard."

So, I thought, "OK, well, I'll be the evil bastard."

And it was all the things that weren't happening in other bands. We wanted to sound dangerous. These groups would get to the lead break and you would hear this pretty little solo and I wanted to hear divebombs and guitars smashing into the amplifiers.

IAN HILL
Judas Priest

Some people thought our name was blasphemous and everyone went through the fad with the Ouija board or whatever, but we were not digging up skulls or dancing on people's graves. We weren't like that at all.

GARY HOLT
Exodus, Slayer

We were all listening to the early Mercyful Fate demos. I was like, "Who's this fuckin' dude reciting the Lord's Prayer backwards? He's awesome."

As kids, we didn't delve too deeply into Sabbath's lyrics but we all thought it was Satanic. Actually, it was quite religious. I guess you could call it cautionary metal warning you of the impending return of the one so below. All that stuff had a huge influence on us in the beginning.

KING DIAMOND
Mercyful Fate, King Diamond

I had a lot of experiences with the supernatural, especially in this apartment in Copenhagen where this early stuff was written and that's what the song "A Dangerous Meeting" is about. It's actually a warning that says, "Hey, don't mess around with this shit. Evil is real and it will bite you in the ass."

And the thing is, when you go on a Ouija board or try to contact spirits some other way, you never know what's speaking to you. And if it feels mocked or disrespected, it can give you answers back that will ruin your life because for the next twenty years you'll always be wondering, "When is that thing going to happen?" Your Ouija board spells out, "You will die from serious sickness" or something, and you're just waiting around for the day you will be sick.

ROSS THE BOSS
ex-Manowar, Ross the Boss, The Dictators

None of us were into the occult, but all these other bands in the mid-'80s were singing about Satan. So we figured if we wrote a Satanic song it would have to be the greatest ever written.

We got *The Satanic Bible* by [the founder of the Church of Satan], Anton LaVey, and we read a bunch of it so we would know what we were talking about and we used some of the words from that in "Bridge of Death" [from 1984's *Hail to England.*] We had the vocals all treated with effects and we said shit like, "Impale me on the horns of death / Cut off my head, release all my evil / Lucifer is king, praise Satan."

I still think that stands as one of the best songs anyone ever made about Satan.

MARK MORTON
Lamb of God

I never delved too deep into the occult. It just didn't speak to me. Sometimes it bordered on silly for me. It seemed very *Dungeons & Dragons* and fantasy-based. I had friends who adopted that as a way of life. It's never been like that for me, as much as I like some of the bands.

And it's funny because Lamb of God used to be called Burn the Priest. Some people thought we were being Satanic and blasphemous, but it wasn't like that at all. The name was a reference to smoking pot.

KIRK WINDSTEIN
Crowbar, ex-Down

I was raised Catholic. I went to Catholic school and they made us go to church. I wasn't religious or anything, I just had no choice. And for me, listening to Satanic lyrics in metal didn't scare me away from anything or draw me to practice the occult. It was just a natural progression for me—metal turning darker and heavier.

Venom did *Welcome to Hell* and *Black Metal* and then Slayer came along with stuff like *Hell Awaits*. The lyrics and imagery never had any effect on my enjoying the bands or wearing their merchandise.

At this day and age, I wouldn't wear a Cradle of Filth shirt that said, "Jesus is a Cunt," but as a young dude, I was fine wearing Slayer's Slaytanic Wehrmacht shirt and not worrying about it. The darker the music and lyrics, the heavier and scarier it all was. For some reason, there's something scary about Satanism and Satanic imagery.

DANI FILTH
Cradle of Filth

I extol the virtues of what we sing about, but then things can be categorized and namesakes are given to things that are really representative—Satan as an archetype, for example.

When we made shirts that said, "Jesus is a Cunt," we were making a statement about adversity. People have come up to me over the years and said, "Yeah, Jesus was a right cunt!" And I'm thinking, "No, you don't understand."

Jesus was just a renowned figure, and he does live on in millions of people's hearts. So "Jesus is a Cunt" is just a very apt comment about adversity. It could have been anyone. It could have been Mohammed is a fat cunt. That's not the point. It was a bit tongue in cheek as well because the front depicted a masturbating nun. So it could be interpreted as finding Jesus in a woman's vagina.

DAVE WYNDORF
Monster Magnet

God knows I tried to harness the power of the devil, but, you know, the Big Guy has never come through for me. I mean, I played with Satan a lot, and it got me in trouble.

On one of the first singles we had and the first album, the tag was, "It's a Satanic drug thing, you wouldn't understand."

And it was like: "Satan, c'mon! I'm calling to you. Please help me. Let's suck Satan's cock, everybody! Let's go!"

So, it was out there, and some people thought we were deadly serious about it for a while. They didn't get the fact that I was just fucking around.

We were touring in Europe, and there were certain Satanic people coming to the shows. One time, a girl came backstage. She was sleazy looking but really hot. She had a big afro, and she was from Trinidad or something but she had a German accent. She was very exotic, erotic, and cool.

She said, "I like you!"

And I said, "I like you, too."

One thing led to another, and we were back in the hotel room. Under closer inspection, she seemed really dodgy. I thought maybe she was a druggie or something, but the vibes weren't good. It was understood that we were gonna do it. She took off her clothes, and I saw this giant fuckin' pentagram on her back and she said, "Fuck me! Fuck me in the ass for Satan!"

I got scared. I think the druggie vibe turned me off. If I would have been drunk or high, I might have gone there, but I wasn't so I thought, "If I fuck her in the ass for Satan, Satan's going to give me some horrible disease."

The vibe was not right. I couldn't do it. She was there wagging her behind, and I was like, "Holy shit!"

I ran in the bathroom and got a small bottle of shampoo and lubed it up and put the bottle in her ass. Then, I grabbed my bag and ran out of the room. She seemed to be having a good enough time with the shampoo bottle, so I guess it was okay.

GENE HOGLAN
Dark Angel, Testament, Dethklok, ex-Death, ex-Strapping Young Lad

I was fifteen when I heard Venom and I didn't really know what to think about God. I didn't have a religious upbringing, but when I'm listening to Venom sing, "Do you believe in God? / He's chained up like a dog," as a teenager I'm not hedging my bets.

I'm thinking, "Well, if there is a god, he's probably not gonna be real happy with me listening to this."

But when you're young and agnostic, but you've got guys preaching, "Satan is the way," you're like, "Okay, I'm gonna go buy that *Satanic Bible*."

[Slayer guitarist] Kerry King actually gave me his copy of *The Satanic Bible*. They were in the recording studio for their first album, *Show No Mercy*. He had the *Satanic Bible* there and I was thumbing through it thinking, "Wow, there's actually some cool stuff in here. This looks like my thoughts."

Kerry said, "Go ahead and take it. I'm done with it. Enjoy it."

I've still got that. I would strut around and let that thing hang out of my backpack.

One time I had a copy of it and I was on a flight with the guys from Strapping Young Lad. I pulled it out and started reading it, and [bassist] Byron Stroud goes, "Dude, could you just leave that home on the next flight, please?"

He's not a Christian either, but he's like, "I don't need someone chanting to Satan thirty thousand feet in the air."

KING FOWLEY
Deceased, October 31

I had read in *Kerrang!* that Venom was the sickest shit ever. So I went out and got *Welcome to Hell*. I saw the gold goat on the cover and it was giving me a creepy vibe. I put it on and immediately and I was like, "Man, this shit is crazy!"

At first, I didn't know if it was for me. It was so raw. I was listening to "Sons of Satan" and it sounded like chainsaws fucking. But I kept listening and looking at the artwork on the album sleeve. Then I got to side two and heard the backwards message on "In League with Satan."

I was freaking out, thinking, "This is weird as shit."

The record finished. My ears were ringing because I was playing it really loud. The loudness offset my nerves. I was sitting there and all of a sudden I heard a noise: BOOM-KA-KA-BOOM-BOOM-BOOM! I thought, "What the fuck was that?"

I was on the second floor of the house in the corner of my bedroom. I had locked the door, so I opened it up and walked out and the attic stairs [which were usually lodged in the ceiling] had come down. I thought, "How the fuck did the attic stairs fall down?"

I figured it was just gravity, so I put the stairs back up and walked back into the room. About five minutes later I heard the loud noise. I looked out the door and the stairs were down again. I said, "Fuck this," and left them down.

I locked my door, stayed in my room and looked at my wall. Then I took the Venom record and turned it over so I didn't have to see the goat's head.

I woke up in the morning. It was a beautiful summer day. I heard the birds chirping. Then I turned over and I saw the goat's head. I thought, "Wait a minute. That record was upside-down when I went to bed last night."

I opened the door and the stairs were back up! I looked out the window and nobody was there. I was so freaked out. My mom's car wasn't there so I knew she was out. I was alone and totally freaked out. I opened the window and jumped out onto the porch. I went down the street in shorts and nothing else. I killed time until my mom got home. I got home six hours later at about four in the afternoon and I saw my mom.

"Where have you been all day? We've been home since noon," she said.

"Yeah, I saw you weren't there this morning so I went out," I said.

I was getting ready to tell her the story about the stairs and she said, "By the way, why are the attic stairs down? When did you go up there? Put them back up."

So I went upstairs and they were down again. The last time I had seen them they were up and there was no one in the house to pull them down again. I still love Venom, but I felt like some force was trying to tell me something.

CRONOS

The occult is perfect for heavy metal. It fits in with all the icons this music draws from. You couldn't have sheep and flowers onstage singing fucking, "Hell yeah, Satan!" We have the big demons and the dragons and the snakes and the flames and the torment and the devil. And it's all part of the imagery of that. But since day one we said we are the horror movies of music. If Black Sabbath were Hammer Horror, Venom are the *Evil Dead*. If I was a practicing Satanist, I wouldn't be in a band playing music. I would take being a Satanist seriously. Making music takes a lot of time, but we've always said rock and roll is our religion. We don't dance around campfires or sacrifice virgins. We're not out to hurt anybody. Yes, we're out to shock people. Yes, we play extreme music and we may sing about things that might make some people uncomfortable, but that's because we're appealing to people who aren't interested in the norm. If you want the norm go listen to an Elton John album. Go buy Britney Spears. We are the extreme of the industry and happy to be that.

RICHARD CHRISTY
Charred Walls of the Damned, ex-Death, ex-Iced Earth, ex-Public Assassin

I was staying over at my grandparents' house the night Geraldo [Rivera] did a special on Satanism. It was a big deal in the late '80s and Geraldo was talking about Satanism and heavy metal. My grandma said, "Richard, you should watch this because you listen to some of that kind of music."

She wanted me to watch it as a warning. But I was already excited to watch it because they were going to have King Diamond on there and I loved King Diamond. I just didn't want to tell my grandma that. I had to hide my excitement when King Diamond came on the show. So it was a little uncomfortable to watch that in my grandma's house. I had to pretend I was really interested in how serious it all was.

When I was in high school in the late '80s, people were terrified of Satanism, but they didn't realize that the more you rail against it, the more kids are going to get into it. And even if they're not into it, they're going to say they are just to freak out the older generation.

We'd go around saying shit like, "Hail Satan!" just to freak people out.

We weren't really into the occult but it got a rise out of people and we liked that. And it was a good way to get the bullies to leave you alone. A lot of bullies don't want to fuck with weird people because they're unpredictable and a lot of them thought that if they teased you, you'd do some sort of Satanic ritual and put a curse on them.

MICHAEL SWEET
Stryper

I'm a big fan of Black Sabbath. I met Tony Iommi and he was nice. I've also met Ozzy. But for a period of time, Ozzy Osbourne didn't seem to like us.

He said we were using God to make money. I think that's pretty hilarious coming from a guy who has used the devil to make money his whole life.

We were friends with White Lion and there was a time they were opening for Black Sabbath at Irvine Meadows and we were backstage with them. Ozzy's tour manager came up to us and said, "You're gonna have to move." And we moved over about ten feet.

And he came back and said, "No, you gotta move again."

"Well, you're not telling anyone else to move. Where do you want us to go?" I asked.

"You just gotta leave this area," he said.

So we left and then Ozzy came through.

Another time we wanted to get an autograph from Ozzy and his tour manager went over to him and Ozzy shook his head no. Obviously, Ozzy had some kind of resentment toward us. I have no idea why. Hopefully, he's outgrown that.

ZAKK WYLDE
Black Label Society, Ozzy Osbourne

When I was working on the *Ozzmosis* record with Ozzy, we were in New York City and we were talking. I had Anton LaVey's *Satanic Bible* with me and Ozz goes, "Zakk, you know if you're reading this it means you're practicing it."

I go, "Yeah, I completely agree with you Ozz. I noticed [Black Sabbath bassist] Geezer [Butler] has been thumbing through my *Flex* [body building] magazine. I guess he'll be competing at this year's Arnold Schwarzenegger's Classic!"

And then Ozz goes, "Anton LaVey? Where have I heard that name?"

"Remember when the first Sabbath album was released and Warner Bros. had that record release party for us on California Street out in San Francisco, where there was this black house? That belonged to Anton LaVey."

"Oh, he had the bald head and the goatee thing," Ozzy said.

Geezer and I both went, "That's the guy."

"Oh, no wonder the album didn't do as well as it could have," Ozzy said.

WILL CARROLL
Death Angel, ex-Machine Head

When I was a kid, a whole slew of us were out drinking on a Saturday night. We decided, "Hey, let's go to Anton LaVey's house!"

He used to live in the Church of Satan on California Street in San Francisco. We piled in a bunch of cars at one in the morning and drove out to his house. It wasn't hard to find. All the other houses in the area were blue or yellow. This one was pitch black, even the windows. It stood out and had a church-like roof. Everything about the house was different.

We were looking at it and going, "Whoa, I wonder what's going on in there?"

"Jesus Christ rules!" someone shouted, just to fuck around.

This pale, white lady came out of the front door wearing an apron.

"You better get the hell out of here!" she yelled.

She was horrifying. It looked like she had no blood in her body whatsoever.

DAVID VINCENT
ex-Morbid Angel, Vltimas

My personal beliefs are what they are. It's something that after years of study and meditation and introspection, I have my world view. It's not for everyone and with certain types of knowledge there are additional responsibilities and the only thing I want to share is what's in my lyrics. I don't proselytize other than what I say in my lyrics. That's always been the best solution for me.

People like Anton LaVey and Aleister Crowley are fellow journeymen. Dr. LaVey did it in a very interesting way because of his world view and where he was coming from. He was a carnie and he made it fun and entertaining. Crowley had his own way of thinking as well, but both of them are important people to discover on the journey.

ERIK DANIELSSON
Watain

The Church of Satan represents the far less spiritual and much more man-based ideology, while true Satanism is based upon the acknowledgment of powers that are greater than man. And that the aspiration onto God-dom is something that is not attainable by every man that walks on earth, but rather by the select. To me, The Church of Satan, has blasphemed the name of Satanists for many years. They can think whatever they want, but to me, I think it's very wrong to call a manmade ideology Satanism.

ROGER "INFERNUS" TIEGS
ex-Gorgoroth

I am a Satanist, yes. I wouldn't go as far as claiming to have had any paranormal experiences. It's just a question of how I regard myself when it comes to fitting in with the world.

For me, LaVey's kind of Satanism is completely different. It's a different species and it's incomprehensible. The most central point in my existence is a belief in God, and I do not position man or myself to be the center of the universe. I regard myself within a frame of the Proto-Gnostic myth. I have a sense of understanding, of being thrown into an existence which is not in any way complete. I don't have any feeling of being fulfilled. I still have an idea of a god and a return and a set of views on how to conduct myself. There are many paths leading in the same direction and Satanism works fine for me.

DANI FILTH

I would say my belief system is more classical—more Crowley than LaVey. Crowley was always misunderstood as being the personification of evil, and he even played on it by calling himself the Great Beast. But he had his own brand, Magick, which was neither good nor evil. It was "Love under will, do as thou wilt."

If you have a very fixed idea of what you're about and what you can achieve, and you don't really live by religious rules or society's general rules because laws are made for the majority, not the minority, then you create your own freedom. You have the moral majority and they make up laws. And if you trespass over them you become the bad guy or the scapegoat. We live our lives as we see fit, which is the essence of modern Satanism. I'm not saying that we're Satanists. I think to label anything is to become narrow-minded. But I think that's how we tend to get labeled as such.

And also, we prefer Darth Vader in *Star Wars* as opposed to Luke Skywalker. We just like dark romanticism as it were.

ADAM "NERGAL" DARSKI
Behemoth

I deal with the universe on many different levels. One of those levels that's the most earthly and carnal is satanic because Satanism is all about being carnal and hedonistic and I'm all about that.

But there are other more spiritual levels that have nothing to do with Satanism. I'm very into Paganism because Paganism is all about being respectful toward nature and accepting things as they are and keeping the right balance. That's what the Christian religion brutally destroyed. But I can't say I'm a paganist because there's so much Satanic attitude in my life. Of course, I don't want to end up in just one category because I think human beings are too complex for that.

GLEN BENTON
Deicide

At first everyone is intimidated or scared of me. But once they meet me, they realize I'm not some psycho, I'm just a normal individual. By the definition of Christianity, I am a Satanist. But am I putting goatskin leg pieces on and dancing around the fire? No. Am I a free thinker? Yes.

I'm ordained at several Satanic institutions out there. I didn't pay the [$225] membership fee [to the Church of Satan] to get my card. I think any organized religion is hokey if you've got to pay to belong. So, I don't know what that makes me. Do I believe in the Commandments of God? Fuck no. If Satan jumped up right now and asked me to do something, I would probably do it nine times out of ten. The thing is, I do believe in good and I believe in doing good. Now, do I believe that if my neighbor's a fucking asshole, I should like him and turn the other cheek? Fuck that. If you want me to treat you good, you have to earn it.

BEN FALGOUST
Goatwhore, ex-Soilent Green

I read a lot of books concerning the dark arts. I'm interested in it and it influences things I write, but I've never taken part in any rituals.

This has nothing to do with the occult, but NoiseLab Studios, where we did *Funeral Dirge for The Rotting Sun* in 2002 was apparently haunted. They had two levels. The bottom level was a studio and the top was a living area. One night me, [guitarist] Sammy [Pierre Duet] and the engineer [Dave Reynolds] were listening to something. We turned down the music and we heard a lot of footsteps upstairs. It sounded like twenty people running around. There was a spiral staircase in the back so we went up to look and there was nothing there. It was completely silent.

Then we went back downstairs and we heard all this running around up there again. As the story goes, back in the day the house was a bookie house and a bunch of mobsters came in one day and shot up and killed a lot of people.

MIKE IX WILLIAMS
Eyehategod

Because of our name, some people think we're gonna be all Satanic and evil and loud. Really, we're just loud. I've met a fair number of people in the underground who are into worshipping the devil. That's silly to me. It's just as silly as somebody worshipping God. It's pointless.

TOMMY VICTOR
Prong, Danzig, ex-Ministry

I used to be really interested in the occult. I have a lot of books in storage and I've got tons of Aleister Crowley, like *The Equinox* and stuff, which I think is a lot of nonsense now. But I was intrigued by it, definitely. I was tempted to try out some of the rituals. Like the *Ordo Templi Orientis*. I was interested in seeking them out, maybe, or *Thessalonica*, but I never did it.

PAUL LEDNEY
Profanatica, Havohej

My mom was a student of the occult and she had some bad stuff happen to people around her. Somebody's neck broke one time. So, I was really interested in it.

I started researching it when I was twelve or thirteen, and I started doing some of the rituals. Researching that stuff has its own place, but in the end, I don't know what people get out of it. I don't believe in the spirit world at all. My attitude kind of bums people out. I've never seen anything happen or been around anything supernatural. So when we say we're all about blasphemy and desecrating the church, it's because we think it's a phony money-making scheme. And I feel the same way about black magic. We call it play-acting.

Up to her dying days, I tried to ask my mom what really happened when she was practicing the occult and she wouldn't tell me. I know a lot of bands we come in contact with fully believe in that nonsense. I guess I believe in God but I don't believe we have any way to contact or get in touch with that force. So, I'm more of an agnostic than an atheist. But I'm definitely not a Satanist.

ERIK RUTAN
Hate Eternal, ex-Morbid Angel, ex-Ripping Corpse

I used to go to this occult bookstore in New York called The Magickal Childe. I've read much of Aleister Crowley and *The Satanic Bible* and *The Necronomicon* and other occult books and things about mythology because I was always interested and inspired by spirituality in general, in different ways. I was never a practicing Satanist, but I was involved in learning about occultism.

ZAKK WYLDE

The Magickal Childe was one-stop for all religions. It had books about Christianity, Judaism, Satanism, Wicca, Voodoo. They had everything.

I saw a poster of Aleister Crowley, so I asked the salesman, "Boss, how much for the poster?"

"That's $6.66," he said with no sense of humor whatsoever.

"Here's $7.00. Keep the change," I said with a smirk.

I hung the poster in the studio with pictures of Jimmy Page and Jimi Hendrix. Ozz was telling me all these funny stories about when he used to go out with Jimmy Page and John Bonham in the early days of Zeppelin and Sabbath. And he looks at the poster and said, "Zakk, who's the bald-headed cunt on the wall?"

"Ozz, you don't know who that is?" I said in disbelief.

"No. Who the fuck is it?"

"Ozz, you've been singing about him since 1980," I said.

"Ohhh. Who the fuck is it?"

"That's Aleister Crowley."

He went up close to it and took a good look at him and said, "Oh, is that what he fuckin' looks like?"

Everybody thought of Ozz as this Satan guy. The Prince of Darkness. Fuckin' hysterical.

ADAM "NERGAL" DARSKI

In Hebrew, Satan is the open hand. This short description says it all. I'm the open hand. Satan stands for freedom and liberation. I couldn't agree with that more. But on the other hand, Satanism is also limiting in a way because it carries its own set of constraints.

In my interests about life and the spiritual side, the idea of Heaven and Hell is a fairy tale. But, of course, we can treat seriously even fairy tales because we, as humans, give power to things. So if I decide heaven and hell are real places, I make them real to me. It's all up to us.

There are people who say Satan is anti-humanistic. I disagree. To me, it's all pro-man. It's a very vital, very positive character that is just misunderstood. But this is the meaning that I give to it, so it's all about interpretation. That's what Nietzsche used to say. Everybody has his own opinion. Some people tend to bend to other people's opinions and accept them without question. I've always been about questioning authority, questioning the laws, questioning everything that's thrown at me.

CRIK DANICLSSON

There is no such thing as brands of Satanists. There is Satanism and there are other things. We represent Satanism in its purest form, which is the very basic belief that creation, as we see it, is the bastardized work of the force that the Gods, that the Yahweh or the Buddha or this cult of mankind, has worshipped, while Satanism is the religion that uplifts and canonizes and worships the gods that have always been shunned in the world's religions because they represent the counteractive forces of these creative gods. They represent the opposition and eventually the destruction of that creation. That is the only intention of the Greater Gods. And to me, because the things I want to destroy are the limitations of the God within me, mankind is a limitation to what works in my heart. In that sense, the Satanist acknowledges himself to extend and transcend the human ego, that, for example, the Church of Satan is very fond of, and that they, themselves make Godly. To me, the human is something that must be defeated in honor of the god inside me, in honor of the black flame inside.

MARK MORTON

The occult and the paranormal are different things. We've played a lot of different places and some of them are old buildings. Sometimes there is something I can't quite put my finger on. You'll walk into a place and just have this powerful feeling that there's some sort of presence there. It might be different cold patches or something. You'll go, "Man, this place is haunted." And you'll ask one of the locals and they'll say, "Oh hell, yeah." So I do feel a little bit of that sometimes but it's nothing I've ever got down the rabbit hole with.

MAX CAVALERA
Soulfly, Cavalera Conspiracy, ex-Sepultura

My mom was really into spirits and she was able to receive signals and talk in the language of the spirits. I was wearing a Venom shirt once and she became possessed and freaked out. She was cursing in a different language and pointing at the shirt. So I took the shirt off and tossed it out the window of my house and she stopped. It was like a scene out of *The Exorcist*. Sometimes I think that shit's really crazy and it's real.

DINO CAZARES
Fear Factory, Divine Heresy, Brujeria, Asesino

In the '70s my mother had multiple sclerosis, but nobody knew what it was. So my father decided to take my mother to witch doctors in Mexico. Me and my brother were kids. We drove deep into the mountains of Mexico and there were only two lanes of traffic. When we finally got there, me and my brother wanted to play with firecrackers, but we didn't have any matches. So we decided to go back into the house where we were staying and look for matches.

I opened up a door and I saw a completely black room. My mother was in a chair with a white sheet over her and there were all these candles around her. There was a woman all in black with a veil on reading stuff to my mom that sounded like some sort of prayers. I figured I should grab one of the candles so I could set off the firecrackers. But then the woman picked up a candle and lit the bedsheet on fire that was over my mother and it burned. I freaked out, but my mother wasn't burned at all.

Years later, I was fifteen and we were in the hospital with my mom. While she was there, these women from Mexico came to visit her and they were wearing the same outfits as they had when we saw them when I was a little kid. They gave her a rosary. They read some prayers and then they left. And as they left, one of the old ladies gave me a hug and kissed my cheek. That night my mother died. I asked my dad how my mom died right after these women came to see her and he said, "They knew."

"Well, how did they know?" I asked.

"I don't know. I didn't call them," he said.

I took the rosary.

In 1998 we were on tour with System of a Down, (hed) P.E., Spineshank, and Static-X. Everybody was sharing one semi with all the gear in it. We pulled up to this hotel in Philly. We were all in the hotel room. The next morning, we got a call saying the semi had been stolen. Everyone's gear was gone. I was freaking out. I told my guitar tech, "You know what? For good luck, I put the rosary inside the cavity of my guitar where the electronics go. And now it's gone."

"No it isn't. I have that," he said.

"Really? Why'd you take it out?" I asked.

"I was working on your guitar last night and I took it out and I have it in my work briefcase in my room."

The rosary was the only thing I got back out of all the million dollars' worth of shit that got stolen.

CHUCK BILLY
Testament

I'm part Native American, but I had never really been in touch with that side of my heritage. I wasn't really spiritual at all, but I had friends who were. Testament played a show in L.A. in the late '90s, and I went out to eat dinner with my friend Nancy at the Rainbow after the show. She had been telling me for months that there's a guy named Charlie whom she wanted me to meet. At dinner that night, she said, "I had a dream that you and Charlie were sitting around a fire putting on warpaint going into battle together."

"Whatever, Nancy. You're crazy," I said.

Then, this guy Charlie showed up at my door unannounced one day after I was diagnosed with cancer. I felt like we immediately knew each other.

"I'm here to give you a healing," he said.

I lay down in the middle of the floor, and he brought in a flute and an eagle's feather and started circling me chanting and playing the flute. I had never had a healing or done sweat lodges. But at the point when he started chanting and had his eagle's feather, I was totally on this journey flying through the air. I heard the wolves and the wind and howling and all this stuff. I was just floating in space. Charlie took the eagle's feather and swooped it across my body, and I felt something move from my chest to my stomach.

He sat me up and said, "Okay, I want to tell you some stuff that's not going to make any sense to you, but when things start happening, they're going to start falling into place and you're going to understand."

The one major thing he told me was, "The wind is going to be your spirit guide."

Then, he left as quickly as he showed up. A couple weeks later, we had a barbecue, and there were a bunch of recyclable beer cans on the side of the house. It was a real windy night, and I woke up because the furniture was getting thrown in the pool and making noise.

I went downstairs and heard clinking and clanking. When I looked out the back window, I saw a funnel cloud of beer cans flying around. I had been having stomach problems all that week. I sat down on the toilet and let something out of my body, and right when I did that the wind stopped and the beer cans hit the ground. And I had a sensation that something left me. I felt like the sickness was gone, and I had an overwhelming sensation that I was better.

I ran upstairs an and told my wife: "Hey, I'm not sick anymore. I don't have cancer anymore."

"Whatever, go to bed," she said.

That week, I went to my doctors for my regular blood tests and they were shocked by the results. "Wow, your tumor is not cancerous anymore," they said.

I never told them what I was doing or what was going on. And they went, "Wow, that's strange."

I had started chemo the week earlier. The doctor said that after 12 weeks of treatment there was a chance my tumor might not be cancerous. He couldn't understand how the cancer was gone in a week. But I still had this big tumor . . . [to be continued]

JOHN GALLAGHER
Raven

Something really crazy happened to our old drummer Joe [Hasselvander]. I didn't see any ghosts myself, but he was almost thrown out of his house by the spirits of haunted tarot cards. It sounds insane, but he showed me a wooden bathroom door and there were clearly markings on one side. There was a goat's head and there was someone's face that looked uncannily like [Metallica's late bass player] Cliff Burton, [who died in a bus accident in Sweden in 1986].

Cliff owned part of this deck of cards, which had been found in Cortland, New York. The landlady gave him some of them and Joe had some of them, some of them were left behind. [After Cliff died,] Joe took the cards, bound them in a Bible, tied them up, put rocks on the Bible, and drove it from Virginia all the way up to Salem, Massachusetts. He gave it all to a paranormal guy and said, "Please take this shit off my hands."

The spirits pretty much left Joe alone after that. It's a crazy story, but I saw some of the evidence.

JOEY JORDISON
ex-Slipknot, Murderdolls, Sinsaenum, Vimic

The first couple weeks we were working on *Vol 3: The Subliminal Verses* at Rick Rubin's [live-in mansion] studio, [guitarist] Mick [Thomson] and I were staying at the very top of the house. At 9 a.m. my door would swing open and his attic door would open as well and there was never anyone there. We didn't realize until a week later that we were all getting up at 9 a.m.

So it seems like something happened in the house at 9 a.m. a long time ago. The house has been there since 1918, so there's obviously some fucked up history there.

Sometimes I'd be sitting there listening to music and I'd see a body shape float across my wall and there was no light coming in to cast a shadow since I blocked out the windows with black velvet. The whole time we were there, lights would go on and off. But it was a good environment for us. It was great for the creative vibe.

ADAM JARVIS
Misery Index, Pig Destroyer, Scour

I went to Philadelphia to watch Pearl Jam play the album *Ten* in its entirety. I was staying in this weird, circular hotel and after I got my room, I wanted to find ice. I took the elevator down and I stopped at every floor and none of the ice machines were working. So I took the stairs and went down to the bottom and the floor was abandoned.

There were all this fuckin' trash and broken beds. There was a hallway and I turned the corner and got this really weird feeling. I thought, "I'm not supposed to be down here. Where am I in this hotel right now?"

It was circular, so I really didn't know.

I decided to turn around and get the fuck out of there and as I turned around this shape that was almost like a shadow went right in front of me. I felt like a terrified, five-year-old schoolboy and I took off running to try to find somebody. It was one of the weirdest things I've ever seen.

MARK MORTON

I lived in two houses when I was a kid in Williamsburg, Virginia and my mom and I felt pretty sure there was some kind of a ghost there in one of them. It had a full-length attic across the house and sometimes when nobody was home you would hear defined footsteps up there. Sometimes a lamp up there would go on and off by itself. One time it was on and it wouldn't turn off so I unplugged it and it stayed on.

SAM RIVERS
Limp Bizkit

I used to live in Jacksonville, Florida in the late '90s and would come to work in L.A., so our record label rented me a house that I stayed in when we were recording. It seemed like this super-cool, '70s-style place, but when I went to stay there with my security guard, I was so scared. And, with a 350-pound guy staying with me I shouldn't have been scared at all.

The master bedroom was so creepy I couldn't go in there at all and my cat, which was also there with us was super bugged out. It used to run around the house and play and any time it started running toward the master bedroom it would literally start scooting its nails like a cartoon, as if to say, "No way, I don't fuckin' want to be here!" And it would run out and come and get underneath the covers with me.

Every night I slept on my couch with the covers over my head. We found out that the place was a '70s playboy house where they held crazy coke parties. One of the former guys that owned it was some sort of a mobster. The basement of the place was all a dirt floor and when I walked around there I would get horrible feelings. It felt like people were murdered or buried there.

There were a couple times I would see little orbs and little things on the ground that were moving and dark figures going across to the back where my room was. My wife saw figures in other places in the house, too. It was awful to be in there, which sucked because the house was so beautiful.

CHRIS VRENNA
ex-Nine Inch Nails, ex-Marilyn Manson

We were staying at the Tate house in California where some of the Manson murders took place. There was one night [Nine Inch Nails' frontman] Trent [Reznor] went into his bedroom. He had the master bedroom in the main house and I had the master bedroom in the guest house. We were done for the night. He went to his room to work on lyrics and I headed back to the guest house.

I walked across the lawn between the front house and the back house, which is where that Steven Parent kid was killed. He was living in the guest house and watching the property. All of a sudden, this white circular light with a silhouette of a body in the middle popped on up against the wall of the guest house. I turned around and I could see the beam of light that was hitting the wall and inside that light was the shape of a female in a dress. I thought there might be someone in our yard 'cause sometimes either Nine Inch Nails fans or Charles Manson fans would want to get onto the property and take pictures. I thought there was someone behind me and there wasn't and when I turned around again the white light was completely gone.

"That was really messed up," I thought.

I went to bed, woke up the next morning and Trent was there with [producer] Flood.

"Man, the strangest thing happened to me last night," I said.

"Me, too," said Trent. "I was sitting there working on lyrics and [my yellow lab] Maise was there with me. All of a sudden all the fur on her bristled and she sat up and started howling at the ceiling."

That was way out of character for that dog.

"Well, that's weird," I agreed. "Now let me tell you what happened to me."

I told him the story, then I asked him what time Maise got freaked out. It was the exact same time as I saw the girl in the light. We both went, "Okay, wow" and we never talked about it again.

KING FOWLEY

I moved into a ranch house in about 2007. One day, I was standing in front of my open refrigerator looking for something to eat. I looked down and I saw a pair of feet below the kitchen door. I looked up and there was a girl standing right there in a yellow dress. I went, "What the fuck?"

I closed the door and she was gone. But I heard her running around my house, which wasn't very big. I looked around but I could not find her anywhere so I just let it go.

Two weeks later, I walked through my house and I could see the girl's reflection on the jukebox glass. We locked eyes through the reflection. Then she ran back to the spot by the kitchen door and started giggling. Then she was gone again.

A few weeks after that, I came home on a Sunday night and my roommate was playing guitar really loud at midnight.

"What's up?" I asked.

"Dude, there's something in this house," he said. "First, something was looking at me outside my window and then I saw something that looked like a girl run through my door."

"Oh, really," I said. Then I told him what I had seen before.

"Dude, you should never have told me that," he said. "Now I gotta move out because I'm freaking out."

The dude was petrified.

I went to bed kind of laughing because I wasn't scared of her at all. It was more just bizarre to me. As soon as I opened my door to go to the bathroom the next morning, she ran by me again.

A week later, I was outside and I told my neighbors what I saw and they said, "Oh, that sounds like our former neighbor Joe's daughter. He used to live in the house with her and she had cancer and died there in her mid-30s."

"Really?" I said.

"Yup, she died right there on your couch. She had on this yellow dress and her bangs were cut."

I was freaked out. I got ahold of Joe and he came over to the house. He was almost eighty years old by that point. He said, "I've got some stuff in the attic. Can I go up and get it?"

I said, "Yeah, let's go."

We went up to the hot attic and he pointed to an old Army trunk and asked me to grab his dog tags and some old pictures. Then he said, "Did I ever tell you I had a daughter?"

"No," I said. I hadn't told him anything I had seen in the house.

"Yeah," he sighed and then handed me a picture. Not only was she in the yellow dress with the same haircut that I saw her in, but she was looking right at me the way she did in the jukebox glass. It was almost like she was saying, "Here I am. See. This is me."

I made peace with her then and there and I never saw her again.

WILL CARROLL

In school, we heard about this house in San Francisco that's supposed to have a huge painting of Baphomet on the side of it, so we naturally had to go Satan-house hunting. Someone said he knew where it was and, sure enough, we found it on a dead-end street. On the front of the house were these screaming faces with whited out eyes. The front of the place looked like it had a meat locker door. It was metal with a round window. There was a locked gate in front of the house so you couldn't get to the front door, but between the front door and the gate were a bunch of mannequin body parts. I wondered what kind of a fucked up person lives in a place like that.

It was 2 or 3 a.m. by this point, but some of us still wanted to see the Baphomet at the side of the house. We went around in the pitch black with just a lighter to guide the way. Suddenly, there it was with wings and horns. It creeped us out so we all ran back to the front of the house. Just as we were getting ready to leave, the lights in the upstairs room turned on and there were a goat skull and a pentagram hanging on the wall. That was enough for any of us. We all ran to our cars and took off and never talked about it again.

CHRIS VRENNA

Being in the house where Sharon Tate was murdered by the Manson family was interesting. When we worked on *The Downward Spiral,* Nine Inch Nails fans would come up to the house, but we would also get Charles Manson fans visiting because of the history of the place. The house was on a hill and people would park their cars at the bottom of the hill and climb the gate. They'd scurry through the brush up the front of the hill and end up in our front yard. I can't tell you how many times I'd walk in and go, "Fuck, who are you?"

ERIK RUTAN

Somewhere in Europe in the '90s, a guy cut a pentagram into himself and then threw the blood all over the drum kit. Our tech lost his shit on this guy, who was bleeding everywhere. Some people are into some pretty dark shit, but people that are interested in it and people that live it are different things.

CHUCK BILLY

[countinued] . . . Since the thing with Charlie [the Native American healer who treated my cancer] went so well, I went to L.A. to see a medicine man and get [another] healing in the Santa Barbara mountains. I went there with a friend and my son Cody, and it started raining really bad. There were floods, so we stayed at Nancy's house. In the morning, we got back in the car and headed toward the top of the mountain. We went west toward the ocean, and as we were climbing up the road and getting closer to the exit, a hole in the sky opened up and all of a sudden it was sunny and 70 degrees. We got off at the exit, and it started hailing on us. Fifteen minutes later, it started snowing. And then, the sun broke out again. We were going through all these weather changes in an hour's drive.

We finally got there, and we got out of the car and stood in the snow. We stripped down to our boxer shorts with towels around our necks. We had never done this before and had no idea what to expect. I asked Cody, "Are you cold?"

"No, I'm not cold at all," he said.

It was fucking snowing. We should have been freezing.

We went to the sweat lodge and did the ritual. I was told that younger kids bring a lot of power and energy to a sweat. So Cody did it with me, and we did a healing ceremony after that.

When we left, we drove up to the foothills of the Sierras, and my friend Tommy's uncle had a friend named Lupon who was a direct descendent of Geronimo. He had studied medicine under this guy named Rolling Thunder, who was a famous medicine man in the '60s and '70s who hung out with the Grateful Dead and all these famous rock stars. The guy lived with a bunch of wild wolves and there were some big wolves up in front of his house. A man there told me: "If you walk out to the wolves, and they don't show aggression, you can pass through. If they show aggression, get back in your car. You can't see him."

So, I went and my son stayed in the car. I got through, and the wolves didn't bother me. So I went back to the car and got Cody to go to the medicine man with me.

Over ninety minutes, the medicine man taught me how to focus my energy on a part of the body, putting a mental circle around it. He told me to envision a powerful color, a healing color in my mind, and to use that energy. Then, he said, "Before you do that, envision that you're reaching your arms thirty feet down below the ground and grab the earth to get connected with the energy there and concentrate on shrinking the size of the tumor." At that time, my tumor was too big for an operation, so we needed to shrink it. I followed his direction and we spent the weekend up there. I meditated in the backyard by myself and over about two weeks, I focused my energy the way he taught me to. When I went back to my doctor, the tumor was almost gone and they successfully operated on it and removed the whole thing. Knock on wood, I'm completely cured.

ERIK DANIELSSON

Some people would say we ascribe to a hedonistic lifestyle, yes. I don't really view my life like it's a funny anecdote. To me, life is a battle. It's strife every day, and I don't want to put it in a humoristic context because it's very far from that. We are living four persons in the quarters of Watain. And we don't go out. We stick to our own world, which we have created, which means there are no addresses of the members who live in that place. Outside of the music, there are no reports on what we are doing or not doing. The statistical consequence and the lifestyle consequence of being a Satanist is to detach yourself as much as you can from the bonds of society. Society will always be an enemy to us and we will always be the enemies of society because society represents a microcosmic aspect of law and order, the same law and order that the universe once was built on. Society is another desperate attempt to try to patronize things, to try to put things into shape and form. We, as much as we can, distance ourselves and alienate ourselves from what people make of ordinary life.

There is ritual involved, but for me, it seems very awkward to talk about these kinds of things with people that I don't know. I'm sure that people don't talk to strangers about what they do in bed with their wives, and this is a bit the same thing to me. Some doors should be locked for the sake of both parties.

ROGER "INFERNUS" TIEGS

I think many define black metal in a different way than I do. I really don't identify myself with most of the people involved in the scene. I prefer my own company and most of my own contacts are people not being involved in the metal scene.

There is a certain understanding in the decadent rock culture that indecent behavior should be something acceptable within the circles of being defined as black metal. I think that's completely wrong. Black metal's not supposed to be like that. Many people in the scene, to me, represent a drive toward fucking groupies, drinking, being morons, living the rock myths. And that's just not good enough. It's un-satanical by definition. It's something I regard as destroying oneself, and it's inappropriate. I do regard everyone to be responsible for whatever they do. I take responsibility for myself in a way which differs from many others in the scene.

CHAPTER 7: CAUGHT IN A MOSH

Diving Into the Pit & Living to Laugh About It

With their third full-length album, 1987's *Among the Living*, everything clicked for New York thrash band Anthrax. The record was faster than the band's first two releases and the group sounded angrier and more defiant than ever. One of the many highlights on the disc was "Caught in a Mosh"—a churning, roiling number based on a true story. The cut remains a stand-out of the band's live set and encapsulates the energy and spirit of late '80s thrash.

Being a dedicated fan of thrash metal doesn't require entering the mosh pit, the rotating circle composed of lurching, colliding, arm-swinging headbangers. But for those who crave heavy-duty physicality along with blaring, chugging rhythms, crashing around inside the pit can be a great way to vent pent-up anger and aggression and escape within a swirling mass of semi-orchestrated chaos. As anyone who frequents the pit knows, there are unwritten rules to being caught in a mosh: Don't dish out more than you're willing to take; if someone's delivering cheap shots or injuring fans, help other moshers eject him from the pit; if someone falls, pick him up. Even those who adhere to the rules are sometimes met with accidental kicks to the head from soaring stagedivers. And those who stagedive do so at their own risk. There's no guarantee divers won't be clocked by bouncers, or flub a leap and crash into the barrier between the audience and the crowd. Then there are those that clear the barrier only to crash on the floor. Even the largest pits sometimes fail to catch divers, and if moshers already face the serious possibility of getting trampled without even ascending the stage, divers who find themselves on the ground in the middle of a swirling pit are even more likely to be injured.

Plenty of moshers emerge from the bit with battle scars they're proud of, but some scars never fade and, in retrospect, many pit-dwellers would have been happy to have exited the pit fray with mere cuts and bruises. Bands that have been around for a while have likely seen dudes in wheelchairs being passed around overhead. As strange as that seems, lots of musicians have witnessed ever weirder activities in the mosh pit.

DEE SNIDER
Twisted Sister, ex-Widowmaker

Mosh pits and stage diving go hand in hand nowadays. I invented stage diving in the '70s after a guy in the audience threw a beer bottle at me and I decided to swan dive into a crowd of a thousand people or more to confront him because he was pretty far back. But when I dove the crowd parted.

I didn't realize that human nature says that when nobody else had ever swan dived off the stage before and you suddenly see one hundred eighty pounds of silver lamé coming your way, you move out of the way. I hit the floor with a thud. The next day we had to cancel multiple shows and then the band got a bodyguard because they told me I couldn't be doing security anymore.

BEN FALGOUST
Goatwhore, ex-Soilent Green

I saw D.R.I. early on the *Crossover* tour in 1987 playing with Kreator and Holy Terror at the Storyville Jazz Hall in New Orleans, and it was the first time I saw a fully formed mosh pit.

Kreator was touring for *Terrible Certainty*, and when they started playing, a giant pit broke out that reminded me of a huge hurricane vortex that was spinning in a circle. No one really called it a pit back then. It was just chaos.

Then when D.R.I. hit the stage, people were lined up to go behind the PA, get on the stage and dive into the crowd. It was a carnival of insanity. The pit and the stage diving were in full rotation. There was constant diving from each side of the stage and everything kept moving. What was really amazing about it was that no one was getting hurt. No one diving off the stage even fell through onto the ground. Everyone worked within this chaos as a unit and it kept going through the entire show.

For a while I just watched from the side, then I went into the pit, full-tilt. And then I dove off the stage. Everything. After it was over, I just thought, "Holy shit, that was fucking amazing." It was astonishing seeing that kind of velocity and movement.

GLEN BENTON
Deicide

When we played South Korea, I was onstage and there were fifty thousand kids there. Four different pits were going at the same time and thousands of kids were going insane. The force of those pits was so powerful that people that didn't want to be in there were getting sucked into it like it was a tornado. One second they'd be watching the show, then you'd see this confused look on their faces right before they got dragged in.

SCOTT IAN
Anthrax, S.O.D., The Damned Things

"Caught in a Mosh," is about our guitar tech Artie Ring. We were playing at the Rainbow Music Hall in Denver, Colorado, in '86, and a kid climbed onstage and fucked up my pedalboard. Artie ran out to push this kid offstage and the two got tangled up and fell into the crowd and got sucked up by the pit. One second Artie was there, the next he was gone. Eventually, Artie climbed back onstage. We finished the show and got on the bus. The next morning Artie came crawling out of his bunk and he could barely move. He was holding his back, hunched over, and when I asked him what was wrong and he said, "Oh, man, I got caught in a mosh."

We thought that was the funniest thing we'd ever heard because Artie was my height and skinner than me. The last place he'd ever wanted to be was in a mosh pit getting trampled. Immediately, a light bulb went on over my head. "That's a song title, right there, song title."

AARON TURNER
Isis, Old Man Gloom, Sumac

Isis rarely inspired a mosh pit, but once in a while it happened and one of the places it happened most was Gothenburg, Sweden.

Once, we were playing there and one second I was doing my thing, and the next, I looked down and Cliff, our keyboard player, had been pulled off the stage by one of the more enthusiastic members in the pit. Cliff's keyboard and some of his pedals went along with him.

JOHN GALLAGHER
Raven

The first time we really started seeing moshing was the second time we came around with Anthrax in 1984. We played The Kabuki Theater in San Francisco.

We had a whole bunch of strobe lights we purchased for the tour. They were about five hundred dollars each and within the first three minutes, they were all destroyed. These guys were just banging their fists on the stage and on whatever was there and the lights were history. We didn't even know about stage diving back then so we had no idea how to react. One-by-one, people kept coming up onstage. We just stopped playing, stood next to them, looked right at them and said, "Can I help you? Get the fuck off my stage right now before I kill you."

And they were looking at us like we were strange.

But it was like, "Listen, we're not a fucking punk band. You want to get on stage? Learn to play. Earn it."

That didn't go down so well with a lot of people. But that was our attitude and, to a large extent, it still is, because the way we jump around and thrash around onstage, you're liable to get banged in the head with a guitar anyway, even if it's not intentional. We didn't encourage it, but if it happened, it happened.

BILLY GRAZIADEI
Biohazard

Our mosh pits were no joke and there was tons of serious violence. Over the years, there were stabbings and shots fired. Dudes would put razor blades between their knuckles and go to town when the New York-style fist-swinging started. In the [New York club] The Ritz in the early '90s, I saw one dude with huge slices down his back from his shoulder to his hip. Someone had cut three giant X's in him, which was fucked up.

For a lot of people, the pit was a fun and energetic release for kids. But on the deeper levels of hardcore, through violent times, it was more about beef—settling beef and starting beef. It was a weird mixture of oil and water that didn't work. Thank god the violent element dissipated over time.

EYAL LEVI
Dååth

When we were in Mexico City in '07 with Dark Funeral, I saw guys crowd surfing with brass knuckles on. They were just punching the shit out of everyone as they surfed across the audience. I saw at least three different dudes fly by like that and they'd swing at everyone around them and then they were gone.

DAVE PETERS
Throwdown, ex-Eighteen Visions, ex-Bleeding Through

When I was sixteen, I was at a Sick of It All show when a fight broke out and I got hit in the head by a pair of brass knuckles that had been filed down. I had these two star-shaped holes in the side of my head and I had to leave the show early because they wouldn't stop bleeding. I went to the doctor and he had to cut hair off in order to stitch up my scalp.

"Did you get stabbed with a screwdriver?" he asked me.

My biggest fear was that my parents would find out what happened because I didn't want them to ban me from shows. I came up with this elaborate story that I was stage diving and I landed on the shoulder of this punk guy who had spikes on his jacket. I went with that story and my parents still don't know I got into a fight at that show and got hit with brass knuckles.

Another time, a fight broke out and a friend, who meant to hit someone else, accidentally hit me on the top of the head with a bike lock and it split my head open. I figured, "Shit, this is the final straw. If I come home with another head injury my parents will say it's too unsafe for me to keep going to shows."

So I borrowed my friend's insurance card and ID and said I was him. I paid for the hospital bill with cash and had the bill sent to my friend's house. I never told my parents about that, either.

DAVE WYNDORF
Monster Magnet

We were playing a club in Vancouver that was so crowded and steamy. There was this stifling, muggy atmosphere, and there were so many people packed in there that the people in the crowd could actually crawl up one another so the actual height of the crowd at any given moment would vary.

I dove from the stage onto the highest peak of the crowd and was lifted up. I saw pipes on the ceiling so I grabbed them, and then the wave receded and left me hanging with a far greater distance to fall than I thought there would be. I knew I wasn't going to fall sideways, I was going to go down standing and I didn't think anyone would catch me. And they didn't. I had to go through the people instead of on the people and wound up like a garbage bag on the floor.

JIMMY BOWER
Eyehategod, Superjoint Ritual, Down, ex-Crowbar

There was a dude in the late '80s from a pretty big band and he used to have combat boots with chainsaw blades nailed to the front of them. He'd dive off the stage and cut people—not by intention—but if you saw this person in the pit or onstage, you got out of the way. All the hair metal dudes would come with their girlfriends and stand in the back. So we'd go back there and knock their drinks out of their hands.

DINO CAZARES
Fear Factory, Divine Heresy, Brujeria, Asesino

You name it, we've seen it. I've seen people jump off the fucking stage and nobody catches them and they land on their backs or on their heads. Next stop: the emergency room. That's happened a million times.

During the *Digimortal* album cycle, one guy in Italy dove offstage but he didn't quite make it back to the pit. His whole body smacked into the barricade and I literally saw the main bone in his leg break. It snapped right in front of me. The crowd parted, the emergency team came through and they carried the guy out with the bone still sticking out.

DEZ FAFARA
DevilDriver, ex-Coal Chamber

We were onstage and there were about three thousand kids in the audience. One kid was crowd surfing and he got dropped. Next thing I knew, I saw people standing around him and that didn't look so good. So we stopped playing and said that we needed an ambulance. I looked at the kid and his femur was busted. He looked right back at me and I tried not to show him how disgusting I thought it looked. If you've ever seen a broken femur, it's unreal. The thing was just popping out. We sent some hoodies and t-shirts to him in the hospital.

BRANDAN SCHIEPPATI
Bleeding Through

In 2003, we were on tour with Underoath and we were playing a floor show in Long Island when this kid broke his leg in the pit. He just lay there and he was still singing along and people were moshing over him and he refused to be moved. It was kind of funny 'cuz he was just sitting there with his leg snapped and he was still singing along. He was there for two songs before he let people take him out to an ambulance.

KYLE SHUTT
The Sword

We opened for Clutch at the Garage in Glasgow, Scotland in 2007. When Clutch went on, I was in the balcony watching the show and this dude got up in the front row and propped himself up with his knees on the barricade. Then he just did this Jesus Christ pose thing in front of [vocalist] Neil [Fallon]. He fell forward, trying to get on the stage but he landed face-first on one of these diagonal forty-five-degree angle metal barricade braces. It busted his whole face open. It's the most blood I've ever seen coming from a person. Neil was just standing there staring at him. No one knew what to do. You could actually feel the pain in your own face.

MATT BACHAND
ex-Shadows Fall, Times of Grace

Shadows Fall did a show with Hatebreed in Northampton, Massachusetts, on Halloween in 1999, and some dude tried to stagedive, but he didn't land right and somehow his ear got torn right off. We stopped the show and security scrambled around on the floor trying to find the kid's ear so they could sew it back to the side of his head. Eventually, they found it and the show continued.

MATT PIKE
High on Fire, Sleep

We were somewhere in Texas touring for *Death Is This Communion*. While I was playing, I saw some kid get his nose ring ripped out. It went through his whole septum on the bottom, and I was like, "Fuck, bro!"

He came up to me after the show and wanted an autograph.

PAUL LEONEY
Profanatica, Havohej

I was at a Morbid Angel show in New York City and somebody's bracelet somehow caught on another guy's face and ripped the whole top of his face off. For some reason, the guy came up to me and said, "Dude, is my face okay?"

"Yeah, you're fine," I said.

But I couldn't look at it so I turned away. There was blood everywhere and you could see the fat cells in the guy's head right by his eye. You could almost look into his head. The guy I was with said to me, "Dude, that wasn't good," and I said, "I know. It's fucked up. But he'll see it when he goes to the bathroom."

PAUL RYAN
Origin

We were playing in Rochester, New York, and about midway through the set this dude in the pit got his head busted open. He was bleeding all over. The girl standing near to him had this look of horror on her face. So it blew my mind when she walked up to the guy, placed her hands on the dude's face so they'd get covered in blood and then smeared her bloodied hands all over her own face.

At the end of our set, she said to me, "I missed prom for this and it was so worth it."

ROBB FLYNN
Machine Head

In Finland, back in 2003, there was a kid up front and he was punching himself in the face to the music the whole fucking show. He'd stop in between songs for a second and then we'd start playing and he'd start punching the shit out of himself again, and he was all bloodied up. I went over there near the end of the show, and I was like, "Are you all right? Is everything cool?"

And he went, "Yeaaahhhh!"

I was like, "All right, killer."

He's feelin' it. There's nothing you can say. That's his thing.

KING FOWLEY
Deceased, October 31

We played the Rock and Roll Hotel in Washington, D.C. with Pig Destroyer. When we were finished, we were getting ready to walk out and this disgusting smell swept through the whole place.

I said, "Man, it smells like a disgusting fart in here. Did someone shit themselves?"

"Dude, you didn't see what happened?" someone said.

"No," I replied.

"While you guys were playing, this guy fell down and all of a sudden all this stuff started coming out of his asshole," The guy said.

Somehow, this dude's lower bowels exploded and all his organs were coming out. He was shitting out his intestines and all this blood and other stuff. I'm kinda glad I didn't see that, but I sure smelled it.

KYLE SHUTT

We played a tiny bar in Grand Rapids, Michigan, in the spring of 2006. We were playing "Iron Swan" from our first record and the place erupted. There was no barricade at the club and the stage was only six inches off the ground. A kid jumped up from the crowd and he hit the stage with his right hand in between his middle finger and his ring finger. It split his hand down the middle. It was so disgusting it was hard to keep composure there was so much blood.

Instead of going to the hospital, he wrapped his hand and watched the rest of the show.

Afterwards, he hung out and he wanted us to sign a record for him. We were like, "Yeah, anything for you, man. Just don't sue us!"

I signed the record with my name and then I wrote, "Thanks for the blood."

CAM PIPES
ex-3 Inches of Blood

In Fargo, North Dakota, we did an impromptu basement show and before we went on, there was a guy there wearing full hunting gear. He came up to us and said, "I just went hunting today and I've got a surprise for you."

During the show, he split to his truck and came back with a garbage bag. He brought it into the pit and took out a deer's head that he had just killed. This thing was fresh, dude, the tongue was hanging out. And he raised it up in the middle of the pit and let all the blood drip on his face. The thing stunk.

"Wow, you're right, man," we said. "That was a surprise."

JESSE KORMAN
The Number Twelve Looks Like You

I always wind up in the middle of the pit during our set and when I've been out there, I've seen guys pull out their dicks, a dude dry-humping some girl, and someone eating a hotdog with mustard all over his face while people slammed into him. I've even seen a mother carrying her baby. But the strangest thing was one time I looked out and there was a girl with her eyes rolled back and she was shaking violently like she was possessed. That was freaky.

DEREK KERSWILL
Tangents, ex-Unearth

I once saw two people making out in a pit. They were really passionate and then some kid came up and drop-kicked both of them to the ground. That wasn't nice but it was pretty funny.

KARL SANDERS
Nile

We were playing in Atlanta and there were a couple in front of me, a super-hot babe and her boyfriend. He had managed to hike her skirt up and was having a go at her right there in the front row. If you can pull that off at a Nile show, more power to you.

ROB BARRETT
Cannibal Corpse

I recall somewhere in Texas, there was a couple in the front row up against the barrier, totally going at it while we were playing "I Cum Blood." I could tell that it was for real because they didn't stop moving after the song was done.

ALEX WEBSTER
Cannibal Corpse

We were playing a show in the late '90s in Sweden when all of a sudden, this naked guy ran by me and jumped into the pit. I just remember thinking, "Man, I'm glad I didn't have to catch him."

TONY FORESTA
Municipal Waste

During *The Art of Partying* era, we played in Miami at this old punk club called Churchills. A few songs into our set a really beautiful, tall, long-haired lady came out in a flowing dress. She went right into the middle of this big circle pit, pulled her dress up, squatted down and started pissing while everyone was moshing around her. It was a good amount of peepee, too.

"Holy fuck! That was amazing," we said to one another.

And then she just sauntered off into the night.

GUY KOZOWYK
The Red Chord

At Ozzfest, there was this heavy metal grandma in the front row, and I was thinking, "If I'm gonna get somebody to flash, ever, it's gotta be this lady."

We were rockin' out and I told this lady to just dump 'em. I said, "C'mon, lady. Get 'em out."

And she did. She pulled out her tits and they went over the barricade right down to the ground. It was like flipping out a couple of plastic grocery bags full of water. Everyone was just astonished. I felt a strange sense of satisfaction that day that I haven't felt in a long time.

PHIL SGROSSO
As I Lay Dying, Wovenwar

Most of the time I don't notice anything that happens in the crowd. But when we headlined our first show in Bangkok, I saw a guy in the pit whose hand was on fire. He was waving it around like a madman. I just stared at him for ten seconds hoping no one's hair would catch fire.

BOBBY THOMPSON
Job for a Cowboy

The craziest pit I've ever seen was during a Slipknot show when they were on tour with Lamb of God and Shadows Fall. Dudes were getting smashed. Every few minutes a fight would break out in the middle of the pit. I saw about ten dudes get knocked out.

Then, about halfway through the show, some guy lit his shirt on fire and swung it around his head. This inspired a bunch of other people to join in. Most of the flaming shirts ended up forming a smoldering pile in the middle of the pit. It took security forever to break through and stop the insanity.

JOSH JAMES
Evergreen Terrace

We were playing Atlanta, and in the middle of the show the crowd parted and the moshing calmed down. Suddenly, a kid ran through the pit area wearing nothing but a thong made to look like a miniature tuxedo. He made his way to the front of the crowd, pulled out his balls, poured rubbing alcohol on them, and set them on fire. Then he tried to pat the fire out, but the flames only got bigger. Soon, he was freaking out.

A friend ran up with a tub of ice cream and gave it to the guy to sink his balls into. I wouldn't have believed it if I hadn't seen it.

AARON TURNER

I was traveling around with Cave In around 1998 and they were playing Philadelphia. There was a large, apparently insane and possibly homeless woman who wandered into the venue, entered the pit, and was dancing around in a provocative fashion. At some point, the entire audience parted, and we could see she had disrobed from the waist down and had exposed her rather formidable backside to the entire room and caused a mass panic.

MAYNARD JAMES KEENAN
Tool

I saw a guy in a wheelchair once and that didn't make any sense. I just remember thinking, "What are you doing up there?" He was in the wheelchair and they were lifting him across their heads, crowd surfing the wheelchair guy. It just didn't seem logical to me. My Spock brain was frying. The image is still burned in my mind.

TOMMY VICTOR
Prong, Danzig, ex-Ministry

Early on in our career, we were supposed to play with Blood Feast. They booked the show and it was at a pizzeria in Bayonne. This guy bought the pizzeria and had a side room with a little tiny PA back there and a disco ball on the ceiling. It was a Jersey Italian guy and I don't know what he thought. Maybe he figured we'd be playing Four Seasons covers.

The dude was in his early forties and he had a bunch of tough guys in there with him. As we loaded in, he said, "Aw, man. What is this? Look, I don't care what you do. I don't know anything about what this hard rock thing is. But as long as nothing happens to that disco ball, I'm cool."

I said, "All right."

We went on and started playing the first song "Freezer Burn" off *Force Fed* and there were fifty kids there and they went crazy. They were chicken fighting in the pit. These guys were on top of each other and one of them punched the disco ball. It unhooked from its anchor, flew across the room, and landed by the owner of the place. It didn't break, but the dude lost his fucking mind.

He ran onstage, grabbed me and said, "That's it! That's it! I want you guys out of here!"

The mosh pit was crazy enough for him to end the show and it cost me a hundred fifty bucks to play half of a song because we had to pay this guy to get out of there alive. It was totally like something out of *The Sopranos*. I don't even think Blood Feast played.

ROBB FLYNN

I remember one kid was running around the pit with a dead dog and smacking people with it. It was this little black dog that was totally in rigor mortis. At first I was like, "Man, what is that?" I thought it was something obvious like a shirt or a jacket but then I looked closer, and, yup, it was actually a dead dog.

JAMEY JASTA
Hatebreed, Jasta

A drunk guy snuck his pit bull into the pit at a show in New Jersey in '96 or '97. He was a total fucking idiot. The dog didn't like the loud music and didn't understand why people were hitting each other. So the dog went crazy and started biting people. One guy got bit on the ass really bad and had to go to the hospital and get shots. Luckily, it was his ass. It could have been the other side.

EMIL WERSTLER
Dååth

When we played Ozzfest in Connecticut, people in the crowd were surfing trashcans into this whirlwind pit. And they weren't empty. Garbage was spilling out of them and people were getting covered with empty cups, napkins, leftover food—whatever was in those cans. When it first started happening it was hard to figure out what was going on.

"Is that a garbage can in the pit?"

I did a double-take and realized it was and then suddenly there were a bunch more.

MARK MORTON
Lamb of God

The wall of death was frightening to watch. Obviously, it's a tradition that came out of the New York hardcore scene in which the crowd is split in two and the right side all go to the right and the left side all go to the left. Then on cue, everyone runs straight for each other like a big game of rugby and collides in the middle.

When it's going on, it looks like a scene from *Braveheart* or something. It became almost a staple at our shows. At first, it was something we would initiate when we played "Black Label," but it became so ferocious in there that we actually stopped asking crowds to do it because we were literally concerned for the safety of some of the people on the floor. I was genuinely worried that people were getting really hurt. So I was relieved when we stopped doing that.

ADAM DUTKIEWICZ
Killswitch Engage

On the Warped tour, we did the chickenfight wall of death, which was pretty sweet. We had everyone get on someone else's shoulders and then do the wall of death like that. It was dangerous as fuck, but nobody got hurt, so it was all good. And it was funny, so that's something right there.

GUY KOZOWYK

During Mayhem, we got these retarded walls of death going. Some days we'd play on the second stage right before Five Finger Death Punch went on the main stage. They got so big during that tour, there were days that by the end of our set there were as many people waiting to see them as there were standing there watching us. So it was kind of like the wall of death was already set up for us. We had this big open space between the two stages and there were people on each side.

So we started calling out the Five Finger Death Punch crowds, and we got our fans to back up and their crowds were less than enthused sometimes because they were waiting to see a band, they weren't looking to get into this moshpit ritual. So basically you had The Red Chord's wall flushing over into the Jägermeister stage. When we did signings, we'd see some of these kids with mangled arms and legs and this eyeball looking thing sticking out of their foreheads going, "Yeah man, I totally ran face-first into this dude."

Those were some of my favorite onstage pit moments.

SAM RIVERS
Limp Bizkit

There was a wall of death at one of our shows and, I shit you not, I saw a bunch of girls out there. They started on my side of the stage and I was thinking, "Wow, this is going to be interesting."

Sure enough, we had a breakdown in the song and Fred riled up the crowd. When we kicked into the music again, I saw a whole bunch of these girls charge and when they hit they didn't stop. They just plundered these guys. I thought they were going to run at them and then maybe get out of the way of the chaos. But they were ready to battle. I couldn't stop laughing. I was almost in tears while I was playing. Thank god all the sweat on my face took away from tears of me crying.

TRAVIS RYAN
Cattle Decapitation

We did a one-off show in Nashville and the weirdest thing happened in the crowd. I'd never seen anything like it. Right in the middle of a song, the pit cleared out for a second and suddenly there was a seven-person human pyramid, like you see at cheerleader practice. And all the kids in the pyramid were wearing Cattle Decapitation t-shirts. The kid at the very top had a can of hairspray and a lighter and made a blazing torch, which was a nice touch.

MIKE SCHLEIBAUM
Darkest Hour

At a festival in France, I saw a dude in the pit in a long reclining beach chair holding a beer, and he was being passed to the front of the stage. He stayed up there for a long time and probably had the best seat in the house, and dude, he did not spill his beer. But he did take a pretty hard fall on the back of the head when the crowd decided they didn't want to carry him the whole show.

JONATHAN COOKE
Winds of Plague

I love when people are in costume. I've seen a circle-pitting Jesus and a two-stepping hamburger. But the best was at a Halloween show we played in Anaheim at Chain Reaction. Right there in the pit, Dora the Explorer got into an altercation with a teddy bear and the room turned into a huge all-out brawl.

MIKE "GUNFACE" MCKENZIE
The Red Chord

I went to see Emperor years ago when they toured the States for their *IX Equilibrium* album. Standing in line outside before the show were two kids wearing matching green-hooded capes with gold trim that they had obviously put a lot of work into. A few hours later during Emperor's set, one of the capes landed at my feet, torn to shreds. I guess the fans in the pit were not Renaissance fair enthusiasts.

BEN FALGOUST

We did a show with Goatwhore in Little Rock, Arkansas, at a place called Vinos. The front part of it was a pizza place and the back part was a club. In the back area there was a four-and-a-half-foot Santa Claus yard decoration, which was weird. As we were playing, the pit got crazy and then we started noticing sparks. Someone had picked up a metal office chair and was repeatedly slamming it on the cement floor in the pit, which caused all these sparks. No one was getting hurt so it was cool. Then all of a sudden, the sparks stopped. The next thing I knew, this giant Santa Claus was flying across the room. Kids were bouncing it up and down like a giant beach ball. It was perfect. Goatwhore and Santa Claus.

GLEN BENTON

In Remoutzy, Canada, we played in this big farm building in the middle of nowhere and there was a fuckin' dirt floor there with no less than three thousand people in the pit. Kids were showing up on school buses and they kept coming in. I looked out and there were ten-year-olds, fuckin' dead drunk, laying on the ground. And I saw this big, huge ring dug into the dirt floor.

I thought, "They must run horses around this thing."

I got onstage and the crowd started pitting in that ring. There were three thousand kids stampeding in a fuckin' circle and a cloud of dust coming out. It was like something out of a Western where the Indians are circling around the wagons.

RODY WALKER
Protest the Hero

At a show in Thunder Bay, Ontario, there was a guy in the pit who didn't seem to fit in with the rest of the crowd and he was clearly upset about it. At one point, he took a beer bottle and repeatedly struck a small girl in front of him. After he had hit her about six times, our stage manager, Michael Fairless, saw what was happening and tried to drag the dude out of the crowd, except this guy was much bigger than Michael.

Suddenly, it looked like Michael was going to be the one under attack so two people from the side of the stage came to Michael's aid. They dragged the guy with the bottle up on the stage and threw him down the stairs off the side of the stage. Then security ejected him from the building.

DANI FILTH
Cradle of Filth

We were playing a festival in Finland in 1998. It was one of those nights in the summer when the sun goes down very late and then the moon comes up and then goes down and the sun comes up again all in a period of a couple of hours. So at 2 a.m. it was still basically sunny. Our keyboardist at the time was Lecter, who used to always dress in a grubby clerical outfit and he always used to get bought a huge amount of drinks because he convinced gullible people that he was from a rogue sect of the clergy that was allowed to drink.

At one point in the festival Impaled Nazarene were playing a killer gig. The moshpit was going like crazy. And there was Lecter on a chair right in front of the stage asleep and snoring while three hundred people ran mad circles around him.

MARK HUNTER
Chimaira

I love Pantera, but I've had some bad luck at their shows. They were playing the Cleveland Agora in 1994 during their first run of the *Far Beyond Driven* tour. Pantera played "A New Level," which was my favorite song at the time. I tried to jump up because I was excited, and as I was jumping somebody hit me from behind almost like a football tackle. The guy leveled me and I broke two ribs. I was taken out right away.

Later that year, Pantera played at the Richfield Coliseum. Sepultura were opening and I was running into the arena, right onto the floor, dying to get to the stage when I caught a fist in the fucking nose and faceplanted right on the ground.

WILL CARROLL
Death Angel, ex-Machine Head

I was at a Cannibal Corpse show twenty years ago at Slims in San Francisco. I had just bought a "Changed and Contorted" Cannibal Corpse shirt. The band had just gotten on and they were opening with an instrumental called "From Skin to Liquid." It's a really slow track and I couldn't believe they were playing it live.

I was so excited I ran up to the front of the crowd, which I didn't normally do. I'm a drummer. I don't want to break my ankle. A pit broke out behind me and some guy was falling. He grabbed onto my neck collar to anchor him and keep him up. I started feeling the stitching on my new shirt tearing. I didn't want the dude to go down, but then I looked at my new shirt and thought, "Fuck that!"

I had a beer in one hand and my jacket in the other. My hands were full. So I leaned back and bit his hand until he let go and he fell to the ground and got trampled on.

JACOBY SHADDIX
Papa Roach

In 2005, we were playing this song called "Scars," and there was a girl at the edge of the pit cutting her arms up with a razor.

That was real heavy to me because I was a cutter for a while.

So I was like, "Man, fuckin' A. Somebody give this kid some love."

After the show, I went down and gave her a kiss on the forehead. And I was like, "Cheer up, honey. This, too, shall pass."

CHAPTER 8: RAINING BLOOD

Suffering & Bleeding for Metal

A cornerstone of thrash, "Raining Blood" was a song that the late, great Slayer usually played during their encore. The track was the last on the band's heralded 1986 album *Reign In Blood* and, aside from "Angels of Death," was the only song over four minutes long on the fast, concise record.

There's a saying in tabloid journalism: If it bleeds, it leads. With the possible exception of hardcore punk, it's pretty safe to say metal musicians have bled more for their art than artists in any other musical genre. Some, including Marilyn Manson, Morbid Angel, Shining, and forgotten industrial metal band Malhavoc actually integrated bloodletting into their stage performance. Many others have wussed out and used fake blood. The most dramatic metal carnage, however, is unplanned and happens because of the reckless energy and unrelenting passion metal bands inject into their performances. Stage collisions, prop malfunctions, launched projectiles, and drunken idiocy are primary reasons artists get hurt onstage. Then, there are injuries like bone breaks, contusions and electrical shocks which loosely fit the category definition since they cause pain, and often internal bleeding—well, maybe not shocks, but seeing a singer get zapped and fly backwards is just as dramatic as watching a guitarist take a mic stand to the forehead.

COREY TAYLOR
Slipknot, Stone Sour

I think I almost broke my neck or cracked my skull when I fell off the stage at Ozzfest '99. We were doing a show in either Detroit or Indianapolis and I was singing on a monitor. I slipped and landed on top of my head and twisted my neck. I could move all my fingers and toes so I was like, "Fuck, okay, I'm fine" and I finished the show.

But I've had MRIs and X-rays, and my C5 and C6 vertebrae basically fused together and destroyed the disk in between and the bone was growing into my spinal cord. The only thing I could think of that could have caused that was that fall at Ozzfest. But my doctor said the injury could have happened long before that and over time the bones grew back in an abnormal way.

At least that explained why I was having so many physical problems at the time. The MRI showed that the bone was literally choking off the fluid and damaging the nerves on my spinal cord. My doctor couldn't believe I was walking. That tells you how bad it was. They replaced the disk, jacked up the vertebrae, and shaped the bone back so it wasn't going into my spinal cord anymore.

When the doctors operated they had to go through my neck so they wouldn't sever any of the spinal cord and now I've got this gnarly scar on the front of my neck.

GARY HOLT
Exodus, Slayer

I'm the poster boy of onstage injuries. Nobody can touch me—maybe the occasional dude who's too hammered and falls offstage and breaks his neck. But I've hurt myself bad. I've taken headstocks to the forehead when [ex-Exodus guitarist] Rick [Hunolt] and I both were playing those pointy Jackson guitars. We'd both cut each other open, bleed all over the place, and get butterfly stitches after the show.

In 2011, we were out in Europe with Death Angel, Kreator, and Heathen. I used to drink several shots to loosen up before a show. And I tripped over some cabling from the monitors and I went up completely horizontal in the air and landed flat on my back. [Death Angel vocalist] Mark Osegueda and [guitarist] Rob Cavestany were standing right there on the side of the stage. And everyone was going, "Oh my God. Wow."

I got up and I said, "Oh, I'm fine."

It's crazy. I didn't feel hurt at all. Three days later I got up in the morning and lit a cigarette and coughed and my rib, which I had apparently cracked before, actually broke one hundred percent. I crawled in the back of a bus at 7 a.m. I couldn't even breathe. And there were people there still partying. My tour manager was shitfaced and he'd been Sharpied. He had dicks and boobs and buttholes drawn all over him. I told him I had to go to the hospital and from there I did seventeen shows in a row on morphine with a broken rib.

Playing in pain is just part of the gig. I view it like being a football player. You gotta get out there and play no matter what happens. If I can somehow, someway, pick up a guitar and play, I'm gonna do it. I've read stuff in the metal press all the time about some guitar player who hurt his foot and canceled the next show. I'm like, "Fuckin' pussy. Get out there. People paid money to see you. Toughen up."

BEN WEINMAN
The Dillinger Escape Plan

From day one, it has been absolute chaos. We were so normal in our daily lives since we weren't doing the band full time. We had regular jobs, but then we'd play these weekend shows and they'd be so visceral and violent. We'd be playing in VFW Halls and places that didn't even have stages so there'd be no division between the crowd and us and the mosh pits. We'd be throwing gear, beating ourselves up and breathing fire in these little places.

I'd limp into work all bruised up, with a black eye the next day and it looked like I was a member of Fight Club.

When [vocalist] Greg Puciato got into the band in 2001, it got even crazier. We were colliding with each other a lot 'cause we started getting more and more trance-like. Playing the shows would be almost meditative. We'd lose ourselves and the performances became second nature and truly uninhibited. We would basically destroy each other onstage and be bleeding everywhere from hitting each other by mistake. And then when we got a bigger fanbase, it got even crazier with all the climbing and jumping off huge amp stacks that we did.

I guess I've gotten the worst of that as far as permanent injuries go. I've had broken bones and rotator surgeries and neck problems. People can't believe I haven't been paralyzed by a lot of the shit they've seen me do. But some of the stuff that *did* lead to serious injuries was stuff that I didn't do intentionally. I can usually manage the stage antics. It's the unexpected things that you can't control and you're not ready for.

The worst thing that happened to me was when we were on tour with Between the Buried and Me and Horse the Band in 2005 and we were playing in Anaheim, California, at a club called Chain Reaction. There was a big, heavy, black speaker hanging overhead, which I didn't see, and I tried to jump over something. I jumped as high as I could and the speaker was right over me. I cracked my head open and fractured my neck and I had to get eight staples in my head. The whole crowd was covered in blood. And it was in the first twenty seconds of the set.

KIRK WINDSTEIN
Crowbar, ex-Down

The worst I've ever fucked myself up was with Down in Shreveport, Louisiana on December 30, 1995. The stage was six feet high and it was dark. As we were leaving the stage at the end of the show, somebody moved the staircase over from where it was, but no one told us that. I went to put my left foot on the stairs and there was no step there. My right leg hit the stairs and I flipped over and landed on the palm of my left hand. I thought I broke my thumb. I wasn't really cut up, just sore and bruised so I shook it off and said, "Fuck it, let's do the encore."

As we played "Bury Me in Smoke" I looked at my left hand and it was really swollen.

The next day my right leg from my knee all the way up to my nuts started getting more and more bruised. I thought I broke ribs, too, because I had a cut on my right side right where my ribs were and they were bruised up. That night we had a thirty-minute set so I gutted it out. We got drunk with everybody afterwards.

I got back to New Orleans a day or two later and my right leg had swollen up really bad. I had to have it drained and I had X-rays. Fortunately, nothing was broken, not even my ribs. That was scary because I could have broken anything falling off a tall stage like that.

REX BROWN
Pantera, ex-Down, ex-Crowbar, Kill Devil Hill

I was playing with Kill Devil Hill in 2012 somewhere on the East Coast. The backstage area was up about three flights of stairs and there was a platform at the bottom of each flight. I was coming down wearing boots and I had a coffee in one hand. Partway down my boot slipped and I couldn't catch the railing. I was trying to stop myself from falling. I hit the first platform down the flight of stairs, and it launched me in the air. I came down and thank God my tour manager saw what was happening.

I was cruising at about thirty miles an hour and he caught me mid-flight right before I landed. I was upside-down and if he hadn't been there, I would have landed on my goddamn neck.

Even with him catching me, I fell so hard I broke three ribs—cracked the fuck out of them. I'm sitting there at the bottom trying to catch my breath. My side swelled up like a fuckin' cantaloupe. They said, "We're canceling the show."

"The fuck we are," I said. "I've never canceled a show. I'm not about to start now."

I asked someone in the club to get me a bandage. When he came back I told my tour manager to squeeze as tight as he could around my ribs and wrap the ace bandage around me. He said, "Well, can you breathe? Should we call the paramedics?"

I said, "Let's get through the set. We'll make it a short one. Let's finish the goddamn thing."

I played the show and afterwards I felt even worse. I had to sit up for the next three and a half weeks in the back of a van propped up. I couldn't lay down. I should have gone and gotten the ribs set because they still protrude.

DAVE WYNDORF
Monster Magnet

At the late, lamented Dynamo Festival in Holland, I dove offstage and I had my guitar on. I got wrapped up in the cords and the strap and got surfed back to the stage. A security guard grabbed me to pull me out, but the crowd held on. It was a tug-o-war, and they were equally pulling at me.

I went, "Hold, on, hold oh, hold on, hold on!"

It was like medieval torture, and it broke my rib. I could feel it pop. I got back on stage and finished the show in this crazy pain. I kept going but it took forever for the pain to go away.

ROB CAVESTANY
Death Angel, ex-The Organization

At the end of the show I toss guitar picks into the crowd, like every other band. Usually, there's nothing to it. Then there was the time I tried to hand a pick to a fan in the crowd and I fell right offstage.

It was a pretty high stage and I went headfirst with my guitar on, so I could have been killed. Somehow, a security guard was holding my ankle and I was right above the cement floor. I wasn't fucked up at all. I was completely upside-down with my guitar on the ground and everything was fine, both me and my guitar.

JOEY JORDISON
ex-Slipknot, Murderdolls, Sinsaenum, Vimic

I got my head split open from a flying pipe from a keg [drum] that broke. I've cracked my fucking knuckles on the side of the snare and bled like a stuck pig. It wasn't just droplets of blood, the whole bottom of the drum was painted red with my blood. Another time, I pulled my rack down on top of me and cut my shin wide open and had to have stitches.

[Percussionist] Shawn ["Clown" Crahan] had his fucking ribs broken three times. He's had shin splints. He's had his head cracked open twice. Once, he threw the mic stand up and lay down on his back, and it came back down and hit him in the head and split his head wide open. That fuckin' ruled!

If the music makes you go that fucking insane and you get a battle scar from it, you know it was a good show.

CHRIS URENNA
ex-Nine Inch Nails, ex-Marilyn Manson

We were at the Warfield Theater at the very beginning of the *Downward Spiral* tour. During the second song in the set, "Sin," I had my head turned stage left, and out of nowhere, Trent [Reznor] launched his mic stand towards the drums.

Instead of hitting the cymbals, which would happen from time to time, he overlaunched the thing and it came up over my cymbal stand and hit me square in the forehead. I didn't see it coming because there were purple lights and I was turned the other way. The mic stand split my forehead wide open.

I kept playing 'cause I didn't realize how bad it was. It was like slow-motion. I was trying to shake off the blow, so I looked down and I saw my snare drum filling up with blood. And then I looked up and saw three members of our road crew all running at me with towels. I was like, "Aw, shit. This can't be good."

I almost passed out from the pain, but I got through the song and then we stopped the show for about a half hour.

My forehead was split open right to the bone. They butterfly bandaged me back together and then I went back out and finished the set and went back out and did encores. As soon as the show was over, I got rushed to the hospital and got forty stitches. I had a concussion for the next week and I still have a huge scar over my right eyebrow.

JOHN GALLAGHER
Raven

Our old drummer, Rob "Wacko" Hunter always wound up cutting him-self. We played with Ted Nugent at the Six Flags in Houston. We were on for ten minutes because Rob was punching cymbals and he cut the main artery on the top of his hand and blood was literally squirting out like a Monty Python episode. We had to duct tape him up and get paramedics to treat him. The next day he played very drugged up and bandaged.

MIKE IX WILLIAMS
Eyehategod

I've done the broken bottle to the face thing and gotten stitches a bunch of times. I would just sporadically cut myself during the show. It definitely wasn't every night. But once you cut yourself once, a lot of times it will open up again a few days later. So I'd bleed at a few other shows but not from the actual cutting.

One time in Dayton, Ohio, in the '90s, we had all sniffed a little angel dust before the show because there was a ton of it around for some rea-son. Then, when I was onstage I cut myself on the forehead and was bleeding pretty bad. I went to the nearby fire department and got ban-daged up, then I went to the hospital and got stitches. We came back to the club to pick up our equipment and people there were majorly trip-ping on this angel dust. One guy was staring at a landline phone crying his eyes out, waiting for it to ring.

But the bottle thing got pretty dangerous. I used to break bottles onstage just 'cause I liked the way it looked. But then people started bringing their own bottles and breaking them. I saw a lot of fans with cut hands and faces, and I didn't want to play any part in that so I stopped doing it.

TOMMY VICTOR
Prong, Danzig, ex-Ministry

I got screwed up really bad at the Pinkpop festival in Holland in 2002. I was leaping off a monitor, using it as a trampoline and it wasn't anchored down. The monitor slid underneath me and I fell off the stage and broke three or four ribs. I was in pain for a long time. We had three more weeks to go and I could hardly do the shows.

WILL CARROLL
Death Angel, ex-Machine Head

We went to see a local show in the early 2000s, and afterwards, we went to this house where all the San Francisco metalheads used to party. It was hardcore partying—smoking speed, doing coke, taking pills. We were over there and the host of the party was setting up hot rails. That's where you lay out a giant line of crystal meth and you get a glass tube and a torch. You torch one end of the tube so it gets orange-hot. You put that end to the line and you snort the line with the other end of the tube and the meth vaporizes immediately in your nose. Then you blow out the largest cloud of smoke. It looks like pyro at a Kiss concert and it gets you so high. You're gone for days just from that one hot rail.

I did one, someone else did one, and then this friend of mine, who's in a pretty well-known sludgy, stoner band said, "I wanna do one!"

"Are you sure, dude," I said. "I mean, you're on tour, man. You're gonna be up for fuckin' days."

He was already drunk and he said, "I can handle it."

We torched up the glass tube for him and he said, "Watch this." He accidentally put the scalding orange end to his nostril and it welded to his nose. He screamed and ripped it off and blood spewed everywhere. After his nose finally stopped bleeding and we were able to take a good look at his nostril, the opening looked like a butthole. It was disgusting. That was the last time I ever did a hot rail.

SCOTT IAN
Anthrax, S.O.D., The Damned Things

[Drummer] Charlie [Benante] broke his nose on stage in Japan sometime in the '80s. I was playing drums while we covered Judas Priest's version of "The Green Manalishi (With the Two-Pronged Crown)" and Charlie was playing guitar out front. [Ex-guitarist] Danny Spitz threw his head back while he was headbanging. He didn't know Charlie was right behind him. CRACK! His head went right into Charlie's face and broke his nose and that was the end of the show.

DAVE WYNDORF

I bashed my nose with the microphone while trying to pull this cool Elvis move. I grabbed the mic stand from the middle of it rather than the top, not putting two and two together and realizing that when you grab a mic stand and swing it, the mic on the top of the stand is going to disengage. It swirled around three times and then bonked me on the nose. Of course, it was amplified so everyone could see it and they could hear it too. It was like a cartoon. I told the crowd, "I meant to do that!" but my nose was bleeding like a faucet, which was just humiliating.

BILLY GRAZIADEI
Biohazard

I get low to the ground when I headbang and my face and head are in proximity to people diving off the monitors.

One time in Europe in 1992, the kids were going crazy. I was playing and someone duck-kicked to go out into the crowd and accidentally kicked me in the face. It took me years to get the distance sorted out so I could avoid that.

On one tour leg, [guitarist] Bobby [Hambel] and I had forty-two stitches between the two of us. We kept getting cut up in different ways. Sometimes we didn't even know how it happened. But once, I was kicked in the face and my tooth got knocked out and the side of the canine tooth next to it impaled my lip. I stood up like, "What the fuck happened?"

The tooth that got knocked out was fake. The real one that used to be there got knocked out in a fight years ago. My first thought is that it could be replaced. Then I stood up and blood gushed out of my face and mouth. Something was pulling at my face, which I didn't understand. I looked at the guys in the band and they had these horrified facial expressions. Blood was still pouring down my chin and getting all over me. What happened somehow was my lip got impaled by the tooth so I had to pull my lip down and around the tooth.

I cleaned up the best I could and then I was backstage drinking beer and when I closed my mouth a mixture of blood and beer squirted out of my lip. That's when I figured this was a problem and I had to go and get my lip stitched up.

DAVE PETERS
Throwdown, ex-Eighteen Visions, ex-Bleeding Through

We played Club Krome in New Jersey and Tommy [Love], who was playing guitar for us at the time, used to spin his guitar around a lot like the guy in Biohazard. At this one show, he spun around and I was coming down to headbang, and the headstock of the guitar hit me dead-on in the forehead. The label owner's wife got sick when she saw it happen.

There was blood shooting out all over the stage and spraying out into the front row.

We put a towel over it but we couldn't get my head to stop bleeding. So we had to stop the show and I went to the doctor and got two layers of stitches because the gash was so deep. I had this golf ball-sized knot on my head for the last ten days of the tour. I don't think I talked to Tommy for five days because I was so pissed.

ERIK TURNER
Warrant

There's footage of us performing at the *American Music Awards* [in 1990] and [singer] Jani [Lane] has a butterfly stitch across his eye. That's from Jerry [Dixon] hitting him in the face with his bass onstage. He just split his eye wide open.

JERRY DIXON
Warrant

He was trying to roll me over on his back. It worked in rehearsal but then the butt of my bass hit Jani right in the face. We always said, "If one of us isn't bleeding when we get offstage it wasn't a good show."

One night, we were jamming onstage with Lynch Mob and [Dokken guitarist] George Lynch spun around and his guitar whacked me right in the mouth. It knocked one of my vampire teeth up into my head. I was spitting out all this blood and it hurt so much I almost passed out. I went to the emergency room and they said the tooth would eventually drop back down and that I should have a nice night. So I went back to the bus and just continued drinking. It took about six months for the tooth to stop hurting and fully grow back into my mouth.

JOHN GALLAGHER

I hit [guitarist] Mark [Gallagher] in the face with the headstock of my bass in Frederick, Maryland, in 2018. I just happened to turn around and, BANG, right behind the ear. There was copious bleeding, but we just kept going.

To be honest, I don't know why that doesn't happen more often since we run around and jump and so much on these small stages. Air traffic control has got nothing on us. Mark's no stranger to bleeding onstage. There have been many times when his guitar has a sharpened bridge piece on it and the way he palm mutes his guitar his palm is constantly getting cut up. He keeps filling the wounds with Krazy Glue. But then the Krazy Glue breaks off and all of a sudden there's blood everywhere.

PIOTR "PETER" WIWCZAREK
Vader

One guy was surfing through the mosh pit in Holland and he flew up onstage and hit my face with his feet. My nose exploded and for five minutes I was covered in blood. But we kept playing.

BEN FALGOUST
Goatwhore, ex-Soilent Green

I took a knee to the nose and forehead, but it was my own fault 'cause it was my own knee. I was just jamming and I went down too far when I was headbanging, and the way my leg was positioned [on the monitor], my knee smacked the bridge in between my eyebrows and my nose. That was kinda messy.

GARY HOLT

My spine's a fucking disaster. I need surgery. I have a broken bone in my back that's been broken since I was a teenager. It probably happened from a skateboard accident when I was sixteen or seventeen years old. So now most of the time I'm on tour I have to spend all my free time off my feet or hanging upside-down on an inversion table.

You have to save every ounce of energy for the stage. Because fuck it. Even if I'm hurt, I'm still gonna bang my head and do something visual during the show.

PHILIP ANSELMO
Pantera, Down, Superjoint Ritual, Scour

I beat the shit out of myself for so many years. I had a lower back blowout from jumping off. I had a ruptured disc with no cartilage in between that disc and the next, so it was bone-on-bone scraping, constantly. The pain was maddening. I went to doctor after doctor after doctor thinking, "Hey, maybe they can fix this fucking thing."

And every doctor all across the country turned me down and said get the fuck out of my office.

I was pissed off and extremely frustrated at the time, but I understand it now. When I was so badly injured, back surgery had not advanced to the point to where it reached in 2005 when I finally had surgery. So these doctors in the '90s were saving me from barbaric, torturous procedures. Every doctor I've talked to said if I had surgery in the fucking '90s, I'd be wrecked, ruined, and fucked. The procedures they were describing to me were fucking unacceptable.

Now, I've got six screws and six titanium clamps holding me together back there and I can still perform. I'm not crippled. It took two-and-a-half years to recover. I was back doing shows six months after the surgery, but by no means was it fucking easy. My surgery took seven hours. They have to have your muscles split wide open for that long. Then they've got you on heavy pain medication that you have to kick: lucky me.

DEE SNIDER
Twisted Sister, ex-Widowmaker

Often, I'll come offstage and go, "Oh my gosh, I'm bleeding."

In 2017, we were in Spain playing this huge festival in Barcelona. I was in between songs and I was talking to the crowd of fifty thousand or seventy thousand. All of a sudden, I hear a guitar playing loud. I turned around and looked at my band and they said, "Not us, dude."

I thought, "What the fuck?"

Then I realized we were playing a festival and the stages were side by side and the crew for the band that was coming up next, Europe, was sound checking during our set—loud. I said to our crowd, "Hold on one second," and I wriggled through the scaffolding and got on the other stage. I had the mic with me and I just tore the guy a new asshole. He was terrified. I was losing my fucking mind, saying, "You motherfucker! I'm not shitting on your fucking band, why are you shitting on ours?"

And then I climbed back. We played the next song. I started performing and rocking out and I see I've got blood all over me. I had cut myself on a bolt or a screw climbing through the scaffolding and I didn't even realize it because it didn't hurt. In the heat of the moment, my adrenaline was pumping and I didn't notice that shit.

So I'm going, this is kind of cool. Now I'm bleeding for rock and roll. That is the best.

BURTON C. BELL
Fear Factory, Ascension of the Watchers

In Luxemburg in 2005, there was a problem with the grounding of the stage between the mixing board and my microphone. Everything was fine until a while into the set when the microphone started getting a little damp with my spit. At one point, I brought the microphone to my mouth and I saw this blue spark in front of my face. It was like I got hit by a semi that threw me backwards onto my ass. It knocked me out.

The band stopped playing. Then I opened my eyes and people were standing above me going, "Are you okay? Are you okay?"

I just said, "I'm fine" and walked off the stage.

I went into the dressing room and looked at the mirror and I was completely pale white. It scared the shit out of me.

JOHN GALLAGHER

[Guitarist] Mark [Gallagher] got a good electric shock in Buenos Aires, Argentina, in about 2013. The microphone wasn't grounded properly so he went flying backwards. It knocked him off his feet two or three feet back. He said it felt like a huge punch in the mouth.

"It's okay. I'll fix it," said some guy who worked at the club.

He got some sort of clamp and wiring. He wired everything up.

"Okay, turn everything on," he said.

So we did and all of Mark's equipment and the mixing board blew up.

DAVE WYNDORF

In 1993, I was electrocuted at sound check in Italy. I plugged in, said a few words into the mic. I went to adjust the mic stand. BZZZZZZ! BOOOOM! I fell to the ground. Blue lips. Everything. I could practically see little birds dancing over my head.

For days afterwards, the ends of my fingers and my lips were numb from the electricity and the rest of my body felt like it was humming. Weirdest fucking feeling—not good. Two hours after I got shocked, the sound guy came up to me.

"Okay, so your set's going to be at 9:30," he said.

"Dude! I'm not going back on that stage. Are you crazy?"

"Nahh, we fixed it. It's all right,"

"No, it's not all right. You electrocuted me!"

"Oh, *que sera, sera*," he said. I was livid.

"No, it's not whatever will be, will be! It's what happened to me because of you!"

I begrudgingly did the show and I kept my mouth as far away from the mic as possible.

DAVID DRAIMAN
Disturbed

The night that I met my wife, I took a hit in my right ear because I was using faulty ear monitors. The signal overloaded and the volume wouldn't come down no matter what I did. I either had to pull them out and have to deal with trying to sing over a hundred nineteen decibels onstage or deal with the overload in my ears. I couldn't adjust anything because it was either powered on and incredibly loud or powered off so that I couldn't hear anything.

I muscled through the show and by the end of the set my ears were screaming. The pain was so bad it was maddening. When I was on the tour bus with my wife-to-be, she was watching me pace back and forth spewing every piece of profanity in the entire book. I'm surprised she didn't flee and write me off. I was furious that a malfunction like this could happen and I was embarrassed because I must have struggled the entire show. I couldn't hear myself most of the time and I put up with the intense pain just so I could try to sing better.

It was forty-three fucking degrees and it was raining lightly. I felt like there couldn't be a more cataclysmic combination of events. Then my future wife grabbed me, put her hands on the side of my face and kissed me and I immediately shut up and stopped complaining. Suddenly, everything didn't seem so bad anymore.

TONY FORESTA
Municipal Waste

There have been so many nights I've had a few drinks before we've gone onstage and then I stumbled around, not really paying attention to what I was doing, and wound up falling off the stage. I've blown my knee out, broken my ankle.

When we were in Atlantic City with Gwar in 2006, I took a tumble and their drummer Brad [Roberts] had to carry me up a flight of stairs because my leg swelled up and I couldn't walk. I had to go to the doctor and get it all bandaged. I couldn't walk for the rest of the tour. I was on crutches and everyone was wheeling me around in a wheelchair. Gwar was clowning me. When they did their encore, they would make fun of me by wheeling their singer Dave Brockie [aka Oderus Urungus] out in a wheelchair.

MICHAEL SWEET
Stryper

Years ago, we had these ramps that took us up to the back cabinets and you could go and stand on the cabs. In New York in 1987, our guitarist Oz Fox went up there and wound up tripping and falling off the stage and breaking his ankle. It was close to the end of the set, so we ended the show, then took him to the hospital. We continued the tour with him in a wheelchair.

SAM RIVERS
Limp Bizkit

The first night of Limptropolis in America was in a big hangar, maybe in Portland.

About three songs into the show my bass was messing up. This kept happening at different shows and the manufacturer didn't know what was going on. I didn't know what was going on. The only thing I can think of is that my sweat killed the electronics every single night. I went through twenty of those basses before switching to a different brand. But that night I snapped and smashed the bass onstage. Unfortunately, the neck was so slippery and I was so sweaty that my hand slipped down the neck and caught on one of the tuners, which ripped my palm wide open. I turned my hand over and there's blood squirting in two-foot arcs. I closed my hand and walked backstage. I said, "I don't know if I can play anymore."

I opened my hand and our tour manager saw this blood squirting everywhere.

"Whoa! We've gotta get you right to the hospital!" he said.

They rushed me out the door super-fast, got me in an ambulance. They got onto one street and the driver said, "All lights green."

And we drove on that one street all the way to the hospital. They got me down there in ten minutes and stitched me up. The band kept doing something to bide their time. And back then we didn't have cell phones. They had girls on top of people's shoulders making out to occupy people. But everybody in the crowd stayed and I got back in the ambulance and they raced me back to the venue.

I was pilled out for the pain and I said, "Let's do it."

And sure enough, I got back upstage and I played the rest of the show and I was in no pain. I don't know how I played on those drugs, but it was a rockin' show.

COR>Y TAYLOR

It's hard enough to be onstage in Slipknot with two eyes let alone one. And when you put the mask on with an eyepatch underneath it, that really fucks with your peripheral vision. When I had my original Slipknot mask with the dreads on it, I would whip my head around and headbang and the dreads whipped around and smacked me in the eyes and scratched my corneas. Twice on the first run, my eyes got infected from that, which was fucking hell.

JESSE JAMES DUPREE
Jackyl

Everyone knows I swing a chainsaw around onstage, and during the show I use it to cut up a barstool when we played "The Lumberjack." The saw is real and I've suffered the consequences.

One time, we were out with ZZ Top, and that afternoon before the show the Hard Rock was having an anniversary in Miami that they wanted us to play. They had a huge cake, big enough for someone to jump out of. They brought that out on the stage and wanted me to cut it up with the chainsaw. I was cutting the cake up and making a mess. We were doing "The Lumberjack" song and a guy jumped over the barricade and ran straight at me. I threw my left hand out and I was holding the chainsaw with my right hand with the throttle and when I let go of it with my left hand I revved up on the throttle and the torque of the chainsaw made the tip of the blade raise up and it popped me right on the base of my thumb. It ripped up the flesh to the bone.

That was fifteen stitches right there. I got the stitches and then I had to play that show with ZZ Top, but I couldn't play guitar. I could only sing. So someone else played guitar and it came out okay.

MILLE PETROZZA
Kreator

We played Recife, Brazil, in the '90s, and there was this guy that wanted to sneak in so he tried to jump the fence. But there was barbed wire at the top that totally cut off one of his fingers. And he still watched the show with blood dripping down his arm and over his whole body. I don't know if he stayed to the end of the show, but he definitely didn't want to leave right away.

GUY KOZOWYK
The Red Chord

We played Hellfest in New Jersey around 2003. At the end of our set, one of our friends decided to stagedive. He cross-checked me in the process and I went over.

For a minute I was on top of the crowd, and then I fell headfirst to the floor in a handstand, but instead of my feet being up in the air, my shins were against the metal front of the stage and my feet were still on the stage. I was trying to move my feet but people kept jumping on top of me and as I was trying to pull my leg out, it was getting driven further into the metal corner of the stage by every person that piled on.

By the time I finally slid my legs out I had deep, bloody indentations in my shins that went all the way down my leg. I didn't see any bone, just a bunch of swollen flesh, but there was too much of a bloody mess on both legs to figure out how badly I was injured or if anything was broken.

That was the first day of a five-week tour.

The guys were all calling me BB shins—or Big Bloody shins—for the entire trip. I was just a mess. I used non-stick bandage pads on the wounds, but there was no skin on my legs so there was nothing the bandages wouldn't stick to. I had ripped the skin right down to the muscle. You never realize how much your shins come in contact with everything, or how many people grab your legs during a show until your shins start bleeding through your pants.

TOMMY VICTOR

We were in Wilmington, Delaware, opening for the Bad Brains at The Mad Monk in about 1993. It was right before *The Cleansing* came out. They allowed bottles in there and some dude threw a bottle and it hit me right in the head and knocked me out for about 10 seconds. I had this huge, horrible blue-purple bulge on my forehead from this beer bottle. And you could actually see the copyright symbol embedded into my forehead. You could see a little bit of the "C" with the circle around it.

JESSE JAMES DUPREE

When I cut up a bar stool with a chainsaw during a show, I always used a real stool. Then, when I was at Radio City Music Hall they gave me a balsa wood prop stool. I had no idea they had done that, so when I hit it with the chainsaw the blade went straight through the stool and into my knee. I needed seven stitches for that one.

There were two young fellas right down in the front row that looked like Beavis and Butt-Head. They were all excited to see the blood. I reached down and ripped my pant leg open to see how bad I was cut and then I just kept playing. I was bleeding pretty good, but I was able to get through last bit of the show before getting fixed up.

ROSS THE BOSS
ex-Manowar, Ross the Boss, The Dictators

Manowar went to England for the first time and we played a big show. Everyone from the press was there, *Kerrang!, Melody Maker, Sounds.* This was our breakthrough moment.

We were at the end of our last song and we all raised our swords in the air. For some reason, [Vocalist] Eric [Adams] threw his behind him and it barely nicked me, right in the hairline. It was just a pinprick. I didn't think anything of it. And then I felt warm blood flowing down my entire face. I looked down and my white guitar was splattered with blood. The audience didn't know what to think. Some of them thought it was part of the show.

When I saw how much blood there was I thought, "Oh, my God," and my heart started beating faster, so, of course, my head bled more. I couldn't believe how much I bled from a tiny little cut.

At the end of the song, I went backstage and they bandaged me all up. It was really nothing. But if he had thrown two inches lower it would have killed me because we used real swords and they were sharp.

RICHARD CHRISTY
Charred Walls of the Damned, ex-Death, ex-Iced Earth, ex-Public Assassin

I've had my hair singed by pyro that went off too close to me and burned me a little bit. But I said, "You know what? That's metal." It's metal to get singed by flash pots that go off onstage.

But one time in Public Assassin, a cymbal stand fell off the drum riser and the top of the stand cut a huge gash in our singer's back. He didn't think that was very metal at all. He literally pointed at me during the show and said, "You are buying a drum rack!"

It came down to me buying a drum rack or he wouldn't play in the band anymore. So the next day I invested in the damn thing.

KARL SANDERS
Nile

This wacky looking Wicca chick in Dallas wanted to meet me. She looked like she was going to kiss my hand, but instead of kissing it, she took it and tried to bite a big chunk out of my hand, zombie-style. I realized what she was doing before she was able to get her teeth all the way through. Another half-second and she'd have gotten away with a big chunk of flesh.

I started screaming and security had to come and take this crazy bitch away. I went and got a tetanus shot, so, fortunately, I didn't turn into a zombie.

DAVID VINCENT
ex-Morbid Angel, VItimas

We were playing with Iron Maiden in Mexico and we went to do sound check. The stage was fifteen to twenty feet in the air and there weren't any barriers off to the side of the stage. There were a few monitors but that was it. I remember looking down off the stage and thinking, "Man, that's a hell of a drop."

And the crew's like, "Ah, we're used to it."

We were finishing up sound check and I was trying to grab my stuff. It was a hurry-up-and-get-'er done situation. I grabbed my stuff and they were rolling Pete [Sandoval's] drums off as the next band started setting up their gear. I grabbed all my stuff and I started moving backwards. Next thing I knew, I was like, "Uh-Oh."

I had the wherewithal to throw my bass on the stage and I just tumbled from the stage and landed square on my back. And it hurt. I looked up and there are all these guys around me almost smothering me, shouting at me in Spanish. I was like, "Please, everybody get up. Let me just see if I can stand up."

I was very sore for a period of time, but thankfully I had no major injuries. I was very lucky.

ERIK RUTAN
Hate Eternal, ex-Morbid Angel, ex-Ripping Corpse

We opened for Deicide and Entombed on Metal Alliance. After one of the shows, I was trying to get my gear off as fast as possible. I was holding onto my rack and as I went down the stairs I completely slipped. My sound guy was in front of me and he helped catch me, but my hand was still holding the rack and it got all jammed up. It was a bloody massacre and my hand blew up to five times the normal size.

Glen [Benton] from Deicide asked somebody to get some ice.

I was hoping, "Ahh, it will heal in a day or two."

It took three months to fully heal. We ended the tour early and went home and I had to go through physical therapy.

KIRK WINDSTEIN

Down was playing at the 9:30 Club in Washington, D.C., in 2002. I was on stage right, and as I was playing, I walked over to the left to go jam with [vocalist] Phil [Anselmo]. And as I was walking, I didn't realize how Phil's monitors were set up. I tripped over a monitor and fell face-first while holding my guitar.

My whole bodyweight hit the ground and I've got a substantial amount of body weight. I jumped up and went to where [my tech] Grady [Champion] was standing. He gave me another guitar real quick and I kept playing.

"Are you okay?" Phil said at the end of the song.

"Yeah, I think I'm all right."

After the show, he said, "Dude, I was so afraid to look at you. Out of my peripheral vision, I kinda saw you fall, but I heard and felt it. I just knew you fucked yourself up."

Since I fell on the guitar while holding it, my hands were cut up, bruised and swollen and I was all sore, but somehow I didn't break any bones.

KYLE SHUTT
The Sword

Trivett Wingo, our first drummer, hated the drums. And he hated that he was so good and he took that frustration out when he was playing and I think that's what made him such a powerful player. He would beat the hell out of those things and totally bust his knuckles all the time. He was always totally covered in blood after he played. It was disgusting.

It's funny 'cause he would get grossed out over the tiniest things. I would sneeze or something and he'd go, "Oooh, gross."

And I'd be like, "But dude, your blood is everywhere right now."

CHAPTER 9: DIE WITH YOUR BOOTS ON

Near-Death Experiences & Other Atrocities

One of the pioneers of the so-called New Wave of British Heavy Metal movement, if you don't count Judas Priest (who came earlier), Iron Maiden were a powerhouse from the start, a combination of flashy riffs, twin guitar harmonies, and forceful singing delivered by a charismatic frontman. First, it was the punk-ish Paul Di'Anno, who performed on two albums and helped the band get noticed, and then, the theatrical, vocally superior (to just about anyone) Bruce Dickinson took over. "Die With Your Boots On," a song about stoicism in battle in the face of probable death, surfaced on Maiden's 1983 album *Piece of Mind.* It was Dickinson's second record with the band and showcased his multifaceted vocal style and tremendous range.

Not many metal artists under fifty years old actually die from a cause that's not drug-related or illness-related. There are exceptions. Pantera guitarist Dimebag Darrell was tragically murdered onstage, Ministry and Rigor Mortis guitarist Mike Scaccia dropped dead from a heart attack during a show, and a handful or artists over the decades have died in motorcycle, car, or bus accidents. Aside from those tragic vehicle accidents (which warranted their own chapter, "Highway to Hell"), most metal merchants look death in the face and escape the close call, wiser for the experience, but not necessarily smarter. The folks below survived riots, accidents, shootings, stabbings, and collapsing stage equipment. And usually, they came back for more again and again.

TONY IOMMI
Black Sabbath, Heaven & Hell

When we did the *Born Again* album we bought four cars—a car each—so we could use them while we were recording and on tour. One day [vocalist] Ian [Gillan] had been drinking rather a bit too much and he was going around the track at [Richard] Branson's house and flipped the car and set it on fire. But it wasn't his car! It was [drummer] Bill [Ward's] car.

I don't know how Ian got out of the flaming vehicle, but he just walked in the house and threw the keys on the table. That was just one of the many close calls we escaped from unscathed.

BILLY GRAZIADEI
Biohazard

Violence used to go down all around us. For a while, it seemed like Biohazard shows were the meeting places for different crews to settle their beef and we started getting banned from clubs. At first, it was something that was cool, like watching a hockey fight. Then the shit got ugly and people got really hurt.

We became the soundtrack for the violence in the scene and we soon realized it was going to destroy us or the scene: "I went to a fight and a Biohazard show broke out."

Somebody pulled out a gun at a club in New Jersey and shot up the place. Another time, our friend Archie got beat up real bad outside of [the Brooklyn club] L'Amour by one of the bouncers.

When we played our record release party for *Urban Discipline* at the Marquee in New York in 1992, two dudes walked up to a friend of ours and one had a huge hunting knife on him and stuck our friend in the groin. He pulled the knife up and gutted him like a deer. He survived, but just barely.

ERIK RUTAN
Hate Eternal, ex-Morbid Angel, ex-Ripping Corpse

Ripping Corpse played Club Bené in New Jersey with Biohazard and Morbid Angel in 1990 or 1991, and during the third song I looked out and saw a guy laying on the ground in the pit. He had been stabbed and there was blood everywhere. The next thing I knew, someone was swinging from the theater drapes and a riot broke out. People were throwing chairs and fighting. Even the girls were hitting people with chairs. It looked like an ECW event.

Scott Root, our singer said, "Hey, pack up your stuff! We're leaving. Now!"

We got the hell out of there. It was one of the most insane things I've ever seen. It went from a great show to total chaos.

MIKE BORDIN
Faith No More

Sometimes the most dangerous things can be really funny in a perverse way. In 2010, our singer Mike Patton climbed on top of a Marshall stack that rose up from our stage set. He did a front flip off the amp and as he flipped around his hips like an Olympic diver, he landed right on my drum set. His head hit my right cymbal and his feet whipped over and kicked me right in the side of the head and knocked me off my seat and really stunned me.

It was kind of scary and dangerous, but at the same time, it was hilarious. And it totally felt like a real moment that you couldn't recapture if you tried.

SID WILSON
Slipknot

I was coming down the street on my motorcycle and a guy pulled out in front of me from a side street. He didn't see me and I tried to swerve around him, but he hit his brakes when he saw me, so I clipped his back side and my body slapped up against the back of the car, then flew about thirty-five feet through the air and landed on my face and then slid on my head another thirty feet into a pole and the pole spun me out into the middle of the street. I tried to get up and start my bike again, but I had broken two ribs and punctured my lung. That shit almost killed me. If I hadn't been wearing my helmet I would have been a squashed grape. That kind of freaked the band out a little bit.

FRANKIE BANALI
Quiet Riot, ex-W.A.S.P.

Quiet Riot had just finished doing pre-production soundcheck for the QR3 tour in 1987. I had literally just stepped off my drum seat. I was still on the drum riser when one of the lights, a par can, fell thirty-five feet straight down and destroyed my snare drum. When drummers are sitting down and playing, they lean their head right over the snare. Had I waited another few seconds to get off my seat, the light likely would have taken me out.

ROB HALFORD
Judas Priest, ex-Halford, ex-Fight

One night part of the rigging collapsed and this huge piece of equipment from the lighting truss came soaring down and barely missed me. It was just swinging back and forth. It was on a safety chain, but the moment was reflected upon because if either [drummer Dave Holland] or I had been a couple of inches in one direction or another, we would have been dead. These big lighting trusses have thousands of pounds of equipment and they're just hanging above your head. It's just something you obviously don't want to think about.

ALEX WADE
Whitechapel

We were in Oklahoma on our third ever tour and a piece of the lighting rig actually fell from where it was hanging and barely hit me. It cut me up and bruised my face a little, but it was scary as fuck. If it had been bigger or had hit me more direct who knows what could have happened?

MATT BACHAND
ex-Shadows Fall, Times of Grace

In the early 2000s, Shadows Fall were playing with King Diamond. He had these wooden candelabras on either side of the stage. At the Trocadero in Philly they were up on the PA and the PA there is kind of angled. For some reason, they put them up there so they were slanted.

There were two or three opening bands and as the night went on, they were shaking and moving closer and closer to the edge. Right before we went on, I was at my pedalboard line checking. Our intro music was going on and one of the candelabras fell off and smashed right into my face and then cut open my left hand. I still have a scar from that.

We went onstage and my hand dripped blood the entire set and splattered my guitar. At the end of the show, I wrapped my hand in a big towel since I was still bleeding. Since I couldn't see it I didn't know how bad it was. Then I took a look and I was like, "Holy shit!"

I didn't go to the hospital. I just taped it up tight and I was okay.

BEN WEINMAN
The Dillinger Escape Plan

Once in France, I fell off an old, rusty light [I had climbed up] and cut my whole back open and I broke a rib at the same time. That was gnarly.

Another time we were there, I climbed up a speaker and it started to tip. It was a giant stack and I thought I was going to fall on the ground and crush some people. So I pushed off to save everyone and I went flying off this thing. It was so high up that I could easily have broken my neck. But somehow I threw my hand up in the air and I reached out and there was one of those ropes that people use to climb up on lighting rigs. I grabbed it and swung out of the crowd like Spider-Man.

It was basically a miracle because I didn't get hurt at all and I easily could have died right then and there.

MICHAEL SWEET
Stryper

We had light trusses come down and almost hit us. In 1989, pyro went off too close to my brother [and drummer Robert]. He was literally like a cartoon character. He was all black from the powder and you could see his eyes.

CRONOS
Venom

[Megaforce Records founder] Jonny Z booked us to play two shows in Staten Island with Metallica. Of course, Venom is known for lots of pyrotechnics and before the show Jonny told us that he couldn't get any pyro in America. We couldn't believe it. So we put the pyrotechnics in the back of all the speaker cabinets and we sent the gear over by ship and it took nearly three months to get to America. We had to send the equipment three months before those shows. And when the big truck arrived at Jonny Z's house, we took all the equipment out and we took the screwdrivers out and started taking the backs off the cabinets. And we started pulling out all this titanium and fuses and blasting powder.

Wow. If that that had gone off on that cargo vessel it would have sank in the middle of the Atlantic and no one would have known why. There was enough explosives inside the speakers to totally, totally bring the ship down. And that's what we used at the Staten Island show and we burned holes in the stage so big that the venue was actually closed down after the second Venom show. It's never been used for a concert since.

MANTAS
Venom

We had two pyro guys at the shows at the Paramount Theater in Staten Island. They had these huge boxes at the front of the stage which were full of sand and then there was cast iron containers inside them and they then had the pyro powder put into them. I think there was about eight boxes along the front of the stage maybe and there was three of these containers in each one and the pyro powder was poured into the measured amount and then just before the show to my recollection the second pyro guy went fuck the pyro pots?

So he ran around and filled them up again and the resulting explosion was, fuck me, it was colossal, I mean it took the bass stack out completely. I mean it just fucking wrecked it with the impact.

And at the end of the show there was a hole in the stage, and one of the pots was missing and it was found in the back wall of the balcony. We were very lucky. But you know the whole thing was a huge learning experience for us. It wasn't like it is today. You know, every pyrotechnician has to be licensed and correct and all this kind of stuff.

That's what we wanted to do, though. We wanted to be over the top. We wanted to really go for it.

SAM RIVERS
Limp Bizkit

We used a bunch of pyro. We would mark the areas where the explosions would go off and there were different colors for each song. On your setlist, it would be colored blue, green, yellow or pink and we'd know exactly when those cues were going to be. The pyro guy was on the side of the stage one night and he fired off one of them completely wrong and I almost was in the middle of it. All my hair was singed and my skin got red, but didn't burn too bad. It wasn't horribly painful. Fred [Durst] saw it happening and he proceeded to show the guy that he fucked up by throwing a mic at him.

JOHN GALLAGHER
Raven

Back in 1985, we had a very entertaining gentleman named Arwin working with us. He was a black fellow with wild, curly hair, rings on his fingers, and bells on his toes and he talked like Roger Moore. We asked him to make us a rocket-firing guitar. So he came up with this contraption for one of Mark [Gallagher's] guitars that was basically a three-inch-long socket wrench, which he mounted on the back of Mark's headstock. It was like a mortar. He filled it full of junk.

There was a magnetic switch for a cable that came down the back of the guitar neck and Mark would have this trigger on his wrist. At the appropriate moment, he'd point the guitar at the ceiling, push the switch and KABOOM!

Well, KABOOM! happened, but not as we planned. Mark's headstock blew off his guitar and it was amazing that Mark didn't blow up with it. Flames shot out of the guitar and set the roof on fire. Our roadies immediately grabbed fire extinguishers and frantically tried to put out the flames. We were choking on the fire extinguisher powder. It was complete chaos for five minutes. People were running out of the venue in droves, but we got the fire out.

JEFF BECERRA
Possessed

I was twenty-two years old and I knew I was too young to give up making music and too old to keep fucking off. So I was drinking less and getting clean. I stopped to get a pack of cigarettes on the way home one day and I flashed a $100 bill. On the way out, two guys came running up: "Give me all your fucking money!"

They cornered me between a wall and a Volvo. One guy was covering me from fifteen feet away to keep me from running. And the other gunman was pushing his gun into my stomach and against my chest really hard. I should have just given them the fuckin' money, but I resisted.

They rifled through my pockets. One guy's hand slid right over the $1,300 in my back left pocket. I puckered my backside in so he couldn't get a good feel on it and he missed it. I think he felt intimidated even though he had a gun. First of all, I was bigger than him. I'm six-foot-three and I was looking for an in to try to grab that gun. I wanted to snatch it, shoot him, and possibly shoot through him to the other gunman.

But before I could work that out, he took the pack of Camels from my front left breast pocket, put the gun right where the Camels were and pulled the trigger point-blank. BAM!

The second gunman had a .22 caliber and shot two times in a knee-jerk reaction, POP! POP! He was scared and stupid. A bullet went right by his buddy's head and clicked off my right ring finger backwards and whizzed by my right ear. I held my hand up defensively and prevented the bullet from hitting my forehead.

Then, I dropped like a bag of sand. I knew I was paralyzed . . . [to be continued]

DINO CAZARES
Fear Factory, Divine Heresy, Brujeria, Asesino

We were on tour with Obituary and we were in Kansas City. I used to wear a shirt that said, "End Racism." The shirt was by the record company Alternative Tentacles. One day in Kansas this skinhead jumped onstage and pulled a gun on me.

"Take your shirt off," he said.

I took my shirt off and then security came out and the guy took off running. But I almost got shot because of my fuckin' shirt.

FRANKIE BANALI

A promoter in Germany pulled a gun on me. Quiet Riot were huge at the time and he said he didn't think the band was as big as we seemed to think we were. He was really mad and he said, "Well, I should just shoot you," and he pulled a gun out of a drawer.

I said, "You better make sure you either hit me here (and I pointed to my head) or here (I pointed to my heart) because if you don't, I'm gonna fuckin' kill you."

Then he put the gun back in his drawer and I walked out of the room.

JEFF BECERRA

[continued] . . . The bullet hit my finger and it was hanging off backwards, dangling, and squirting blood out two feet like a Monty Python sketch. I hunched over and coiled up as much as possible. I pinched my right armpit between my ring finger and my thumb and held it tight like a tourniquet, so it didn't keep squirting or I would have bled out.

The bullet that went into my chest busted through the ribs on my front left side and smashed through the lung and stuck between my heart and spine. That numbed everything. I didn't feel the pain except for the actual wound, which smelled like steak and was smoking.

I lay there and the first gunman put his weapon to my forehead and tried to make a kill shot but the gun jammed. He started slapping the side of the gun and it didn't work. Then, he and his partner ran off and the gun must have unlocked because they were shooting over their shoulders and the bullets were hitting all around.

Once they left, I lay there and scooted on my elbows under the Volvo and hid there. I thought, "Well, at least they didn't hit my heart. I know I'm paralyzed, but I'm motherfucking Jeff Becerra and I'll get through this."

Ironically enough, the finger was more painful than the chest. I waited forty-five minutes or so and this little black girl walked by and I said, "Hey, call 911!"

She jumped 'cause she thought I was dead.

She said, "I can't! I live here. These guys will fuck me up!"

I said, "Well, I'll give you ten bucks."

And she said, "ten bucks!" and her eyes got real wide. I reached in really quick with my good hand and got a ten and gave it to her.

Sure enough, twenty minutes later this rookie cop came speeding up and slammed on the brakes. He got out. He had bright red hair and couldn't have been any older than twenty-three.

"This is my first solo call! he said. "I can't believe this is fucking happening!"

"Get me an ambulance," I said.

He had his gun out and totally had my back. He called an ambulance and they showed up another fifteen minutes later. They took me to the critical care facility and that was the beginning of four to five months in the hospital. I'm paralyzed from the chest down and I'm in a wheelchair, but I can still play shows.

WILL CARROLL
Death Angel, ex-Machine Head

Our one and only time playing Bosnia was in 2013. We were onstage and the crowd was moshing and stage diving. But the security guards were in front of us roughing kids up and being really aggressive.

At one point, there were four or five kids onstage running around and jumping off the stage. Our bass player Damien [Sisson] later said he couldn't tell the difference between the security guards and the kids. He was pushing kids off the stage to keep them from getting hurt. And he ended up kicking off one of the security guards. He put his foot into his back and kicked him into the crowd. These were the same kids the security guard was roughing up earlier so they wouldn't let him down. They crowd-surfed him around the venue and he didn't want to be crowd surfing. At the end of the song, he finally got down.

We didn't think anything of it so we finished our set.

After the show, we were in our dressing room for maybe two minutes. The dude came running in and hit Damien with a nightstick in the hip and started screaming at him in Bosnian. Damien walked up to him and the security guy pulled out a gun and stuck it right in Damien's face and then in [guitarist] Rob Cavestany's face. Then he turned and looked at me and I put my hands in the air.

Right then, the promoter came running in and threw himself in front of the gun and started begging him in Bosnian not to shoot us.

Finally, another security guard came in and grabbed the first one and he put his gun away and they walked out.

JOHN GALLAGHER

Our father died and we had to go to England for his funeral. I flew back to America on September 10, 2001, and my brother [and guitarist Mark Gallagher] and his wife flew back on September 11 and, [because of the terrorist attacks that day], they promptly spent the next two weeks in Ganda, Canada, where they diverted most of the air traffic. Then Mark came back and immediately had a car accident. Somebody was driving with their lights off and ran right into him. Mark's head hit the windshield and he had a huge lump on his head.

But he had to go to a job site to pick up money from a friend of his. They were building a huge drugstore at this job site so everyone had to wear a helmet. Well, he couldn't wear one because of the lump on his head from the car accident. He just had a baseball hat on and it actually saved his life.

It was extremely windy that day. They had a huge wall built up that was about a hundred fifty feet long, twenty feet wide, and fifty feet high and it wasn't braced properly. The wind blew his hat off. He went to get the hat and the wind blew it again. He chased it again. And then without warning the whole wall came down and landed on his legs, ripping the calf off one leg and sticking a piece of rebar metal all the way through the other, dislocating both of his feet and a knee. It ripped all the skin off one leg.

Mark called me on the phone laughing.

"What's going on?" I said, expecting a funny story.

"You won't believe where I am right now," he said.

"Where's that?" I replied.

"I'm under a wall. A wall fell on me."

I thought he was joking!

"Ohh, okay. That's good. I'm busy. I'll talk to you later," I said, completely unaware of what had happened.

Mark was in shock so he kept giggling. They had to call a medevac to get him out. At first, they thought he wasn't going to live, then they thought they were going to have to amputate both legs. Then, they said they'd just have to amputate one leg. Then it was, "We can save the legs but he'll never walk again."

At every turn he said, "No, fuck you. I'm keeping my legs. I'll get well."

He proved them all wrong, which is remarkable. He was in a wheelchair for three years. Then we started playing festivals with him in 2005 when he was wearing a Mad Max-style brace. Then in 2009, he started wearing a leg brace. And he gradually got better to the point where he can perform onstage standing up and even run around.

It took the lion's share of nine years for him to recover. He's still got some issues. His knees and ankles hurt all the time, but you'd never notice it. And we're still touring like crazy and recording, which is really a miracle.

BILLY GRAZIADEI

One time, me and [Biohazard vocalist] Evan [Seinfeld] went out with some friends to this after-hours place called The Cooler, which was in the meatpacking district in the West Side of New York City. The underground clubs there started at 2 a.m. and they went until noon.

We came out all fucked up at 7 a.m. A couple dudes I was with were getting coffee. I was with my homegirl Chris, who was this skinhead chick from Pennsylvania. We were on 14th Street and Eighth Avenue. She was talking to a hooker on the corner.

"How can you do that? You're demeaning women. You're demeaning yourself. Get a job. Don't sell your body," She said.

The prostitute said, "Fuck you, bitch" and pulled her skirt up. She had a giant cock swinging in the fucking wind.

Chris kicked her in the balls and the hooker ran away down the street. Chris ran after the hooker. My friends and I chased Chris to try to stop her. Suddenly there were three or four prostitutes standing together. They threw a bottle at Chris and it smashed at our feet.

Now we had beef with these prostitutes, so we started chasing them. They went across the street and down an alley, then they stopped. They weren't scared anymore, which raised a red flag in my brain.

"Nah, they've got something planned. Let's go," I said.

We turned around and walked back to get the car and [Biohazard vocalist] Evan [Seinfeld] split to get his ride. He had a Cadillac that his father gave him. It was his Dadillac. He put air shocks in the back and the shit was jacked up so high the front bumper scraped the ground when you crossed the street and the back was at what seemed like a 45-degree angle.

The rest of us started walking the other way.

Suddenly, my buddy grabbed me by the chest and yelled, "Run!"

I looked at him for a second confused and he turned and pointed at a hooker running across the street with a nine millimeter pointed right at us. She was only a few feet away and screaming.

The whole thing ended like a scene from a fucking movie. This hooker pointed her gun at us and suddenly Evan tore around the corner in his Dadillac as we were running back to 14th Street. He stopped, we jumped in the car and we escaped with our lives.

MIKE IX WILLIAMS
Eyehategod

I didn't use to give a fuck about anything. I didn't care about destroying my body with drugs and alcohol or dying early. It just didn't matter. I guess I had a death wish for a while. I had anxiety and depression, like a lot of people, and I had that attitude that I was a punk rocker and I didn't think I'd live to thirty.

But as life goes on, you find people who you love, and they don't want you to go anywhere. It depends on meeting the right people. I guess I did, and when I got a little older I kinda realized that I wanted to live. It was a gradual thing.

The band got more serious and started becoming more like a career, and we all wanted to play good shows and make good music. That became like a real job, and we enjoyed it because we weren't always wasted. I started cutting back on the drugs and alcohol, and started to do shit that was fun instead of self-destructive. Now, I'll have a glass of wine or two, but that's about it. I don't do hard drugs now, and I haven't been drunk for years. It's just not worth it. Not at this age.

DAVE WYNDORF
Monster Magnet

We were in Milton Keynes, England, two days before we were going to do the Big Day Out festival. I looked at our scheduling, and we were in the afternoon. I was like: "Aww, they fucked us over. We're playing for thirty minutes at 2 p.m." Manson and Metallica went on way later.

I thought: "This was our big shot. We should be further up the bill."

I got madder and madder, and I decided, "Fuck, we've gotta do something those motherfuckers are gonna remember."

At that point, I had a burning guitar onstage. I would wrap it in t-shirts and staple them to the guitar and soak it with gasoline and light it on fire. Sometimes, I'd hold it over my head and the flames would rise about ten feet. I'd swing it around or swing it at people if I could. But I decided to up the ante for this show. I told the tour manager to go out to the British equivalent of Linens 'n Things and buy a lot of sheets. And I decided to wrap the monitors and mic stands in sheets and set them on fire, too, during our cover of the MC5 song "Kick Out the Jams" so we could have as much real fire on stage as humanly possible, not this fuckin' fake pyro shit. I told them the stuff would burn off really quick and wouldn't hurt the monitors, but I didn't know that for sure. I was just guessing.

God bless the techs. They wrapped everything in the sheets.

When I lit my guitar on fire for these shows, the burst was so big. Everybody had cans of charcoal fluid to soak all the sheets. The plan was that I would use the guitar to light everything else.

I told all the techs, "If the flames aren't high enough, just keep pouring the lighter fluid on there."

It was like Dresden! I didn't know that since we were outside and there was air displacement, everything became a vortex. All the separate flames from the mic stands and the monitors went into one whirling flame. It was fuckin' explosive! The smoke was coming up in these toxic black clouds. I went, "Holy shit!" and ran off the stage.

I knew there would be mean angry men coming to beat me senseless for setting the festival stage on fire. They came down. They chased us. Cops arrived. Our tour manager threw us under the bus. Cooler heads prevailed. One of these guys who was stage security went to bat for us. He told the cops everything was under control, and it looked worse than it really was.

We never even got a bill. But it was fucking great.

I talked to someone afterward and said, "How'd it look?"

And he said, "Man, it looked like a plane crashing onto the stage." And I was right, the fire wasn't on the equipment, it was in the sheets, so the fire never got to the amps or damaged anything.

DAVE MUSTAINE
Megadeth, ex-Metallica

It was 1992 in February. We were touring and I was up in Eugene, Oregon, and a concert barricade broke, the fans rushed the stage, we ran out to the bus, the bus took off.

We canceled the tour because the drug use got so bad with me eating Valiums all the time. My wife didn't like the smell of alcohol on me, but I was too keen to be defeated by something as simple as the smell of alcohol, so I got Valiums. I overdosed, and my heart stopped. They had enough time to call from the hospital where I was at and to tell people that wanted to visit that I had died, and don't bother coming. Obviously, they revived me.

BOBBY LIEBLING
Pentagram

I was awake around the clock smoking crack for six days straight before a gig at the Black Cat in Washington, D.C., in January 2005. I didn't have any water, no food, not a minute of sleep for a week.

I was debuting a brand-new band at a packed house and I had just taken my methadone. The combination of everything in my system gave me a nervous breakdown of stress and exhaustion. I just blacked out. Then I seized because I had all the drugs in me. I walked up on the stage and the next thing I knew I woke up the following night at Howard University Hospital wondering what had happened.

I asked the nurse what day it was and she said it was Sunday. And the gig was Saturday. My mind went, "Oh no, oh no. Something happened. I missed the gig."

I wasn't aware that I came out onstage twice and fell into the drum set. Then I was rushed off and I flatlined twice on the way to the hospital.

MAX CAVALERA
Soulfly, Cavalera Conspiracy, ex-Sepultura

When I was a teenager, I was going record shopping in Sao Paulo and there were all these skinheads hanging around the store and fucking with the longhairs. I had all this vinyl under my arm and I was ready to go to the subway to get to the bus station. All of a sudden, I saw twenty skinheads running toward me with knives. I ran for my life and then entered this guy's coffee shop. It was an old man and I asked him if I could hide behind the counter. The guy was really cool. He said, "Yeah, yeah. Go, go."

The skinheads didn't see me duck into this shop so they didn't catch me. When they were gone, I went back to the bus station, came home, and I still had my treasure from the day's hunt.

PAGE HAMILTON
Helmet

We played at Roseland Ballroom in New York on the *Betty* tour. It was the last show of a leg of tour. The guys in the crew got shaving cream pies and I looked around and everyone in the band is getting smashed by these pies. I foolishly decided I was not going to get hit by a shaving cream pie so I dropped my guitar and dove over the barricade into the crowd.

It was a really violent pit. I had this really heavy cord around my neck with my now ex-wife's name on a ring that I wore around my neck. They completely tore it off me. I thought the crowd was going to tear me limb from limb. I had these giant red welts on my neck and these fingernail gouges under my armpits and chest.

I should have taken the shaving cream pie.

GENE HOGLAN
Dark Angel, Testament, Dethklok, ex-Death, ex-Strapping Young Lad

Dark Angel was playing the Whisky in L.A. in 1986 and the band that went on before us had a drummer who lit his sticks on fire. Okay, whatever.

Then we got onstage and I looked down and there was a cup that was filled. I thought, "Great, my tech Ray got me a glass of water."

We were about to start playing and I reached down and started drinking. Then I noticed these black little beads crawling down the cup as I'm drinking and I felt the liquid on my lips and it didn't feel like water. It felt all greasy. It had no taste so I kept swallowing it. And then I suddenly realized that it was kerosene or some other flammable liquid that the drummer for the opening band had dipped his sticks into it before he set them on fire.

People ran up to me after the show, "Oh my God, we heard what happened. Are you okay? Do you need some milk? Do we need to induce vomiting?"

And I went, "I don't know. I feel okay."

And for some reason I was fine.

DAVE PETERS
Throwdown, ex-Eighteen Visions, ex-Bleeding Through

We played the Showcase Theater and they have a rail there that goes behind the crowd. People would stagedive from both directions. There was so much liability I can't believe they ever had it that way because people would dive from this railing backwards. Tons of people got hurt and collided in mid-air.

One time, I jumped out in the crowd and people grabbed the mic. I was climbing back onstage and someone dove from that back rail and landed on the back of my neck and head. I had never been knocked out before. This was the only time I had ever had my light switch flicked off. It was like a dissolve at the end of a movie. Everything went white and then there was a pinhole and I didn't hear anything except humming.

When I snapped out of it, I was looking around. I didn't know how long I had been out. But I was looking around concerned, wondering, "Oh my God, did I get knocked out in front of everyone and ruin the show?"

But I had only been out for a split second. I climbed back onstage and finished the song and played the next song.

BEN FALGOUST
Goatwhore, ex-Soilent Green

Goatwhore were in Europe with Sepultura in February 2018. We shared a bus with Obscura and Fit For An Autopsy. The trailers are different over there. They have these big metal trailers and the doors are these ramps and they have this hydraulic system so the doors can come down. The doors weigh three hundred pounds or so but with the hydraulic system one person can open and close it.

We were in Rome on the fourth show of the tour and I went out to open the bus and the hydraulic system went out and the whole door came down and knocked me in the head and threw my back. I landed on my leg and foot. I broke my right leg and my left foot. I stayed out there on crutches and sat on a head case every night and did the rest of the tour, which was actually really good.

CHUCK BILLY
Testament

I went to the hospital 'cause I was experiencing a shortness of breath. My doctor sent me to have a biopsy, and they discovered I had cancer. They showed me an X-ray of the tumor, which was near my heart and was the size of a squash.

"Tomorrow, you're starting chemotherapy," said my doctor. It kind of went in one ear and out the other. I went home, and my wife said, "Well, what'd the doctor say?"

"Oh, I've got cancer," I said.

That's when it hit me. I sat on that couch, and me and her cried for that whole day. I felt sorry for myself that night, and then I went to bed and woke up in the morning pissed off. I said: "I'm gonna beat it. I'm gonna kick this fucking thing." That's when I got mentally ready to go. I started on the twelve-week journey on chemo. At that time, my tumor was too big to operate on. But I also underwent a Native American ritual, and, by the time the entire process was done, the tumor had shrunk to the size of an orange and they were able to operate on it and remove it. That was in 1999, and all my tests have been normal since then. Thanks to this spiritual Native American experience, I'm completely cured.

SAM RIVERS

I got liver disease from excessive drinking. I was diagnosed in 2011. I didn't really get what was happening back then. I stopped drinking and battled the liver disease for a bit. I got clean for about nine or ten months and went on tour. I was super clean, but my home life wasn't that great at the time and as soon as I got off tour I started drinking, and then drinking more. I fell right back into being a horrible drunk again.

It got so bad I had to go to UCLA Hospital and the doctor said, "If you don't stop, you're going to die. And right now, you're looking like you need a new liver."

I fought liver disease for a couple years and it won. I had to get a liver transplant in 2017.

I got really lucky. The doctors said I was literally the sickest person in the hospital. I had just been with my doctor, who's a surgeon, for so long, that he had the authority to get me in. I had been so close to the list and he just used his power to push me to the top because I would have died if they didn't do the transplant right away. Being so sick made me a priority. People with liver disease have a very low immune system, so they're susceptible to anything.

Right before I went in for the transplant, I got bit by my cat and I got food poisoning and I got cat scratch fever, which dropped my white blood cell count so low that I fell down, hit my head really bad and was rushed to the hospital. As soon as I got there, I guess I was trying to pull off all the tubes and electrodes that they had on me.

I don't remember any of that.

So, they put me under an induced coma for two weeks until they found a liver and then they pulled me out. But the liver wasn't a match. Then, one came in for somebody else that wasn't a match for *that* person, so the doctors held it and, sure enough, it was a perfect match for me.

As I started healing and I was beginning to walk and do rehab, I learned about people that were there for eight months waiting for a new liver. I was just blown away. I was like, "Wow, I've already got mine and these people have been waiting so long." They're seriously close but they just can't find the perfect liver for them.

ERIK RUTAN

I had E. coli poisoning in 2002. I think it came from a bad steak and I haven't eaten any red meat since then. We were in North California traveling to Portland. We stopped at a truck stop and I had a T-bone.

By the time we got to the hotel I was shitting my brains out every five minutes and it was just pure liquid. We were supposed to play that night.

I went, "I don't know how I'm gonna play."

I got so dehydrated I passed out and had to go to the hospital. I stayed overnight and they put me on an IV and gave me medication. We had to cancel the show and, man, there's nothing worse than canceling a show. I had to be on a special diet for a month.

KING FOWLEY
Deceased, October 31

I was playing basketball and I thought I'd hurt my leg. My leg was all swollen. Then my mom died and I didn't care about my leg. I was grieving and didn't care about anything.

A couple months later, I was sitting there and my second leg was so big I was in tears. The motherfucker was so hot you could cook an egg off of it. Finally, it passed.

Then about three weeks later I couldn't breathe. So I went to the emergency room and "Nope, there's nothing wrong with you," they said.

One doctor there actually said, "Listen to you talk. You're hyperactive. No wonder you can't breathe. I couldn't breathe either if I was talking like you. You don't take a breath."

He did a chest X-ray just to make sure I was okay. There was nothing wrong.

Four days later I still felt like shit, so I went to my son's mother Carrie's doctor.

"You have asthma. It's that simple," they said.

I knew that wasn't true. They gave me the fucking purple Advair thing you see on TV. I sucked on that a couple times. Nothing happened.

The next day I had to go to Milwaukee to play in both my bands, Deceased and October 31. I went to meet everyone on the plane to go there.

"Look, I'm sorry. I think I'm going to die this weekend. But whatever. Let's go," I told everyone.

I went up there and somehow got through both shows but I still felt terrible. Then I was talking to a friend there, who was a doctor.

"When you get back, go to the hospital and have them check for a blood clot in your lung," he said. "It sounds like a blood clot that was in your leg and it busted off and now it's in your lung. If I'm right, it was a DVT and now it's gone into what they call a pulmonary embolism."

I took the plane home and, on the way, my legs swelled up again. The next morning, I felt like a fish out of water trying to breathe. I went to the hospital. A lady saw me and said it looked like my friend was right and I had a pulmonary embolism.

"We're gonna do a CAT scan and we're going to do a VQ scan on your lung," She said. After the test she came right back in. "Give me your right hand. I'm running an IV now. You've got a blood clot in your lung."

"What do you do now. Do you cut it out?" I asked.

"No, we don't do that and we don't want to push it through any further. We want it to dissolve right where it is."

They did more tests and they realized I was beyond a pulmonary embolism.

"Your lung is no longer blocked," the doctor said. "Your lung is dying. It's like you had a heart attack in your lung."

They put me in a hospital room for seven days. All these doctors came in to try to figure out what caused the infarction to my lung and they couldn't find anything. All my vitals were fine. So they sent me home.

"If you feel weird or if your legs swell up again come right away."

I went back to the hospital thirty-nine times between August 2002 and the middle of 2003. Finally, they sent me to a respiratory doctor.

"You've got the lungs of an 80-year-old woman," he said. "You may never get your lung power back."

"I'd rather be dead if I can't play music," I thought.

I couldn't even walk stairs.

Nine months went by. I busted my ass to work my way back from that. I started walking and then jogging. I built my shit up and I came back stronger than ever, healthier than I've ever been. For all of 2003, I was okay. It was a miracle . . . [to be continued]

PAGE HAMILTON
Helmet

We were in Canada driving from Vancouver to Calgary. We were going through the Canadian Rocky Mountains and it was a blizzard. We ended up getting to Calgary. [Drummer] John [Stanier] is leaning over and saying, "Man, I've got a stomach ache. Pull over."

So I gave him some aspirin. Don't ask me why. I'm not a doctor.

As it turned out, he needed to have emergency appendectomy surgery in Calgary. We had to leave him in Calgary. Tour over. We had done twenty-two shows in a row starting in Cleveland.

The first day of the tour we had an absolute blizzard and I thought we were going to drive off one of these cliffs into one of these great, beautiful lakes. But we made it. And the next day I wake up and John's like, "I'm in the emergency room."

And I went, "Ha, ha, ha, that's funny. Let's eat."

It turns out he *was* in the emergency room. So we ended up driving to Minneapolis, which is where our label Amphetamine Reptile was, and we stayed there for a few days. And John's parents had to fly him home, because we didn't have the money.

BUZZ OSBORNE
Melvins

One time in the early '90s I didn't know what was wrong with me. I was in Eugene, Oregon, on our way to Spokane. At first, I thought I threw my back out. Then I had waves of insane pain and I thought I was dying. I was pouring sweat. By the time we got to Spokane and went to soundcheck I was in so much pain I skipped soundcheck and went to the hospital.

I told them my symptoms and the doctor said, "We can't do anything until we figure out what's wrong with you."

They did all kinds of tests and X-rays and I was writhing in fucking pain. Finally, a nurse came in with a huge syringe and nailed me with a big shot of Dilaudid. Then she told me I had a kidney stone. The doctor showed me that I had blood in my urine and I was trying to pass the stone.

So I went back just in time to do the show and I was fucking wasted. I was able to play, but that opiate-based painkiller did a number on me. I got a giant prescription of codeine. I broke up all the pills into pieces and I only took one at a time.

The doctor said, "You gotta jump up and down, drink tons of water and you'll end up passing it."

I had to pass that fucking thing while I was on tour. And the doc told me I might have another attack. So I took little tiny pieces of codeine 'cause I was worried I would run out of them in the middle of nowhere. I'm not sure when I passed it. You gotta pass it through your dick. God, it's fuckin' horrible. But eventually, it quit hurting.

SAM RIVERS

Eight weeks after my liver transplant, I had to have open-heart surgery. When you have a liver transplant, doctors tell you to expect something to happen within the first year after the surgery and, most likely, it will have nothing to do with the liver surgery. For me, it just happened to be my heart.

I didn't have a heart attack. I was just having erratic heartbeats and wasn't feeling myself. The doctors did tests and said, "Yeah, your valve is a little leaky."

Unfortunately, they had to open me up. They put an artificial valve in and before the surgery, they said, "Get ready because when you get this surgery, you're going to feel like you're twenty years younger."

And sure enough, I got that surgery done and I went home a few days later and I was ready to go. I was jumping off the walls.

KING FOWLEY

[continued] . . . I went to bed one night in 2004 and told my son's mom my back hurt. I had never had a backache in my life. I somehow got back to sleep. I woke up and my back was killing me.

So I checked my phone and some girl texted me. I went to text her back three or four times. She wrote, "I can't understand what you're saying."

I could think, but I couldn't type. I figured I must still be asleep or real tired. So I went back to bed.

I got up again and there was a knock at the door. It was my stepdad and one of his friends.

"What's wrong with you?" he asked.

"What do you mean?"

"You look weird."

I looked in the mirror and my whole face was drooping.

Later, I saw Carrie again. "Something looks wrong with you. Are you okay?"

"I don't know."

"What do you think's wrong?" she asked.

"I don't know."

"What's the cat's name?"

"I don't know."

She was afraid I had a stroke. We went to the hospital and they checked me in. The fucking doctor I had seen for my lung two years earlier said, "You've had a stroke, man. It could have been caused by the blood thinners you were on for your lung infarction."

He had left me on blood thinners for one year. Normally I would have been furious, but I said, "Whatever man."

I wasn't mad. I felt happy. The left side of my body was destroyed and I'm left-handed. I didn't lose my memory, thankfully, but I lost my physical mobility on my left side. And I said, "Fuck this. I've been through so much already. I don't give a fuck."

I went to the Kmart with Carrie and my son and I got lost. I couldn't find them. My mind just wasn't working. Finally, they found me and Carrie said, "You gotta stay with us."

A couple days later, I went to the store and had a shirt made that said, "Don't fuck with Strokey."

And I told my band I am not taking time off again. We were practicing for our new album, which we were getting ready to demo. I went in and did the demo and I screamed into the microphone while this music was in my headphones and I remember my body going, "What the fuck are you doing to me?"

But I didn't care. I just tried to sing through the stroke.

I was physically just mush. I had to go to therapy and to like pick up quarters and throw balls. I busted my ass again to come back. I sat there on death's door. I was thirty-four years old. But I was happy for some reason.

The neighbors said, "We're so sorry. We heard about your stroke."

"Yeah, isn't it great?" I said with a smile.

"Oh man, this motherfucker's lost his marbles," They must have thought.

"Dude, you're done. Your career is over. You can't come back from this," my roommate said.

I proved him and everyone else who doubted me wrong. I definitely lost about twenty percent of my brain. There's a big spot missing on my brain scan X-ray. The side effects were hard for the first few years and in the beginning, they were excruciating. If I did anything, like dribble a basketball or anything to fuck with my left side it burned really bad. It was like having a papercut from my toe to my eye. If I went to take a shower, the water would feel like forks going through my skull. I couldn't put my head on a pillow. It was the worst torment ever.

"There's no medicine on earth—not the heaviest cancer medication—that will help," my doctor said. "You have to ride it out."

Luckily it went away after two weeks, but it was the worst two weeks of my life.

Everybody has their shit and life is life. Some people just get dealt worse hands. But you gotta keep on truckin'. Life doesn't give a fuck.

One of my favorite quotes was from Katharine Hepburn. She said, "Life is a son of a bitch. In the end, it kills you. It always wins."

BOBBY LIEBLING

I was a junkie, so I had all kinds of near-death experiences. Heroin's not like other drugs. It's something you need, not want. And when you need something you stop at nothing to get it and you do as much as you can and sometimes you do too much.

Many people who have died, then been revived, talk about the tunnel of light, and that's all true. You see a tunnel and at the end of it there are amoeba type-things. One I recognized as having my grandmother's face. But they're translucent and out of focus and they kind of glob together like a Sixties liquid light show. Everyone is beckoning you with their hands, telling you to come to the light. And you're sliding down the slide, tranquil as a baby.

But then, it looked like there was a kaleidoscope closing up the hole in the middle with these flaps like a propeller, and it felt like I was getting sucked back up a sewage pipe and I realized I was alive.

For all intents and purposes, I should be dead ten times over. But it wasn't my calling yet and God saw that there was goodness under all the callouses and let me live.

CHAPTER 10: THIEVES

Stealing for Food, Gear & Kicks

The opening track from Ministry's 1989 album *The Mind Is a Terrible Thing to Taste* was the first solid indication that the Chicago-based band had fully transformed from its dancey synth-pop roots to a style more firmly based in crushing industrial thrash metal. "Thieves" starts with a menacing staccato riff and evolves into a wild-eyed ride through surging guitars and menacing distorted vocals and includes samples from Stanley Kubrick's *Full Metal Jacket* and a Richard Nixon speech. "Thieves" was more than a heavy song about political manipulation and hypocrisy, it was storming new statement of intent—to destroy all that had come before.

Many, if not all adolescents go through a period—however brief—of kleptomania. At a time in their lives when it seems like they have little control over anything, including the changes in their own bodies, stealing candy from a shop or changing price tags at a department store gives the thief a feeling of power, and, if he gets away with the heist, the accomplishment is accompanied by an endorphin rush comparable to drug high. For developing bands, stealing can serve a different purpose. Some groups that haven't gotten noticed yet literally have to steal to survive. Others have stolen to construct stage sets or score better instruments. More than a few have taken from their fellow man to score drugs. And then there are the thrill-seekers that aren't much different than the average teenager stealing just for kicks. Sometimes, getting away with taking shit for free is simply a matter of opportunity and convenience, but sometimes it's a challenging ordeal and if everything goes south there can be severe consequences.

COREY TAYLOR
Slipknot, Stone Sour

I used to walk to school every morning and the first thing I would do is hit that convenience store right across the street from my house. I would

232 ⚡ RAISING HELL

fill my pockets with candy bars, then I would go to school and sell them for twenty-five to fifty cents apiece so I'd have money to buy cigarettes or actually get some food. It's kind of amazing I never got caught. When I was a teenager, I didn't have any money so I learned how to steal cars. Me and the people I hung out with on the street would either sell them or trade them for drugs. The nicest car we ever got was a '78 Impala, which we probably got a grand for. And then I think we just wasted it on narcotics. Shitty cars were easier to get a hold of because nobody cared about them. But they didn't make us much money at all.

AL JOURGENSEN
Ministry, Revolting Cocks

I used to steal cars and go on joy rides, but I never profited from it. It was more of a primal instinct. I was bored and I knew how to steal cars. Back then it was so easy. All you needed was a screwdriver. Pop the ignition and you're in. But out of principle, when you're on the road and in the middle of Kansas or something, and you're in these fucking redneck truck stops at three in the morning and everyone gives you funny looks, you've got to make a statement. So, on principle alone, I make sure I shoplift something. I don't think I've ever been in a truck stop where I haven't shoplifted a pair of sunglasses. It's just my thing. But that's the extent of my stealing. I don't steal from people I know and I've never stolen drugs from anyone. That I can say, because I've been the recipient of many a drug heist and I've always hated it.

It's such bad karma to steal from heroin addicts.

That's just gross because what makes you think you need it any more than the next person? You need that so you're not sick and you immediately put your needs above another person who owns those drugs to make sure he's okay. And you don't give a fuck? I don't think that's cool at all.

ROB HALFORD
Judas Priest, ex-Halford, ex-Fight

We were like thieves in the early days of Priest. We would nick anything that wasn't secured or nailed down—tables, chairs, silverware, and glasses. Invariably we nicked stuff at the very end of the show so we were able to leg it out of the venue while we were being chased by either the management or the bouncers.

"You'll never play here again!"

Once, we were playing a gig in Wales and there was nothing to steal, so we got into the catering part of this club and stole these giant bags of shrimp. We pigged out on raw shrimp after the show, which is not a very good idea, especially after you mix it with all the other liquids you consumed. Needless to say, it can cause some undesired stomach problems.

GLENN TIPTON
Judas Priest

Back when we were starting out, there used to be a big cage around the bar and the first ten or fifteen minutes after we arrived was usually spent trying to extract what we could in the way of whiskey and spirits from the bar with specially made tools with duck pincer clamps on the end so you could pick things up. Also, we'd never turn down the chance for a free mic. We could get thirty pounds for a Shure DJ mic in any second-hand shop. The DJ was the enemy in those days. He was the bringer of un-live music, so he was a target. Usually, he was a nice guy, so it was a shame.

He'd come around and say, "Have you seen a Shure mic anywhere?"

And we'd say, "No, sorry, no."

And then we'd go sell it.

MAX CAVALERA
Soulfly, Cavalera Conspiracy, ex-Sepultura

I stole my first microphone. We were broke and our gear was all shit. So we made a plan. There was this new wave band that was playing for free in Bello Horizonte, [Brazil]. We went to the show. They were horrible. We snuck in there and got right in front of the stage. And I told my friends, "When the lights go dark, lift me up on the stage so I can steal the microphone."

The lights went out, the guys tossed me up there. I grabbed the mic, shoved it in my pants and did a little bit of a stage dive into the new wave crowd. Then I went home to celebrate with the new mic—Shure '58, awesome.

GARY HOLT
Exodus, Slayer

Even as Exodus made a name for ourselves when [early vocalist] Paul Baloff was in the band, we would be in clubs or at parties and we'd take whatever we wanted, like alcohol and microphones. Or we'd go to the little small local music store and if we really needed something, we'd just sort of lift it—like strings or effect pedals if we could get to them. We didn't even consider it stealing. We considered it rightfully ours.

In California, near where we lived, we had a local liquor store called the Wagon Wheel that burned down. We had nothing to do with that, but we waded through the burnt rubble of this condemned building, risking life and limb to get to the alcohol. The bottles with plastic caps were all melted. [Guitarist] Kirk [Hammett] had this old Buick Skylark. We called it the Skymobile. And we filled his trunk with gallons of whiskey bottles with these black melted caps on them. We were scavengers. It's part of what made Exodus great, that hunger and ambition.

DINO CAZARES
Fear Factory, Divine Heresy, Brujeria, Asesino

We were working on our first record with producer Ross Robinson and he was friends with Blackie Lawless [the frontman] of W.A.S.P., who owned Apache Studios in Hollywood. We didn't have a lot of gear back then and [vocalist] Burton [C. Bell] found this equipment room that had a bunch of gear.

We needed a new bass head and a cabinet, so we ended up taking it from Blackie Lawless and we had it for a long time. He had a bunch of stuff in that room so I'm sure he didn't miss it. We actually used the gear on the album *Soul of a New Machine*, so it came in useful. I think we needed it more than Blackie did.

BUZZ OSBORNE
Melvins

We have been involved in a little bit of theft when we needed to be, but I never stole some band's gear or stole guitars from someplace. I never kicked in the door of someone's practice space and stole all their shit. I knew people who did that kind of stuff. Some people I know went to jail for doing that. I always thought it was bullshit. It's hard enough to try to survive as a musician without having your gear stolen. Jesus Christ, go steal something else. I was more along the lines of stealing gear from a practice place, like a PA or something, but not from other bands.

FRANKIE BANALI
Quiet Riot, ex-W.A.S.P.

Before we were making any money, I used to go to the Mayfair Market in my sweatpants and I would tie the bottom of the sweatpants up with shoelaces so they would be really tight. I walked up and down the aisles and ate whatever unperishable food I could. Then, I would steal a couple of steaks and stick them down my pants and walk out, go back to the band apartment and cook steaks for the guys.

ROSS THE BOSS
ex-Manowar, Ross the Boss, The Dictators

When we were in the Dictators, we were starving. So if we went to the grocery store, I'd grab some cans of tuna fish and pocket them. And I'd get some hot sauce and M&Ms and we'd buy some spaghetti 'cause it was really cheap. My specialty back then was pasta with really hot chili sauce and M&Ms. The chili sauce satisfied the craving for spice and the M&Ms were sweet. So you'd eat a little of that and you'd feel full.

KIRK WINDSTEIN
Crowbar, ex-Down

Way back in the late '70s and into the early '80s, I would jack little things from the store. There weren't any surveillance cameras back then so I'd take candy, snacks . . . and beer. I had a winter jacket and the bottom of the pockets had ripped so there was a huge space there. I'd go by the beer section of the store with a group of guys and they'd all take single beers and cram them in my jacket and then fill up the whole back of the thing. Then we'd leave and they'd walk right behind me so no one could see the shape of these cans poking out.

PHILIP ANSELMO
Pantera, Down, Superjoint Ritual, Scour

One night in 1989, Kirk from Crowbar was down visiting me as he would do quite often. We were over at Dimebag Darrell's house and we'd been drinking our motherloving balls off. We were in Texas so there was a cut-off time. I think it was Sunday night at 11 p.m. Well, 11 came and went and we were still rollin'. Dimebag busted out some Valiums. He'd keep them stashed for special occasions. We were drinking, taking Valium and feeling great.

But then the hideous, abysmal realization of having no more beer hit us.

Well, we couldn't have that so we painted Kirk Hulk-green, put tight cowboy jeans on him, boots and a long, dark wig, fake moustache, cowboy hat, and a button-up long sleeve and we drove down to the local mart. Kirk walked in casually dressed like the Western Hulk and grabbed two 12-packs of cheap beer, put another under his arm and trucked out of the store.

Thievery and wildness and drunken barbarity from a bunch of morons in Dimebag's yellow Camaro.

The dude would blaze and burn that car through people's yards and do donuts on their lawns and tear off. This night was no different. We tore ass home and cut through people's front yards and made it back with no trouble. And then we drank the beer.

TREVOR STRNAD
The Black Dahlia Murder

We were so broke I used to steal hot dogs in gas stations. That was my go-to tour move in the early days. I ate the hot dog while I was looking around at the other snacks. And sometimes I could even get two. And then I'd just pay for my Cheetos—or not. It was almost foolproof. If I got caught somehow, I'd just go, "Oh, I forgot. Here's a dollar."

DEZ FAFARA
DevilDriver, ex-Coal Chamber

When I was homeless, I used to steal from the AMPM at the end of Sunset and Western that was right above the bridge of choice [that] I was sleeping under. I wish I could go back and find that guy who worked there and thank him 'cause he knew what was going on. He would see me and a couple of other degenerates coming in late at night and he would turn around while we took stuff. We didn't abuse the opportunity. We just grabbed a hot dog or a burger so we'd have something to eat. I think the dude knew we were only taking what we needed so we wouldn't starve.

MIKE IX WILLIAMS
Eyehategod

Sometimes, I'd be so broke that I'd go to the store down the street and steal a couple eggs from a carton and go home and boil them. That was dinner. But also, I used to shoplift for fun just to see if I could get away with stuff.

One time, I grabbed forty packs of cigarettes from a store and I got away with that, which was kind of exciting. My big thing was going to Tower Records and stealing CDs. I did get caught there one time, though. I never stole an instrument from a music store, but I always wanted to. I had a friend who did that. He brought an empty case into the shop and put a guitar in the case and just left.

DANI FILTH
Cradle of Filth

We were recording our first album. I remember being in a pub and back then the band didn't have any money. I lived in a nice apartment but didn't have much in the way of furniture so I acquired things. I scored a very nice mirror that way at my friend's university. We went there to do a photo shoot and just walked out with it. If you're walking out with something quite large people don't automatically assume you're stealing it. Otherwise, why would you be stealing a large mirror in broad daylight?

When we were doing our first album, we were in this very nice Yorkshire pub and they had a Victorian or Georgian thing for getting rid of the ashes or putting in your bed to heat it up. It was worth quite a few quid, but it was really long like a broomstick. Who the hell could nick that? We had to literally walk out of the place with it through every part of our clothes and down our trousers. And then, adding to our chances of getting caught, our guitarist, Paul [Allender], who was a bit inebriated, decided to take it and smash a few car windshields as we went by.

MATT BACHAND
ex-Shadows Fall, Times of Grace

We used to ransack dressing rooms that had anything leftover in them after the artists left. We stormed into Willie Nelson's dressing room the night Shadows Fall played Milwaukee. A friend of mine worked at the Pabst Theater down the street. Willie had played there and was gone, so we ran over and stole all his dressing room leftovers. There was stuff from the deli tray and the veggie tray and snack food. But Willie did not leave the booze behind. It can definitely be risky to eat from a deli tray, but when you're making $50 a night and you've got ten hours to drive, sometimes you roll the dice.

MORGAN LANDER
Kittie

Mostly, we stole alcohol from our parents. We started the band in 1996 and we didn't start to get good until 1999. That's because my parents would leave the house on Sunday and we would just steal alcohol and get drunk before practices and then play badly. By the time we were touring we had a little money so we never had to steal to survive. But there was a period of time where I was a bit of a deviant and I'd steal a necklace from the mall or something. And I never got caught.

PHILIP ANSELMO

Would stealing one's PA system from one's future high school to sing through be considered pilfering? Uhhhh, that happened. I've only stolen a few times in life. I don't really admire thievery. But man, I was about to go to this high school and I heard through a friend of mine that there was a door that was broken. There was a way in. He knew where the PA system was. We could go there. We could get it out. We could steal it. We had my friend's big green monstrous car with this huge trunk.

So sure enough, we drove in and we rolled out four cabinets with two tweeters. When we stole this thing, our trunk was wide open and we had to maneuver our way underneath a chain link fence on a busy corner where cops were constantly turning and driving. This is the type of shit you can only get away with when you're in your teens. I can't even imagine trying to pull this wild caper these days.

REX BROWN
Pantera, ex-Down, ex-Crowbar, Kill Devil Hill

We always needed gear and I was in the school band, which had tons of stuff. So, on Friday afternoon I'd leave the window open to the music room. Then I'd take my mom's car late at night and drive it underage and go get some of the band gear through the window. We'd practice with it and then put it back in Sunday night before the band leader even knew what happened. It wasn't like I was thieving because we got everything back. It was more like borrowing without permission.

BEN WEINMAN
The Dillinger Escape Plan

A long time ago, way before Dillinger started, a friend of mine and I wanted to start a band but we didn't have any money for gear. I had a really horrible guitar that I used and a cheap guitar head, but we didn't have microphones. So we went into a church during the day and put a stick in the doors to keep it from locking. Then, we'd come back at three in the morning and break in and take the microphones and the PA.

I'm not proud of it, but for my first bands, I used this PA and microphones from a church.

ROB HALFORD

Sometimes stealing could be constructive. We'd play a venue and if they had a few lights, we'd always nick one. Our first lighting rig was put together from nicking this lamp and that lamp from all of these little clubs. We felt, well, if we take just one, they won't miss it, which invariably, they didn't.

REX BROWN

We'd go to Home Depot and take scraps of wood. We took a few at a time so we wouldn't get caught, and eventually we had enough wood to build a whole stage in Dimebag Darrell's fucking garage.

DAVE ELLEFSON
Megadeth

We never stole anyone's equipment or did anything malicious like that. But yeah, if there was an opportunity, we took it. If there was a piece of plywood that seemed like it was blowing in the wind, we grabbed it to use to build a drum riser. Everything was a bargain and everything was a negotiation to try to get it.

We built our first stage set in [Slayer guitarist] Kerry King's backyard. Before we went up and played our very first shows in February of 1984, Kerry was filling in on guitar for us, so he somehow convinced his parents that we could bring these stacks of plywood down there and build our stage in his backyard. We painted them black and borrowed every single Marshall amp that we could from Kerry and Slayer's other guitarist Jeff Hanneman. And we borrowed stuff from Jim Durkin from Dark Angel.

We were all friends, so we borrowed everything we could from every cool metal guy in Los Angeles County so we could have a stage set up for our debut in the Bay Area.

FRANKIE BANALI

We recorded the *Metal Health* album at a small studio and I got a really, really big sound drum sound on that record. But it didn't come easy. There was shag carpet on the walls and a drop-down acoustical tile ceiling that wrecked the sound. So I borrowed a station wagon from a friend of mine and, in the middle of the night, I went to a construction site and made off with probably 20 sheets of plywood. I brought them down to the studio the next day and lined them up on the wall so I'd get a better drum sound that wasn't dampened by the carpet and the walls.

When you're young and you need something all you need is a friend with a station wagon and another friend with a bolt cutter. Then, the sky's the limit.

BRETT CAMPBELL
Pallbearer

As a struggling band, we got stuff stolen from *us* a bunch. That sucked because at that point we weren't making any money on tour. We had almost all of our guitars stolen and all of our pedals. It had taken me ten years to get the pedals I had. I was so pissed.

SCOTT HEDRICK
Skeletonwitch

[Ex-vocalist] Chance [Garnette] and I were in our friend's place in Austin in 2008 drinking beer. Our van and trailer were across the street in this apartment complex. This guy who was there walked carefully by us because he didn't want to wake anyone up, and then he went outside to take a piss. When he got back in, he went up to us and said, "Dudes, I think someone's fucking with your trailer."

We immediately sprinted down the driveway and we saw this one guy in a pickup truck parked perpendicular to our van and trailer, and another dude was kneeling down by our trailer hitch. As soon as the guy heard us running through this gravel driveway he jumped back in the truck, which was already running, and he and his buddy took off. They had busted off the lock on our trailer and they were trying to jack up the trailer and hook it up to their pickup so they could drive away with the whole thing. We caught them just in time.

PHILIP ANSELMO

On this particular tour we did with Megadeth, my boxing coach could not come and Dave had a karate sensei with him. Me and this guy started talking and working together a little. I started boxing with the guy, and he showed me some of his karate moves. We got tighter and tighter, and he started hanging out with us more and more and partying with us a little here and there.

The next thing I knew, he was drunk with us almost every fuckin' night. Oh, my God! I stole Mustaine's trainer away from him and got him drunk! It was a little dramatic there for a little while. Dave was definitely pissed off, but I had a smile on my face the whole time.

SCOTT "WINO" WEINRICH
The Obsessed, ex-Saint Vitus

One time when we were on tour in Europe, we lost the axle bearing on our touring vehicle and we were stuck. Our intrepid Dutch road guy had spotted the exact vehicle that we needed a bearing for back in his hometown.

So we camped out in this German city and he went back home and yanked one off this vehicle in the middle of the street and then put it on our van so we could continue the tour.

BURTON C. BELL
Fear Factory, Ascension of the Watchers

In 1993, we were on tour in a van with Obituary and we were in Atlanta at the Masquerade. I was the main driver and one of our headlights went out. I wasn't going to drive with one headlight. We were done playing and Obituary were onstage. No one was in the parking lot so I combed through it and looked for another van. I brought my pliers and screwdriver, found a matching van, and I took out our bad headlight and took their good headlight and replaced it with our bad one. Then I went to our van and we had a working headlight again. Thank God no one saw me.

THOMAS GABRIEL FISCHER
Celtic Frost, Triptykon

Switzerland was a very conservative country and when you had long hair you would be beaten up almost every day by the other people, even by adults. And there was only one other guy in that farm village that dared to have long hair and he was half Indian/half English. And of course, because we both had long hair and we both were outcasts, we bonded immediately. He had an older sister who listened to hard rock. He would steal some of the cassettes from his sister and we would listen to the music. One cassette that he stole had Pink Floyd *Wish You Were Here* on one side and on the other side was Black Sabbath *Vol. 4*.

And from that petty theft, I discovered both Pink Floyd and Black Sabbath, two of the most important bands in my development as a musician.

MAX CAVALERA

Sepultura's bassist Paulo Jr. used to work at Cogumelo Records [which put out our first record *Bestial Devastation*]. They sold other records besides the ones they put out and they left it up to Paulo to close the store, which was a big fucking mistake because we were all in there. Before we'd leave, I'd grab a whole crate of records to take home. It was all stuff that I wanted and they had it.

BRETT MICHAELS
Poison

I stole a Kiss *Alive!* album from Sears. That went over big when my dad made me return it after I bragged that I stole it. So I brought it back with my tail between my legs.

KYLE SHUTT
The Sword

When I was 15, I used to shoplift CDs. It was really easy to steal them. You'd just peel the little security tag off and walk out with it, but they caught me on camera three times doing that and finally they busted me. They called my parents and the cops. I had to go to teen court and expunge it from my record. I was trying to steal NOFX's *Punk in Drublic* when they got me.

KING FOWLEY
Deceased, October 31

I used to sell CDs to survive. I could get five dollars apiece at these stores that sold new and used CDs so I'd steal them new from one store and bring them to another to sell them. Then the stores started getting in on it. They'd give me lists of titles they wanted me to find.

They'd say, "Okay, on Tuesday the new Metallica's coming out and I need 50 copies. I'll give you $350 for 50 copies."

We'd go in these stores wearing sweatpants and we'd load them up. I could get, like 20 at a time. I'd hit 4 or 5 stores a day I did routes. I'd go to Pittsburgh and do all the stores up there, then Richmond and do those, Southern Maryland. I would say I did at least $250,000 of business over 10 to 15 years. At one point, some of the store employees who were in on it told me they had these new things called alarms manufactured inside the CDs. So they started giving me these demagnetizers to use in the store. Or they told us to put them in these aluminum foil bags that would not set the alarms off. It was a good racket.

BOBBY LIEBLING
Pentagram

I needed money for drugs and I got the money from hustling, selling things, tapping my folks, stealing—every rotten thing you can do. I did everything shy of selling my ass. And if it was trouble, count me in because I wanted my drugs. I was totally married to the drugs for forty years before I got clean. I could be so rich right now. I made millions, tens of millions of dollars—sometimes in cash—five-figure millions at a time running cocaine for the Medellín cartel during the Escobar years. And I blew it all, every dime of it on my own personal whoring, car-buying, house-buying for my friends, buying Ferraris and chinchilla coats and diamond rings for broads and flaunting it.

I was 25 years old and we were running across from Bogotá and back in a Cessna every week and splitting $20 million cash three ways (laughs). And I shot it all up. I'm not proud of it at all.

AL JOURGENSEN

Sometimes I've tried to steal shit just because I was drunk or I thought it would be funny. I tried to steal a giant duck from the hotel bar at a

Sheraton in North Carolina during Lollapalooza and the police caught me. They literally drew guns and they were ready to shoot me as they were saying, "Put the duck down and put your hands in the air!" It was a 50-pound wooden duck. I was drunk as shit and for whatever reason I wanted it in my hotel room. I wasn't going to take it with me on the bus. It was a pretty strange night. It was the same night I had the first mother-daughter threesome I ever had. And I was with the mother and daughter as we were going into the hotel.

I said, "Can you two wait a minute? I really need this duck."

I don't know why it was so important. The security guard was there, but he didn't have a weapon. He told me to stop, I told him to fuck off. So he went and got the real police. Three cops with guns surrounded me. I guess the duck was really important to the hotel. One of the cops shouted, "The duck stays here!"

KING FOWLEY

We were staying at this hotel and I saw a Ms. Pac-Man machine. I thought, "I want this motherfucker." I was on the second floor, but I was like, "You know what? I'm just going to open the window and drop it out there and if it breaks, it breaks. If it don't, I'm good." I dropped the motherfucker out the window and somehow it didn't break. I put it in the fucking van and I was home free.

RICHARD CHRISTY
Charred Walls of the Damned, ex-Death, ex-Iced Earth, ex-Public Assassin

In the early '90s my band Public Assassin had a gig in Jefferson City. After the gig, we were driving by a junkyard and there was a coffin just sitting there.

"How could we not just take this coffin?" I thought.

It was just begging to be stolen. Here we are a death metal band in the middle of the night and there's a coffin right there in our faces. Like that's not a sign? So we took it.

I think it had been used, but I doubt anybody was ever going to use it again to bury one of their relatives. We took it back to our practice space in Springfield, Missouri, and we got tons of use out of it. I would actually sleep in it around Halloween to get in the mood for the holiday. Me and my buddies filmed low-budget horror movies and we used the coffin a ton for that. We took band pictures with the coffin. So even though I still feel guilty that we stole the coffin, we gave it plenty of heavy metal love. I think the coffin really felt appreciated.

JEFF WALKER
Carcass

I have the hat that [former Brujeria multi-instrumentalist], El Cynico used to wear. Then, when I played a gig four or five years ago in Rio de Janeiro in a real ghetto of a sports hall, someone got onstage and stole the hat and it disappeared. At one point there was a guy on stage with a gun threatening whoever had stolen the hat, saying that he was going to kill him. And this guy turned out to be an undercover cop and a Carcass fan!

Three or four months later, I got the hat back. A friend of mine saw it at a party in Rio and managed to steal it. There's been quite a history of theft behind that hat so today I consider it my lucky hat.

PAGE HAMILTON
Helmet

I wouldn't say we were officially stealing. We would rent vans in Minneapolis, Minnesota because it was actually cheaper to fly to Minneapolis, rent a van, drive it back to New York and pick the band up than it was to rent a van in New York. We learned how to disconnect the odometers so we couldn't get charged for all the miles we put on the van. We tied the odometer with a piece of wire to the bottom of the frame and every couple of days someone would have to climb underneath the van and spray WD-40 in the hole where the odometer went. We did that regularly because we would come home from a tour and we would each make $500 for the month we were away. Half the band would end up losing a job because of the tour but everyone was really dedicated. So the last thing we needed was the cost of paying thousands of miles on the rental vans. We would have made zero dollars.

SCOTT IAN
Anthrax, S.O.D., The Damned Things

As a little kid, I would steal comics from the comic book store. But I grew out of that quickly once I understood the consequences of getting caught. I never did get caught. But I heard about what happened to friends of mine who got caught. They'd hold you at the store and call your parents to come get you, or worse, they'd call the police. I knew that was something I didn't want anything to do with.

AL JOURGENSEN

When we were in Barcelona, I tried to steal a 400-pound bull out of a restaurant. The band and crew were eating there and I was just admiring this fuckin' gigantic bull. It looked about the size of the Merrill Lynch bull. Me and three of the members of the road crew actually made it out with the bull. But when we got it outside, we realized that it wasn't going to fit in the luggage bay of the bus. So we moved it to right outside of the doorway of the restaurant.

When you're involved in chemical abuse and you're being impulsive, you're not really thinking about the ramifications of your actions. I never meant any harm with any of these stupid thefts. I was just being an idiot. Seriously, I don't like theft as a way of life or a preconceived agenda.

ROB HALFORD

One night we were coming home from a show in London around Christmas time and we didn't have any money for a Christmas tree, so we pulled off the M1 motorway. There were various Christmas-y looking trees there. We sawed two or three of those down.

While we did that at four in the morning, all these eighteen wheelers passed us honking their horns.

We cut these trees down and stuck them in the back of the van so we all had a Christmas tree that season. When we got up the morning after we cut them down, we looked at what was lying on the floor in the living room and it was completely covered in black soot and diesel and oil and shit from all the traffic that had gone past it. There was not a bit of green on it anywhere. It was the embodiment of the grime and the filth and soot of the Midlands.

By the time we had a few trinkets hung on it, it looked a little bit festive, I suppose.

MICHAEL SWEET
Stryper

My brother was fascinated, and still is, with yellow and black. When we were young, we used to go out and steal road signs that were yellow and black. We'd go out late at night and bring out tools and unscrew the bolts and take them down and put 'em up on our garage studio wall. And of course, that yellow and black look became a big part of Stryper's image.

DEE SNIDER
Twisted Sister, ex-Widowmaker

Very specifically, we stole police barricades. We put them in front of the stage and covered up the word "Police." So they just said, "Keep Back."

We used them in our show because they looked cool, but also because we knew human nature. The minute you put a barricade up and tell people to keep back, they immediately go up to the barricade to see what the hell they have to keep back from. So right from the start we were playing to nobody, but the nobodies who were there were immediately drawn to the front of the stage.

They'd be like, "What's going on? Keep back? Why? Is there a crime scene here?" The barricades drew the audience in every time.

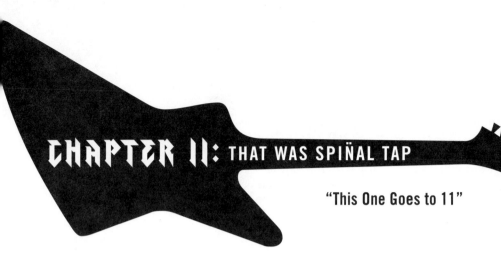

CHAPTER II: THAT WAS SPIÑAL TAP

"This One Goes to 11"

The album *This Is Spiñal Tap* was the soundtrack to the mockumentary of the same name and contained metal song parodies with titles like "Big Bottom," "Tonight I'm Gonna Rock You Tonight," and "Sex Farm." The album, which featured an all-black cover like the controversial *Smell the Glove* record in the movie, was the perfect accompaniment to the film—positioned so much like a real metal album that it kept the nagging "are they or aren't they?" question alive in the heads of fans who saw the movie and thought there just might really be a British band called Spiñal Tap.

All of the misfortune the band experiences throughout *This Is Spiñal Tap*, including malfunctioning stage props, disastrous promotional appearances, and mid-tour lineup shifts are both funny and entirely plausible. Clearly, the co-writer and director Rob Reiner is not only familiar with the traditional music documentaries he parodies, but he's also familiar with the lifestyles of musicians and bands and many of the predicaments they encounter on endless international tours. Reiner chose a perfect cast of actor/comedians and encouraged his actors—Michael McKean (David St. Hubbins), Christopher Guest (Nigel Tufnel), Harry Shearer (Derek Smalls), David Kaff (Viv Savage) and Ric Parnell (Mick Shrimpton)—to improvise dialog to fit the absurdity of the scenes. Had the actors turned their noses up at the music that their imaginary band was supposed to be celebrating, the movie wouldn't have worked. Instead, the entire cast embraced their characters and treated all the ridiculous antics and circumstances as realistic situations, which, in the world of metal, they are. Granted, it's unlikely that any metal drummers have spontaneously combusted, but countless bands have gotten lost underneath the stage, stood slack jawed as record label promoters and publicists proposed one inane idea after another and dealt with inadequate hotel and backstage accommodations. Ask any metal musician if he or she can relate to *This Is Spiñal Tap* and many will tell you it's the story of their lives.

REX BROWN
Pantera, ex-Down, ex-Crowbar, Kill Devil Hill

Let me put it this way. [Pantera drummer] Vinnie Paul, God rest his soul, thought *This Is Spıñal Tap* was an actual movie, not a satire until I said, "Vince, it's a joke. It's a spoof." He thought it was about a real band. But you can understand why. Everything that happened in that movie is based on shit that happened or easily could have happened to any touring band. We were a professional touring machine and Spıñal Tap shit happened to us every day.

RICHARD CHRISTY
Charred Walls of the Damned, ex-Death, ex-Iced Earth, ex-Public Assassin

With Iced Earth, we had an amazing Spıñal Tap moment in Greece in 2002 on our last show of the tour. Some of the road crew had a tiny Stonehenge monument, which they lowered down to the stage in the middle of our last song just like in the movie. We were all dying laughing. It was hilarious. I don't know if *This Is Spıñal Tap* is that popular in Greece because our singer Matt Barlow had to explain to the crowd why we were dying laughing and why we could barely finish the song. A lot of people in the crowd just looked confused.

TOMMY LEE
Mötley Crüe, Methods of Mayhem

For our farewell shows, we built this Crüecifly rollercoaster that I was strapped into. Every day, I looked forward to getting into the thing. That was my time to fly over everybody's head and get an insanely awesome bird's eye view of the arena. I'd high-five the scoreboard on the way out and on the way back. I loved that shit, dude. We knew we wanted to make a movie of the concerts, so we filmed all three nights. And on the last night it broke down! I was hanging there upside-down and had to be rescued. We were talking about not using that footage of the thing breaking down and using the shots from another night. And I said, "Hell, no. That was New Year's Eve and that's how it went down." I actually think it was fuckin' hilarious. It was totally Spıñal Tap. And it's definitely in true Mötley style. If it can go wrong it'll go wrong.

FRANKIE BANALI
Quiet Riot, ex-W.A.S.P.

We had this big elaborate stage set for the *Condition Critical* tour. We had multiple levels with ramps and an elevator shaft-type system. At the start of the show I would count off the first song and we'd start playing. [Vocalist] Kevin [DuBrow] was in the center elevator, [bassist] Rudy [Sarzo] was in the left one and [guitarist] Carlos [Cavazo] was on the right. We spent hundreds of thousands of dollars on that stage set and on the very first night, instead of projecting them to the top of the platform the elevators only got high enough to show the tops of their heads. I started the song and I expected them to come running down the ramps around me and go up to the front of the stage, but I didn't see them so I kept playing. Then I turned around and all I could see was what looked like three severed heads at the top level and then them trying to crawl out.

DAVID DRAIMAN
Disturbed

When we did our tour for the *Believe* album [in 2002], I would come down from the rafters on this giant "Believe" symbol. It was supposed to be this big, dramatic entrance and I don't know how many times it got stuck or just didn't work. We paid all this money for the thing and it worked properly maybe thirty percent of the time. When it worked, it worked great and looked awesome, but it got stuck part of the way down about seventy percent of the time. When it got stuck, I'd have to start the song from atop the "Believe" symbol and wait until the techs got it working again before I could get down to the bottom of the stage. Fortunately, it always eventually came down so I never had to climb down from the thing or be rescued.

JERRY DIXON
Warrant

From the moment we started playing shows, we built this big, giant Western saloon and we said, "Come hell or high water we're bringing this son of a bitch to the Troubadour [club] in Los Angeles" We had risers and lights in it. We had our crew guys and band guys and we made this stuff during the week. We'd load this shit up in everybody's Volkswagens and bring it down to the Sunset Strip and set it up wherever we were playing. Sometimes the doors fell off and there were other problems here and there but for the most part, it was nothing that we couldn't fix with duct tape. And once it was fixed it would usually be good for the whole show and give us that extra visual appeal that made the show more complete.

DANI FILTH
Cradle of Filth

In 2007 we were touring the States with 69 Eyes and 3 Inches of Blood supporting us. We did a gig in Anaheim at a House of Blues. I don't know how we got talked into it, but this guy sold us on a big inflatable castle to use onstage during the show. He said, "We'll bring it down. You'll love it. It's inflatable, but it doesn't look inflatable. It looks like a real castle. It's really rugged and you wouldn't be able to tell it's blown up, but you can blow it up in twenty minutes so it's easy to use." Of course, it was total shit and it looked just like a huge bouncy castle. The walls were round and puffy and it took up most of the stage. 3 Inches of Blood were in absolute hysterics when they saw it. It was just awful.

WILLIE ADLER
Lamb of God

There was a really important show we played at L'Amour in Brooklyn. Before we went on, we were all like, "Okay, we gotta put on the greatest show ever." We had labels that were checking us out, including Nuclear Blast. And within thirty seconds of the first song, [vocalist] Randy [Blythe] knocked himself out. He stage-dove and kind of tripped. The next thing I knew, he was out like a light and he was being carried out. I thought, "What is going on? Of all the shows for this to happen!" But the crowd was totally cool about it. Without any planning, this dude from the audience came up onstage and sang the whole set and he killed it. And in an interesting twist of irony, the people from Epic Records asked us to dinner. When we were there, they said it was by far the most dangerous thing they'd ever seen and they needed to sign us immediately.

DEE SNIDER
Twisted Sister, ex-Widowmaker

We were headlining in 1984 and I think it was in Cleveland, of all places— "Hello, Cleveland!" We didn't get a soundcheck so I didn't know that the place we were playing had an arena on one side and a theater on the other side. They build it like that so they could have a theater show by setting up one way and by setting up the other way it would be an arena concert that would accommodate a lot more people. When we started our shows, I was always the last one to go out on the stage and that night I was waiting for my musical cue. I heard it and I went running out and there was an empty theater and an empty stage. I was completely disoriented and confused because I could hear the band playing, I could hear people cheering, and there was nobody there. Before I could wrap my brain around what was happening, a roadie came over and grabbed me and yelled, "The other side." I didn't know there was another side! He pulled me out and threw me out there on the big stage. There was a full arena and the band was playing the first song. I joined them just in the nick of time.

WILL CARROLL
Death Angel, ex-Machine Head

When I was in Vicious Rumors, we played the Wacken Festival in 2002. I had just seen Candlemass and I walked over to the other stage to watch Destruction. On the way, I saw [guitarist] Rick Hunolt from Exodus, who were playing that year. We walked over together. It had been raining all weekend and all morning so there was mud everywhere but there were still thousands of people in the crowd. Rick's not that tall and I'm kind of short so we couldn't really see the stage.

"Fuck, this sucks, man. I can't see shit," he said.

Then I noticed right in front of us was a mound of mud.

"Dude, how come no one's utilizing that? C'mon!" I said.

We both stepped up on this mound and we were a couple feet higher than everyone else. We high-fived each other, started watching Destruction and all of a sudden—BAM!!—someone shoved us off of the mound from behind. I turned around and it was some woman and she was screaming at us in German. She pointed at the mound. We were confused for a second so we looked back at the mound and someone rolled it over. The mound turned out to be a fat guy with no shirt on and mud all over him. We had been standing on him watching the show!

GARY HOLT
Exodus, Slayer

We left [drummer] Tom Hunting at a Midwestern Roy Rogers truck stop for eighteen hours in around 1987 when we were touring for *Pleasures of the Flesh*. We stopped there to get some food and this was before the era of cellphones so there was no way to communicate with the bus. Everyone got off at this Roy Rogers, including Tom's drum tech, Todd, who was also blonde. And for some stupid fucking reason, Todd crawled into Tom's bunk. The tour manager did a headcount and he counted Todd before Todd got into Tom's bunk. And then the tour manager opened the curtain, saw what he thought was the back of Tom's head and counted him again. So he thought everyone was there and we left. We didn't realize Tom wasn't with us until we got to the next venue. He had used a pay phone and called management to tell them that he was not on the bus. He was sitting this truck stop with no money and no jacket. Some people fed him out of the kindness of their heart. We had to cancel the show and go back and get him.

JOHN GALLAGHER
Raven

We had these ramps that had Lucite tops to let the light shine through. They were an inch and a half thick. My brother [and guitarist] Mark was jumping up and down on it and he broke it and went right through. The jagged part of the broken Lucite hit the top of his leg and he had a red and purple bruise the size of a pancake for the rest of the tour.

MATT HEAFY
Trivium

We were playing on a really crappy, old stage in Rochester, New York once and all of a sudden my entire leg fell through. I didn't get hurt. I was just scuffed up a little bit. But I couldn't get out by myself. So [guitarist] Corey [Beaulieu] grabbed my arm and helped to pull me out, which was more than a little bit embarrassing.

GLENN TIPTON
Judas Priest

We used to go to this pub that happened to be in the center of the Hells Angels chapter. They were having a festival not too far from the studio where we were recording so we got to know them a bit. We'd talk to them and they invited us over to their headquarters. When we got there, I saw the leader had this incredible chopper. The forks on it just went on forever. I was looking at it and he said, "Oh, you've got songs like 'Hell Bent for Leather' and 'Leather Rebel.' You must be able to drive a bike."

"Yeah, I can drive a bike," I said without thinking.

I have got what we call track bikes, which go through forests. But I'm not a road bike man. The guy threw his keys at me and said, "Feel free."

I couldn't very well step down from that. I'd gotten myself into trouble and dug a bit of a hole. I thought, "It can't be too difficult." So I started it up. Fortunately, it was a key start not a kick start. I put it in first gear and went across this field, and halfway across was a great big mound of rubbish. I managed to turn around it a little bit because I could turn the machine left okay but I really couldn't turn it right. I realized I was in over my head so I drove the bike just far enough to be out of view.

"Okay, I'll put it in neutral and then I'll do a three-point turn until I face the other way and I'll go back as if I've driven all the way around the field," I thought.

As I was turning it around, it fell over on my leg and the exhaust pipe started burning through my trousers and burned my leg. I was trapped underneath. I manage to get up. I was covered in mud. But fortunately, as I picked the bike back up it turned around a little bit and it was still running. So I got back on it, put it back into first and pulled back up to the bikers. It had been quite a long time since I'd vanished, so it appeared as though I'd driven all the way around the field. When I got back to the guy, I accelerated a bit and I did a little bit of a skid to come to a stop and quickly put the rest down. I got off the bike and gave the keys back.

One of the other Hells Angels came up and said, "Hey dude."

"Yeah, what?" I asked.

"I had a guy just this morning who couldn't fuckin' turn the thing right," he said.

That was an experienced Hells Angel who had a bike himself. So that was a real test that I came through with flying colors even though it was falsely achieved. Honestly, I'm lucky I didn't kill myself on the thing.

MICHAEL SWEET
Stryper

We did a gig and there were tons of people in the crowd. There was also a pit bull roaming loose. My brother [drummer] Robert [Sweet] had feathers on his legs and the dog came onstage and started to attack my brother's feathers. He stopped playing drums and sat down. The dog left. So we started playing again and the dog came back. This went on for twenty minutes. Nobody could get this dog under control.

BRETT CAMPBELL
Pallbearer

We were playing Hellfest in France. We had stayed outside Paris and it was a three-hour train ride to the festival grounds. And we had to pick up a shuttle to go to the station. Since the hotel was on my credit card, I was still standing there at the front desk because even though the hotel was paid for they needed an additional three euros for tax. The girl behind the desk took her fucking time and what should have taken five minutes took forever.

While I was working things out with her, everyone else in the band loaded their stuff and the shuttle took off. I don't speak French and many French people don't speak English, or they don't want to. Twenty minutes later I got on the next shuttle and I asked the driver if this was the shuttle to take to go to Hellfest.

He said, "Yes." So I got my guitar and my pedalboard and got onboard. It turned out the shuttle I was on was not going to the right station to get to Hellfest and I couldn't find anybody that could tell me how to get to the place I needed to go.

One person there was trying to help me. I said the name of the city fifteen different ways with different shitty accents and then no accent and eventually, I wrote it down. And he said, "Oh yes," and then he pronounced it just like I had been saying it. He couldn't help me either. Somehow, [bassist] Joe [Rowland] managed to find an Internet [connection] to contact me. I checked my email and he told me the number of the train they had taken. But I still didn't have a clue where I was. Finally, someone helped him figure out how he could find me. Eventually, I met up with Joe and we got tickets for a later train after [drummer] Mark [Lierly] and [guitarist] Devin [Holt] had already left for the festival. By this time, I was completely drenched from head to toe in sweat from walking around this train station with my equipment and I was sweating even more from anxiety. On top of that, I had stress diarrhea so I was dragging all this stuff to find a bathroom to shit into those steel French toilets. I felt like I was completely having a nervous breakdown. If I had just died on the toilet like fuckin' Elvis I would have been completely happy.

Finally, I went with Joe and got on the right train and we got to the festival. By the time we got there, we were literally supposed to go onstage in twenty minutes. We saw Devin and Mark out there talking to somebody, just smoking cigarettes, looking like they were about to freak out. Mark had chewed half off his mustache just from being nervous. It looked like he had mange of the upper lip. I had brought tiny little shot bottles of whiskey from the States, so we did tiny shots for a little stress relief before we went on. We played for the biggest crowd we had ever played for at the time. It was about four thousand people and we went onstage and absolutely destroyed the place.

KEITH BUCKLEY
Every Time I Die, The Damned Things

We had a show with Taking Back Sunday in Las Vegas that was outdoors at the Hard Rock Cafe pool. People from all walks of life are familiar with Taking Back Sunday. Those specificities do not apply to us. It's a very specific kind of person that likes our band and it's not the types of people that would be partying at a pool in Las Vegas on a hot summer night. I looked out when we were playing and I saw people in bathing suits partying. They were in cabanas and they were ordering vodka bottles that come out with a sprinkler. I felt like we were the entertainment at a fucking techno rave or dubstep party. People were grinding in the pool in their bathing suits. There was such a weird, horny vibe.

Nobody could move because we literally played at the edge of the pool and all the people in the surrounding hotels were standing on their balconies watching us. It just didn't feel like anything Every Time I Die should be a part of.

At the end, I said that if anybody liked us that hadn't seen us before, I would happily baptize them into the pool. I got crowd-surfed off the stage and thrown right into the pool and a bunch of people met me down there. It was totally surreal. I was baptizing all these people at this pool at the Hard Rock in Las Vegas.

BEN WEINMAN
The Dillinger Escape Plan

At this crazy show in Sydney, Australia, people in the crowd were throwing garbage cans all over the place. Some people were bleeding from the violence in the pit and we were going nuts onstage. After the show, all these young girls ran up to me and asked for autographs like I was a rock star. I started signing stuff like I'm David Lee Roth, and more kids showed up. I slowly backed up as I signed shit. Then, SHTOOMP. I literally fell into a garbage can full of water and was stuck in it. It was like my ass was suctioned to the sides. A security guard came over and had to help pry me out. It was like, man, I can't savor just one moment of glory. No matter what it is, the world just won't let me have it. So eventually I got out of the trash with a soaking wet ass and I just kind of shuffled away from the crowd.

RICHARD CHRISTY

At one of my very first shows with this band Syzygy back in Kansas, I was playing a keg party at Elm Creek Lake. I was drumming hard and really getting into it. Then all of a sudden I couldn't feel my kick drum. I looked down and my drums had fallen off the stage and were in the crowd. I had to finish the song with only a floor tom and a snare drum while the crowd picked up my drums and put them back onstage. After that show, I started putting a nail in front of my kick drum on the drum riser to keep it in place.

DAVE PETERS
Throwdown, ex-Eighteen Visions, ex-Bleeding Through

Back in 2001, we were going to play a show with Eighteen Visions that we thought was in the heart of Philly. This was before Google Maps. We all piled in one van and drove and drove through rural Pennsylvania. We were running super-late and we figured we must have gotten the wrong directions. The road was lined with trees and there were no streetlights. We went down a small road and there was a dirt clearing. The show was booked on this field in the middle of fucking nowhere. Some guy had a cabin out there and there was a stage and power and they lit the whole place up with floodlights.

We loaded the gear out and there were already a bunch of problems. We were unloading our second batch of gear when we heard one of the floodlights get smashed and a bottle got broken. Then we saw someone running back toward the cabin area bleeding everywhere and shouting incoherently.

We thought, "What the fuck's going on here?"

We found out that the guy who got his head smashed open was the youngest son of the guy that owned the cabin. His dad or uncle came out and he got pushed around by the crowd so he went back in the cabin and came back out with a shotgun. Everyone cleared the area. All the other bands took off. We went to grab our gear and put it back in the van and the guy pointed his gun at us.

"Don't go anywhere!" he said.

"Look man, we just got here," we said. "We don't even know what's happening."

"Those guys knocked my glasses off," he said. "I need my glasses."

We were the only bands that were still there, so we scoured the area to find this guy's glasses while his son or nephew nursed a head wound. The guy was still holding the gun and we were afraid he was accidentally going to shoot one of us.

In the end, one of our guys found this dude's glasses in the middle of the woods and all of a sudden we're buddies for life with the guy. He talked to us about what a shame it was that the show got ruined. We ended up leaving without getting shot, which was nice, but we didn't play the show and didn't get paid.

BUZZ OSBORNE
Melvins

We opened for Nirvana on their very last round of touring. It was literally within three or four shows of them being completely finished. Their crew was not being particularly nice to us on that tour and the Nirvana guys were oblivious to it. Kurt [Cobain] was certainly oblivious as a result of what his lifestyle was like at that point.

We weren't getting paid a lot of money and the crew said if we wanted lights for the show, we had to pay their light person.

"Well then fuckin' turn them on and leave them on," I said. "We don't need a light person."

They said no. It wasn't the Nirvana guys; it was the people working for them.

"Great, we have to pay some fucking asshole to do lights. I can't believe you guys are extorting money from us to do this as well as having us pay to use the monitors."

They wouldn't just leave the monitors off and let us play without them either.

Our set was supposed to go from 8 p.m. to 8:40 because Nirvana were starting at 9:00 sharp. We were all ready to play and the house lights went off. We were there at the side of the stage ready to go on. The audience was cheering. No lights . . . No lights . . . No lights. Suddenly, the audience was no longer cheering, they were murmuring. We sat there for fifteen fucking minutes in the dark because this girl forgot that she had to do lights for us.

Finally, someone reminded her. The lights came on and we got to do a 15-minute set. Did we get our money back? No. We didn't even get an apology.

JERRY DIXON

About ten minutes before we went onstage in Dallas in 1992, I went outside to have a cigarette and I got locked out of the venue. It was an arena show and at those places you're fucked if the doors shut behind you in a remote part of the venue. Sure enough, the door shut and when I realized I was locked out and no one could hear me banging, I walked all the way to where the buses were. No one answered the door there either. I banged and banged until I realized nobody was going to rescue me. I had to walk all the way around to where the backstage area was. I told the security guard I was in the band and I had to be onstage.

"Yeah, right," he said.

"Come on dude, look at me," I pleaded. No luck.

I had to go back around the building to the load in area and I finally got onstage, but I missed the first few songs.

TONY FORESTA
Municipal Waste

We were playing in Seattle back around 2004, and while we played, I lost my backstage laminate. The security knew who I was because they had seen me back there, but they wanted to be dicks. I left for a minute and then came back.

"Nope, can't let you back. You don't have a pass," they said.

"Dude, you're being an asshole," I said. "My shit's back there and I need to get it."

They directed me to go talk to someone and while I was telling him what was going on, one of the security dudes came up to me.

"Can we talk to you for a second?" He said."

"What?"

Right away, a few of them jumped me and gave me a black eye. I punched them back and then the thing just ended. Once the people running the tour found out what happened, it was bad news—for the security dudes, not for us.

MARK SLAUGHTER
Slaughter, ex-Vinnie Vincent Invasion

We opened for Kiss in 1990 on the Hot in the Shade tour. During the show, I jumped into the crowd while I was singing, and a security guard thought I was an unruly fan. He started dragging me out the back of the arena. Meanwhile, I was hitting this guy with my mic going, "No, I'm the singer, you asshole."

We got out the back door and the head of security said to this guy, "What the fuck are you doing?"

I still had a cordless mic so I was able to go on and nobody really knew what was happening besides the people on the stage.

MIKE IX WILLIAMS
Eyehategod

We did a meet and greet in Slovenia, and when we got to this place we saw a line of some people and it went around a corner and we couldn't see any more. We thought: "Oh, cool. There's a line. We can sign some stuff." We got to where they were, and it was literally ten people who were at the meet and greet. The people who showed up felt bad for us, so they went around twice to meet us again.

I thought, "Now you've really made me feel stupid because you come around twice."

They didn't really speak English that well, so they were smiling and looking at us for the second time and I thought, "Hey, I remember you from five minutes ago."

WILL CARROLL

I get myself into stupid situations all the time just by being a goof-off. We were playing with Slayer and while they were on one night, I saw a wheelchair and I jumped on it and started racing all over the place. The backstage area was huge so I was doing wheelies and everybody was taking pictures and laughing.

All of a sudden I heard, "Help! Help! Someone stole my wheelchair!"

This guy was hanging out of the bathroom holding himself up by the door. I rushed up to him and gave him back the wheelchair and I felt like such an asshole.

MYLES KENNEDY
Alter Bridge, Slash

In 2018 we were playing at Red Rocks in Colorado on the Disturbed and Breaking Benjamin tour. We got onstage and started playing. We were rockin' out and it was going well. Then I looked out in the audience and saw people giving us the thumbs down. One guy put his finger to his neck in an off-with-your-head gesture.

"What the fuck's going on here? Do we suck that bad?"

Then I noticed there was a tarp hanging over the side where the mixing board was and the engineer was banging on the top of it. What I didn't know was that the front-of-house sound had gone out. No one could hear us and we were carrying on like nothing was wrong. From the audience's perspective, that must have looked ridiculous.

MICHAEL SWEET

We played for a sold-out arena crowd in Australia in 1988. This guy was standing in front of my feet rocking. He looked like a pirate. Three or four songs in he was screaming and yelling at me and pointing frantically. I looked down at my feet while I was trying to play and I saw something near my foot. About twenty seconds later I hit a barre chord, reached down and flicked the thing and it went into the crowd. It felt like a marble.

Well, it wasn't a marble, it was this guy's glass eye.

He was headbanging and it popped out of his head. For the rest of the set, he called me every name in the book.

BILLY GRAZIADEI
Biohazard

There's a scene in *Spinal Tap* where the guitarist Nigel [Tufnel] is backstage at the catering table and he's complaining about the deli meat being regular sized and the bread being miniature. I swear to God, that same thing happened in Biohazard. I sat there with my jaw open thinking, "Is this real? Are [vocalist] Evan [Seinfeld] and [guitarist] Bobby [Hambel] really standing there complaining about the same shit they complain about in *Spinal Tap?*"

They were saying, "Why is there fucking bread with butter and the meat doesn't fit the bread? What the fuck is that? It's a fuckin' sold out club. They can't find meat that's the right size?"

That was fucking hilarious and, of course, it ended with one of them picking up the deli tray and throwing it against the wall.

PAGE HAMILTON
Helmet

We were playing this club in Raleigh, North Carolina, in the early '90s. We pulled up and the place had a marquee that read, "MTV's HELMENT."

I told one of our big crew guys, "Let me get up on your shoulders."

He said, "Why?"

And I went, "I'm gonna take the MTV off the sign and spell the band's name right."

ROSS THE BOSS
ex-Manowar, Ross the Boss, The Dictators

At one Dictators show, I jumped down onto a platform and I was wearing a pair of black leather pants. They weren't even that tight. But when I jumped, they ripped from top to bottom. My ass was totally hanging out. I went over by the side of the stage after we finished the song and the guitar techs there had black gaffer tape that they used to tape over my ass. They were sticking it to the pants and across my rear end.

DINO CAZARES
Fear Factory, Divine Heresy, Brujeria, Asesino

We were on Ozzy's Retirement Sucks tour in 1997 and we were playing at the San Diego Cox Arena. I was onstage headbanging in front of 10,000 people when the button on my shorts broke and my shorts fell down to my knees before I could catch them. I don't wear underwear onstage 'cause I don't like to get my underwear sweaty. So everyone could see my schlong hanging out.

I walked to the side of the stage with my shorts down to my knees and my tech pulled my shorts back up and then duct-taped my shorts together so they stayed tight enough to not fall down again. The whole time, I didn't stop playing.

ERIK TURNER
Warrant

Everybody does the rock pose that we all learned from [Iron Maiden bassist] Steve Harris—the one where you put one foot on the monitor and one foot on the ground. I did that and suddenly I thought, "Damn, it's kind of breezy and cold out here tonight."

My wife was out on tour at the time and she said, "Hey, your balls are hanging out of your pants!"

The crotch in my pants ripped out and I didn't realize I was flashing everybody in the front row with my ball sack.

MYLES KENNEDY

Twenty years ago, I was touring with my band The Mayfield Four. We were on our way from Rochester to Buffalo. We got in the fifteen-passenger Ford club wagon and started to drive. All of a sudden our tour manager said, "Something's going on with the van."

We pulled over, and sure enough, the van was on fire. It wasn't that bad. We weren't going to blow up or anything, but we weren't going anywhere. We hitched a ride with this family that picked us up. It was totally a Clark W. Griswold *National Lampoon Vacation* moment.

These kids were in the back seat and one of the kids couldn't really talk because his tongue was attached to the bottom of his mouth. But the family was nice to us and dropped us off in Buffalo and we made it to the gig.

BRETT CAMPBELL

[Drummer] Mark [Lierly] has an X-Men power where he can shoot fireballs out of his ass like a flamethrower. We were next to the bus pretty late at night and this woman and some other people were walking down the sidewalk. They didn't really stop but she turned as they were walking. She had a cigarette and she said, "Hey, do any of you have a light?"

Without missing a beat, Mark said, "I've got a light for you."

He jumped up, [pulled out his lighter] and shot a Mount Vesuvius into the air. The woman and everyone in her group sped up and walked right by us.

KEITH BUCKLEY

The first time we ever recorded with Adam D of Killswitch Engage, we were at his studio in Massachusetts. [Guitarist] Jordan Buckley was recording a guitar part on one song and Adam's board lit on fire. Adam was really excited about it. He put the fire out and it didn't do much damage. It hit a few channels he wasn't even using so it became a very funny story; Jordan's hot licks lit Adam's board on fire.

JOHN GALLAGHER

We played in Slovenia on my birthday in 2017. The soundman disappeared before the show and I wanted to check my headset mic. I tried to come off the stage to find the sound guy and it was dimly lit, so I missed the stairs. It was a six-foot fall down onto the concrete. I had the presence of mind to roll into a ball before I hit the ground and, amazingly, I didn't break anything. Then during the gig, my brother, [guitarist Mark Gallagher] had a bottle of water and he threw it at me, which shorted out my microphone and my wireless system and basically cost me $1,500. No strippers, no wild parties, nothing. So happy fuckin' birthday to me.

GENE HOGLAN
Dark Angel, Testament, Dethklok, ex-Death, ex-Strapping Young Lad

Death played in 1993 in Bilbao, Spain, which we thought would be a nice little town. We pulled up to the venue and it turned out to be this burned out shitty shithole of an ex-church. It was basically this big empty room. We looked around. There were needles all over the ground. The owners told us to go upstairs to our dressing room. So we looked upstairs and there were no dressing rooms. There were just a bunch of wooden planks thrown across the beams in the ceiling.

"That's where we gotta go hang out?" we thought.

There was no working toilet in the place, just a porta-potty in the corner near where we put the merch. We thought, "Hmmm, this ain't gonna work." Our tour manager and [Death frontman] Chuck [Schuldiner] were both like, "We're not playing here."

So they kicked out a homeless guy from a phone booth out front and called the band's agent.

"Hey man, I don't think we can play this place," said Chuck. Then he handed the phone to the club owner and the agent told him we needed to switch venues or we weren't gonna play.

"No, you guys are going to play because each member of the band is going to have a high-powered rifle trained on you until you finish the show," he said. We're going to shoot you if you don't play."

"Uh, that sounds fair to us."

A few minutes later we went up to the club owner and said, "Hey, um, we have to get ready for the show so we're going to go back to our hotel to get some stuff and we'll be back in a little while. Okay?"

"Okay," He said, to our surprise.

Obviously, we weren't going to any hotel. We were gonna hightail it to the nearest border. As we were pulling away, the club owner realized what was going on, so he jumped into his car with two cronies and chased after us. We drove for a while and we saw these police cars. Then we looked behind us and saw the club owner turning onto an off-ramp to get off the highway. I guess he decided not to chase us to the border.

ALEX HELLID
Entombed

The first time we went to Canada there were four of us. Our vocalist [L-G Petrov] had left the band, so our drummer [Nicke Andersson] sang. The second time we were there, it was only three of us because the van was broken into the day before the show and our singer and bassist [Lars Rosenberg] had their passports stolen from their bags. But we needed the gas money to make it to the next show. So we played the show as a trio. [Guitarist] Uffe [Cederlund] and Nicke did the vocals on the first night in Toronto, and then some whiskey was delivered to the table after the show and they thought, "This will do wonders for our voices for tomorrow's show in Montreal."

Of course, it ruined their voices and we had to do an instrumental show that night.

To make things worse, the power kept cutting out. At first, we were happy. We thought there wouldn't be any power so we wouldn't have to play. But the club kept fixing it. People at the venue had been expecting us to be a full band and now there were only three of us. We joked that the next time we would come back as a duo and then as a solo performance.

TONY FORESTA

We played this shitty stoner rock mini-festival in Ohio and the sound guy was being a total dick. He had a talkback mic and his voice was going through the PA. While we were tuning, he would say condescending shit to the band. He had been doing it the whole night to other bands before us. So I walked over to him and grabbed his talkback mic from his hand and threw it in a huge garbage can.

"Fuck you and your shitty attitude," I said.

He was so pissed at me and for the next two bands I watched him have a big hissy fit, looking through all this trash for his mic. He couldn't handle being at the show without his little toy. It just made my night watching this jerk.

KYLE SHUTT
The Sword

The Sword were playing with Metallica in the spring of 2008. We were flying from Saint Petersburg to Riga, Latvia. [Pantera vocalist] Phil Anselmo was on our plane, which was so cool to me since I was such a huge Pantera fan when I was younger. He always seemed like a ferocious badass. So, the flight lands and there was a luggage mix-up, but the only people that lost their bags were me, [The Sword frontman] J.D. [Cronise] and Phil. The three of us were stuck in the baggage area filling out these forms 'cause there was nothing else we could do. Phil had a cut-off-sleeve shirt, cut-off cargo shorts, and he was wearing crocs. To a young me at the time, that was pretty hilarious. I didn't think this was where I'd be ten years after first seeing the Pantera video for "Five Minutes Alone" on MTV. And I definitely wouldn't have pictured him wearing crocs.

WILL CARROLL

I busted my left kneecap in my senior year of high school. I was walking to my car during lunch hour and someone backed out of their space without looking and smacked right into my knee and popped it. I had a cast on for months. And I had a big show coming up at the Omni in Oakland with my thrash band Aftershock. I was able to play the show using one foot for the drums and by putting my leg with the cast on it up on a chair to the side. It was really uncomfortable and looked bizarre, but it worked.

People were like, "What the fuck is this guy doing?"

And then they totally got into it 'cause they saw I could still play and we fuckin' killed it. I was really proud of myself so I decided to stand up and wave to the crowd and give them a thumbs-up. When I stood up, I completely lost my balance and fell right off the drum riser in front of everyone. Right after kicking ass, I totally blew it.

PAUL LEDNEY
Profanatica, Havohej

We were at our hotel in Jersey in 2007 and as I was walking down the hallway I saw two hot chicks in their bras and underwear. One of them went, "Hey, could you help us?" It turned out she was in the room next to ours.

"Okay, what do you need?" I said hoping I might hook up with her and her friend.

"There's something gross on the wall," she said.

"Well, what do you want me to do?" I said kind of annoyed.

"Clean it."

"What are you talking about?" I replied in disbelief.

"Um, aren't you the janitor?"

It was really awkward 'cause we were on one of the top floors and they were in the same elevator with me about ten minutes later going down.

SAM RIVERS
Limp Bizkit

Our stage set on the Family Values tour featured a giant toilet. At the beginning of the show we all climbed up this ladder under the stage and came out of the toilet. Once, Snot's singer Lynn Strait came out of the toilet naked, and I think it was on a bet. Nobody thought he was going to do it and right at the end he said, "I'll do it. I'm gonna do it." And he did, but that couldn't have been worth much. Nobody had money back then.

TOMMY VICTOR
Prong, Danzig, ex-Ministry

Ministry used a real metal fence when they toured for *The Mind is a Terrible Thing to Taste*. They used it for a video and it was something that kids could actually climb on. Frontman Al [Jourgensen] kept the fence that was used in the video and went on tour with it, which looked pretty cool. Eventually, all his shit got pawned or stolen. So in 2007 he said, "We're gonna do a new fence."

He gave $200 to these Mexican goth kids in El Paso who idolized him, and they made this rickety chicken-wire fence.

"Al, kids are going to jump on this thing and it's going to fall and we're going to look stupid," I said.

He got pissed.

"We spent money on this. We're gonna use it."

This was back when he was not eating and he was just drinking wine, and that's all he did. So we're in Charlotte, North Carolina, on the C U LaTour farewell tour. They set up the fence, we started the show and these kids jumped on the fence right away and it collapsed into the audience.

"That's it, I'm not playing anymore," shouted Al. "This is bullshit! Fuck these people."

"What the fuck is wrong with you?" I said. "You're fucking crazy, dude. You gotta go back on. Fuck the fence."

"No. Fuck these people. Fuck this whole place."

He went into the dressing room pulled down his pants down.

"I'm gonna shit right here!" he slurred.

He was grunting and groaning, trying to shit and all that came out was this purple slush. It was so sad.

SAM RIVERS

One time, we started playing a song and I desperately had to shit. There were no toilets around or porta potties so I finished the song and said, "Don't start the next one! Hold on."

There were these little kiddie pools backstage that were full of ice and beers. I didn't care what was in it. I dropped trou and it was going down right there. I finished, pulled my pants back up and ran right back onstage. I think the whole thing took less than a minute.

BILLY GRAZIADEI

Our rider always said, "Deli meat, preferably Boar's Head." That was the brand of cold cuts that we liked.

We once played a festival in Sweden and we walked into the dressing room and there was a huge, awesome spread of deli meat and in the center of this giant tray was a real fuckin' pig's head!

We thought, "What the fuck is this? Sweden is the land of death metal, but this is crazy."

Later, we found out from the people in hospitality that the staff of the place was walking around saying the same thing: "Why does Biohazard want a pig's head?"

JOHN GALLAGHER

We were playing Columbia and the promoter was supposed to pay us before the show, but he had an accident. He fell over and had to have his arm in a cast. He was crying, "I can't pay you right now, but I'll pay you later."

The hall was full of people and we were trying to play hard-ass. Eventually we said, "All right, we will play the gig."

We played the show and then afterwards we took four Marshall guitar amp heads as collateral. The promoter came the next day looking for his amplifiers.

"We don't know nothing about any amplifiers," we said. "Where's our money?"

There was a bit of a Mexican standoff for a while. Then he came up with the money and we gave him the amps back. We got in the van to leave. And as he came over to wave goodbye to us he tripped over, fell flat on his face and rebroke the broken arm and broke his other arm as well.

BEN FALGOUST
Goatwhore, ex-Soilent Green

We played a crazy wedding in New York 2015. The bride and groom had a friend who said, "What do you want for a wedding present?" And the couple said, "We want Goatwhore to play at the reception?" We got contacted about it and I wasn't sure the dude was serious. I said, "C'mon, is this a joke." And the guy said, "No, we're serious. We'll fly you there [from Seattle], feed you, and get you hotel rooms. And we'll pay you some money and fly you back."

The party was at this bar called Lucky 13 in Brooklyn. We set up and there was a lot of family there who didn't belong at a metal show. Then the friends of the bride and groom came and they were more into us. We had a lot of our fans there, too, because we were allowed to announce that we were playing this free show. It got pretty crazy. But the wildest thing was seeing the bride in her gown pitting and knocking dudes over during the show and having a good time. While we were playing, I looked at the groom on the left side of the stage and he just put his hands up and shrugged.

BRETT CAMPBELL

Back when we were running super-DIY, [Bassist] Joe [Rowland] used to have really long hair and it would start to dread almost immediately because we didn't have access to showers very often. Joe had this detangler stuff that was in a spray bottle and he'd use this stuff so his hair didn't look like a beaver tail hanging from his head. We were standing outside the venue before a show and all our gear was on the sidewalk. The road was a mild grade incline. Devin was helping Joe get his hair detangled and somehow Devin, who always wears cowboy boots, tripped over his feet while spraying Devin's hair. As he was falling, he started running down this hill to stop himself from face planting. The mechanical action of spraying the bottle didn't stop, so his finger kept squirting the detangler as he was running down the hill, so he was basically screaming and squirting the detangler into his own mouth as he ran out of control. He looked like a character in *South Park*.

NATE GARNETTE
Skeletonwitch

We drove a shitty-ass Dodge and a little trailer for three years. There was no air conditioning so we'd keep the windows open and hang our arms out the window to feel the breeze. We'd drive through the desert and our arms would get sunburned like a motherfucker. And in the winter there was no heat unless I popped the hood and took the handle for the jack and slammed this little lever. Then sometimes it would kick over and the heat would turn on. We slept in that van every night because we couldn't afford to stay in hotels. One time it was so cold there was condensation all over the inside of the van and our guitarist's [Scott Hedrick's] pillow was frozen to the window. In times like that, the best thing to do was to drink cheap beer until we all passed out and then get up the next morning and drive to the next city.

DINO CAZARES

We played this show in Hollywood as part of Foundation Forum. There was no water backstage in our dressing room, so when we were done I was thirsty as hell. There was a plastic tray full of melted ice in our dressing that had held drinks, but they were all gone. So I thought, "Fuck it, I'm gonna drink the melted ice."

I picked up the tray and put my mouth up to it. And [vocalist] Burt [C. Bell] yelled, "What are you doing?!?" and pushed the tray out of my mouth.

"Dude, I was getting a drink. I'm thirsty!" I said.

"I just washed my feet in there!" Burt said.

DAVE WYNDORF
Monster Magnet

We played the old Masquerade in Atlanta in 1999, and the gig was upstairs in a place that used to be an old factory and they had a big sliding door in the back of the stage, which was shut during the gig. I decided to set my guitar on fire, so I extra-loaded it with lighter fluid because the venue had a tall ceiling and I felt like it could handle higher flames, which would look really cool.

But when the flames were shooting up, the guitar spit these little fireballs. Bits of the T-shirts burned off, and these little balls of flame went everywhere. So this thing is burning really big and shooting out fireballs, and I realized that the flame is bigger than I thought it would be. I looked at the techs, and they weren't smiling. They looked really worried.

I thought, "Oh my God, when is this thing gonna peak."

And it didn't peak.

My techs realized they were gonna have to put out the fire. They were waiting for me to put down the guitar. But it looked so good and the audience was loving it so much, I didn't want to put it down. Then, one of the stage guys from the Masquerade got freaked out and did the stupidest thing he could have done. He opened the sliding door, which created this cross ventilation. All the hot air from the place went right at me and enveloped me, and the flame went over my body. It must have looked cool as shit, but it burned my arms, my eyebrows, and my hair.

If I wasn't sweating like a pig, I think I definitely would have gone up in flames because I wasn't wearing any fire-retardant clothing. But on the whole, I was okay, and it was definitely worth it.

BUZZ OSBORNE

We once stole a whole bunch of gasoline and diesel fuel to make Molotov cocktails, and we were near a nuclear plant. If we got caught, we would definitely have gotten in a lot of trouble. We weren't trying to blow up the nuclear power plant, obviously, but it definitely wasn't the smartest thing I ever did.

MARK SLAUGHTER

When we were teenagers, we were literally lighting our own pyro concoctions in Las Vegas trailer parks. They were controlled experiments to try to figure out how many parts concussion powder to regular powder we should use. My band Excursion almost blew the windows out of a school. We added a little too much concussion powder to our flash pots. The explosion was deafening and the windows shook so much the principal came over and said, "Don't use those again!"

ROB CAVESTANY
Death Angel, ex-The Organization

We were on tour for our first album *The Ultraviolence* and for one show we parked behind the venue. Dennis [Pepa] was bored so he tagged this building with our band name. It was kind of obvious who did it. He took off and the owner of this restaurant whose building he tagged came out back. The dude was a maniac. He had no shirt on and he had huge scars on his chest.

"Who the fuck's fucking up my building?!" he said.

We were pissing our pants 'cause we were the only ones there and he knew damn well who fucked up his building. He made us repaint the back of the building, and Dennis had left so he didn't even have to do it. We were fuckin' pissed because we were doing that for hours, long before our show. Fans were showing up and we were out there painting this building. They were looking at us like, "What the fuck?" But this dude was gonna kick our ass if we didn't do it. That was the *Ultraviolence* tour. In the end, the dude felt sorry for us and he brought us a whole bunch of Mexican food.

DAVE ELLEFSON
Megadeth

The album cover for our first record *Killing Is My Business . . . and Business Is Good!* was absolutely embarrassing. Dave [Mustaine] did a cool drawing of a skull with its eyes covered, its mouth bolted tight, and metal plugs over his ears. It was supposed to symbolize the old saying, "Speak no evil, see no evil, hear no evil." He sent the drawing to Combat Records and said, "We want the cover to look like this, but better."

Fast forward many months. We had a P.O. Box since we were homeless at the time. We were so excited to see the finished artwork. Dave [Mustaine] and I went to the box one day and opened it up and we see a vinyl copy of *Killing Is My Business* and we were like, "What in the world is this?!?" It looked nothing like what Dave gave them. It was a picture of this cheap looking plastic skull with metal hooks keeping his mouth closed and this shitty tin can visor over his eyes—totally low budget. There were chains next to the skull and a knife sticking into the ground and lit candle. It was awful. We immediately called Combat and they had their excuses and their reasons they did such a bad job.

"We have our own artist who does all of our artwork and the costs would have been exorbitant to do it the way Dave drew it."

They didn't even use the right logo. They just used some Gothic font. So basically, they disregarded everything we wanted.

GARY HOLT

I don't think our first record [cover] *Bonded by Blood* came out as bad as Megadeth's or Anthrax's, but it was still pretty awful. The original album cover had a silhouette of us and all these bodies piled all around us. Our label Torrid Records thought the cover was too extreme. That's back when the album was called *A Lesson in Violence*. Then, we came up with *Bonded by Blood* and that all added up to one of the many delays that kept the album from coming out literally two years earlier. I think our *Bonded by Blood* album cover is iconic, but I know it's bad. The concept was awesome—the angel baby and the devil baby as Siamese twins tearing apart from one another. I think the concept was stolen by Van Halen years later on the album they did with the angel and devil twins. But ours didn't come out right. I wouldn't have chosen a baby-blue sky background. It was supposed to look horrific with carnage and dripping blood. But back then we were working with artists we could afford who had an airbrush gun and knew how to do a little painting. At least we had the logo, which I think is classic. The only thing we've changed over the years is we've balanced it out. Looking at the logo, back then we had the right side of the logo smaller than the left. We changed it once and then we went back basically to the original. We just sharpened all the points so it looks like you would cut yourself if you were handling it.

JOHN GALLAGHER

We had an album cover all set for [our 1982 album] *Wiped Out*. We had an awesome atomic bomb explosion. And the label head said, "Nope, you can't use that. It's in bad taste. I refuse."

So he locked me and Rob in a room and said, "Come up with a new cover. You've got two hours."

And that's how we wound up with the two crossing bolts of electricity, one black and one red [against an orange backdrop]. I drew it up at gunpoint, basically. It was that or nothing.

CHAPTER 12: HIGHWAY TO HELL

Why Bands Should Maybe Tour by Train

The song that broke AC/DC in the United States, "Highway to Hell" is about the "Canning Highway"—a stretch of road in Fremantle, Australia, near where vocalist Bon Scott lived. The singer regularly drove the highway to his local pub, The Raffles, and at the end of the trip there was a steep hill. Reportedly, the road was nicknamed the "Highway to Hell" since it was the site of many fatal accidents over the years. Tragically, the 1979 album *Highway to Hell* was the last on which Scott would sing. He was reportedly hammered when he aspirated vomit and died in a friend's car February 19, 1980. Officials labeled the events that happened that night "death by misadventure."

These terrifying road stories in the "Highway to Hell" chapter began as part of "Die With Your Boots On," but it soon became clear that so many bands have had van, bus, and trailer accidents while on tour that there was too much material there to bury it all in another chapter. "Highway to Hell" is colored with humor, but many of the road tales are scary and unsettling. There are anecdotes about impossible driving conditions, near-misses, and full-on collisions that range from surprisingly mild to nearly fatal. There are also stories of wheels that have popped off vehicles, and a bus that burst into flames. Some of the accidents were due to a driver getting distracted or falling asleep at the wheel. Others were caused by the driver of another vehicle. All are sobering reminders of the bravery and dedication of touring metal bands that literally risk their lives every time they hop in the van or get on the bus. Driving from city to city is usually pretty boring (which is why so many young musicians drink and take drugs to kill the monotony). But boredom is a luxury compared to some of the horrific ordeals that have gone down on the Highway to Hell.

KYLE SHUTT
The Sword

Being on the highway is just so dangerous. We have a rule that we don't drive at night anymore just because we've seen so many terrible things happen at night. Sometimes you'll just be driving sixty-five and then a semi in front of you and a little Mazda Miata both try to take the lane in front of you at the same time. The truck takes it and this little car spins out and slams into the median and busts back across the highway like a pinball.

I can't tell you how many times I've seen that happen driving from San Diego to L.A. The car barely misses some other truck and trailer, getting on the freeway and then tries to jump across four lanes and slams into the concrete. I'm surprised more stuff like that doesn't happen.

Grand Theft Auto is one thing. But in real life you have to make it from point A to point B every single time. And people are on their phones all the time or they're drunk. As far as being on the Autobahn going 150 miles-per-hour five feet away from a semi directly in front of you, you have to be okay with the idea of perishing in a ball of flames. It's like, "Okay, everything could end right now. All it would take is one little thing for everything to end in a heartbeat."

RANDY BLYTHE
Lamb of God

Once, I was the only one up on the bus and we were in Oklahoma somewhere at 9 a.m. It was snowing and I was in the front lounge reading a book and kind of falling asleep. All of a sudden I heard our driver Jesse go, "Aw, shit." And then I heard him say, "Hold on, boys!"

All of a sudden WHAM! I looked out the window right as this truck came flying across the highway all the way across the median and slammed right into the side of our bus. He lost control in the snow going about fifty or sixty and slammed into the bunk area right where our guitar tech Larry was sleeping. Luckily he wasn't hurt, but it scared the living crap out of him.

Then BLAM! There was this huge explosion [from the truck]. Everybody was up. We were all okay. The side of the bus was kind of mauled. The guy's truck was totaled.

We talked to the cop. He told us the guy in the semi was having a bad day. His wife had divorced him and left him and he was driving home from bankruptcy court, having declared bankruptcy just that day. He was on his way home when the accident happened. He told the cops, "I wish I had just died."

MARK MORTON
Lamb of God

When people think of bands on tour buses they think, man, you made it. Well, there are different versions of tour buses. Some of them are very nice. Some of them are old and aren't nice.

One of our early tour buses was very old and everything was leaking. It was basically an old rolling camper. We had a Croatian bus driver named Mario. We were in the Midwest and the weather was really bad. There was snow and sleet coming down. One of the windshield wipers wasn't working, the other was intermittently working and the defrost was broken. The driver had a T-shirt and he was constantly wiping the condensation and haze off the window. It was terrifying.

NATE GARNETTE
Skeletonwitch

We had just played at the Grog Shop in Cleveland in 2004 and we were driving back to Athens so we were somewhere like Marietta. We were on an onramp to get on a two-lane freeway and this guy just zipped by us going the wrong direction. Fortunately, he wasn't in our lane or we totally would have crashed head-on.

Me and [guitarist] Scott [Hedrick] just looked at each other and went, "Wait. Was that fuckin' real?"

It really freaked us out but at least we were wide awake for the rest of the night.

BRETT CAMPBELL
Pallbearer

We were touring with Enslaved in 2013. It was February and we had gone into Canada. We got stuck in a blizzard in Winnipeg. They were in a bus and we were in a $1,100 Dodge van. It was twenty below zero and we weren't going anywhere.

So we pulled into this old, creepy hotel and Enslaved's bus got stuck. The back wheels were frozen. While they were pulling out, [drummer] Mark [Lierly] was pissing on the wheel to try to unfreeze it.

"You gotta stop that. If the driver sees you, he's gonna murder you," Said the tour manager.

They finally got out and we were stuck in Winnipeg for another day. They went on to Toronto and Montreal. Leaving from Winnipeg to the show the GPS said it was thirty-hour drive and we had thirty-three hours to do it. I had slept all day so I was well rested and ready for the night shift.

Right before sunrise, we were in North Carolina around one of the Great Lakes and I kept seeing salt trucks. I'm driving fifty-five miles-per-hour and I started passing these salt trucks. I saw a group of two and then another group of two. And I guess I passed the first salt trucks that were sent out on the road because suddenly there's no salt and the roads were in shit condition. I hit a patch of black ice with this $1,100 van and a U-Haul. The van started to turn and everyone woke up screaming, "What the fuuuuuck!"

The van and trailer started to tip and go up on two wheels. I was trying to correct my steering and we went 180 degrees on the interstate and ended up facing in the wrong direction. As soon as we stopped, two semis that had been right behind us came barreling by. If we hadn't slid over to the shoulder of the road we would have been vaporized. After that, a pickup truck was careening toward us and it nearly capped our front end 'cause he went out of control, too. Luckily, there was an exit ramp five hundred meters from where we were so I turned around and very carefully pulled off the interstate into this gas station and waited for my heart to stop doing blast beats. The sun was starting to come up so we sat there in the parking lot for about two hours watching cars slide off the road, one after another.

JOHN GALLAGHER
Raven

Back in 1984, we left Neat Records and we took all of our equipment out of the building and took it to a music store down in Sunderland ten miles away. We drove back over the Red Heath bridge in Newcastle which was over the Tyne River. It's a good one hundred feet up and it was very windy. We were driving a twenty-seven-foot truck, the wind picked up and all of a sudden we were on two wheels for about two hundred yards and in serious danger of flying off the bridge. Three of us were leaning the other way, screaming when the truck righted itself back on four wheels. That was one of the scariest things I've ever experienced.

ERIK RUTAN
Hate Eternal, ex-Morbid Angel, ex-Ripping Corpse

We were on tour in Midwest Canada and it was snowing so bad I said, "Listen, we gotta pull over."

We were running out of gas as well and nothing was open. We pulled into a gas station and slept there. The next day we woke up and there was a mountain of snow that had fallen. We got gas, got back on the highway and kept driving.

As we were driving, we saw three eighteen-wheelers and some cars flipped over. Nobody was on the road and it was still snowing.

"What the fuck?" I thought. "Why is nobody out here?"

We drove for about forty-five minutes and didn't see a single driver. We turned on the radio to get a weather report. They had closed down the freaking highway because the weather was so bad and there we were driving with a van and trailer not even realizing what had happened.

CHRIS URENNA
ex-Nine Inch Nails, ex-Marilyn Manson

After *Pretty Hate Machine,* Trent went to New Orleans and I went to Chicago and did Die Warzau's second record *Big Electric Metal Bass Face* with them and then we went on tour. We had a bus and two crew guys were driving around an eighteen-foot box truck with all the gear. We had just played Denver and the next night we were playing Minneapolis. We all went to bed on the bus and when we woke up the next day at noon we were in this parking lot.

We were like, "Where are we? Shouldn't we be in Minneapolis?"

"Guys, sit down," said the bus driver. "I'll explain."

We were only thirty miles from where we were the night before. He said that a black ice storm hit in that part of the country and everyone else from all the other vehicles was in the hospital. As soon as the freeway opened, we went to go get them. We drove down I-90 about an hour down the road we looked off to the side and saw an eighteen-foot box truck on its side, nose down in a ditch. It was our gear truck and the driver and passenger were in the hospital.

When we got to the hospital we found out that the opening band were in one of those fifteen-passenger rental vans and it had rolled six or eight times. A boom box went flying over the seat and dislocated one guy's shoulder. Those guys were still in the emergency room and we didn't yet know what condition they were in. Our two drivers were okay. They climbed up and out of the truck. We were so freaked out. Everyone had bumps and bruises and black eyes. A lot of our gear got destroyed. We canceled the last two shows and piled everyone onto our bus. We drove twenty miles-per-hour and it took us three days to get back to Chicago.

BRETT CAMPBELL

On the way back from recording *Foundations*, we were driving from Portland back to Little Rock. We got stuck outside of Denver for several hours. We sat there waiting along with ten million other cars. It took three hours to make it one mile. The roads were finally cleared off by the salt trucks and we were inching along at five miles-per-hour. And after sitting in a dead stop for three hours we finally started moving and started to slide right away toward the edge of a cliff. There was no barrier. There was just the road and then a sheer drop into death.

We were drifting to the right and the trailer started sliding sideways. We jackknifed and the corner side of the trailer shattered the back driver's side window of the van as we slid toward our doom. We stopped sliding right at the very edge of the cliff. We could see over the side to the bottom of the mountain. [Bassist] Joe [Rowland] had to drive back into traffic, which was all going two miles-per-hour, to turn us around. And it was a very cold drive back with no rear windshield.

NATE GARNETTE

In the winter time, semi-truck drivers think they're invincible. I'll be driving slow as shit and they'll fucking honk their horn and swerve around to pass me.

One time in Nebraska in 2008, we were touring with Job for a Cowboy and a semi driver passed me, jackknifed and went off a giant hill on a road with no guard rails, just cables. All the cables snapped and one almost blasted out our windshield. Who knows what happened to the guy in the semi?

ROB ZOMBIE
White Zombie

We were driving in Europe once and our bus driver smashed into something but kept driving and it tore the whole side of the bus off. It opened like a can of tuna fish.

Fortunately, no one got hurt.

Another time, we were pulling out of New York and our bus driver decided to drive up the off ramp and go screaming into oncoming traffic. Fortunately, we got him to turn around before we were in any real danger. And then there was the time that we were driving into Manhattan and we had the air conditioning units on top of the bus. And we went,

"I don't think we're gonna fit through the Holland Tunnel."

"Oh, don't worry about it," he said. "I've been driving a long time."

CRRRUUUNNNCHHHHHH!!!!

He tore everything off the top of the bus and there was Freon spraying everywhere.

DAVE WYNDORF
Monster Magnet

Five years ago, we were in Belgium and our bus driver fell asleep. I saw the whole thing in slow motion. We drove into a guard rail and scraped along the side of it. There were sparks and broken glass, and the mirrors tore off the bus. I saw the whole goddamn thing happening in slow motion. It was like that scene in *Goodfellas* where they're talking in a diner and the camera's going both at the scene and away from the scene at the same time. The driver woke up and steered the bus back onto the road, so no one got hurt. But the guy didn't even apologize.

ALEX HELLID
Entombed

We got a bus to tour Europe. The first show was in London. After the show, we went to leave the country and as soon as we got to the other side going into France, our driver crashed into a low bridge. It wasn't just a flat bridge. The height was okay, but the side was curved. He saw that it was coming and thought we'd make it, but we didn't. The whole side of the bus got pushed in.

I was awake, but some of the guys were sleeping. And there were bunks up on the sides so people woke up with a real shock. Lars, our bass player, was in his bed and he woke up covered in glass. He wasn't too chuffed about that.

It was crazy. That was our first bus and it didn't last long. We had to get another bus and we went with that for a few days. And then it fell apart. One of the axles actually fell off while it was driving. It felt like we were riding around in death traps on that tour.

MARK MORTON

Back when we were still traveling around in a van we were going down Interstate 65, and the lug nuts broke and the wheel came off. We skidded down the breakdown lane and we came to a stop. I can't remember if we called a tow truck or if we had a spare, but it was amazing we didn't crash.

RANDY BLYTHE

We were coming back from a Philly show and there was this hitchhiker on the side of the road. He looked like a hardcore kid so we picked him up and he got in the van with us. He turned out to be a straight-edger. He wanted to go down to North Carolina and we were going as far as Richmond. But he got in anyway and immediately noticed all the empty beer bottles. Pretty soon we were partying in the van, 'cause that's what we used to do—like fucking idiots. We were pounding beers and there were eight of us crammed in there smoking weed and cigarettes and this guy, who was obviously clean and sober, was getting more and more uncomfortable. We were raging drunk and even the driver was probably hammered.

Finally, the van started making a funny noise. We were in Maryland and going about forty miles per hour when the rear wheel just flew off. We were grinding down the road on three wheels. The van almost tipped over. We were all laughing because we were having a good ol' time. But this poor kid was fucking terrified.

We called our buddy to come tow the van. We told the straight-edge kid, "Look man, we got a buddy coming. He's gonna tow us and you can ride with us."

Seconds later, that dude was gone. He ran to the other side of the road and we never saw him again.

MATT BACHAND
ex-Shadows Fall, Times of Grace

We were driving on our way to Ozzfest in 2004 and the wheel came off the bus. We didn't realize it at first. We were cruising down the highway at seventy miles-per-hour and the front left wheel snapped right off and it was gone. It was five hundred yards into the woods.

I woke up and we were kind of sideways. How the hell I slept through that, I have no idea. Some people didn't. We ground up a nice long chunk of highway.

The state trooper showed up and looked and the bus, then looked at us and said, "You all should be dead."

He didn't understand why the bus didn't flip over.

We kept that driver for a long, long time because he was able to keep the bus upright and keep control when we could have had a really bad accident.

KING FOWLEY
Deceased, October 31

We went to play Huntington, West Virginia, one night in the late 1990s. We were up near the Ohio area, so the weather is really bad. We got close to the venue and all of a sudden this crazy fucking downpour came. I was like, "Ah, shit" because it was so heavy.

The promoter picked me up and said, "All right, you ride with me."

So we drove and it flooded so quickly that the guy said, "Man, we have to go under this bridge to get to the club."

I was like, "What are we gonna do? There's water everywhere!"

And he said, "We're gonna drive through it!"

Of course, his car got stuck. The whole car was completely submerged in water. I had to get out of the fucking car and swim to the other side of the bridge. This guy had just bought two hundred dollars of import CDs back when they were thirty-five dollars a pop and we saw them floating away in the water.

I had to go dry off to play the show and I don't know what kind of funky-ass water it was because there were fish in it. I said, "How did fish get in here so quickly?"

And the promoter said, "Yeah, this is a freaky town. There's a lot of weird floods."

It took almost a year for his car to dry out enough that it would start again.

TOMMY VICTOR
Prong, Danzig, ex-Ministry

Danzig was supposed to play this Force Fest in Mexico City in 2019 and it was comparable to the Battle of Verdun in World War I. There was so much mud and the rain was horrible. The weather was apocalyptic.

There are areas of Mexico City that might as well be Los Angeles, but for the most part it's the third world and when these storms hit it's a real muddy mess. It was like Armageddon. Everything was melting in the rain. There were more than one hundred thousand wasted people trying to get into the place. The roads into the stage area were impossible to traverse so the driver of our van drove through this food court area and almost ran people over. Then the driver told us that the only way he could get us to the stage was to floor the van right through the crowd.

We were hydroplaning at eighty miles per hour and then we smashed into a tree. When we got out, we had mud up to our knees to get to the stage. And we never got to play because Slayer wanted us to go on after them and we said no fuckin' way, but they didn't care. They did it anyway. They said, "Fuck you guys. If you don't want to go after us then you're not playing."

They had enough power to make that happen. So by the time they finished, the show was over. They were the headlining band and there was no way we were going on after them. No one goes on after Slayer.

ROGER MIRET
Agnostic Front

Once we were traveling through Washington State in the middle of the night and I heard "KA-VARROOM!" I had been resting at the time, so I slowly emerged from my bunk and I saw these fuckin' antlers sticking right through the front windshield of the bus!

The driver was standing outside on the cold road looking at the animal. Its huge antlers looked like barbed spears. I asked the driver what happened and he said this giant elk started charging alongside the bus on the freeway and when it got ahead of the bus it turned around and ran straight at us! The driver was almost cut up by the horns when they went right through the windshield before the driver hit the brakes and the elk fell onto the highway.

The driver called the state troopers and they showed up and said the size of the deer was world record for the state of Washington. The cops took out a giant knife that looked like a machete and cut off the deer's fuckin' head. Then the troopers carried the head to their big pick-up truck and left the body right there in the road.

They told us we could have the dead deer if we wanted it. We had killed it so by hunter's law it was ours—even though the thing, more accurately, committed suicide. The body of the elk was way too heavy to move and none of us wanted it so we left it there and drove away.

It was a really dangerous drive. The front windshield was still attached but it was spiderwebbed with cracks and pretty much destroyed. We taped it up so it wouldn't shatter inwards and we made some calls and checked in with garages and junkyards, but no one had a replacement windshield for a tour bus.

Over the next few days, we drove from Washington to Colorado and the driver had to crane his head to see out of the part of the windshield that wasn't so badly cracked. He drove really slow and we played two shows with the bus like that before we were able to get the windshield replaced.

ERIK RUTAN

In 2008 we were in Colorado in the middle of nowhere and there was a deer in the middle of the road. I know how to handle this kind of thing. I slowly pulled into the right lane and as I was passing him I looked at this deer which was to the left of me now. We locked eyes for a second and then he was behind us.

We kept driving and suddenly the deer ran head-first into the back side of the van. He literally committed suicide. To this day there's a huge dent in the back side of my Mercedes-Benz Sprinter tour van. He was in the clear! I don't know what the hell he was doing.

MÅRTEN HAGSTRÖM
Meshuggah

We were in the middle of South Dakota in the middle of the night when the bus started swaying all over the road. We were rolling over in our bunks, and we thought we were going to crash. But we didn't crash and the driver finally pulled over.

As it turned out, the bus had smashed into a giant deer that went right into the windshield and crushed the front of the bus. We were all shaken up but the driver could still drive so we kept going.

The next day, we were in Boulder, Colorado, and our driver was picking out pieces of deer and bloody fur, and ordering new pieces to fix the bus. We thought that was the end of that, so we went in to do our show and some interviews. When we got back later that night, we found out that [Tool guitarist] Adam [Jones] had taped the front half of a plastic deer to the front of our bus. It was such a coincidence that we ran into a deer and then Tool happened to have this thing lying around to put on the fucking bus. The driver thought it was so funny he kept in there for about eight weeks and we got pulled over a couple times because of it. Then our driver would tell the cops the story and they'd just shake their heads and walk away.

DINO CAZARES
Fear Factory, Divine Heresy, Brujeria, Asesino

Five years ago, we were in Europe and our bus driver reached down to get a candy that he dropped. The bus swerved over and plowed into this other car. We were all in our bunks asleep since this happened in the morning. The whole side of the bus was fucked up, the windshield was gone. The other car was like a sardine can.

Luckily, everybody was okay. But everything on the bus was destroyed. And there was glass everywhere. We all had to step very carefully but no one got cut up.

PAGE HAMILTON
Helmet

We were the middle band on a three-band bill with Ministry and Sepultura. We were in a van and we had a full box truck. I didn't want to get a tour bus. We had gone gold and we were doing well, but I still had [indie rock figurehead] Steve Albini's words ringing in my ears, "Don't sign to a major label, don't tour in a bus, don't do this or that."

It turned out to be stupid. We had two crew guys and [drummer] John [Stanier] in the Ryder box truck. And John's girlfriend was in Baltimore or D.C. so he wanted to spend more time with her. The rest of us got in the van and drove to our next gig in Chapel Hill, North Carolina.

And then we got a call in the middle of the night that one of our guys had fallen asleep at the wheel and rolled the truck into the median. Thank god there was a grassy, wooded area between the north and southbound lanes. Otherwise, the wreck could have killed them.

The truck rolled a couple times. The driver was in a coma and paramedics had to airlift him to Richmond, Virginia. John had broken ribs and Keith Bornzen, our drum tech, had broken legs.

Obviously, we were done for that period of time. Ice-T's band Body Count filled in for us on the Ministry tour. It was a really rough time.

That's when I decided to let [guitarist] Peter [Mengede] go because he got a separate tour bus and drove to Florida to be with a girl rather than go with us as a family to visit our friend, the driver, who was in the hospital in Richmond. Family comes first and people's lives come before anything.

The dude had some issues after the accident. He didn't feel the same and he was under a lot of stress so he quit. We hired him back but he was frustrated. He felt like he couldn't do the job anymore because we had gotten pretty big. So he decided to leave. But he became friends with another popular '90s band that opened up for us on that first *Meantime* tour. And he started dating one of the members of that group. He was straight-edge with us. He never even drank a Coca-Cola. But apparently he started doing heroin and he OD'd on the bus with this other band. I've never gotten over losing that kid. He was just a fuckin' sweetheart.

GEORGE "CORPSEGRINDER" FISHER
Cannibal Corpse

We were going through Quebec and we had this bus driver who could not stay awake. He would have to repeatedly pull over all night long to keep from passing out and getting into an accident. On a day off, he pulled over on the side of the road into this soft gravel and the bus started tilting. I woke up and I couldn't get out of my bunk. It was the middle of the summer and there were all these flies and bugs buzzing around.

"George, get out of your bunk," yelled the tour manager.

"Why?" I asked.

"We gotta get out of here before this bus flips over and rolls down a hill!"

We eventually flagged some people that were driving by and they took us a couple miles down the road to a burger joint. And we were able to find a garage there and get the bus towed out of the gravel.

BEN FALGOUST
Goatwhore, ex-Soilent Green

In 2001, Soilent Green were on tour with Morbid Angel, Deicide, Zyklon, and Exhumed. And we were on I-90 after leaving Seattle. We were about sixty miles from Spokane, Washington. We had a day off at that point to head down to Denver. The weather was really bad and our van we hit a patch of black ice and slid down the highway and flipped over.

Our bass player Scott [Crochet] broke a scapula bone in his back and our guitar player Brian Patton fractured his collar bone. The rest of us had to get the gear and rent a truck and head home. Everything was totaled. I had to crawl out of the window and the snow was blowing sideways into my face. Luckily, there was an ambulance that was not far behind us and they saw us crash. They pulled up and brought us to a little hospital near Spokane.

We sorted things out from there and got the two injured guys back home. Luckily enough the trailer top got torn off, but the way everything was packed in the trailer everything stayed perfectly solidly packed. Even

288 ⚡ RAISING HELL

without a cover on the trailer, there were still bars in place so all the equipment worked when we got it home and tested it . . . [to be continued]

DINO CAZARES

We were in England during the summer festival tours in 2010 on the *Mechanized* tour. We were dropping off our drummer's girlfriend at the airport. We had to get on the M1 freeway.

For some reason, the driver kept using the emergency brake to slow down. It made the brakes so hot that the wheel well started to catch fire. The guy pulled over and said, "Everyone get off the bus!"

We were all sleeping. I put my clothes on and grabbed my bag and backpack. By that point, the smoke was coming into the bus. We all got off and were standing out in the middle of the fucking freeway. We could see the flames coming out of the side of the fucking bus.

One of the techs said, "Let's unhook the trailer."

They unhooked the trailer and pushed it far enough back that none of the gear got torched.

Then someone went, "Where's our merch guy?"

He was still in the bus. One of our techs wrapped a shirt around his face to cover his nose and pulled the tech out in his underwear. He got drunk the night before and was passed out. If someone didn't realize he was missing he would have been dead.

GENE HOGLAN
Dark Angel, Testament, Dethklok, ex-Death, ex-Strapping Young Lad

I thought, "Oh we must have bumped into the wall." All of a sudden, the bus stopped. My lady said, "You know what? There's smoke drifting into my bunk."

It was four in the morning. My tech came running back, "Bus is on fire. Everyone off!"

We all jump off the bus, but our merch guy remained sleeping on the bus. He was brand new to the tour. We had just met him, so when we did a quick headcount he wasn't really on anyone's mind.

We were watching the bus burn up and then my tech went, "Wait a minute, Zeke, the merch guy.!

My tech ran back on the bus, which was now ablaze, and this guy was still sleeping right through it. Our tech had to pull Zeke out by his chest skin. And he said later that the only reason he remembered Zeke was still on the bus was because as we were standing there watching the bus burn, he thought, "Hey, where's the guy that shared his drugs with me last night?"

So, in essence, drugs saved Zeke's life.

BEN FALGOUST

[continued] . . . Five months after we crashed in Soilent Green, we were back on tour with Gwar. I was driving and I'm pretty sure I fell asleep at the wheel outside of Chicago and I ran into the back of an eighteen-wheeler that had stopped. The whole front end of the van smashed in on me. I broke both legs and both ankles. I went through nine surgeries. I tore my left heel off so they had to reconstruct that.

We had a guy filling in on bass named Johnny Modell. He broke his collar bone.

I spent two weeks at the hospital and then my parents drove up there in a mini-van with a mattress to bring me back home to New Orleans. And then I had to get involved with a hospital there, where they did additional procedures. I had to spend a year in a wheelchair and then years after that going to rehab.

But I started going back on the road again. I didn't have any fear or reservations about it.

ERIK RUTAN

In 2003, on the *King of All Kings* run, we were touring in the winter with Dying Fetus, Kataklysm, and Into Eternal. We were driving a van through Madison, Wisconsin, and I was sleeping on the back bench. Someone else was driving and I just remember laying there and all of a sudden hearing somebody saying, "Oh shit! Oh shit! Oh shit!" over and over again.

That woke me up and I could feel us going off the road. I felt us sliding and then the trailer coming with us. I looked up from my laying position, and we were going off the road and the trailer forked, swung around and hit the window of the conversion van right where I was sleeping. I got knocked out and woke up with my face in a broken windshield. There was glass all around me and snow coming down. The impact was so strong I got knocked from the back of the van all the way to the front. And the van was in a ditch on the side of the road.

I thought everyone was pretty much okay. I had so much adrenaline pumping through me and it was freezing. I got out of the van. Paramedics and cops came and once the adrenaline started wearing off I realized I was seriously injured.

I went to the hospital and they discovered I had a chipped vertebra and my whole body seized up with whiplash.

The tour was over, the van was totaled. Some of the gear was smashed. We ended up going home and I had to go through physical therapy for three months. It was six weeks before I could even feel my fingers. I was lucky to survive. The doctor said that if the driver had been going five miles per hour faster, I might not be here. Two miles down the road was a fifteen-car pile-up accident so who knows what would have happened if we hadn't gone off the road? We might have crashed into that.

JOHN BAIZLEY
Baroness

We most definitely weren't on a highway. We were going through little neighborhoods in Bristol, England. It's an old country, the system for roads there was not set up in a particularly clever or grid-like pattern because the country doesn't really allow for it. They can't really widen a lot of those roads and we're on this tiny little road in a big 1983 Mercedes bus. We took a left turn and we were on the top of a hill. I saw a sign that said, "Next two miles twelve percent downgrade."

I reacted internally thinking, "That's very steep and it's a very long hill. We shouldn't be here."

In America, commercial vehicles can't go on anything steeper than an eight percent gradient. So, it was way steeper than any major highway you would go on and this was a country road. There was a stone wall on one side and a steep hill on the other. Very quickly I heard some sort a mechanical malfunction noise that was deep and rocked the chassis of the bus.

Immediately we were in accident mode. [Guitarist] Pete [Adams] was awake in the back of the bus and our front of house guy, Loopy, was in the back lounge as well. I was in the front. Everyone else was asleep. There are times in life when we know we are about to get hurt and I knew this was one of those moments and I almost had a mathematic grid in my head which was percentage points of this working out okay in the long run. And if the brakes hadn't gone, we would have been rolling along at one hundred percent.

As soon as the brakes hit it was ninety-nine and every second for the next two minutes as we careened down this hill the chances of survival got much, much closer to zero.

Eventually, I was positive we were all going to die. We couldn't swerve because we would have flipped the bus. The only way to slow down the bus was to run into a vehicle, which would have killed them.

Our driver was losing control. His emergency brakes failed. The bus pre-dated the secondary braking system that is now mandatory on all buses. When the brakes were gone and the emergency brakes were gone and the steering wheel became very difficult to maneuver, all the systems of the bus that would allow us the control to not crash were gone. They were out the window. It took me thirty seconds to realize all of that and then there was another minute-and-a-half of time where I was just thinking about what should be done.

"Should I try to jump out the bus? No. That would feel like leaving my friends behind. Is there anything I can do to help us? No. What should I be doing?"

I instinctually started calling everyone to wake up, which came out more like, "Everybody get up. We're about to get into an accident. Get yourself ready."

And it was much louder with all kinds of swearing.

A minute or forty-five seconds before the actual crash that really disturbing, magical thing happened, where time stopped and each second felt like a full minute. I had no idea what to do. Mostly everybody was waking up but they certainly weren't recognizing what was happening. At the bottom of the road there was a vaguely T-shaped intersection—which I was told later was a very busy intersection—which luckily wasn't filled with cars, and a stoplight, which was red. We went through the red light at about sixty or seventy miles-per-hour through a metal guardrail like it was made of warm butter. And very immediately the four wheels of our full-sized motor coach were in the air.

I was watching from just in front of the halfway point of the bus. I saw the little, teeny wispy tops of spruce trees whip the halfway point of our windshield and I was sure this was the last moment of our lives. I looked at the driver, he looked at me. I said goodbye to him.

I looked to the back of the bus. Everybody was acknowledging in their own way and going through their own way of saying, "Well, this is it. I guess it's been a good run until now. I hope this is quick."

That's still a source of huge discomfort for me to have gone through that because my attitude was, "I hope this is quick. I know it's over and I'm totally fine with it. I'm not scared. I just don't want to suffer. I just want this to be the end and lights out." . . . [to be continued]

ADAM JARVIS
Misery Index, Pig Destroyer, Scour

In 2007 me and [guitarist John] "Sparky" [Voyles] were hanging out in the bus lounge while we were driving somewhere in England. I went to take a piss and all of a sudden the bus slammed on its brakes. That's one of the worst feelings in the world. You can't see what's about to happen so you just find the "Oh shit!" handle and hold on for dear life. We came to a screeching halt. With piss all over me, I stepped out of the bathroom and saw this car that was completely mangled fifty feet in front of the tour bus. I looked at Sparky and he had this wide-eyed stare.

"What the fuck happened?" I asked.

"Dude, as soon as you went to take a piss it was like something from out of *Fast and Furious* or *Final Destination*," he said. "I looked out of the side window and there was a car in midair flying past the tour bus."

By the time I got out of there, the tour bus driver was already out of the vehicle going up to the car. The diver of the car was obliterated drunk and was literally in the back of the car by the time the car landed and somehow he was still alive.

"Hey, man. Have you been drinking?" our driver asked the guy, who was all discombobulated and fucked up. "Look man," continued the driver. "If I was you, I'd piss the fuck off."

The dude literally climbed out of the back of the car and took off running down this median and disappeared into the woods.

GEORGE "CORPSEGRINDER" FISHER

We were on the road in late 2008 in the middle of the night driving in Europe and there was a car pulled over in the emergency lane. And then someone who was trying to help them pulled over right next to them, not in front of them or behind them. We came around a turn and the driver locked up the brakes and the bus screeched to a halt.

[Bassist] Alex [Webster] was standing up talking me with and [drummer] Paul [Mazurkiewicz] and our old sound guy. Alex almost went flying down the hallway of the bus, but he was able to catch himself. I was up against the wall, so I smashed my head, but I was fine; I have a really hard head. But, man, if we had hit that car who knows what would have happened.

JOHN BAIZLEY

[continued] . . . We were flying over these trees and there's a little stream with a road on either side and then a bridge off to the right. We managed to stick our bus directly over these spruce trees, which kept us from going over toward the bridge or the stream. I think the spruce trees saved all of our lives.

We crossed this little river and the bottom of the chassis of this 1983 bus was so heavy and dense that there wasn't any rolling from side to side. There was no lateral twisting or bending. We went straight up and straight down and the nose of the bus came down first. It hit the ground and I had this moment where I thought to myself, "Okay, I'm still alive," and I remembered hearing all these people say that drunks in accidents tend to have a higher survival rate because their bodies are loose.

So as much as I could, I tried to relax and loosen up my body. We hit and I went like a fucking bullet right up to the windshield. I hit the windshield so hard that the entire front windshield of a full-sized bus cracked. I saw all the little cracks spreading out from the side of my face because my head hit first. The whole windshield of the bus popped out almost cleanly and I popped out with it because I was going that fast.

However, because of the physics, I was also bouncing back from it. So when I landed I was back in the bus looking at the windshield, which was ten or fifteen feet in front of me.

I surveyed my body and immediately saw my left leg was bent in a very unnatural direction so I knew that was broken.

My right leg seemed to be okay.

I looked at my right arm. It was mostly blood and glass but my fingers were moving. I could move my arm straight out.

I tried to move my left arm straight out but I couldn't. I looked down and I saw the one image that's easily the most traumatic from the whole experience. Halfway down between my shoulder and my elbow, my arm was completely broken in half. My left hand, which should have been directly in front of me pointing straight was bent 180 degrees backwards behind my back and my left hand was almost in my right pocket from behind.

I could feel it was like when you bend a water hose and the water stops. I could feel that with my artery.

I whacked the hand with my right fist. It snapped and broke again but now at least it was on the left hand of my body. I grabbed my hand, which had no feeling whatsoever. It was like grabbing a cold stranger's hand. I broke it two more times and pulled it into my chest. And I had my hand on my elbow, pulling it into my ribcage.

For the next four hours I wouldn't let go. I held it tightly because when a bone snaps it's not a clean shearing. You've got a bunch of jagged pieces sticking in you which is excruciating. Every time I felt one jagged outcropping of bone scraping against another it was disgusting and nauseating and it makes me shiver to think about that feeling.

For a split second, I was positive I was dead. I had what most people consider a near-death experience. I saw the nothing that I now believe exists beyond death and when I was conscious and in the moment again I was in tremendous pain but also overcome with the really bizarre, absurd joy that all of a sudden I was feeling pain.

And I could smell gas and diesel fuel and blood and the food from our bus and all those weird smells that metal makes when it bends. It was a really potent moment. And there is no amount of adrenaline that overrides that pain, so I was miserable.

Very quickly there was a group of local people helping us out. A lot of the band members and crew members that weren't as injured as some of us were helping to get everyone off the bus and safe. And then they got me off and took me to the hospital and fixed me up.

And the fixes they made weren't exactly perfect. I don't exactly love the new reality of the state of my left arm, but it took three days for them to figure out how not to amputate it and that's better than not having it.

Who knows how or why we survived because it seems miraculous.

CHAPTER 13: SYMPHONY OF DESTRUCTION

Trashing Hotels, Venues & Buses

A prescient political song about a mass population being led to ruin by narcissistic politicians, Megadeth's "Symphony of Destruction" appeared on their 1992 album *Countdown to Extinction*. The jagged, mid-paced tune was the first single from the disc and helped propel the record to triple-platinum status, making it Megadeth's most successful release.

Being in a popular metal band affords musicians the luxury of living the dream exemplified by the phrase sex, drugs and rock and roll. It also makes many rockers act like children. There's certainly a loss of inhibition that comes with alcohol and drug use, which could account for the destructive tendencies of metal bands. Seeing home videos of their idols smashing gear, throwing TVs out the window, and trashing everything in sight surely has a pronounced influence as well. However, destroying hotels, buses, and dressing rooms comes at a price. Bouts of demolition sometimes result in being banned from a hotel, terminated by a bus company, thrown off a tour, or spending a night in jail. Then, there're the actual damage expenses, which are typically charged directly to the rowdy rockers, often at inflated prices. Such costs have been insignificant for huge bands like Judas Priest, Scorpions, Guns N' Roses, Metallica, and Pantera. For everyone else, unless they happened to run into a crazy fan who gave them permission to smash up his or her place (which has happened a surprising number of times), symphonies of destruction usually ended before the final movement.

ROB CAVESTANY
Death Angel, ex-The Organization

What's so crazy is that we grew up at a time when we thought we were supposed to destroy dressing rooms and smash shit when we were on tour.

We were absolutely trying to emulate what the bands that came before us did and what we thought we should do. So we tried everything we could think of to fuck shit up. We destroyed countless dressing rooms and hotels. We smashed all the lamps, turned over the mattresses, flipped over all the tables and chairs, threw shit around, and broke shit. We'd be wasted and laughing at how destructive we could be.

When we recorded *Act III* in 1989, we were living in an extended stay hotel. In the middle of the night, our bass player Dennis [Pepa] took a 10-foot-tall tree that was in this huge planter and dragged it out of one room and into another. He shoved the soil and some branches into the toilet and plugged it up. The next morning, we threw it two stories off the balcony down to the pool area below. People were lounging down there and the tree landed on a table right near them and smashed the table to bits. We were so stupid. We could have killed those people but we didn't even think about that. We hid in our rooms laughing our asses off, thinking no one was going to catch us. But they did and we got busted and had to pay a bunch of money.

ZAKK WYLDE
Black Label Society, Ozzy Osbourne

Me and Ozzy were on the tenth story of a hotel in Prague and we threw the television out the window at 3:30 in the morning. It was bolted to the fucking stand, so I had to rip it out before we threw it out the window.

But the explosion it made when it hit the ground was worth it. Ozzy and I were lying there crying on the ground.

He said, "Zakk, I've heard a lot of things in my life, but I've never heard anything as great as when that hit the fucking ground."

We also totally destroyed the room. The hotel management said it was so trashed they couldn't use it for a month. Afterwards, Mom—Mrs. O— called up my wife Barbara Anne and said, "Well, the two fucking morons, the gruesome twosome, are at it again."

Ozzy was already paying $1,000 a night for the room, so it set the Ozz back about $41,000, which is what the hotel charged him because they said it would take them 41 days to get the room ready for other guests. And it set me back $10,000 for that piece of shit TV. It was bullshit. Me and a friend could have had that place cleaned up in about three hours and had the windows fixed after we visited Home Depot to get some screws and glass and shit. And it was a tube TV, so it had to cost about $200. We could have fixed everything and bought them a new flat screen TV for under $1,000.

That was the last time I threw a $10,000 TV out the fucking window. That was back in the drinking days, so that kind of thing will never happen again. But I'll never forget the sound that fuckin' TV made.

DEVIN TOWNSEND
Strapping Young Lad, ex-Steve Vai, ex-Wildhearts, Devin Townsend Band

During a show when I was singing for Steve Vai, I shot a fire extinguisher into the crowd for fun and it was filled with toxic fluid instead of this fluffy foam. I didn't know what to do so I ran backstage. I felt like an idiot and I was really upset and I didn't know how to articulate that, so I started kicking stuff backstage and smashing things to bits. I saw a full garbage bag and I decided to destroy it so I kicked it and jumped I picked it up and threw it around the room.

Later, I went back onto the bus.

"No one talk to Steve right now," said the guitar tech. He's furious."

"I know," I said. "I can't believe I shot that fire extinguisher at the crowd."

"Oh no, dude," said the tech. "He doesn't care about that. He had $2,000 worth of leather boots and perfume in this black plastic bag backstage and somebody smashed it all up."

GARY HOLT
Exodus, Slayer

Decades before I joined the band, Slayer played a show at Ruthie's. The night before the show, we met up with them and their guitarist Jeff Hanneman gave us permission to trash his hotel room. Before all the words came out of his mouth, we were taking out a wall. We nailed pizza to the ceiling and destroyed the television. And they had this giant bag of popcorn that was the size of a laundry bag. It looked like it was snowing there was so much of that shit flying through the room.

That night, Jeff gave me the upside-down cross stage prop that's on the back of their album *Show No Mercy*. I used it to rip the mattresses apart. And I had that thing in my possession until the late '90s. Then I moved houses and afterwards it went missing. That's one of my greatest regrets in life, losing that thing after more than 15 years.

GENE HOGLAN
Dark Angel, Testament, Dethklok, ex-Death, ex-Strapping Young Lad

We were staying with Slayer at a friend of theirs' place and this party happened with this mother/daughter groupie, weird tag team family. The mom and daughter would both go to the shows and pick up guys and do their thing.

The next morning, [Slayer vocalist and bassist] Tom [Araya] got a phone call from the mother, who was at her house. She was freaking out.

"Oh my God, the Exodus guys just tore up my house! she shouted. "[Vocalist] Paul Baloff kicked the shit out of my refrigerator and broke all these doors and the TV and trashed the place. He grabbed some kid and tied him up and started pounding on him. He tried to set his hair on fire."

Tom and I drove over there just to see the aftermath. Of course, there was nothing we could do about it. The place was pretty wrecked. I'll never forget, Tom came out and said, "Damn, those guys are gremlins!"

ROB CAVESTANY

We grew up in the Bay Area in the height of the thrash scene and Metallica kind of took us under their wing as their little brothers, so we had a front row seat to all the craziness. We were so young I couldn't drive yet. I was fifteen and we were at a party somewhere around the Bay Area. We had a friend, Randy, who drove. He was kind of nerdy and got picked on a lot, but he didn't realize people were having fun at his expense.

Randy drove us to this party and there was a pinball machine there. People were playing pinball. Then [Metallica frontman] James [Hetfield] and [Exodus vocalist Paul] Baloff came into the room and picked up a life-sized ceramic doll. The thing looked like a jester and two of them swung in down on the pinball machine and smashed all the glass, ruining both the ceramic doll and the pinball machine.

Everyone was like, "Oh, shit!"

The room immediately cleared out. And when I turned around, I saw Paul poking Randy in the chest with a fork and James was standing there cracking up. I ran over and saved the dude. I told James and Paul that Randy was a friend and our driver so they backed off. But Randy was nearly in tears.

JIMMY BOWER
Eyehategod, Superjoint Ritual, Down, ex-Crowbar

We were on our first tour and we stayed at other people's houses. What people will let a group of guys do to their fuckin' houses blew my mind. We stayed at this one chick's place in North Carolina and everybody was wasted. She was stupid as fuck and she said, "You all can fuck up my house. I don't care."

We were out with Buzzov*en and we just demolished the place. That kind of thing would happen nightly and that was pretty much my introduction to touring. I wasn't a big drinker in the beginning 'cause I was driving. But it was fun to wreck stuff.

TONY FORESTA
Municipal Waste

One time early in our career, we played inside a burnt down house. The place was basically unlivable anyway, so we lit a couch on fire and threw it out the window. Another time, we were at this guy's house and he gave us an axe and let us chop down his front door. It's amazing what kind of destruction people will get into when they're get caught up in the moment.

WILL CARROLL
Death Angel, ex-Machine Head

When I was in Machine Head, I played drums on the band's first ever U.S. headlining tour, which was the last run for the *Burn My Eyes* cycle. The tour was incredibly long. We did twelve weeks with Stuck Mojo opening and it was brutal.

It was the first tour I had ever done so I was a total greenhorn. First of all, I wasn't much of a Machine Head fan. I kind of lied that I knew all their shit to get the gig. I really didn't know much of their music, but they hired me anyway.

In the middle of the tour, we were in Vancouver, Canada. It was the only night of the tour that we got hotel rooms, and that night Neurosis happened to be in town and they were friends with Machine Head [frontman] Robb Flynn. So they played, too. After the show, we were hanging out in the bus getting hammered because the next day was a day off. The guys from Neurosis came on the bus and all of a sudden there were fifteen people raging. We started throwing food. It all began playfully. Someone threw a grape at someone else. All of a sudden, Robb opened a giant four-liter bottle of cranberry juice splashed it all over the TV and the stereo on the bus and everything started shorting out.

That was everyone's invitation to have a full-on food fight. We could have gone into the hotel room and destroyed that like most bands. That would have been the smart thing to do, but instead, we had a raging party on the bus.

Since I was the new guy in the band I took the lead from Robb, who was the team captain. We ripped down the curtains and wrecked the front lounge. After the ten minutes of chaos ended, the guys in Neurosis looked at the damage and went, "Oh, shit!"

And then they bolted.

Robb was laying there laughing and drinking until he passed out. I was the last one awake on the bus. I looked at the damage and thought, "I'm not getting caught sitting up here. No fucking way!"

The bus was destroyed. It was raining grapefruit juice and orange juice from the ceiling.

I got out and went to my hotel room and waited for the phone call. Sure enough, an hour later, the phone rang. It was Machine Head's bassist Adam Duce.

"Will, were you on the bus last night?" he asked.

"Uhhh, yeah."

"Was Robb on the bus, too?"

"Yeah."

"What the fuck happened?" asked Adam, knowing damn well that we trashed it.

I didn't want to rat out Robb so I didn't say anything.

"Get down here right now! We're having a meeting in the hotel lobby," Adam said.

I got dressed and went down. Everyone from the whole tour was sitting in a big circle in these chairs looking bummed out. I sat down.

"What's going on?" I asked as innocently as possible.

"Don't act stupid, man," said our tour manager. "You know what's going on. We're getting kicked off the tour. The bus company's already pulled the bus. They're taking it within the hour after they clean it!"

That's when Robb, who was sitting next to me, elbowed me and looked at me and started laughing. I was like, hey man, if you're still laughing, I'm still laughing.

Robb didn't blink an eye. He didn't care. He knew we'd get another bus, no problem. And we did! We had another bus within five hours. It was a brand-new bus with a whole new bus company.

And then we lost *that* bus three weeks later because of Adam. The bus was in a Walmart parking lot overnight while the bus driver went to a motel to shower or sleep. We were just sitting there in the middle of the parking lot and Adam figured out how to get the bus running. He turned it on and we drove all around. When we got back to the parking lot he tried to park it exactly the way it was before, but he couldn't. So, the moment the driver saw it he knew we had moved the bus. We got kicked off that bus, too. And then came bus number three . . .

BILLY GRAZIADEI
Biohazard

On one tour with Slayer, there was non-stop wreckage. I tipped over Pepsi and Coke vending machines when I was wasted and all the glass would smash, which I thought was funny.

One night, I threw a beer bottle at Slayer's tour bus. It sailed across everyone's heads and hit the window in the perfect spot just as [Slayer guitarist] Kerry King was walking to the bus from backstage. The thing completely shattered. Kerry was freaked out and covered in glass. It was great.

But it wasn't great when the bill came.

The bus window cost me about three thousand dollars. At the end of the tour, our tour manager sat me down.

"Okay, here is a list of all the things you broke," he said. "Here's a list of damages. This is from hotels. This is from venues . . ."

Oh well, easy come, easy go.

REX BROWN
Pantera, ex-Down, ex-Crowbar, Kill Devil Hill

When Pantera were in Tokyo in 1997, our assistant and my bass tech went out and got these little plastic guns. They were semi-automatics that would put a whelp on you. Well, me and [guitarist] Dimebag [Darrell] had to one-up them, so we went to the department store and got these fully loaded little Uzis that would shoot thirty rounds a second. I bought two thousand rounds of ammunition and me and Dime shot fruit and watched it explode. We shot light bulbs and anything that had glass. We destroyed about thirty thousand dollars' worth of shit in this hotel room.

We were knocking on the crew's rooms and opening fire. We went postal in this real, real nice Hilton. We got banned from all the Hiltons in Japan for the rest of our career. I had to call the head of the Japanese record label and apologize.

"Sir, it was just a prank that went terribly wrong," I said. "I'm very, very sorry."

[Drummer] Vinnie [Paul] and [vocalist] Phil [Anselmo] were so pissed at me and Dime for the whole rest of the tour. We had to be on our best behavior. But, of course, we went back to the department store and bought a ton more of these toy guns and smuggled them back into the country.

CHRIS URENNA
ex-Nine Inch Nails, ex-Marilyn Manson

I first joined Manson in 2004 because [drummer] Ginger Fish fell off the stage in Germany and broke his arm and several other bones and was in the hospital for a while and obviously couldn't play. While I was in the band, we played Auckland, New Zealand, in this theater that was over one hundred years old. Manson was mad about something so he started throwing stuff around. While he was throwing this tantrum—it was kind of an accident, but—he had something in his hand, raised it overhead, and smashed off one of those Mercury-controlled fire detectors that had the water sprinklers. As it broke off water started pouring into the basement of the dressing room in this beautiful 1800s-built wood theater.

The floors were filling up with water. He flooded the whole place.

They had to call the fire department, which off the water main. Manson's little hissy fit caused five figures of damage. Needless to say, we were immediately escorted off the property and barred from ever playing that venue again.

DAVID VINCENT
ex-Morbid Angel, Vltimas

Our first European tour with Napalm Death was interesting to the point where we made a joint t-shirt that said "Napalm Death/Morbid Angel Smash Team." It had a skull with crossed baseball bats. If we didn't like something, it was history no matter what it was. If the TV didn't work right, out the window it went. Turn a light switch on . . . if the bulb was burned out the entire fixture was eighty-sixed. It was stupid, childish shit that cost us far too much money. But we all had a good time.

MATT BACHAND
ex-Shadows Fall, Times of Grace

One of the first nights we were out with Damageplan toward the end of 2004, Dimebag Darrell was on our bus and for some reason, Damageplan were leaving an hour before we did. The tour manager came up and said, "Dime, it's time to go!"

He didn't want to go. We were hanging out and drinking Black Tooth Grins (Royal Crown or Seagram's 7 with a splash of Coke).

"Nah, man," he said. "I'm hanging out with my buddies. I'm not going anywhere."

"Dime, it's time to go!"

"Time? Fuck the time!" Dime shouted.

Then, he put his fist through the clock in the front of our bus and it shattered everywhere.

He looked at us and said, "Oh, is your driver gonna be mad at me?"

Of course, the driver comes back and goes, "What the fuck happened?"

The next day Dime stopped somewhere and got a new clock and handed it to us.

"I'm sorry, guys. I got carried away."

The next night the same thing happened. Our bands were both leaving at the same time, but we were drinking and he just looked at the clock and decided to smash it again. This went on for weeks and weeks. Every night turned into broken clock time, and the next night we'd have a new one.

The last time, Dime went out and got this really nice stainless-steel clock with a thick glass front, not the little cheap ones they usually have on the bus.

"I swear I'm not gonna break this one," he said.

Well, he put his fist through that one, too and the slivers of glass cut up his hand. The next day he said, "Aw, how am I supposed to play? My hand's all cut up."

We taped up his hand.

"C'mon, man. Get out there and do your thing!" we said.

And he did.

KING FOWLEY
Deceased, October 31

In 1992, we played this place in Washington, D.C., called The Safari Club, and at some point this guy we called Tony Pitmonger and a few other dudes decided to climb up into the roof of the place by ripping the ceiling out. Little by little, they tore out these tiles and climbed up. Before long, they were up inside the fucking roof and pulling on all the wires and messing with the electricity.

"What the fuck?" I thought as they tore the place apart.

Then, the whole PA fell over and it landed on a dude. He had a big lump on his head and had to be taken out. Then, all the electricity shut off and the whole ceiling came down. End of show.

I think Tony and his friends broke all the wiring for the entire building.

The crazy thing is the owner didn't care. This was back in the days when you'd play these really small foreign places where the guy just wanted to get you to pay for drinks. He didn't give a shit what happened. You could shoot heroin in the bathroom. You could bring twelve-year-old kids in there as long as they bought drinks.

So, we would trash these places.

"If they don't give a damn, we don't give a damn," we figured.

We did these five-dollar, all-ages shows and brought three hundred kids to a restaurant that only held a hundred fifty people. It was so ass-packed that you could get away with anything, including climbing into the roof.

PAGE HAMILTON
Helmet

We were opening for Faith No More in Worcester, Massachusetts. Our dressing room was like a grand ballroom with puke-green walls and chandeliers. There was all this booze and food laid out.

Our merch guy, Greg, decided to start throwing food at the wall.

We were drunk and Faith No More was onstage and we were dying laughing, throwing tomatoes and fruit against the wall and watching it splatter. Henry [Bogdan], our bass player kind of snapped and he started grabbing beer bottles and whipping them against the wall, one after another. We were shielding our eyes and the bottles were knocking out the chandeliers.

Our manager at the time came in and said, "Uh, we just got this bill for ten thousand dollars."

All of a sudden the situation went from drunk idiot fun to, "What the fuck?"

WILL CARROLL

We played the House of Blues in Orlando when we were on tour with Anthrax in 2011. The show was almost over, so everyone was grabbing their stuff out of our dressing room and bringing it back on the bus. Then someone from the staff locked the door to our dressing room and my bag was still in there along with a lot of other people's things.

"Hey, our door is locked," I said to a security guard. "We need to get our shit out."

They gave me the runaround. After thirty minutes, I kicked in the door and it busted right off the hinge and shit went flying everywhere. It looked really cool, but I didn't mean to cause that much damage. I grabbed my stuff and some other things that were left and then I picked the door back up and positioned it right back on the hinges even though it was totally broken. I put the broken wood back in like a puzzle piece and stuck it back to the wall. It looked perfect! You could never tell it was totally broken.

I took off.

Then [bassist] Damien [Sisson] forgot he left something in the fridge so he went back there. "Oh no, the door's gonna collapse when he pulls the handle and we're gonna get in trouble," I thought.

But when he got back there some security guard was being yelled at by his boss. They pinned it on that guy for being too rough with the door. It was so perfect.

DINO CAZARES
Fear Factory, Divine Heresy, Brujeria, Asesino

Back when we were working on our first album, me, [producer] Ross [Robinson] and this other guy picked up these chicks who had a hotel room on Sunset Strip. We went in there thinking we were all gonna get laid.

When we got back there, these girls were in the bathroom fighting over who would end up with who. They were taking forever. So we just said, "Fuck this" and went into their hotel room and destroyed it.

We threw everything out the fourth-floor window: the TV the bed, the chairs, the lamp. And they were still in the bathroom yelling at each other when we were done, so we took off.

A half hour later, we called the room to see what happened. The sheriff answered. I don't know if they got in trouble, but we didn't go back to find out.

TOMMY VICTOR
Prong, Danzig, ex-Ministry

Ted Parsons, who was the original drummer in Prong, would get crazy when he was drunk and the next day he would never remember what he did. And he would never admit to it. He would laugh, but he'd insist that a lot of the shit he did didn't happen.

We were at the Hilton in London. We had a week off for some reason and over a three-day period Ted drank so much and then seemed to think he turned into a professional wrestler. There were light fixtures that would come out of the wall and they had them in the corners of the room. He was treating them as turnbuckles in a wrestling ring. And somehow he got up on these things and propelled himself onto the bed and tackled other people in the room. He was suddenly Roddy Piper or something.

It wasn't long before all these fixtures ripped out of the wall. The guy was 225 pounds.

There was shit thrown out of the window that night. There were drugs and girls. Then, when Ted's room was trashed, the party gravitated into my room. It just kept going and they tried to kick us out of the hotel. In order to escape arrest, I had to disappear for a couple days. I was with this girl and we were so afraid to go back to the hotel because from what we could tell everyone was going to jail. It was absolutely ridiculous how much damage they did.

But Ted somehow got out of it.

He would destroy shit and occasionally we'd get a cleanup bill but for some reason, we didn't have to pay for the damage at the London Hilton and I was basically a fugitive from the law for no reason.

Everyone thought I was a party pooper because I usually didn't smash anything because I was always afraid of getting in trouble. I guess that came from going to Catholic school. I was afraid of the nuns and it got into my head. I could feel this actual presence come up to me and go, "Oh no, here we go. We're getting into trouble again."

WILL CARROLL

In 2010, we played a three-week tour of South America. We were in Sao Paulo and everyone had his own hotel room, but whenever people want to party, they always came to my room 'cause I'm a party guy and I don't care about keeping a clean room. So everyone was in my room and we were drinking and blasting music.

There were two beds and I was jumping back and forth from one to the other. I was catching air really high and slamming on the other bed like a wrestler. Everyone was laughing and cheering and I was going higher and higher.

And then I jumped from one bed and landed in the other and it went, GWOOOOOOOMMMM! It turned into a bed taco with me in the middle.

"Pull me out, pull me out!" I yelled.

I had to be extracted from the bed. When I got out, I looked at it. The frame was cracked in half. Everyone left the room. Party over.

I tried to doctor the bed the best I could, but it wasn't working. So I tried to be real sly. We were staying at the hotel for four or five nights and this was night number two. The next day I went to the promoter.

"Hey man, do you think I could switch rooms?" I asked. "I don't like my bed. It's kinda lumpy and I haven't been able to sleep well."

"Yeah, 'cause you broke it," he replied. "I know the whole story. You jumped on your bed and busted it."

I just walked away. I couldn't lie my way out of that one.

The next day, there was a memo from the tour manager saying, "We've been kicked out of this hotel. Everyone grab your personal effects. We're moving to a way less nice hotel down the street."

I went downstairs with all my stuff and everyone was pissed at me. There was a business center down there in the lobby. I sat down and logged into the computer to check my email. And while I did that [Death Angel guitarist] Rob Cavestany walked up to me and said, "Hey asshole! You realize we're all leaving 'cause of you, right?"

I just nodded and said sorry.

We had to drag guitar cases and our luggage down the street from one hotel to the other.

TONY FORESTA

On the first Municipal Waste tour, we were all wrestling in our hotel room. I kicked my friend, our merch guy, in the chest. He's a big boy and he flew backwards into the wall and went right through the sheetrock and into the bathroom.

"Fuck. What are we gonna do?" I said. "This is going to cost a bunch of money."

The next day, we went to check out and we knew they'd find out about the damage we caused so we told the front desk that we put a hole in the wall by accident.

"Oh, don't worry about it," said the dude behind the counter. That happens all the time."

So we decided to get the fuck out of there before they checked the room and saw how big the hole was. Amazingly, we never had to pay for it.

PAGE HAMILTON

Our first ever show with [guitarist] Chris Trainer was a warm-up gig in 1997 before the tour. *Aftertaste* was done and we were playing in New Jersey at this little place where I could step from the stage to the bar. It was a packed, cool little dive. I was so excited to see Chris onstage. He was having fun moving around. We got along so well.

I was laughing onstage and, somehow, [drummer John] Stanier thought I was mocking him. I wasn't. I was just laughing because I was having fun. Plus, we hadn't played for a while so I was really excited. After the show, John was furious.

He yelled at me for making fun of him. I told him I wasn't laughing at him and then we started fighting for real. We were shoving each other and overturned a table of beer bottles and started smashing stuff. [Bassist] Henry [Bogdan] put his arm around Chris and took him out of the room.

In the end, John and I totally destroyed the dressing room. I guess instead of hurting each other we took out our anger on the room.

JOHN GALLAGHER
Raven

I was at a party in Amsterdam. During the course of the evening, every available bike and motorcycle was thrown into a canal. Why? I don't know. I guess it just seemed like the thing to do. We were just there.

Being the Boy Scouts that we were, we didn't contribute to the destruction. Most of our destruction takes place onstage.

I remember we played with Tank and the brothers [guitarist Peter Brabbs and drummer Mark Brabbs] were running around like crazy backstage, getting into everything, breaking it, and causing all kind of trouble. And then when they got onstage, they just stood still and did nothing. We're kind of the opposite. We would smash guitars and equipment, burn stuff up onstage, and then look for a cup of tea after the show.

BUZZ OSBORNE
Melvins

I got all that kind of large-scale vandalism out of my system when I was fifteen. So when I was thirty years old, I kinda sat there thinking, "Nah, this isn't for me." I'd rather have the weirdest thing about me be my art.

The audience doesn't see all this destruction. Who's it for?

When you're fifteen years old and jammed full of adrenaline and you're going through puberty it makes more sense and you kind of have an excuse to want to break things. So, I always imagined that these destructive rock guys didn't do that sort of thing when they were teenagers and it's a new thing for them. I just find breaking stuff to be relatively boring. When you're having tantrums and destroying shit as a thirty-year-old man, you just look silly.

CHAPTER 14: LAUGH? I NEARLY BOUGHT ONE

Pranks, Practical Jokes & Other Antics

For bands including Ministry, Prong, Swans, and Cop Shoot Cop. Killing Joke have been a force of musicality, spirituality, and innovation since their 1980 self-titled full-length debut. *Laugh? I Nearly Bought One!* is a 1992 compilation that includes songs from almost every Killing Joke album through 1990's *Extremities, Dirt and Various Repressed Emotions.* The collection includes the song "Eighties," the main riff of which Nirvana nabbed for "Come As You Are." Had Killing Joke not been such huge fans of the Seattle grunge band, Nirvana might have lost millions in a lawsuit, but the British pioneers decided not to take legal action.

Fans that attend the last show of a tour can pretty much expect the headliners to play a practical joke on the opening band. Sometimes, the opening bands also mess with the headliners and usually it's all good-spirited fun. But sometimes the pranks are mean or destructive, either accidentally or on purpose. Other times, they're entertaining to the bands involved but they can ruin part of the show for the crowd members who came to see a band play a particular song without having it marred by uncontrolled laughter, unanticipated sound effects, or stunts that make the musicians unable to play. Still, some fans consider it a once-in-a-lifetime opportunity to see their favorite band's hit single collapse like a pyramid of canned foods. If being on the road for so months at a time inspires metal bands to coordinate elaborate onstage pranks, it also contributes to the passive aggressive jokes artists play on one another all tour long. It isn't just inter-band pranks, either. Lots of musicians get their ya-yas by humiliating friends and strangers alike, which is one reason why he who drinks with mischievous artists should be careful not to pass out, lest he wake up covered in obscene Sharpie doodles.

ROB HALFORD
Judas Priest, ex-Halford, ex-Fight

By the time we had a bit of money, we got a very bright orange Volvo. Once, we pulled this thing up to a traffic light. Glenn had a really hot meat and potato pie. This big, burly biker pulled up beside us and was revving up his bike and looking at us. For some reason, Glenn was just possessed and threw the pie at this guy and caught him on the back of the neck.

It was scalding, boiling hot!

This biker started screaming at us.

"Drive, drive, drive!" shouted Glenn.

Whoever was driving kept meshing the gears and we kept sputtering and starting and sputtering and starting. The biker guy got off his bike and he was holding this huge piece of biker chain. He started thrashing the Volvo in the middle of the street with all these people looking at us. We managed to get the car going again and we drove away. Thank God he only hit the car with the chain and didn't follow us when we left.

GLENN TIPTON
Judas Priest

It wasn't a meat pie, it was a French loaf. We were coming back from a gig one night and there was a bunch of Hells Angels. As they passed by the window of our car I reached out and hit one of the Hell's Angels with a loaf and it broke over his helmet.

It really was meant as a joke. I didn't think he would take it personally. It's only a piece of bread.

About ten minutes later we pulled up to some traffic lights and these bikers with chains surrounded us. They were prepared to beat the shit out of our car and change its shape. It was an old Volvo, which I hated, anyway, so they just made it look better, in my opinion.

For five minutes, they reigned havoc upon the car and then drove off. We're really fortunate they didn't drag us out and stab us.

We did throw a meat pie at a Teddy Boy once. The guy had sneakers, the long three-quarter coat with the velvet collar and his hair was like Elvis's. We didn't throw it at his face but he wasn't very pleased. He chased us up the road, but again, we got away.

TONY IOMMI
Black Sabbath, Heaven & Hell

We were recording *Born Again* at Richard Branson's house. We played so many pranks on each other there that we went overboard, literally. [Vocalist] Ian Gillan had a big twin-engine boat parked outside on the river. [Drummer] Bill [Ward] and a couple of us went in with a chisel and chiseled through the bottom of Ian's boat and sank it.

Of course, Ian got up in the morning and went, "Someone's nicked me boat! Me boat's gone!"

He didn't know it was underwater. He had this massive guy that worked for him driving up and down the river trying to find the boat. And then when he found out what had happened, he was furious. The pranks kept getting worse from there. We didn't kill each other, but we could have.

VINNY APPICE
ex-Black Sabbath, Heaven & Hell, ex-Dio

There was a rehearsal place in Sound City that was across the street from a parking lot. A guy named Brett worked there and he had his office set up just so— a lamp, a desk, a chair—the whole thing. We went in there and turned the vending machines upside-down to get some fucking candy outta there. We opened the pinball games and made it so the balls wouldn't go down the chute—so you could play forever. Sometimes we punched holes in the wall just for fun.

"Hey Brett, we need some beer. Can you go to the store for us?" we once asked him.

He got in his car and ran to the store and we took his whole office and put it out in the parking lot in the same exact position. We got the electricity going too, so the lamp was on outside. It was nighttime, too, so it was perfect. Everyone got a good laugh out of that.

SCOTT IAN
Anthrax, S.O.D., The Damned Things

We pulled off the greatest prank on Slayer in Miami on the last date of the Clash of the Titans tour. Back then, Slayer never broke character and never smiled. It was all pure evil and they always pulled it off. It was amazing.

We thought about what we could do to break the façade onstage.

So we asked one of the guys in our crew to go to a supermarket and get the biggest fish in the place. This thing was, like, two hundred pounds.

The lighting guys put it up in the rigging and attached fishing line to it. We told them to lower the thing when Slayer began playing "Angel of Death." So, [guitarists] Kerry King and Jeff Hanneman burst into that classic riff that opens the song and our guys started to slowly lower this humungous fish. By the time [vocalist and bassist] Tom [Araya] made that horrifying scream that comes right before the vocals kick in the thing was right in front of his Tom's microphone

We were laughing our asses off the whole time. Slayer tried to keep their composure, but they all started cracking up, too.

DAVID VINCENT
ex-Morbid Angel, Vltimas

We were touring with Black Sabbath and Motörhead and there was one day when we went into catering and they were serving chicken. I grabbed a few pieces and sat down where everyone was eating. I cut into the chicken and it was severely undercooked, to where it was bleeding. I raised all kinds of Cain about that. I yelled at everybody. I don't think anybody was near as upset as I was and I have a loud voice so it kind of stuck in people's minds.

The last day of the tour, Motörhead attached a whole chicken to a string up in the rafters on the light truss. While I was singing, the techs lowered this thing down to where it was right above my head for virtually the entire show and I didn't notice it.

Everybody else did, though, and they were laughing.

"What the fuck is so funny?" I thought."

It never dawned on me to look up.

FRANKIE BANALI
Quiet Riot, ex-W.A.S.P.

W.A.S.P. was opening for Quiet Riot and their singer Blackie Lawless used to do this thing where he'd turn this skull prop upside-down and it would have fake blood in it. He'd show it to the crowd and then pour all this blood into his mouth.

One night I decided to exchange the fake blood with hot sauce. I have never seen demon eyes quite like that in my entire life.

So, for payback, he had the road crew go out and get a couple dozen chicken carcasses, which they kept tossing at me as I was playing. At one point, there were more chickens on the drum riser than drums.

GARY HOLT
Exodus, Slayer

We played some jokes but they were usually pretty normal. They weren't on the level of [Guitarist] Phil Campbell from Motörhead. He was legendary for pulling pranks.

He once rode out on a horse while Testament was onstage.

One time we did something cool at one of these Christmas festivals in Portugal in the early 2000s. There were about ten bands playing. [Exodus guitarist] Rick [Hunolt] and I got control of the smoke machine and we hammered the button down on the thing when Grave were onstage and wouldn't let it go until there was so much haze you couldn't see anything. We set off every fire alarm in the place. They came at us and we acted all innocent.

"What's wrong? Why are you so angry?"

The venue was just a step or two from totally evacuating the place. It was awesome.

DEE SNIDER
Twisted Sister, ex-Widowmaker

Back in the '80s, everyone was partying, going to strip clubs, and sleeping with lots of girls. And I was straight in the sense that I was married and faithful and I didn't drink take drugs or go out to strip clubs.

So, when we toured with Ratt they filled our dressing room with dildos and sex toys and put pornographic pictures all over the walls. That's the only prank anyone's really pulled on us because I absolutely forbid anyone from doing pranks onstage. It just ruins a show for an audience that paid to see a real concert. So I make it clear that I will come and get anybody that pranks us. I will hurt them and find their family. But the Ratt thing—that was kinda funny.

JOEY JORDISON
ex-Slipknot, Murderdolls, Sinsaenum, Vimic

When I was in Slipknot, we all had fun pranking each other. [Vocalist] Corey [Taylor] is fucking terrified of sharks. One time, I got up early and went to a theatrical shop and bought a six-foot shark prop. I stuck it in his bunk before he got to the bus. When he saw the shark he almost passed out. It rocked.

CORY TAYLOR
Slipknot, Stone Sour

I used to do this thing called the rhino. I would wait until the last show of the tour and I would go onstage naked with socks duct taped around my Johnson so it looked like a rhino horn. And I'd go on and jump up and down and freak out the opening band.

At one point, I wandered on stage like that with a case of beer and started handing cold beers to the band while it was playing. Everyone onstage was looking at me like I was fucking crazy and people in the audience were losing their fucking minds.

GEORGE "CORPSEGRINDER" FISHER
Cannibal Corpse

We played in Italy with Dark Funeral, Marduk, and Vomitory. During our set Vomitory came onstage in just their underwear and they put their hands around each other's waists and did a train across the stage. They all stood there in their underwear while we played "Covered with Sores." Then everyone but their old lead singer Marten left. Marten stayed, took his underwear completely off. He swung it around for a while and did a little dance, then left butt-naked.

ERIK RUTAN
Hate Eternal, ex-Morbid Angel, ex-Ripping Corpse

Morbid Angel were playing the Trocadero in Philly and it was the last show of the tour. Our crew decided they were going to come out with socks on their cocks and do a train. Five of them walked across the stage while we were playing. And my mom was there that night.

I was dying inside, but they got offstage and my mom came to the side of the stage and those guys were standing there and she knew some of them.

So they had an interesting conversation.

TOMMY VICTOR
Prong, Danzig, ex-Ministry

In about 2006, Ministry had this road manager that we terrorized. Al [Jourgensen] told the guy he was going to fire him unless he drank a whole bunch of absinthe. The guy guzzled this absinthe and we saw him change. It hit him like a hit of acid.

He was praying to God and was a complete mess.

We totally terrorized the poor guy. He vomited everywhere. He was on the bus naked. We drew all over him, we put cigarettes up his ass and took pictures of him. It was horrible stuff. And he didn't even know he was naked. We told him he had to go check into a hotel and he went into the hotel naked covered with obscene drawings.

FRANKIE BANALI

We made sure that everyone we toured with got excessively drunk and passed out. And then, they might wake up with their pants down and a mustard bottle hanging out their ass and we would take pictures and put them up backstage. Or someone might hold a big fake penis next to someone's face and take pictures. That was our idea of fun.

KIRK WINDSTEIN
Crowbar, ex-Down

Crowbar played a gig around 2001, and I went back to Dimebag Darrell's house with him and [his common-law wife] Rita. We were doing our usual thing, drinking Black Tooth Grins and slamming Coors Lights. We were jamming on guitar and I was getting pretty drunk. Dime was feeding me shots. Of course, if Dime was giving you a shot you were gonna fuckin' do it.

I ended up passing out.

"All right, K. Windstein, lemme get you back to your hotel. It's five o'clock in the morning," Dime said after waking me up. "You got a fuckin' gig tomorrow, boy."

"All right man, I had a great time."

He gave me a Pantera T-shirt and he dropped me off at my little Motel 6. I made it to my room and passed out.

I got up in the middle of the night to take a piss and I turned on the fucking light, bleary-eyed. I glanced in the mirror and it scared the living fuck out of me. Dime had taken a Sharpie and drawn the full Gene Simmons makeup on me. I had Sharpie permanent marker black lipstick. The whole nine fuckin' yards.

I went, "Oh my God!" and stumbled back to bed and passed out again.

In the morning I got in the shower and I scrubbed with a washcloth to the point where my skin was swollen and getting rashes and that shit would not come off. I went through two or three boxes of baby wipes. I washed my face at the venue all day. It took a good week until all the marker finally went away.

BUZZ OSBORNE
Melvins

We played with Isis on their last-ever tour. On the last night, we went out with water-soluble ink pens and wrote all over their vans, "Boston pigs suck" and "Fuck you, pigs" and all this horrible shit.

They were loading out and their vans are covered in these hostile words. Try driving through town like that. They were pissed, but we thought it was funny. And when they realized that it wasn't permanent marker they calmed down a lot.

BRENT RAMBLER
August Burns Red

We were in Australia playing the Soundwave Festival in 2014. It was in Adelaide and the dressing rooms were in an old historic jail. We were getting ready and our tour manager thought it would be funny if he shut the door of our dressing room.

"You guys are locked in jail now," he said.

The thing is, the door actually locked.

"Okay, don't worry," he said. "I'll go and get the key and come right back."

The place was ancient and the room we were in had a solitary confinement door, which didn't have any bars on it. Our tour manager went downstairs.

"Hey, man I closed the cell door on the band as a joke and now they're locked in there," he told the guy that was there. Can I have the key to get them out?"

"We don't have a key," the dude replied. "Why did you close the door?"

"I don't know," he lied. "It's a dressing room and the guys are changing."

"No, you're not supposed to close the door."

So our manager came back and said, "Guys, there is no key. We're working on some way to get you out."

We were supposed to go onstage and play in, literally, fifteen minutes and we weren't even close to the stage. Our tour manager started trying to get the door off with a screwdriver. He was unscrewing the outside lock. And the owners of the place were yelling at him saying, "This is an antique jail. You can't take the lock off!"

"I don't care. My band's locked inside," he said. "I will tear this place apart if I have to."

But he couldn't get the lock apart.

At that point, we were just worrying about getting out, let alone playing our set. Meanwhile, the guys in Five Finger Death Punch are filming the whole thing and thinking it's hilarious.

Finally, some guy said, "I have the jail manager's son's phone number. Maybe we can get hold of him."

They called him and fortunately, he was there. He didn't have the key, but he was able to get hold of the prison master and the guy had a skeleton key for all the cells. They unlocked the door, we all got into a shuttle and went straight to the stage. Our intro was just finishing when we got there and jumped onstage and started the show.

WILLIE ADLER
Lamb of God

We were in Sweden with Slayer and Children of Bodom on the Unholy Alliance tour and the show was being broadcast nationally over the radio. So me and [bassist] John [Campbell] thought it would be funny to come up with some line in Swedish and hand it to [vocalist] Randy [Blythe], saying, "Oh, this means you guys are the best."

We talked with one of Bodom's guitar techs and asked him how to say, "Now everybody please cum on my belly."

We wrote it out phonetically and handed it to Randy right before the break in the set.

So he said it to the crowd and . . . crickets.

It was so quiet.

I was off in the wings laughing my ass off. Randy didn't know what he had actually said and we didn't tell him until after the set. He was absolutely outraged.

BILLY GRAZIADEI
Biohazard

I'm fluent in Portuguese and I speak some Swedish and Spanish. I love learning different languages. When we went to another country in the early days, I used to find a cute girl and ask her how to say things in her native tongue and I'd learn how to say them. I practiced, took notes and then I'd say a little bit to the audience. At first, it was simple things like, "How you doing? It's great to be here. Make some noise." And then it got to be sentences. I tried to say something to the crowd in Serbia and that was insane.

When we were in Sweden once, [vocalist] Evan [Seinfeld's] ego got the best of him and he wanted a little more of the limelight. He asked some Swedish friends of mine to help him talk to the crowd. He was trying to jump on my coattails.

"Don't help him for real," I said to them in Swedish. "Everything he asks, tell him something different."

He wanted to say, "I really love being here" and I had them teach him, "I love young boys." And it went on from there.

We get onstage and I spoke to the crowd.

He said, "C'mon, lemme do it. I want to talk to them."

"Do you remember how to say what you were taught?" I said.

He said he did and then he started to walk over to the mic. I just couldn't go through with it.

"Don't do it! Don't do it!" I said.

"No, I got it," he said. "I got it."

"No, bro. Trust me. We fucked with you. It's all a joke. You really don't want to say those things to a crowd."

So he didn't do it. But he was bummed.

MORGAN LANDER
Kittie

We toured with Shadows Fall, Killswitch Engage, and Poison the Well. On Poison the Well's last day, we were at the Whisky in Los Angeles and we decided to send them off with a bang. We hired male strippers and paid them a bunch of money to go onstage like they were going to stage dive, but instead of diving, they went up there and started taking their clothes off. It was fucking amazing. The guys' eyes were popping out of their heads. The strippers fully stripped down and they were dancing around. God, we were laughing so hard.

SAM RIVERS
Limp Bizkit

If you take a whole bunch of Niacin you'll break out almost into hives and you'll turn real red and itchy. It's not dangerous, but if you don't tell somebody that you've dosed them with Niacin, they don't know what the fuck happened and they usually freak out. I'd never heard of that until it was done to me when I was eighteen and we were recording our first record, and then I ended up doing it to other people a lot.

Our first producer Ross Robinson did it to most of us in the band because he was all about the vitamins back then. He was such a health freak.

"Hey guys," he told me and [drummer] John [Otto]. "This is a new vitamin. It's incredible. You gotta try it."

So we did and he didn't say a word.

After we finished tracking John and I were having a few beers in the back next to a little shed. He went to the restroom and I went out to have a cigarette. Then, when we both walked back into the room we saw each other's arms and faces. We both had beers in our hands.

"Oh man, it's the beer!" we concluded.

We seriously thought the beer was tainted.

Everybody else in the studio had already been pranked so they were in on it. We ran into the control room and yelled at everybody not to drink the beer. We were itching and our bodies were getting all hot. We thought we were going to have to go to the hospital for food poisoning. They all started laughing and we had no clue what was going on.

"No, dudes, we're dead serious," I said. "Put down your fucking beer!"

"No, dude, Relax," someone finally said. "Ross played the same joke on all of us and you were the last to get pranked. You haven't been poisoned and the itching will go away."

That was the worst prank anyone's played on me. So, of course, I had to pay it forward.

TREVOR STRNAD
The Black Dahlia Murder

It was horrific. As I Lay Dying put a dead, pregnant possum on our windshield under the windshield wipers. The animal had these little white pieces squirting out of it all over the place. We didn't know who did such a disgusting thing but we eventually figured it out.

MORGAN LANDER

We toured with Blackguard and The Agonist. The drummer of Blackguard, Justine, despises octopi, so we went out and bought an octopus and put it on her cymbals. She had to go out there with a dead octopus. That was pretty gross, but we thought it was hilarious.

DEVIN TOWNSEND
Strapping Young Lad, ex-Steve Vai, ex-Wildhearts, Devin Townsend Band

Steve Vai played *The Tonight Show with Jay Leno* in 1983 when I was singing for him. And me and my buddy were backstage. We felt like the staff were full of themselves. So we went into the green room and I said, "Let's just fuck with them. We can cover up the windows and take photos of me naked all over the room."

Halfway through this craziness, I decided to stick the receiver of the house phone up my ass. We got a bunch of photos of that and it was really funny.

The next day I got a phone call.

"I can't believe you did that!" one of the guys at management said to me.

I played innocent: "Did what? We didn't do a thing."

"Yeah, you did. They caught the whole thing on hidden camera."

I got mad shit for that.

Afterward, I got Dunlop [Manufacturing] to make me some guitar picks that said, "Don't use Jay's phone."

DAVE PETERS
Throwdown, ex-Eighteen Visions, ex-Bleeding Through

One of the roadies' stepdads worked for the telephone company. When you're up in those cherry pickers working on the top of the telephone pole, typically guys don't come down to use the bathroom. They have these bags they pee in. So our roadie got a bunch of them for us to use during the tour. It's better than trying to pee in a bottle 'cause there's this silica stuff on the bottom that turns your pee into gel.

One time, these guys in front of us were pacing each other and going fifty miles-per-hour on both lanes of the road. We couldn't get around them. We were running late for a show and they just wanted to be dicks by blocking us behind them. We finally got around them after some evasive, dangerous driving, and one of them flipped us off and threw something at the van.

So, one of us reached into the back and grabbed one of these pee bags and threw it at their car. It couldn't have been more awful and perfect. The guy had his window down a little bit. It caught him right on the corner where the windshield meets the hood. The bag ripped and this pee gel flew into this guy's car through the passenger window. It got all over him and the inside of his car.

GENE HOGLAN
Dark Angel, Testament, Dethklok, ex-Death, ex-Strapping Young Lad

Dark Angel was really, really into the urine bomb. If we ever drove with another band, chances are somebody would get a piss-filled balloon whipped at them at some point or a Big Gulp cup full of urine thrown on them. That was our big move. Usually, the urine bombs were directed at each other more than anyone else.

In July of 1987, we were traveling to Texas in two vans, one for equipment and one for the band. We were driving in the blistering heat with no gas stations for miles and miles and I had to piss really bad. I grabbed a Big Gulp cup, peed in there, and filled that up.

I told whoever was driving, "Hey man, pull up to our other van."

I tossed the cup of pee out the window and it landed perfectly on the rim of his door. Our tech was shirtless. He had his window open, arm hanging out the window. And he was soaked with urine. Our tour manager Tony was in the passenger seat and as soon as our tech got hit, the guy said to Tony, "Oh my God! You don't think that was piss, was it?"

Tony leaned over and smelled him and said, "It sure smells like piss."

The poor dude. There was not a gas station for miles.

SAM RIVERS

I had irritable bowel syndrome (IBS) when I was younger and I couldn't wait to make it to a rest stop. Since you can't shit in the toilet of a bus, I'd bag it and throw it out the window. Or I'd squeeze the poop bag out of the little vent on top of the roof of the bus.

Usually, it would land by the side of the road, but one time I tossed it out and it landed smack on the windshield of a driver behind us and freaked the fuck out of him.

It wasn't an intentional prank, but we all laughed our asses off.

SCOTT IAN

When we were in our hotels, we use to throw water at people and that quickly escalated to piss and shit. We were total degenerates with no concern for who was going to have to clean up for us. One trick was to get someone's key when they were out and sneak into their room and shit in their garbage can. Then you'd fill the trash with hot water and turn the heater on full blast. Whoever your target was—and we were all victims at one point or another—would come back to their room six or seven hours later and open the door to a hot, nauseating wave of human excrement. [First published in the book, *I'm the Man: The Story of That Guy From Anthrax* by Scott Ian with Jon Wiederhorn.]

RICHARD CHRISTY
Charred Walls of the Damned, ex-Death, ex-Iced Earth, ex-Public Assassin

My band Public Assassin played a gig at a community center in Joplin, Missouri, in 1993. We were so bored. There was nothing to do backstage.

There was a kitchen and an oven there, and for some reason, our lead singer said to me, "Why doesn't someone take a dump in a Folger's can and we'll cook it?"

I was happy to oblige.

We put it in the oven and set it at 400 degrees. Then we went onstage and played our show. The community center started filling up with smoke. The smoke reeked. And we were making jokes onstage like, "Wow, this gig is the shit" and "Man, this shit is smoking today, right guys?"

It was a pretty stupid thing to do but nothing caught on fire. And, fuck, when you get bored on the road you do some pretty crazy shit.

DEVIN TOWNSEND

We did a tour with Meshuggah in America. During the last show, we were onstage and they started screaming through our monitor wedges to try and distract us. For a whole song, it was just them screaming and everybody was trying to keep themselves composed.

So during the third song of their set, [drummer] Gene [Hoglan] and I walked over really slowly while they were playing and covered everything with toilet paper. And then Gene stood there totally stoic, with his sunglasses on while he held toilet paper between two fingers.

I took a shit in a bucket, then took the toilet paper from Gene, wiped my ass with it and threw it on the drummer [Tomas Haake's] kit.

He was so confused, it was awesome. He was looking at me and he had this expression that just said, "Why would you?"

BEN WEINMAN
The Dillinger Escape Plan

For one of our earliest tours, we went out with Botch and Converge. Those bands would prank each other the whole tour and we just tried to stay out of it. But eventually we got wrapped up in it as well because they would throw eggs at one another and we ended up getting covered in eggs. Our drummer was super-pissed. And then Botch and Converge were shooting fireworks at each other, which was crazy.

We left the tour early to play the Milwaukee Metal Fest, but right before we split, someone took a big shit in a cup and I put a note in it that said, "Thanks for putting up with all this shit." I hid it in their van in the bottom of this big bag of food. It was August, and it took them over a week to find it. They were throwing up it smelled so bad. They didn't know what it was and they couldn't find it. They were smelling themselves to see if it was them and washing their clothes.

Finally, [bassist] Brian [Cook] found the cup of shit and was like, "Whoa!" He was dry heaving and freaked out.

We toured with them a couple times after that and I was really waiting for them to get back at us, but they never did because I think they were scared.

They were just like, "Let's let it go and leave them alone because they're obviously not afraid to escalate things."

ERIK TURNER
Warrant

We toured with Mötley Crüe and one night Tommy Lee came in and left a sandwich on the table in our dressing room.

It was a shit sandwich.

He had taken a shit and put it on bread and taken the time to put mustard and lettuce on it. He came in, dropped it off and ran out.

So [singer] Jani [Lane] took a Hershey bar and rubbed it all over his face so it looked like he ate the sandwich. He went into Tommy's dressing room and everyone had a good laugh.

GEORGE "CORPSEGRINDER" FISHER

One night when we were touring with Obituary, guitarist Allen West came out with a pair of underwear with a melted candy bar smeared all over it. I was standing there singing and he walked up to me like he was serving me dinner. He held this messy underwear and looked at me. "What the hell have you got there?" I thought. Instead of giving it to me or rubbing in my hair or whatever, he just smiled and threw it into the crowd.

WILL CARROLL
Death Angel, ex-Machine Head

Death Angel guitarist Ted [Aguilar] used to guitar tech for Obituary. He told me that a former member of the band used to shit in a bag backstage and then go behind the drum set while the support band was on and throw the bag into the crowd on a regular basis. That's kinda funny and disgusting at the same time.

MARK SLAUGHTER
Slaughter, ex-Vinnie Vincent Invasion

When we were touring with Ted Nugent in 2004, our last show ended in Las Vegas and since that's my home I called a buddy of mine who went to a costume shop and rented a panda suit for me. I dressed up in this panda suit and threw my backstage pass over it. I walked through the crowd and waved at people. Then I walked into the backstage area and knocked on Ted's door.

Ted opened it, looked at me, and stepped back.

He carries, so he put his hand on his gun.

"Hey, Ted! Gimme a hug!" I said.

I pulled the panda head off and he said, "Mark Slaughter, you crazy son of a bitch. I thought you were one of those PETA fuckers and I was going to have to shoot you."

"Ted, I'm the one white meat you don't eat," I said.

DEVIN TOWNSEND

We were in Germany with Steve Vai and the keyboardist had a bunch of fart samples on his keyboard. MTV was taping the show so I thought it would be funny if I went to the front of the stage and held the mic up to my ass while he made the fart sounds to make it look like I was farting.

MATT BACHAND
ex-Shadows Fall, Times of Grace

We were out with Slipknot in 2005. Me and [guitarist] Jon [Donais] were always running around with [their drummer] Joey Jordison and talking about '80s hair bands because we loved that shit and everyone else seemed to hate it. We were talking about '80s-era Kiss. Everyone said, "'80s Kiss sucked. It's all about '70s Kiss!"

But we were all about '80s Kiss. We'd run into the dressing rooms every night blasting '80s Kiss, bumming everybody out. The last two shows of the tour we put a band together that we called '80s Kiss and opened the last two Slipknot dates. Joey dressed up like [drummer] Eric Carr, I was [guitarist] Vinnie Vincent, Jon was Paul Stanley and their tour manager, Sully, was

Gene [Simmons]. We went all out. We had the rigging set up so we could lift Gene up in the air thirty feet. We all did really shitty makeup jobs and used pieces of cardboard with "'80s Kiss" spray painted on them as a backdrop. It was so hokey. Everyone in the crowd was looking at us confused. The only ones into it were the old dogs that were there with their kids.

We played three songs, "Tears Are Falling," "Lick It Up," and "Heaven's on Fire." Jon was in total Paul Stanley mode. He was yelling things like, "Hey, section 318! I see you back there. You're louder than the PA, man!"

And people in that section were looking at each other like, "What???"

One of the shows was in Madison, Wisconsin, and he got up on the mic and said, "Madison Square Garden, I'm talking to you!"

MARK MORTON
Lamb of God

We toured with Slayer and Amon Amarth in 2019. And Amon Amarth had this big Viking boat as part of their stage production. Before the last show of the tour a bunch of band members and crew from the other bands got ahead of the game and ordered a bunch of oars and toy fishing rods. So, during our last night with them a dozen of us stormed their boat and rowed it and fished off of it for the last song of the set.

JOHN GALLAGHER
Raven

We toured with Running Wild, who have lots of pirate themes in their music. They had a Viking ship on their drum riser with a figurehead in the front. When we were in Barcelona we were wandering around in the upper reaches of the loft and found this gigantic clown's head, so we put it on the figurehead of the ship. When they saw it they were laughing so hard they couldn't play.

Another show on the tour, [drummer] Joe [Hasselvander], who is roughly the same size and has the same hairdo as their guitarist Rock 'n' Rolf, grabbed one of Rolf's two identical Explorer guitars and put on Rolf's huge jacket. Then Mark walked behind him and imitated every move he made for half the song. Rolf couldn't figure out why the crowd was laughing.

RICHARD CHRISTY

I grew up on a farm in Missouri and I quickly learned you gotta kind of make your own fun there. So I've always been up for any sort of crazy hijinks.

I've never been afraid to run around nude.

When I was in Europe playing drums in Death, I wore a super-tight thong with my balls hanging out. [Frontman] Chuck [Schuldiner], [bassist] Scott [Clendenin] and [guitarist] Shannon [Hamm] got such a kick out of it. I don't think the fans really understood what was going on. But it was very comfortable.

JERRY DIXON
Warrant

We were always screwing with each other, for sure. One night, [Michael Foster] the drummer in Firehouse and myself were in my room partying. And he mentioned that he never trashed a hotel room. Immediately I went, "Oh, we're gonna change that."

So, he and I threw the TV, the chairs and the furniture out into the Ohio River.

The next day we called the Firehouse guys in and told them that because of what Michael and I did, our managers thought we shouldn't be on tour anymore together and they should go home.

Michael turned green. He went, "Whaaaatt? Oh my God!"

And then we started laughing and he realized we were fucking with him.

KYLE SHUTT
The Sword

We played a tour with Seemless and Lacuna Coil and on the final night when Seemless was going on, the drummer, Derek Kerswill (ex-Unearth) started the count off for the last song and as he did that a Lacuna Coil crew guy grabbed the ride cymbal and walked off with it. Thirty seconds later another guy came on and took the crash cymbal. Then, a guy grabbed a floor tom. They took his whole drum kid apart piece by piece until all he had left at the end of the song was a kick and snare.

MYLES KENNEDY
Alter Bridge, Slash

While we were playing our last song the headlining band Fuel and their crew came out and started to slowly unplug each of our instruments and amps and took things off piece by piece until I was just standing there like an idiot.

PAUL LEDNEY
Profanatica, Havohej

I have a really high-frequency sound that I bookmarked on YouTube. It's really high pitched and it makes people nauseous. So I'll put it on my iPad and play it in the green room and walk out. No one's puked, but I've made a lot of people uncomfortable.

You start to feel the high-pitched sound in your jaw. Some people can hear it and they think something's wrong and start to panic. It's barely audible but even if you cover your ears you still hear it. It goes in through your eyes and if your mouth is open it goes in there.

So I won't ever come forward and say, "Hey, I did it" and laugh about it. It's more of a real-life torture thing that I'll pull from time to time. It doesn't work on my band. My guys know as soon as I pull out the iPad what I'm up to and they leave.

DAVE ELLEFSON
Megadeth

The pranks usually came from the guitar techs messing with us. They'd put Bengay in a certain guitar player's high-top shoes so when he was onstage his feet would be killing him. And we found out that one tech would spit in one of the guitar player's water bottles because he hated him.

We were on tour with Iron Maiden one time and their crew came out while we were playing and dressed up like women and danced around us just to punk us. But it was done with love. They weren't dumping bags of flour on us onstage or anything.

DEZ FAFARA
DevilDriver, ex-Coal Chamber

The last night of a tour, we were in Washington at the 9:30 Club. We went upstairs and filled, like, three hundred tiny little Dixie cups with baby powder and sat upstairs on the balcony. The minute the opening band started playing, we dumped all these cups on them. It ruined all of the gear, it ruined all the monitors, we got sued and we had to pay the club for the monitor system and everything. Pranking always went bad with us. We always took it overboard.

GARY HOLT

Pranks with us usually amounted to shaving cream pies in the face and we put a stop to that. A crew would usually do that to us on the last day of the tour and then they'd go home. They were paid employees of the band, but they didn't clean the shit that got all fucked up by these pies. We'd take a couple of weeks off and go back to rehearsal and our gear would be all covered in dried up crust and shaving cream.

We said, "If you're going to be pulling this shit and not clean up the mess before the gear goes back in the cases we're gonna be fighting."

KYLE SHUTT

I got to pie three out of four members of Metallica. If you're in Metallica and it's your birthday you get pied and it's been that way for thirty years. They make it an epic thing so you never know when it's gonna happen.

[Bassist Robert] Trujillo was first. They would always end with "Seek and Destroy," and they would put the house lights on and drop down a bunch of big inflatable Metallica beach balls. That's when we would pull the trigger. The house lights were up. Everybody was singing "Happy Birthday" to Rob and then "Seek and Destroy" started, which was our cue. We were hiding under the stage and we came out around every corner, each of us with two pies in hand. Trujillo was covered in pie and everyone had a great time.

A couple months later it was Kirk's birthday. Before the show there was a meeting: "Okay, we're gonna pie Kirk [Hammett]. There's just one rule. Don't hit his guitar."

Me and Kirk had become buddies at that point and it was my personal mission to pie him. This became the whole point of my life. I had two pies in hand. I snuck up behind him and right when I threw the pie he spun around and faced me and my pie flew through the air slammed right into his guitar.

It was like one of those slow motion "oooohhhh, nooooo!" moments.

I felt so bad. But then I threw the other pie and got him in the face.

Lars is hard to pie. We had all the pies hidden underneath the stage where all the propane was for the pyro. We figured we'd get him after "Seek and Destroy" was over, which was a little different. Lars runs for two hours a day. He has a jogging regimen and he's really fast and in shape. So we wanted to get him while he was sitting down playing.

That motherfucker. He knew we were coming for him. He could sense it. He was on a rotating drum riser that was on the stage in the round. He turned around at the end of the song and saw us, and he made it all the way across the other side of the stage, down to the barricade, and then all the way behind us before we even knew what was going on. He hightailed it out of there.

Someone eventually got him on the back end, but it wasn't me. So I really only pied two Metallica guys.

They weren't on tour when James [Hetfield] had his birthday so I couldn't get him either.

WILL CARROLL

Five or six years ago, Death Angel did a European tour and someone kept filling my water bottles with vodka when I was onstage and that suuuucked, man! After a three or four-song stretch with no breaks I was dying for a gulp of water. I turned around and grabbed my bottle, took a huge swig and spit it up all over myself. Someone kept on doing that and I never found out who it was.

DAVID DRAIMAN
Disturbed

We were brutalized on Ozzfest the first time we played the festival in 2000. We got pranked, pranked, pranked. Every single drum head on Mikey [Wengren's] kit was covered with talcum powder; someone filled all of our water bottles with vodka. In the middle of one of our sets, one of the guys from the Deadlights came up and wrapped us with diapers while we were playing. Another time, someone came out while we were playing a song and tied our ankles together with duct tape. It was merciless.

MORGAN LANDER

We were out on tour with Disturbed and our last show was in Montreal. At the very end of our set, they all came out and poured gallons of milk all over us. I couldn't shower because there was no shower at the venue and there was no time before we had to leave. As time went on that night and into the next day driving home, the milk started to get sour. I reeked so bad. It was horrible.

DINO CAZARES
Fear Factory, Divine Heresy, Brujeria, Asesino

When we played with System of a Down we threw powder and food condiments on everybody. It wasn't a well-planned joke, but it ended up good. The last show was San Francisco and there was a restaurant inside the venue. So we took all the mustard, ketchup and mayonnaise and threw it all over them along with a bunch of powder. Then they turned around and did it back to us. It turned into this wild food fight.

FRANKIE BANALI

When Quiet Riot opened up for Iron Maiden in 1983 their drummer Nicko McBrain came out on the last show and sprayed silly string all over me to the point that I looked like I was in Funkadelic. I had so much of that shit in my hair and, of course, I couldn't get it out.

So, after we finished playing, I went and acquired two dozen raw eggs. While Maiden was playing I sat behind Nicko and every time he did a drum fill, I popped a raw egg on his head. It was brutal. I don't think he's ever forgiven me for that, but we're still friends.

WILL CARROLL

In about 2012 we were in Germany on our way to the airport. It was the end of the tour and we were getting ready to fly home. We stopped at this gas station right outside the airport. I hopped outside the bus with my flip-flops, my shorts and a T-shirt on. I didn't have my phone or my wallet because I was just running in to use the bathroom. I was only in there for a minute or two, but when I got back out the bus was gone.

I started losing it. I started screaming, "Oh my God, nooooo!"

I was yelling at myself like a crazy person. I was freezing cold and I didn't know what to do. I thought they had left without me but all they had done was pull the bus on the other side of this huge divider at the gas station to trick me. And they were all filming and watching me lose my shit.

KIRK WINDSTEIN

We toured a bunch with Pantera over the years and everything with Dimebag [Darrell] was crazy. One time we were playing in St. Louis with Pantera at the beginning of the *Far Beyond Driven* tour and they had just taken off. This was right before they started playing arenas.

We were at this really old theater and we were jamming. Normally, people pull stunts at the end of a tour. This was just some regular Tuesday evening gig. But that's the way it was with Pantera.

They had this huge PA and monitoring system on tour with them that was really loud. We were onstage jamming and all of a sudden, I feel like something's come off the roof. These things were falling all over.

"Man, there's so much fuckin' low end in the mix the paint is literally coming off the ceiling," I thought.

I'm rocking out and getting into it. Then I glance off to my left and there's Dimebag with a fuckin' VHS video camera filming us. I thought that was peculiar, but I keep playing and then the ceiling really started flaking off.

"Damn, this place is getting ready to cave in," I thought without realizing what was really going on.

Pantera had gotten a bunch of plastic garbage bags full of little, bitty Styrofoam balls. And they got the guys up in the lighting rig to cut open the bags and pour these things on us. It got to the point where I couldn't play the guitar because the entire fretboard and neck and strings were covered. Every time our drummer would hit a drum Styrofoam would go flying everywhere.

We just ended up stopping the show and cracking up.

"Oh, you got me again, motherfucker," I said.

We played in Kansas City the next day and our crew had to get a dry-vac and clean out all our instruments. This Styrofoam was everywhere. It was inside the guitar pickups, stuck under the strings. You can't believe how much of that shit there was.

MIKE IX WILLIAMS
Eyehategod

Dimebag Darrell was always playing with people and having a good time. He'd give people money for doing stupid shit. Like, if you ate a giant cake with apples baked into it, he'd give you $500. When we were on tour with him, he dressed up like a janitor with his hair put up in a hat. And he walked around the auditorium with a broom and swept up trash. If he ever felt bored, he'd come up with something funny or weird to do.

On what was supposed to be our last date of the tour with them—we actually got added for another month—we were onstage playing our normal set, and all of a sudden there were these huge styrofoam airplanes coming at us from all directions and tons of silly string. They did something to all the instruments and made them sound all shitty through the PA.

VINNIE ABBOTT
Pantera

When we toured with White Zombie, both of us were blowing up at the same time and we had a lot of fun. We butted heads a few times with Rob, but that's kinda normal.

They had this big devil's head and Dime would go up there and put black duct tape over one of its teeth so it had a black tooth. Shit like that would piss Rob off to no extent.

One night he got mad because somebody took his bagels out of his dressing room. So the next night we got a bunch of bagels and duct taped them to the sink in his dressing room. He didn't find that funny, either.

SEAN YSEULT
White Zombie

Pantera were constantly trying to entertain us. They played for the audience, but if you were in the wings watching they'd play to you the whole time, too.

Sometimes Dime or Phil would point at me and then fall down and I'd stand there cracking up.

Phil was constantly streaking for no reason at all. We'd be in our dressing room ready to go onstage and he'd run in and streak around the room butt naked with a big grin on his face. He used to do this thing where he'd pull his dick around into, like, a coaster, and he'd put his beer on it and come into the wings and show everyone, "Hey, look how I'm balancing my beer."

He would do that all the time during the show—anything to make us laugh.

PHILIP ANSELMO
Pantera, Down, Superjoint Ritual, Scour

At the end of the tour, we were playing our last song and everyone in White Zombie and Trouble came running out in bald caps with their shirts off and stupid shit written across their stomachs and these big dildos between their legs.

Rob Zombie came onstage in a fuckin' ape suit and [bassist] Sean [Yseult] was dressed up like Dimebag. She had a fuckin' fake beard and a cowboy hat and shorts. I guess that was their way of trying to get back at us.

ROB ZOMBIE
White Zombie

It was almost like we were attempting to destroy each other's shows all the time. In St. Louis, those guys rigged a snow machine above the stage so it was snowing during our set. And at the same show, we had found life-sized cardboard cutouts of movie stars and we had them up above their backline so it looked like there was a giant puppet show going on during their whole set.

When we were in Tokyo with them, we brought a huge banquet table filled with food out in the middle of the stage and ate dinner while they were playing. It turned into a huge food fight. The promoter was furious and he said, "You have disgraced this stage."

PHILIP ANSELMO

We toured with Type O Negative when they were doing well. Pete Steele was a big muscular ladies' man at the time. I used to catch him in the middle of singing the most romantic bullshit, and I'd hit him in the head with asparagus.

And we had this big old rubber alligator that we'd throw at [guitarist] Kenny [Hickey] and trip him up with it. He'd grab that motherfucker and hum it back at us. This thing weighed about three pounds and was sharp as fuck.

We were playing Vegas, and at the end of the tour they got us back so bad. They gave kids in the audience rolls of toilet paper. So we started playing and the next thing we knew, mountains of toilet paper were flying all over us. It was getting wet and it felt like plaster. We were falling down and getting covered up in the shit. I think we made it through a song and a half. Poor people in Vegas.

REX BROWN
Pantera, ex-Down, ex-Crowbar, Kill Devil Hill

Dime would prank the fuck out of everyone. He always had something up his sleeve that would make us laugh. And if he was down about something, we would pick him up. That's the way we were. We were a family. If somebody was down, well, either they deserved it and you would kick them even harder or you would bring them back up.

TOMMY VICTOR

Any of the pranks that we played in Prong weren't that good and when bands did shit to us we just got angry. When we were touring with Pantera in 1994, we got destroyed a bunch of times. We played this place called Johnnyland in Corpus Christi. It was an outdoor gig in this giant sandbox and Pantera rolled out barbecue equipment during our show and they would not leave. Dimebag had a chef's hat on and they were grilling hotdogs. Their whole crew was up there completely destroying our set. This wasn't even an end-of-tour prank. It was right in the middle of the tour.

And they continued doing shit like that. They would throw marbles out on the stage while we were playing. And we were just idiots anyhow so we could never do anything to top them, whether it was the band itself or any of their pranks.

Vinnie was a huge Dallas Cowboy fan and we'd get into arguments about football all the time. So we got a bunch of Houston Oilers uniforms and gear and real pig's heads on sticks and we ran out onstage at the Nassau Coliseum so we got back at them a little bit.

ERIK TURNER

At the end of our *Cherry Pie* tour we had Trixter and Firehouse opening for us, so on the last day of the tour we totally bombed both of them with everything we could think of. We dumped flour on them from the lighting rig in the ceiling and put oil on the floor so they were slipping all over the place. They tried to get us back but I don't think our security let them get to us.

MICHAEL SWEET
Stryper

We went on tour with White Lion and we did lots of pranks. We'd get them one night and they'd get us the next night.

We discovered were could key up on our CB radios and it would come through [White Lion guitarist] Vito Bratta's amps. He'd be out soloing during a show and we'd go, "Breaker one nine, breaker one nine," and it would come out louder than the solo.

We drove four remote control cars out on the stage during their set.

And then they started getting us back.

My brother used to climb a pole to get to his drum set. They started putting Vaseline on his pole so he couldn't get up to his kit. Then next night we covered the stage with between two hundred and three hundred laminates sticky-side-up. When White Lion ran out the laminates stuck to their boots. And the boots got bigger and bigger with each step. They looked like cats trying to kick tape off of their paws. It was the funniest thing I've ever seen in my life.

The next night they poured a giant box of Cheerios over my brother's head.

[Singer] Mike Tramp came out with a devil's mask on throwing out *Penthouse Forum* magazines. That was the stunt that took it over the top. And that's when the tour managers met and said, "All right, let's call a truce here."

RICHARD CHRISTY

When Death was on tour with HammerFall we convinced our bus driver to stop at a Waffle House after every show. If you ever go to Waffle House there are about ten songs on the jukebox that are about Waffle House. The people who work at Waffle House hate these songs because drunk people come in and play them over and over and over again late at night. The songs have names like, "Special Lady at the Waffle House" and "Waffle House Hash Browns (I Love You)."

We would go and play these songs again and again every night and laugh our asses off. People working there would see these crazy long-haired musicians and the employees were always intrigued. I always made it a point to ask one of the employees if I could have a piece of Waffle House clothing. They would usually give me a visor or a pin.

But by the end of the tour, I had a full Waffle House manager's uniform from these nice Waffle House people giving me articles of clothing. When HammerFall played on the last night of the tour, I walked out as a Waffle House manager with a full plate of food and offered every guy in the band some Waffle House food. I don't think the crowd knew what the hell was going on.

After Death played, we came on as The Waffle Heads. I wore nothing but suspenders, a G-string, Groucho Marx funny nose glasses and a Waffle House hat and members of HammerFall joined in for a song called "Let Your Tongue Run Over My Bunghole" by this crazy, perverted band The Perpetrators.

ROB HALFORD

If we were lucky enough to get a shitty hotel room for the band and crew, we'd go in there to sit down before the show and Glenn was always

338 ⚡ RAISING HELL

throwing around waste basket bins full of water. He'd always time it so whoever was walking three or four stories below would get drenched. We'd all be peeking out over the edge just as the water hit the unlucky person as he was walking along.

There used to be these Teddy Boy types, as we would call them. They were always dressed up in their Sunday best, strolling around really cocky. Glenn totally clobbered this one guy. He was fucking drenched and we were just howling. We heard him yowling and screaming.

And Glenn said, "The screaming and yelling seems to be getting closer."

So Glenn put his head out the window and saw that this guy was actually climbing up a drain pipe on the side of the hotel trying to get back into the window where Glenn had done a Niagara Falls deal on him.

GLENN TIPTON

It wasn't a waste bin, it was a polythene bag of water that I dropped on the Teddy Boy and it exploded on his head. You can just imagine this guy at home having a shave and getting dressed up, and then that happens on the way to wherever he was going.

We all ducked out of sight and after about five minutes we looked out and he was scaling the hotel wall from the outside. So we shut the window and went to someone else's room on the other side of the hotel.

We got a phone call from the manager and he said, "There's a guy here covered in water and he said you guys did it."

And I said, "No, we've been in this side of the hotel in this room for the last two hours just jamming away."

We had to be very careful when we went outside that he wasn't lurking around.

BRETT CAMPBELL
Pallbearer

We were touring with Bask and Kayo Dot and right before the tour began we did an in-store signing and [guitarist] Devin [Holt] found *The Best of Wrestlemania* DVD for $1. We had a TV in the van so we watched that entire thing and the whole tour became super wrestling-themed. All the dudes in Bask and Kayo Dot were also super into wrestling.

There were several nights when we would get shitfaced and wrestle. My elbows were black from all the elbow drops on the ground or the concrete.

We kept getting more wrestling DVDs as we went along. We were on the road for a month and the last day of the tour we were in Knoxville,

Tennessee, and we just decided to come out shirtless to Shawn Michaels' theme "Sexy Boy."

Right before our last song, the lights went out and the sound of breaking glass comes on. It's the Stone Cold Steve Austin theme and Bask and Kayo Dot came out dressed as different wrestlers and gave us a heavyweight champion belt that they had made early on in the tour. We smashed a bunch of beers and got soaked and we were really sticky when we played our last song. The night devolved into one giant free-for-all wrestling match on the floor of the venue between the bands and the staff at the venue on the concrete floor. I was unbelievably sore the next day.

WILL CARROLL

The drummer for Stuck Mojo showed me a cool trick once. He took the skin off the top of a snare drum, put a ping-pong ball inside and then put the head back on and tightened it. He did it to one of the local openers and at soundcheck the dude hit the snare and the ball bounced around like crazy and made this insane sound: "DING-A-BAKAA-DINGA-DINGA-BACKA-DINGA!" That was funny as shit.

JOHN GALLAGHER

The last night of a tour with Saxon we were playing and all of a sudden these weird techno noises started coming out of our speakers. Saxon's soundman had taken our kick drum and run it through all these processors, which made all these bizarre and off-putting noises.

Ha, ha. At first, it was funny.

Then, when it went on for two minutes I said, "I don't know who's doing this but if you don't stop it right now I'm going to track you down and beat the shit out of you."

DEE SNIDER

The big problem with pranks is these are inside jokes. Your audience isn't in on. I've heard the stories.

[Bassist] Mark "The Animal" Mendoza told me that when he was with the Dictators they toured with Uriah Heep and Foreigner. And on the last night of the tour Foreigner was doing "Feels Like the First Time," which was the big hit single. One of the bands bypassed the soundboard and the roadies sang the song. Now the audience didn't see the roadies they just saw Foreigner up there and they heard this horrible singing. It's very funny to talk about, but to the audience this was the big hit and it sounded like dog shit. They didn't know what was going on.

And then when the Dictators were on, Uriah Heep dumped potatoes on them. Dick Taters-potatoes. And it interrupted the set. Again, the audience did not know what was going on. There wasn't an announcement that went, "Tonight's the last night of the tour so pranks will be played."

It's not like that at all. It's just a ruined show for an audience that paid to see a real concert.

DAVE WYNDORF
Monster Magnet

Our old drummer, Jon Kleiman, met his match with our tour manager. Jon liked to buy fireworks and blow them up wherever he could. His idea of a good night off was to have a couple beers and hang out at the hotel room and throw firecrackers out the window. And he'd buy BB guns and shoot stuff. But he didn't deal with trouble well. He'd get drunk and not realize he was getting into trouble. I kept telling him if he threw firecrackers out the window, we were going to get fined.

"Nah, they'll never catch me," he said.

So, my tour manager went through great pains to draw up these very legal-looking papers from Dallas, Texas, that contained an accurate record of him shooting off firecrackers in every hotel, and it pointed out that they had pictures from security cameras. It said he was going to have to come to Texas and go to court. The fine was something nuts, likes $25,000. The tour manager started mailing these fake legal papers to Jon's home, and Jon's mother forwarded the mail to him. Jon bought it hook, line, and sinker. He'd get a new letter about every week. And our tour manager, Shane, had the date all planned out, so the band would be as far away from Texas as possible when the imaginary court appearance came up. Everyone was discussing how long we should let it go without telling him 'cause he was definitely getting unwound. Shane finally told him, and Jon freaked out.

GLENN TIPTON

The best prank we ever pulled on our tour manager Dave Corke in the early days happened when we were in a plane that was like a jumbo jet. As we came into our descent somewhere on the East Coast, we said to the captain, "Hey, our manager Dave is really scared of flying. Can we play a practical joke on him because he plays them on everyone else?"

"What do you mean?" the captain said.

"Can we say the plane is going to crash into the North Sea," I asked.

"No, of course not! You can't do that."

We pleaded with him.

"Look," he finally said. "If you can get the head air stewardess to confirm to me that everyone on the plane knows that it's only a joke, we'll make some sort of announcement."

We okayed it with the air hostess and then went around to let everyone in on the joke except Dave. They were all into it and agreed to act like they thought the plane might crash.

Then, all of a sudden, Dave saw all these people looking very worried and he grabbed me.

"What's going on?" he asked, fear burning in his eyes.

"Well, we're short on fuel and there's a possibility we're not going to make it," I calmly said.

Just then, the announcement came on: "Ladies and gentlemen, there's absolutely no cause for alarm."

We knew Dave would freak out when he heard that. He was wearing these glasses that got dark in sunlight, so his face went so white his glasses went dark. We were sitting in the back, facing each other. Rob [Halford] was on one side, I was on the other side of Dave, and there were three other people across the table.

"Could you please fasten your seatbelts?" said the stewardess.

Dave couldn't find his buckle, so he strapped his belt over Rob and into my buckle. We were strapped together like triplets just about to be born.

"Please remove all your objects from your pockets, she said over the intercom.

Dave was throwing all this loose change and his comb. He was starting to panic.

"Please remove your shoes," said the air hostess.

Dave had Dessa Boots on, and to this day I have no idea how he pulled them off his feet without undoing the laces. He just went from bad to worse and in the end, he lost it completely. He went delirious, then passed out. It was a little like the movie *Airplane!*. Everyone was queuing up to slap his face and bring him around.

After we landed safely, the airport's medical people carried him off on a stretcher.

As he was coming round, we were all there.

"Guys, what did you do that for?" he asked.

"C'mon Dave, you're the worst practical joker ever," I said. "You play jokes on everybody all the time. Look what we just done for you. You were going to die in a plane crash and we flicked our fingers and you're alive. It's a joke. You should be happy."

But he never saw it as a happy moment.

SCOTT IAN

Tony Iommi once said something to me that wasn't a practical joke, but it showed his sense of humor. He knew I'm this huge Black Sabbath fan—I mean, who isn't? We were both in L.A. for a radio event or something. I got onto a freight elevator to go to the street. On the way down, the elevator stopped at another floor. A security guard walked in and gave me a once-over.

It was just me and [my wife] Pearl [Aday] standing there.

The security guy turns around and said, "It's okay."

"Who the hell's getting in this elevator?" I wondered.

And then in walks Tony Iommi and his entourage. I couldn't believe it.

"Oh my God, Tony! Hi!" I said.

"Hello Scott. How are you?" he replied, the total gentleman.

Of all the people who could have walked into the elevator, Tony Iommi would have been my number one pick!

"You know, you just made my day. I'd rather you walk in than Stephen King, and he's my favorite writer."

I mentioned to Tony that we were going to see him when Sabbath played the Hollywood Bowl and that I was totally looking forward to it.

"I guess I'll see you there," I said.

Tony looked at me with a deadpan expression.

"Oh, I'm sorry Scott. We've had to postpone."

"Why?" I asked.

"Yeah. Something with Ozzy, you know? I hope you can make it to the postponed date."

For a second there I was super bummed and then he looked up at me and smiled and said, "Gotcha!"

"Gotcha? Holy shit. Don't do that." I said.

The fact that he took that time out of his day to even play a practical joke was amazing to me.

And he had the biggest smile on his face.

"Gotcha."

CHAPTER 15: FIGHTING THE WORLD

Security Scraps, Band Brawls & Nazis, Oh My

Unrepentantly praising the endurance and durability of metalheads and chastising those who marginalize the metal genre, "Fighting the World" is an anthemic microcosm of the Manowar ethos. The song is the title track of the band's fifth album, which arrived on the bloodstained battlefield in 1987. While it failed to connect with the masses, *Fighting the World* hit the bullseye for loyalists, who remain as devoted to Manowar as Dave Matthews die-hards are to their favorite artist.

For established bands, throwing down against smack-talkers is inadvisable in today's climate of opportunists and ambulance-chasing lawyers. Put simply, those with wealth that deliver beatdowns likely will be delivered legal paperwork. Less successful bands have a little more latitude when it comes to kicking ass and getting away with it, but it's still risky business.

It hasn't always been that way.

Back in the '80s, the metal world was like the Wild West. Clubs didn't need expensive liability insurance, so artists could get away with unpredictable, even dangerous behavior without later seeing themselves on YouTube busting heads and facing the consequences. Before the internet, musicians were often lauded for attacking unruly fans, belligerent interviewers, dudes in other groups, and even their own irritating bandmates. Now, fights are fewer and further between, which is probably a good thing for the survival of metal. But it's sure cool to look back at some of that old footage.

DEE SNIDER
Twisted Sister, ex-Widowmaker

You can fight internally with your bandmates but ultimately, you're family. If someone on the outside tries to start something, the entire family goes, "What did you fuckin' say? You're not in the family. Get the fuck out of here!"

Twisted Sister was a band of brothers, and I was the head brawler and during our earlier days of touring, I was security. I would jump off the stage nightly and get into fights with people in the crowd who were starting up with us. There were a lot of hecklers or people who thought that we were just there for their amusement, especially because of the way we looked, with the outfits and the makeup. If you didn't smack them down, other people would join in.

So, the minute somebody would say something or do something, I would dive off the stage. I had many a fight in the crowd.

FRANKIE BANALI
Quiet Riot, ex-W.A.S.P.

For some reason, a promoter in upstate Washington really took a disliking to [vocalist] Kevin [DuBrow], and he was trying hard to pick a fight. Kevin was not about to back down but before they could start throwing punches I got in between the two of them because I noticed that the promoter was wearing a knife and his hand was on it.

Kevin was street smart, but he wasn't a big-time brawler and wouldn't know how to fight a guy who had a knife. He probably would have gotten stabbed, so I had to break up their scuffle and take a risk that this guy was going to stick the knife in me instead of putting it into Kevin. Fortunately, he never pulled the knife.

TONY IOMMI
Black Sabbath, Heaven & Hell

Early on, some guy wanted to stab me. We were playing the Hollywood Bowl and that was at a time when people thought we were evil Satan worshippers and all these Satanists were angry that we didn't support their cause, we just made music.

Backstage that night, someone had drawn a red cross on the door of our dressing room, which was strange. But we knew there were a bunch of nutters that were into us so it didn't seem like a big deal.

Then, during the show, my gear started acting up and I was angry. So I kicked over my amp and started walking off the stage. And suddenly, a guy comes towards me with a dagger. Somehow, he got past security, but when I knocked over the amp, fortunately they saw him hiding there and took him down.

ROB CAVESTANY
Death Angel, ex-The Organization

We had a show in Amsterdam at the Paradiso and some dude came up onstage with a massive knife. I don't know what he was doing up there but a security guard saw the knife and tackled the guy. He went down and dropped this huge fucking knife right on the stage in front of me. I kicked it to the side of the stage and we kept on playing, but I couldn't help wondering what would have happened if the security guard hadn't tackled the guy.

SCOTT IAN
Anthrax, S.O.D., The Damned Things

We played with Maiden at Irvine Meadows in Southern California in 1990. A couple songs into the set somebody started throwing firecrackers onto the stage. We stopped the show and I told the crowd that if they kept tossing firecrackers onstage, we were gonna walk. I told them they should police the situation themselves and if they saw who was throwing these things, they should either take him out themselves or get security.

We started playing again and two minutes later, BANG! BANG! BANG! BANG!, another whole pack of firecrackers came flying onstage. They were blowing up all round us and we were ducking our heads and running away from the area the noises came from. So we stopped again.

All the house lights came up.

"Okay, that's it. Fuck you," I said into the mic. "We're not going to stand here and take this shit! It's dangerous."

Then off to the left, about eight or ten rows back, a whole bunch of people were pointing at this one guy and a couple of people were holding him. Security came running down the steps, grabbed him and started walking him down to the front between the first row and the barricade. They were going to take him all the way across the front row in front of the barricade to get him out the exit at the other side of the venue.

As they got him to the front of the barricade, I lost it. I fuckin' threw my guitar down, jumped down to where he was and started swinging. Security let go of the guy. To me, that meant it was on.

The two of us were swinging at each other, but before I could do any damage, something came flying off the stage and past my head. It was [bassist] Frank [Bello] and he delivered a flying Jackie Chan dropkick on this guy. Frank fuckin' nailed this dude right in the chest and the guy went down hard.

At that point, security grabbed the dude and dragged him out of the venue. Me and Frank climbed back onstage and the whole crowd—fifteen thousand people—were chanting, "KICK HIS ASS, KICK HIS ASS."

I still had that crazy fight adrenaline running through me. I walked up to the mic and said, "Okay, anyone else?"

I got a big fucking cheer and then we finished our set.

After the show, the head of security of the venue came in and said that the police were there and they wanted to talk with us.

"Great, we're gonna get arrested for assault," I thought.

I walked in the room with the cops and they asked us if we want to press charges on the guy. They didn't even care that we beat the crap out of him. We told the cop that we thought the guy learned his lesson and that as long as he was away from us we didn't want to pursue the matter any further.

ERIK DANIELSSON
Watain

One time when we played in Salt Lake City, some big skinhead guy came up to the stage and spat at me in the face during one of the songs. I took my bass and smashed it into *his* face. He fell down, of course, and that act was kind of like pushing a button.

The next thing I knew, I was in the audience and everywhere I looked around me was a total fucking riot—an out-of-control western bar fight.

And then I remembered, "Ah, we're doing a concert here."

I turned around and saw the stage was empty except for two Flying V guitars. The guitarist and drummer were smashing the hell out of people in the audience and the other way around. That was a really good night filled with power. We took the skinhead guy down and he went away in an ambulance. We took out some of his friends as well. And I don't think they will come back to one of our shows.

DAVID DRAIMAN
Disturbed

We played the Rolling Rock Town Fair in 2004 along with Velvet Revolver, Sevendust, Three Days Grace, and some other bands including a group called Finch.

Now, about two years earlier, Finch decided to be cute and try to get their five minutes of fame—even though I'd never met them and didn't know them—by saying in the press that they wanna put a bullet in my head and rip the piercings from my chin.

Needless to say, I didn't take it very well. Neither did [our guitarist] Danny [Donegan] or anyone else in our camp.

So, there we all were at the same show. There was a rotating stage, so one band could go on after another without waiting for anyone to break down and set up their gear. Danny and I had no intentions of getting into a fight with anybody. We just wanted to enjoy the day.

Three Days Grace were onstage, so me, Danny, and his wife went up on the deck to watch. Danny's wife was holding their eight-month-old baby girl. I was holding Lisa, my first Akita [dog]. I wouldn't have gone up there with my dog if I wanted to fight and Danny certainly wouldn't have gone over with his wife and child.

While Three Days Grace were playing, Finch were in the back of the rotating stage setting up. They saw us standing there and they started flipping us off and being idiots and talking to each other and laughing. As the stage started turning, the guitar player, [Randy Strohmeyer], walked over to Danny

"Don't you guys realize what a joke you are?" he said.

"I think the joke's on you, motherfucker," Danny replied.

The next thing I knew, the guy threw a fist and Danny dodged it and Danny leg swept the guy. While Finch's guitar player was getting into it with Danny, some fucker decided that it was okay to get to me by shoving Nicole to the side. She fell on the floor holding the baby.

I lost my Goddamn mind.

Lo and behold, that was the moment when the stage turned to face the crowd while me, Danny, and later our manager, Jeff Battaglia, took on Finch, all their crew and twelve security guys that stormed the stage. Their guitar player came up behind me and hit me on the back with his guitar. Jeff grabbed him. I hit him with everything I had. I found the fucker who grabbed and shoved Nicole and put him in a choke hold and didn't let go. He started to turn purple and five security guys tried to get me to break my grip. I wouldn't release the guy.

Then the promoter ran up, a look of desperation on his face.

"David, David!," he said. "You made your point. Let go, let go, let go."

"Nope, this fucker's going to sleep or he's going to die—one of the two."

"Look, just let him go. Let him finish the set," the promoter pleaded. "Whatever you wanna do with him after the set, that's up to you, okay?"

"Okay, fine," I said. I let go and security pulled him away.

Finch went running off to their bus. By that point, the guys from Sevendust heard what happened and they came running over to help us. We had a small mob standing outside Finch's bus and they wouldn't come back out. They were putting their butt cheeks up to the bus windows and being idiots, and we were shaking the bus and pelting it with rocks.

Then, the state police showed up and told us to cease and desist. They were ready to put me in handcuffs. I gave them my hands and said, "Go ahead."

"What's your name, sir?" a cop said.

"I'm David Draiman. I'm the lead singer for Disturbed and guess what? We haven't played yet. You think these forty thousand people came here to see Finch? You want to take me away? You wanna go ahead and stop the show? Be my guest. You'll have a riot on your hands. But go ahead and arrest me."

I was fuming. The cop reconsidered his options.

"Sir, what do I have to do to calm the situation?" he said.

"You need to get those people out of my reach. You need to get them off the premises now. If I can't get at them, nothing's going to happen. If they are here, they're dead. I don't care that you're here and I'll probably go to jail."

We were all furious. It's one thing to insult me, it's another thing to be an idiot. But to shove a woman and her child to the ground crosses every line there is in the world.

At that point, four state trooper vehicles escorted the tour bus off the town fair premises. Disturbed performed as scheduled and it was one of the best sets we've ever played. And whether Finch want to admit it or not, we sent five of those guys to the hospital and I escaped with skinned knuckles and a tiny scratch on my neck.

Finch press statement from 2004
While we were setting up, one of the members of Disturbed, Dan Donegan, was harassing us from the side of the stage. Before we were to play, Randy walked over to Dan to explain that the comments he made a few years ago were a joke, and to give him a friendly handshake. Dan proceed to assault Randy, and Disturbed's singer, David Draiman, attacked Mike Herrara (our drum tech), which caused a fight to ensue. We want everyone to know that Finch did not start this fight. However, we do not take kindly to being assaulted or having our lives threatened.

RICHARD CHRISTY
Charred Walls of the Damned, ex-Death, ex-Iced Earth, ex-Public Assassin

Public Assassin was driving to a gig in Oklahoma and this van full of rednecks started following us. They'd seen some long-haired guys at the gas station and they wanted to beat the crap out of us. They were driving right up on our bumper. And they got really pissed when I put my ass and my ass cheeks up against the back window of the van and spread my bunghole, so they tried to run us off the road.

We pulled into another gas station and me and my bandmates all had to grab weapons because we didn't know if these guys had guns. I picked up a tire iron and I was ready to use it. Luckily, some of our friends were traveling with us so there were about eight of us. There were only three or four of them. They calculated the odds of walking away victorious.

"Aww, fuck this," one of them said. And they took off.

So I got to scare some rednecks away in Oklahoma with my bunghole, which I'm still proud of.

JOEY JORDISON
ex-Slipknot, Murderdolls, Sinsaenum, Vimic

There were times when [Slipknot percussionist] Shawn ["Clown" Crahan] put me in a fucking wooden box and sat me in front of the stage before the show. I would be in there for three fucking hours just waiting to play. Then, they'd let me out and Mayhem would ensue. I felt violent and psychotic.

Right before the show, we purposely went out and looked for fights with other bands. We went up to bands we didn't like and stood right in front of them. They'd laugh uncomfortably and exit out the back door, looking like they were gonna fucking cry.

I remember standing in a pile of snow and punching my fist into a guy's car window telling him to get the fuck out. I can't remember if I did more damage to my fist or his window.

KING FOWLEY
Deceased, October 31

In the early '90s, the death metal scene took off and bands like Morbid Angel and Deicide suddenly got big. We were on Relapse Records coming up the ranks and we would go and play with some of these bands. Most of them were cool and they were on the same level. We were all nice, unified underground spirited people.

But some of these bands got cocky.

We've had run-ins with Morbid Angel—mainly [guitarist] Trey Azagthoth. I can't stand the guy. He's a piece of shit. He's one of the weirdest fuckin' heinous dudes. In 1989, I got a call from Morbid Angel. I was friends with their guitarist Richard Brunelle from our tape trading days, so we were cool. One day Richard called me up. [Vocalist] David Vincent and Trey Azagthoth were also on the line. They were looking for a drummer and they were considering me.

"Well, thank you guys and I wish you well, but Steve [Souther] is my buddy and we're gonna make it or break it together in Deceased," I said.

They were pretty cool about it.

Then later, Richard said I kinda hurt their feelings.

"Look, why don't you guys get in touch with Chris Reifert, man? He was in Death and he can help you out," I told Richard.

It turned out they did get in touch with Chris, but then they found this monster drummer named Pete Sandoval, so it worked out for them. I figured everything was good between us. But I guess I was wrong . . . [to be continued]

DEE SNIDER

When we played the Reading Festival, we were getting bombarded with all kinds of shit. You've got tens of thousands of people throwing things.

At that point, I was notorious for jumping into the crowd to deal with the bad apples. But when there are that many people, who do you beat up? Instead of diving into the crowd, I decided to call out the entire audience and challenge everyone in the crowd to a fight. I did it and they believed me, which just stunned them.

They were laughing going, "Oh my God, this guy's fucking nuts. He's not kidding."

"That's it," I said. "One at a time. Side of the stage after the show. Let's do it!"

So the show did go on and there were no fights. And [Motörhead's] Lemmy Kilmister, who was a fan, came out for the final song with [guitarist] Fast Eddie Clarke and Pete Way from UFO. and we did "It's Only Rock'n'Roll (But I Like It)," which was the capper. We had already won the crowd over with our attitude but when those guys came out we reunited Motörhead [guitarist] Fast Eddie [Clarke] and Lemmy, who were at each other's throats at the time, having just broken up., It was one of the crown performances of the event.

JOHN GALLAGHER
Raven

We played The Orpheum Theatre in Boston with W.A.S.P. and Saxon in 1987, and there were Slayer fans throwing nine-volt batteries at us and whatever else they could get their hands on.

We had a song that we would briefly stop in the middle. That night, we extended that gap, put down the guitars, climbed over the barrier,

"Okay, who's first?" I said. "I'll fight every one of you miserable little motherfuckers right now."

And they backed off. That earned us some respect and enabled us to continue the show.

We used to play for punks in the '70s that fuckin' hated us and let us know it, so we're not scared of anybody.

KING FOWLEY

[continued] . . . In about 1990 or so, we were on the same bill as Morbid Angel at the Deathfest in Michigan. When we got there, the promoter, Sandy was in tears. She said, "Man, Morbid Angel are so demanding."

[Their guitarist] Trey Azagthoth literally said to her, "If I don't have a coffee in my hands in forty-five seconds we're leaving."

"Is this motherfucker serious?" I said.

"Yeah, he's been doing it all day."

I went backstage and saw Morbid Angel acting like fucking rock stars. Then I saw their singer David Vincent.

"Hey King Fowley," he said. "Can I talk to you?"

I went over there and got ready for whatever crap was coming.

"You're not using your banner," He said.

"We're not? Who said?"

"I said because we're using ours and we're the headliner."

"You know, Dave, you're established. People know who you are," I said trying to butter him up a little. "We're here to make a name for ourselves and having a banner up there would really help. Can't we just put our banner up for our set and then we'll take it down. You can put yours up. I'll even help you put it up?"

"Nope, that's not gonna work," he said.

"Well, we're using it, man," I insisted.

Things were tense for a minute, but by the time it was our turn to play, not only did we use our banner but David went out with me, climbed the ladder and helped me put it up.

"I like your attitude, man," he said. "I like how you go for it and you're all in."

"Yeah, man," I said. "I'm not trying to cause a problem. I just want to do what's best for my band."

After our set, I helped him with the Morbid Angel banner just like I said I would. We were okay after that but Trey was still rolling his eyes every time he saw us and being an asshole. And that grudge went on forever.

ROSS THE BOSS
ex-Manowar, Ross the Boss, The Dictators

The Dictators had the same management as Blue Öyster Cult and Uriah Heep, so we would open for those guys all the time. Sometimes, the crowds were totally loving it, but some people didn't really get the kind of punk metal that we were playing. The boos we got at some of those shows were so loud it was unbelievable. Sometimes they threw things at us.

[Our singer Dick] Manitoba enjoyed antagonizing the crowd, which didn't make them like us anymore. Once, one guy got so angry, he charged right at Manitoba and a security guy right in front of him clotheslined this guy and he was out.

GENE HOGLAN
Dark Angel, Testament, Dethklok, ex-Death, ex-Strapping Young Lad

Everyone in Dark Angel were a bunch of brawlers. My first incarnation of Dark Angel had Don Doty on vocals. He was a scrapper. He wouldn't back down for anybody. [Guitarist] Jim Durkin was a fighter. My second singer [Ron Rinehart] could throw a punch, too.

One time we went up against the whole San Diego punk rock contingent and I was still in high school! It was 1985 and we were the co-headliners of an all-day punk rock festival at the Jackie Robinson YMCA. This was back before the crossover scene had taken its upswing [with bands like Corrosion of Conformity and D.R.I.]. Our shows featured so much aggression and hostility.

Every night, I would grab the mic and call the crowd a bunch of pussies and poseurs just to rile them up. Don would do the same thing.

Don came up to me before this San Diego looking a bit unsure of himself.

"Have you taken a look around this place? We are definitely in the minority. Maybe we should hold off on the insults."

"No. Let's do our show like we always do," I said. "Call them a bunch of pussies. Call them a bunch of idiots. Call them a bunch of losers. Just get them into it."

"Okay," Said Don reluctantly.

Two songs into the set Don started berating the crowd and calling them a bunch of punk rock idiots. Usually, our crew was tucked behind the amps. I looked over and I saw that they had drifted onto the stage and there were people jumping on the stage and trying to take cracks at our guys.

Suddenly, mayhem broke out. Don kicked a dude in the face and then a wave of people descended upon the stage. There were about one hundred punkers against eight or ten of us. My tech, Ray Sanchez—the Satanic Hispanic—got absorbed off the stage into a sea of punkers. And then Don got cornered by six dudes. They were brawling and it looked like something out of a Bugs Bunny cartoon. Fists, dust, legs and then here comes Don crawling out from the mass of bodies that are still punching something.

I couldn't figure out who they were still attacking since Don wasn't there anymore.

I jumped off the stage and right into this dude who grabbed me from behind my neck and kneed me in the balls. I had so much adrenaline flowing, I didn't feel it at all. Right before I took him out, he looked at me in utter bewilderment, like, "I just kicked you in the balls. Why aren't you going down?"

The cops came and broke up the brawl. And after the adrenaline wore off I was hurting bad.

DEZ FAFARA
DevilDriver, ex-Coal Chamber

Coal Chamber did an outside show somewhere in Wisconsin. There was a generator for the event that blew and all of the gear shorted out, including the equipment that we needed to play.

"Look, you just blew all of our presets—everything," I told then. "We can't play,"

That's when the guy running the event went onstage and told the crowd we were a bunch of pussies and we weren't gonna play.

Me and [guitarist] Meegs [Rascón] heard him and immediately ran out of the bus. Meegs punched the guy onstage in front of thousands of people. And then I grabbed the dude and threw him into the pit, headfirst.

Pretty soon, the cops were parked next to our bus and we were being interrogated. I don't know why, but the cops went back to their car to check on something. So the bus driver took off and we rolled. A minute later, we were out of their jurisdiction.

But consequently, the promoter wanted all these damages. We had to come back later and do a show for that guy or he was going to sue us.

ADAM JARVIS
Misery Index, Pig Destroyer, Scour

We played with Intronaut in this bar and grill in Louisville, Kentucky, and there was a strict curfew. We were onstage and this guy said, "Last song."

We gave him the middle finger and he unplugged us.

Next thing I knew, I turned around and I saw [guitarist] Sparky [Voyles] storming across the stage at this guy. Sparky started choking this dude out, then slammed him against the wall and screamed, "You don't fucking unplug us, motherfucker! You're gonna blow our amps out, asshole."

I was afraid the venue was gonna call the cops. But people from the club came over and separated Sparky and the dude and told everyone, "Show's over. Get the fuck out." And we got away.

BEN WEINMAN
The Dillinger Escape Plan

In about 1999, we were at a place in Connecticut called Toad's and I invited a guy from another band onstage to fight because he was fucking with my gear and mouthing off to us the whole set and trying to fuck with me. We had even played with his band in the past. He was drunk and stupid and at first, he was just heckling us between songs. I ignored it. But then in the middle of "Destro's Secret" I saw him pouring beer on my effect pedals.

Our gear malfunctioned enough on its own back then so we definitely didn't need someone fucking with our shit. I stopped the song and smacked him across the face with my guitar and he grabbed it and tried to drag me into the crowd. Finally, I wrestled it out of his hands.

"Alright, motherfucker! Why don't you come up onstage?" I said. "If you want to be an asshole come do it in front of everybody."

He came on and I took my guitar off and swung it at his head like a bat and then [vocalist] Dimitri [Minakakis] clocked the dude across the back of the head with his microphone. The crowd parted and the guy ran out of the club screaming. And then we just kicked right back into the song where we left off as if nothing had ever happened.

KING FOWLEY

In the early '90s, we played a show at Coney Island High in New York City with Nile and Morbid Angel. Nile had just joined our label, Relapse. They were sharing a room with us and Morbid Angel had their own room. [Morbid Angel vocalist] David [Vincent] was out of the band at this point and [guitarist] Trey [Azagthoth] was pulling the strings.

When we got there we had to sign a fucking contract that we could not sell our merchandise within one mile of the club.

"Where is this coming from?" I asked.

"Morbid Angel says you can't sell anything here," said the club manager.

"Do we want to sign this or do we want to walk?" I asked the other guys in my band. I was pretty disgusted by that point and I could have gone either way.

"Let's just sign it, man," agreed the dudes. "People are here to see us. Let's just play and then we'll leave."

We signed the shitty agreement.

Deceased went onstage and did really good. The crowd wanted an encore but Trey gave the sound guy the "cut them" signal with his hand across his throat. I wasn't in the mood to fight so we went downstairs to our dressing room. Nile was onstage and we started playing a drinking game with some people. We closed the door. All of a sudden someone kicked in the door.

"You guys gotta be quiet," he said. "Trey said to be quiet."

"What?" I replied. "We're not bothering nobody."

We were yelling "Warhead" or "Chemical Warfare" or whatever you do when you're drinking, but no one could hear us outside where Nile was playing.

Then Trey came in.

"Hey man, what are you doing here?"

"What do you mean?" I said unsure what the fuck he was talking about.

"Oh, Deceased are playing?" Trey asked with complete disinterest.

I shook my head.

"Dude, you were just there! You told them to cut us!"

He left the room.

Paul Bearer from Sheer Terror was one of the security guards that night. He was the next person to come in to wreck the party.

"Hey man, what's going on? This guy's pissing me off. Can you just settle down?"

"What are we doing wrong?" I asked.

Then we figured, fuck it, let's just get our shit and leave. We stood up and all of a sudden the lady who ran the place walked in and said, "Morbid Angel want you kicked out of the building."

"You gotta be fuckin' kidding me," I said.

"No, I'm dead fuckin' serious. What do I owe you, some piss for gas money?"

She handed me $50. I took the fuckin' money, threw it in her face, spat in her face.

"Fuck you and your club," I said.

And we walked out.

BILLY GRAZIADEI
Biohazard

From the moment we came out, we had a big following in the hardcore scene and these Nazi kids would come to see us, which we didn't understand since half of our band was Jewish and we sang about everything Nazi skinheads were against.

We always seemed to end up fighting these dudes.

We played Airport Music Hall in Allentown, Pennsylvania. During the show, our [black] friend Chris dove into the crowd and got jumped by five or six white power skinheads. They had been standing in the crowd doing Sieg Heils. They roughed Chris up a bit, but we didn't see it. He got out of the pit and in between songs he told us what happened.

So we went on the mic and talked shit about the skinheads and then they all tried to get to us. I jumped down into the photo area between the stage and the barricade. Six to ten dudes pushed their way through the crowd and ran up to the barricade. They were doing Sieg Heils right in my face and tried to grab me.

I kept playing, but I was fucking pissed off. Their fingertips were right by my mouth. One dude with driving gloves on put his hand too close to my face and I bit his hand like a Pitbull and shook it. I wouldn't let it go. Finally, I stopped playing and put my hands out.

"C'mon motherfucker!"

I thought we were going to get in a big brawl, but they just stood there.

"Fuckin' pussies!"

We went back onstage and finished the show.

At the end of the night, we were upstairs and hung out with every-body. And security came up to me.

"Hey, some dude wants to talk to you," someone told me.

"No, I'm up here. It's all good," I answered.

"No, I think you should deal with this privately," the guy said.

I went to see the kid and it was the leader of the Nazi clan. He had the same gloves on and a white tank top. He was at the bottom of the stairs.

"You got a problem, bro?" I said.

"No, I just want to apologize. I want to talk to you," he replied.

"Sure, come on up."

He came upstairs to the dressing room.

"You know, your black friend? We had a problem with him. And it's okay. We don't have any problem with black people. It was just him."

I couldn't believe my ears.

"Well, first of all, if you say *that* you clearly *do* have a problem with black people."

"No, no. It's really not the blacks we have a problem with," he repeated. "It's the Jews."

"Really?"

[Our drummer] Danny [Schuler] and [vocalist] Evan [Seinfeld] were also in the room. I turned around and looked at them and they came over.

"Oh, really, you got a problem with Jews? We're Jewish," Evan said. "What's your problem?"

"Oh, no, no. It's not *you* guys. It's not *all* Jews. It's just the ones who own the banks."

The whole room broke into laughter. It was a joke. The guy was harmless.

"Look man," I said. "Every time you get called on your shit, you change your tone. What's your deal?"

He said that was just how he was raised and his father was a racist and a bigot.

"Well, why do you have to be that way also?" I said. "You can think for yourself. That's what this kind of scene is all about."

It kind of ended there. And hopefully, he went home and thought about what we said and maybe learned something.

PAGE HAMILTON
Helmet

We were in Cleveland on the *Meantime* tour. It was the second to last show and there were three guys doing the neo-Nazi Sieg Heil thing. I stopped the show and put the lights on and had them thrown out. This was early on and I was so unaware that some people would still do that.

That happened one other time many years later.

We were in Hamburg, Germany. We were playing this old punk rock song. This shirtless skinhead said something anti-Semitic to me. I grabbed his arm and pulled him in.

"Hey man, we don't roll like that," I said. "I love everyone. You're welcome to stay if you act cool."

The kid left the pit and within twenty minutes I saw him back in the pit with his shirt on, peacefully co-existing and moshing with the rest of the crowd. I'd like to think it was I had some sort of effect on him. My approach over the last ten years has been to kill them with kindness. Maybe they took a wrong turn somewhere in life. And if you say, "Hey, that's not good. That's not constructive. That's not right," maybe they'll see the light. I think that's preferable to berating them and telling them they're assholes because I think that's what they want, anyway.

MIKE SMITH
Suffocation

Back in 1993, we played Philadelphia and about fifteen Nazi skinheads tried to bogart our slam pit by standing in the middle of the floor and throwing up the Heil Hitler sign. We immediately stopped the show and asked them if they were sure that was the route they wanted to go.

And it turned out they really didn't have the manpower or the true desire to try to push their views across. So they backed down. We didn't have to fight them and they immediately felt the unity of the death metal community. They got roughed up a little through the rest of the night and I never heard from any of those people since.

JOHN GALLAGHER

We opened for Testament in 1989 and when we got to Brooklyn we played L'Amour. The club was always a great place for us to play but this time it was a totally different audience and they had no interest in us. They got really antagonistic towards us, but we just kept playing.

At one point, Mark broke a string and some guy in the front row grabbed the string and wrapped it around his hand. Mark looked at him and went, "Okay." He shrugged and pulled the guitar back. You could see sausages fly through the air as this guy's fingers were all cut to ribbons. The stupid idiot.

PHILIP ANSELMO
Pantera, Down, Superjoint Ritual, Scour

We were so over the fucking moon to be invited to open for Judas Priest on their European tour for *Painkiller*. Pantera could play an entire set of Judas Priest covers.

But good God, what a disaster that tour was. The crowds didn't get it. They hated us 'cause we were different. We were new. Nobody knew who the fuck we were and they didn't want to listen to what we were doing. They wanted to hear the old sound of traditional heavy metal—everything that I was trying to destroy.

So, in a weird way, it was mission accomplished. It was perfect. They booed us. They threw things at us.

In one city, there was a bearded fuck in the front row who had been flipping us off all night so sure enough, I got right in front of him. And, man, I was wearing this old Saint Vitus shirt. It was a relic. And this motherfucker grabbed my shirt and yanked it hard right towards him, which was a complete mistake.

Oh my fucking God. I grabbed this motherfucker.

"Let go!" I growled.

And he pulled again.

I knocked him cold with one, swift left hook. It was beautiful. And what else was beautiful was he was so sandwiched in with people that his body would not drop to the floor so he was sound asleep, leaned over but unable to fall. And all around him everyone's eyes lit up and they were like, "Wow, this guy's serious."

And yes, we all just learned a dirty, valuable lesson.

Three songs later, I looked out with a bit of concert to where that guy had been standing and sure enough with a fuckin' jaw swollen up like a melon he had his fist in the air and he was headbanging. Somehow we won him over and not one year later, [after the release of *Vulgar Display of Power*] we would go back to Europe and be conquerors.

ERIK TURNER
Warrant

Somebody was messing with [bassist] Jerry [Dixon] on the Sunset Strip and it looked like there were going to be some fists thrown. Then [our drummer] Steve [Sweet] grabbed the guy and slammed his head into the bumper of a car and just knocked the dude out before he could hit Jerry. It was funny because Steve is the most mild-mannered, quiet guy you'll ever meet.

WILL CARROLL
Death Angel, ex-Machine Head

Death Angel went to Greece and this woman wanted to take us out sightseeing the day of the show. When we were on the public transportation train, some guy who looked like a junkie was eyeing everyone in the band and saying angry-sounding stuff under his breath and spitting on the ground.

We were like, "What the fuck's that guy's problem?"

We went to another train and he followed us. Then, he got off at the same stop. He followed us up the stairs out of the station and onto street level. That's when [guitarist] Ted Aguilar, who's usually the most passive dude, got into a kung fu stance and said, "C'mon motherfucker, let's go!"

The junkie guy was swinging his keys and we didn't know if he had a knife. Ted was ready to go, but it was [bassist] Damien [Sisson] who ran up and grabbed him and threw him down the staircase. The dude rolled to the bottom and got up and wanted to fight some more. That's when the police came and arrested this guy.

GARY HOLT
Exodus, Slayer

In Exodus, we played a show in 2008 in Mokena, Illinois, at a place that's now closed, called the Pearl Room. It's documented in our live DVD. The security guards were manhandling the fans. Someone did a stagedive and a guard started beating on him and threw him out so we stopped the show.

Then we played "Piranha" and invited everyone onstage to stagedive. There were kids coming up in droves. The club freaked out and turned off the PA. The whole place erupted and everyone was beating on each other. It was awful and it all started with the meathead fuckin' security roughing up some kid.

After the show, the people who ran the club politely asked us not to use the footage from the fight and we said, "Nope, we've got it documented. It's going on the DVD."

ROB CAVESTANY

During the last show of the *Act III* tour, we were in Seattle and we were headlining over Forbidden and Sanctuary so we had prepared an especially long set.

During our first song, someone stage dived. As he was jumping into the crowd, someone in security pushed him hard. The audience opened up and the guy landed on the floor and broke his neck.

That was the end of the show. I heard he didn't die, but he probably would have been fine if that security guy didn't push him so hard.

TOMMY VICTOR
Prong, Danzig, ex-Ministry

We had a show in Boise, Iowa, during *The Cleansing* era that was total pandemonium. Half the crowd wound up onstage and they all started fighting with the security guys. One guard was right in front of me. I pushed a kid to the side and when this security guy grabbed the kid, the mic stand hit me in the mouth. People were banging into it for the whole show and it was smashing into my teeth. So I grabbed the mic stand and threw it and it hit this other security guard in the face and he was all bloody. We had to stop the show early and I had to run for my life and hide.

GLEN BENTON
Deicide

We played a gig in Cleveland years ago, and there were these two big rednecks doing security. They were fucking the kids up and being pricks.

"Yo, man, you need to knock it the fuck off or I'm gonna turn these kids loose on you," I said to them between songs.

They didn't stop. They kept punching people.

So I told the kids to rush the security and fight back. They yanked the feet out from under this one dude and he hit the fuckin' stage hard. Then they inched him into the crowd and he was gone. There were kids piled on top of him, pummeling the shit out of him. And when the security guy to the right of me got pulled down he looked like a fuckin' cat that was getting ready to fall into a swimming pool. He grabbed onto the floor and he tried to hold on like it was gonna fuckin' save him. He clawed at this thing with a look of fuckin' terror on his face. His fingers were slowly pried off of it as they pulled him into the pit and pummeled him. It was fuckin' great!

TONY FORESTA
Municipal Waste

My biggest problem is that I can't help myself when I see security guards fucking with fans. A lot of times they don't know what the fuck they're doing or they're bullying little kids or harassing fans for crowd surfing.

It's like, "Dude, this is a metal show. That shit's supposed to happen. Your job is to try to make sure everyone is safe, not to hurt people."

A lot of security guards know their role and they make the show better. They make sure the kids have a good time and don't get killed. It's when they're there to kick ass and make sure no one is dancing that I get crazy. There have been lots of times I've dove into the crowd and gotten into scraps with security guards. And there have been times I've been dragged out and beaten up. But if that, in any way, helped someone realize security guards are supposed to help you, not hurt you, then it was worth it.

PHILIP ANSELMO

When I first joined Pantera nobody knew me. They didn't know my personality, they didn't know my strength, they didn't know my weaknesses, they didn't know anything about me. I had a chip on my shoulder and I was in a brand new town in Texas so I had my guard up.

The band took me out one night to this place they hung out at. I had been there a couple times before. But this time a couple of their friends came up to me wide-eyed: "Oh my God, Donnie Hart's here." He was Pantera's previous singer.

Back in the day, Pantera's singer was Terry Glaze. After he quit, the band went through five different lead singers, including Donnie, just trying to stay relevant. Then, I came along.

The thing is, Pantera classlessly left Donnie Hart hanging. Instead of giving him a courteous call and saying, "Donnie, we want to thank you brother but I think we found our guy and now you can go back to your band Assassin. We wish you well," they kind of just blew him off. So he was angry.

I was there. Therefore, I was the object of his scourge. I was the witch in the witch hunt—a very familiar feeling I've had through my life. He was eyeballing me all night long from across the room.

"Oh God, why?" I thought. "Not again."

And then it happened. I had my dick in my hand and I felt the eyeballs. I look up and there he was. He had cornered me in the bathroom, this fuck. So I shook it out and zipped up.

"What the fuck are you looking at man," I said. I was pretty sure what was gonna come next.

He started up with me right away and I pulverized him. And then in came his bass player. I pulverized *him*. Here came his guitar player. I pulverized *him*. Enter his other guitar player. I pulverized *him*. Here came his drummer. I knocked him out cold.

And Pantera, all their friends and the rest of the bar stood back in awe at the new guy.

REX BROWN
Pantera, ex-Down, ex-Crowbar, Kill Devil Hill

When he was fighting Donnie Hart and those guys I tried to jump in and help Phil.

"Let me do it!" he snarled.

The guy was eighteen years old. He knocked four dudes into the dirt—into a ditch at the back of a fuckin' club. That's when we knew that we had someone that we could fuckin' rely on.

JOHN GALLAGHER

Once, some guys were flipping off [guitarist] Mark [Gallagher] so he dove into the crowd and landed on top of them. He's a big guy so that literally squashed all dissent. He didn't have to throw a punch.

Another time, something like that happened in Spain and Mark dove but the crowd moved out of the way. He landed on the ground like a crushed bug. He got up very slowly. Luckily it was the end of the show. He has never done it since.

KEITH BUCKLEY
Every Time I Die, The Damned Things

We were in the UK, and we were walking around for a while. Then we came back to the bus after a show and someone was just sitting there in the RV eating our food. We made quick work of him and some of his friends and that was kind of fun. But I sort of respected him in a way. This dude had got some serious balls. He just walked onto a stranger's bus and made himself a sandwich like it was the most natural thing on earth.

So we kicked his ass and his friend's asses. Afterwards, we were a little concerned about other people coming, so we got out of there real fast.

ALEX WADE
Whitechapel

We played this hole-in-the-wall Veteran's Hall, in Vestal, New York, and during the show a kid got thrown through the air onto our merch table. The table broke in half and our merch went flying everywhere. Then, the guy who threw the kid ran over and grabbed the broken table and threw it at the crowd. It turned into an all-out brawl and everyone ended up fighting.

A toilet in the bathroom ended up getting broken in half and water spewed all over the room. One kid got stomped unconscious and was dragged outside like a ragdoll, I seriously thought he might be dead.

WILL CARROLL

After a show in New Mexico, [guitarist] Rob [Cavestany] and I were hanging outside the bus drinking and talking. Some fans came walking up. There were three or four of them and they were drunk as hell. They didn't speak English very well and they were hanging on us saying, "Death Angel, Death Angel" and taking pictures.

They kind of overstayed their welcome. And then one of them walked up to me and tried to grab my beer bottle out of my hand.

"Whoa," I said surprised. "What the fuck are you doing?"

I pushed him off. He came walking back up to try to grab it again, so I punched him in the throat. He went flying back and landed flat on his back and hit his head on the street.

"Oh shit, it's on!" I figured.

But his friends realized he crossed a line so they grabbed him and got the hell out of there.

RICHARD CHRISTY

I was playing in this joke punk band called Pisser. We played at a coffee shop in Joplin, Missouri, which is the last place I would think there would ever be a massive brawl. We were paid in espresso. We actually drove from Springfield, Missouri, to Joplin to play for two espresso shots each. But they were the only ones that would let this band play because we did covers of songs by G.G. Allin and Cocknoose.

We all dressed up in goofy outfits. I was basically naked, like usual. We started playing and these jocks came in and didn't like the way we looked and they felt threatened by seeing my balls hanging out of a G-string so they tried to start trouble with us. It was pretty comical seeing my friend, who was wearing a Tinker Bell costume, defend himself from a dude trying to beat him up. Pretty soon we were fighting the jocks and other people in the shop joined in. No one got arrested. But I've never seen a big brawl at a coffee shop since.

KYLE SHUTT
The Sword

We were in Nottingham, England, in 2015 at a place called Rock City on the first Saturday the University was back in session. All the kids were so ready to party. It was totally sold out.

By the time we hit the stage everybody was wasted. There was this girl in the front row going nuts, waving her arms around everywhere, annoying everybody around her.

When we came back for the encore after finishing the show, we played "Arrows in the Dark" and the girl got pushed and knocked down to the ground. When she got up she socked this dude in the face. He was standing next to her but he wasn't the one who pushed her. He cocked his arm back like he was going to punch her back, and the guy next to him, was like, "Oh no you don't," and clocked him.

Before we knew what was going on, the entire bar was fighting. It was like an old-timey Western saloon brawl. People were picking up chairs and throwing them. We were still playing because we weren't sure what else to do. I looked down at my fingers to do a solo and I saw a security guard punch a kid. Then I looked back up and someone's had that same security guard in a headlock and the original guy was punching the security guard.

Next time I looked over, our security manager was throwing elbows to try to get everyone to calm down. At that point, we put the instruments down and walked off the stage. Eventually, our crew joined the fight against security. We were out of harm's way at that point, but that was the biggest fight I've ever seen.

KEITH BUCKLEY

We were walking back from a bar in Lancaster, Pennsylvania, in 2009. We had seen this dude and his girlfriend at the show and the guy seemed like a dick. We had all seen him moshing too hard during the show or moshing into people that weren't paying attention.

We go to the bar after and he was one of those kinds of guys that go, "Oh, you're my favorite band. Fuck you, you fucking cock suckers. I fucking love you."

They'll insult you while complimenting you. It's this really weird thing people that feel entitled do. It seems if they like your band they're allowed to insult you 'cause you have this kinship where they can tease you even though that's not the case at all. We got the fuck out of there because the dude was obviously too drunk.

We walked back and went to a different bar and hung out there for a little bit. Then when we left and went back to our bus we saw the guy and his girlfriend screaming at each other in the parking lot outside of our bus. It looked like he was getting aggressive.

"Hey, is this guy bothering you?" I asked, feeling like a good Samaritan.

"No, he's just drunk," she said.

"Oh, fuck you!" the dude said.

I turned to him, squared up and punched him right in the jaw and he stumbled and went down. That was the only time I've ever knocked someone out in my life. But I had just had it with this guy. I was a girlfriend protector that night. I was like, "Wow, that was very cool of me."

ERIK TURNER

We were at a club near Graumann's Chinese Theatre that everybody went to on Tuesday or Thursday night. Somebody [in our entourage] said something to some guy's girlfriend and without even saying a word the guy came up and sucker punched us from the side.

[Singer] Jani [Lane] got punched in the nose. I supposedly got punched, but I don't remember it happening and there was no blood or anything. [Bassist] Jerry [Dixon] got punched.

So, Jani was on a mission to find this guy and finally he tracked him down in a back alley and evened the score. He was wailing on him.

And then we got sued and ended up paying thousands of dollars, which was bullshit. This guy attacked us! That's when we first started hiring security to keep crazies away or avoid situations where somebody comes up and punches you in the face when you ain't looking.

MICHAEL SWEET
Stryper

Before we formed Stryper, we were outside a club in L.A. Mötley Crüe were getting ready to play. We had one too many drinks and [guitarist] Oz [Fox] made some comments about something. Tommy [Lee's] bouncer or bodyguard was this really big guy and he came over and started punching Oz. He was on the ground bleeding and we were getting pushed back by a lot of people. It wasn't a pretty sight. We wanted to get in there and defend Oz but there were too many people there. We stayed there until things calmed down and then we all left.

MORGAN LANDER
Kittie

We've never taken any shit. A lot of times people have grabbed us inappropriately while we were standing in the crowd or they've gotten onstage and groped my chest or ass. Early on, I would crowd surf because I thought it was great, but then it started to get out of hand. People were actually assaulting me. Any time that ever happened, we would always make sure that whoever it was got theirs.

I've kicked dudes in the dick a million times. And my sister [drummer] Mercedes [Lander], especially, was very protective of me. She's younger than me but she's much bigger and stronger and she always felt that if somebody ever fucked with me that she would go after them. I've seen her physically fight men and win.

We've also had friends at shows—both guys and girls—that have backed us up to fight when anything went down.

DEVIN TOWNSEND
Strapping Young Lad, ex-Steve Vai, ex-Wildhearts, Devin Townsend Band

We were playing Atlanta and I was telling everyone to fuck themselves. Someone came to the front of the stage flipping us off and told us we sucked. So [bassist] Byron Stroud knocked him out and then I hid behind a bunch of big guys while the audience took out their aggression on us by throwing shit.

Strapping was full-tilt about facing down antagonistic crowds and we had no intention of winning them over. That ended up being our thing. We went out on Ozzfest as the "you suck" band. It became a weird, ironic parody. I was really uncomfortable with that because Strapping never started with any desire to be amusingly provocative.

GENE HOGLAN

Devin is not a violent guy at all, but we had a brawl in New Jersey at a club called Obsession that shut down the whole show. We weren't even headlining. Strapping was opening for Testament and they didn't get to play. It started because the owner was being a complete dick to us for whatever reason.

"You know I'm not in the greatest mood tonight. I think I'm gonna start some shit," Devin said before the show.

Sure enough, he did. We opened with a song called "Velvet Kevorkian" from *City*. As we were playing it, I could tell that Devin was not singing the lyrics. He was berating someone. The band screamed, "Fuck you" when they should have been screaming the word "Woman." And then our power got shut down.

Devin jumped off the stage and ran towards the front-of-house sound guy. Then, he started duking it out with the club owner. Everyone jumped off the stage and it turned into a big brawl scene in a Burt Reynolds movie. We were pounding on people and I had no idea what we were fighting for, but hell, we were fighting and even Devin was out there. He's not a violent guy at all but that night something got in his craw.

REX BROWN

We were in Amsterdam around '92 and that's when the Dallas Cowboys were on their big run against the Buffalo Bills. We were sitting in the hotel and we had our jerseys on. There were some guys from the U.S. military there and they were Bills fans. As the game went on everybody kept drinking and it turned into a war zone. There were twelve of us against fifty fucking Marines.

There were fists flying, chairs broken over heads, bottles smashed. And then all these Marines started whipping these solid beer mugs at us. When those things start flying through the air, the smartest thing to do is jump under the table and then clear the aftermath. One of our assistants broke his hand. I got hit several times. I can't remember what happened with the other guys.

And our security guard—God bless his soul—he was so fucking high from smoking all that weed in Amsterdam that by the time he got to us the fight was pretty much over. We had our asses handed to us, but we did some damage, also. And of course, the place called the cops and we had to haul the fuck out of there with bruised faces and bloody noses.

PHILIP ANSELMO

It was so crazy in the early days of Pantera because everyone had a different take on me. So it became the go-to guy whenever the Abbott brothers— Dimebag in particular—hade a problem: "Phil, this guy said this to me!"

"Phil . . ." "Phil . . ." "Phil."

I didn't even know these poor guys a lot of the times and yeah, maybe the guy was drunk and mouthing off and, BOOM, it happened. But it got to the point where a couple times there, the guy in question was looking at me with this expression that said, "Dude, I honestly didn't mean anything." He was very rational in his explanation of what transpired and what went down. And knowing Dimebag and a few of his friends, I knew that this guy who was getting begged to get beaten up by me was telling the truth.

So I did not side with Dime on those occasions. I just said the dude Dime had beef with, "Bro, let's just walk away from this situation. Do me a favor. Be the bigger person and let's just have a good night and forget this shit ever fucking happened. . . Very nice to meet you, by the way."

It got to the point when I finally had to say to Dime, "Dude, you're going to have to learn how to fight your own battles that you start."

BEN WEINMAN

In 1998, when we were first starting out, we used to play in Philadelphia a lot and one of the places we played was this squat called Stalag 13. It was like a storefront that a lot of bike messengers, crust punks, and grindcore kids kind of took over, and they put on shows.

They started bringing in heavier bands like Brutal Truth, Today Is the Day, and Discordance Axis, and a lot of those bands drew violent crowds. So a lot of these tough Philly gang guys that just wanted to bash on people in the mosh pit started coming to shows a lot. They were thugs and they would beat people up and put them in the hospital on a daily basis. They didn't care about what band was playing. They just wanted a heavy band that they could beat people up to.

So, naturally, they gravitated to us because we were this heavy, violent group.

One time, we played there and these guys were in the pit beating everybody up, so I took my guitar off and threw it at the biggest gang dude I saw. I straight-up speared it at him and it hit him right in the chest and then hit the floor. The guy was massive. It was like the record scratched and stopped.

"I'm gonna fuckin' murder you!" the guy growled.

And these guys *had* murdered people. So, I just stood there.

"All right, there's nothing I can do," I told myself. "I can't defend myself. I'm one hundred pounds wet. I'm just going to stand here and take it."

I kind of almost closed my eyes thinking this guy was about to charge me. And all of a sudden, the people that ran the club and the people that were part of that scene grabbed all these weapons that they had hidden because they were prepared for this. They were waiting for it.

They were like, "We're going to take back our club and get these guys out."

They had crowbars and baseball bats and even a pit bull. They all formed a line in front of me and just chased these guys out of the club.

"Get the fuck out of here and don't fucking come back," someone said while swinging a bat at a gang dude. "If you're gonna beat up people, do it somewhere else!"

I was like, "Wow, okay."

It was a little difficult for me, though, because I was in a band [and] we were playing shows that were advertised so I knew it wouldn't be hard for these thugs to find me. So there was a period of time when I was horrified to play shows in that area. I thought that any moment those guys might come up and shoot me or stab me.

MIKE BORDIN
Faith No More

We played on that legendary Metallica and Guns N' Roses tour but we were at the bottom of the bill. After Metallica did *The Black Album* we just got crushed. There was no air and no space for us because you had these two insanely overwhelming monstrous giant bands. For the fans, there was no room for anything else. Those were some hard shows to play. It just wasn't a good fit.

To make things worse, our record company suggested that we play this radio station-sponsored concert in a club the night after we'd played with Guns n' Roses. And they very strongly implied that if we wanted any help at all with our next single, "Midlife Crisis," we shouldn't think twice about showing up and kissing ass, which is bad enough on a good day. We totally hate that shit. But when the band is already frustrated and punchy you have the elements there for some real problems.

We got to this club thing and it was a straight rock and roll event where they were playing totally commercial rock music. There were some bands there that were up and coming. One of Rick Rubin's bluesy new rock bands was there with their records.

"This isn't going to be the right thing for the crowd," I told our handlers. "The way the band is right now, the way we're feeling and the energy that we're getting from this club, I'm telling you there's going to be confrontation here. It's not going to be pleasant. Don't make us do this. Really we don't want to do this. It's not the right place for this."

Of course, they made us play and our singer, [Mike Patton], ended up going to the hospital. Someone in the crowd got into a fight with him. There were punches thrown and the guy kicked Mike and hit him with a bottle. It was a fucking battle that didn't have to happen. It was ugly and we knew it would be, but no one listened to us. That's the most adversarial gig I can remember us playing.

Afterwards, we were on the bus and the cops came in and we said Mike had to go to the hospital. Later, one of the guys who had been there that night said it was the best show we'd ever done. I thought that was a bit of a funny way to put it. At the same time, there are elements within our band that absolutely thrive on chaos and confrontation to achieve whatever you want to call it—the random factor. And that's the unpredictable punk rock side of us coming out.

TOMMY VICTOR

We were on tour with Faith No More in 1992 and we got into a huge fight with their crew. We were not happy on that tour. The band treated us like dog shit. We were opening and we had to buy onto the tour. On top of that, we had to pay every day to get catering. They were just assholes.

Mike Patton was the only one we sort of got along with, but that ended, too. I was outside of the stage watching the show and Mike squirted a plastic bottle of Coke at me, so I took the bottle and threw it at him. One of their crew guys came over and punched me in the chest and said, "Get the fuck off the stage" and I swung at him.

I was punching numerous people, who were all attacking me and it turned into this whole brawl and in the end I fell off the stage.

WILL CARROLL

In 2014, Death Angel were in Denver on tour with Anthrax. After our set, some of us wanted to go to another club to see Exodus [bassist] Jack Gibson and [drummer] Tom Hunting play with this outlaw country band called Coffin Hunter. So me, [bassist] Damien Sisson, our tour manager and one of our guitar techs went over to the club.

We were having a blast and the Exodus guys were surprised to see us. At the end of the show, Coffin Hunter were packing up their stuff and getting ready to load out.

"Hey, what's going on outside the front door?" someone shouted. "There's some kind of commotion."

I looked, and I could see our guitar tech. This dude was the worst fucking drunk I've ever seen. He would sleep on the top bunk of the bus and get so drunk he'd roll out and smash to the ground. Or he'd be so wasted he'd wake up and go to the back lounge and pee, thinking it was the bathroom. I saw him outside and it looked like he was wasted and something was going down.

So I went outside and it was a lot worse than I thought. My guys were exchanging words with two biker dudes who looked like they had just walked out of San Quentin. They were huge and scary as fuck. Apparently this tech, who got really lippy when he drank, had gone out and told the bikers they had to move their cars because the band was loading out. The tech took it upon himself to act all tough and tell them that. He didn't even know there was a backdoor to the club and Coffin Hunter had already loaded out.

"What's going on," I asked. No one answered. Instead, one of the bikers turned to our tour manager.

"Where are you from, motherfucker?"

"I'm from Oakland," The tour manager tried to say. Before he even said "Oak-" the biker clocked him in the side of the head really fuckin' hard and he went down like a rock and was unconscious.

This dude was about to kick our tour manager in the face with his boots. I jumped over our tour manager.

"No, man, no," I begged. "Don't fuckin' kick him."

The biker hit me in the side of the head but he didn't knock me out. I stumbled back a little bit expecting the fight to continue.

"Yo, man, let's get the fuck out of here!!" the biker's buddy said and the two jumped in their car and took off.

I had no idea why the dude wanted to leave before him and his buddy kicked the shit out of us. Then I turned around and saw our guitar laying on the ground in a pool of blood.

"Fuck, man," I said. "What happened?"

Damien didn't really know because he had been pinned against the wall by one of the bikers when our guitar tech got hurt. The guy's skull was cracked open. He had to go to the emergency room and he was in the hospital for weeks. It was terrible, but it was also really confusing because I didn't see anyone touch him and neither me nor Damien heard anyone fight him. After putting all the pieces together we came to the conclusion that our tech was so drunk he tripped over his own feet and cracked his head open—all because he mouthed off at some huge bikers.

BRETT CAMPBELL
Pallbearer

[Drummer] Mark [Lierly] and I fell asleep in the van in L.A. because we were smashed. We were staying with our friend Stephen [Lee Clark], who used to be in Deafheaven. Everyone else was already at his place, so when we woke up we decided to walk over there. It was a few blocks away.

We got up, brutally hungover and sweaty from being in a hot van in L.A. in the summer. We looked like shit. We'd been awake for five minutes when out of nowhere this huge dude starts walking towards us from a pretty good ways away.

"Yo, where are you from?" He asked.

"Uh, Little Rock," I said.

"What the fuck are you doing here?"

"We're walking to our friend's house."

The guy took off his shirt off and pushed Mark really hard and kicked me in the ass incredibly hard. My butt hurt for three days. He literally kicked my ass. I guess we kind of surprised him by saying anything. We really didn't want to fight the guy 'cause he was really big and we were still wrecked.

The guy glared at us and then stopped in his tracks.

"Don't let me catch you slippin,'" he said.

And then he walked away. He was clearly crazed. When he asked where we were from I didn't realize he didn't mean that in a friendly, neighborly way.

DAVE WYNDORF
Monster Magnet

When I turned eighteen, I went to a bar to get packaged goods. I was wearing a leather jacket and had a Johnny Ramone haircut, and some guy yelled, "You punk rock faggot!" And then he hauled off and clocked me.

Next thing I knew, I was in a fight in the parking lot. I'm not good at fisticuffs, so I spazzed out and went completely balls-out, berserk gonzo crazy. Then, I lay down on the ground, and as he came near me I tried to kick him in the head. He called me a freak and stood there for a minute not knowing what to do. So, I got up and ran like a motherfucker.

GUY KOZOWYK
The Red Chord

When we toured with A Life Once Lost once, I broke my hand on some kid's head. We were in Ithaca, New York, and we watched this weird hippie guy beat the crap out of another hippie guy for no particular reason. The kid wasn't fighting back or anything. And I was like, "What an asshole. I'd love to slug this guy in the side of the head."

And then, lo-and-behold, a couple hours later we were sitting by the side of the road waiting for this little art space to open up and let us load our equipment in. And the guy we saw before came up with his friend and some girl and he just picked a fight with us by knocking over stuff on our vans. Bob Meadows, [the vocalist] from A Life Once Lost talked smack to him.

The guy made a line on the ground with his foot.

"If you cross this line, it's on," said the crazy hippie.

Bob jumped around like an idiot and crossed the line. So the guy attacked him.

"Well, I really wanted to hit him in the face and here's my chance," I thought.

I started punching him in the face and eventually he curled up a little bit. I couldn't get a clear shot. But I really wanted to hit him again and I didn't want to wait anymore. So I just bushwhacked the back of his head.

It was the stupidest thing ever because my hand exploded and I immediately saw stars. I didn't go to the hospital and my hand turned gray-green after a while because I was in denial of the fact that it was broken.

DEZ FAFARA

There was always this urban myth that Meegs [Rascón] hit me on the head with the guitar onstage and that's why Coal Chamber broke up, but that never happened. The band did get into a fight onstage during a show in Lubbock, Texas. We had been arguing all day. For some reason, the rest of the band decided to fire Sharon Osbourne, who was managing us, and they did it behind my back. I love Sharon and she gave us such a big break by managing us in the first place, so that really pissed me off.

Then, we got onstage for the show and during the first song, Meegs turned to me and tried to stab me with the headstock of his guitar. He wasn't goofing around. He was really trying to hurt me. We started shoving each other.

I left the fucking stage and then came back and said, "This is the last Coal Chamber show ever."

Then we trashed the set and that was it.

MARK MORTON
Lamb of God

We never really fought with other people. We were always fighting each other. We were a rolling tornado. There was that little overblown slap fight [in Scotland] that got a lot of attention. But that was just one of many, many incidents.

Back in the day, there was an element to Burn the Priest and Lamb of God that was dangerous. It felt like the wheels were coming off the van. The train was coming off the tracks. There was that feeling inside the band so I know that feeling had to come across witnessing the band onstage. It was one of those things that drew people to us. There was this combustible element about the combination of us as people and with the music we made and it was real. It was lightning in a bottle for us for a while. It was part of the magic.

JOEY JORDISON

When Slipknot ended our *Iowa* tour we had been working every day since September 1995. We couldn't stand being around one another anymore. We had just had enough.

Me and [vocalist] Corey [Taylor] came to blows one time. Me and [percussionist] Shawn ["Clown" Crahan] have, too, and it fucking rocked. We're brothers, man, and all brothers fight. I can honestly say that if we had tried to put out another fucking record after *Iowa* without taking a break, the band would not exist. We needed time away from one another and I think every Slipknot fan should be grateful to the Murderdolls and Stone Sour for doing records during that time because if that hadn't happened Slipknot might not have made it to our third record.

DARON MALAKIAN
System of a Down, Scars on Broadway

We're really emotional guys and really opinionated people and we like to get our way. So, yeah, there have been times when we fuckin' threw down.

[Once, our drummer], John [Dolmayan] and I were totally going at it. My lip was all cut up, and I took a microphone stand and hit him across the head and his head was all bashed in. [Bassist] Shavo [Odadjian] and [vocalist] Serj [Tankian] were looking at us saying, "Awww, man, we're done. The band's over."

But right after we fought, we took each other to the hospital and got stitched up right next to each other. Both of us were sitting there laughing, saying, "This is one of the coolest moments in the history of our band."

ZOLTAN BATHORY
Five Finger Death Punch

We've had times when we've come to some head-to-head, toe-to-toe scenarios.

Once, Ivan grabbed the head of somebody who is no longer in the band, and he smashed it through the window of the bus while we were driving down the freeway. The bus driver didn't even pull over.

He was like, "Well, that's gonna be $1,000, but he had it coming."

MIKE IX WILLIAMS
Eyehategod

There was a guy that was fucking with us and being an asshole, so I hit him with the mic stand and his forehead just opened up. But the worst fights I ever got in were with [my bandmate] Jimmy [Bower] just because we were both super drunk. We've been in this band thirty years. That's a lot of time to piss each other off, so it was bound to happen sooner or later. Sometimes, I didn't hold back, and I'd punch Jimmy when he was acting up. Of course, we'd make up the next day.

When we were in Mexico, we went over to Juarez from El Paso, Texas. It was me, Jimmy, [singer and guitarist] Pepper Keenan, and [guitarist] Woody [Weatherman] from Corrosion of Conformity. We were going barhopping and getting crazier and crazier. Every time we'd buy a beer, they'd give us a tequila shot to go with it. Within a few hours, we were all fuckin' wasted.

We left a transgender bar and ended up at a mariachi bar, which was kind of a nicer place. Bands were playing. For some reason, I just hauled off and punched Jimmy in the face. The band stopped playing, and all the lights came on in the club. The security put me and Jimmy in full nelsons and threw us out in the street. Jimmy took out his false teeth and put them in his pocket because he wanted to fight me.

I was like, "No, man." And I ran away.

For one thing, I knew Jimmy could kick my ass, but we both also wanted to run across the border before the cops showed up. That's what we were afraid of. The whole time, he was behind me screaming.

JIMMY BOWER
Eyehategod, Superjoint Ritual, Down, ex-Crowbar

Me and [vocalist] Mike IX Williams got in a fight in Juarez when we were on tour with Corrosion of Conformity in 1994 on the *Deliverance* tour. We were in a strip club telling each other, "Oh man, look at your girlfriend up there. Look at your girlfriend."

We kept drinking tequila so we were all wasted. Mike walked up to me a little later and said, "Hey man, what was up with that comment about my girlfriend?"

Before I could say anything, BOOM, he nailed me in my fucking eye. My eye was black. He absolutely egged it. I was screaming at him the whole way to the border. Then I chased him around a hotel trying to whip his ass.

JOHN GALLAGHER

Three dates into the Kill 'Em All for One tour we did with Metallica opening for us, we were in Bridgeport, Connecticut, and [guitarist] Mark [Gallagher] and [drummer] Rob ["Wacko" Hunter] got into it. I was playing a bass solo at the time but [Metallica's bassist] Cliff Burton told me about it later.

Cliff had this really shitty second bass, which was basically made from cardboard. It was in a case and he was upset because they were beating the shit out of each other and stepping all over his bass. It was a fight over nothing, probably instigated by absolutely no sleep. There were no hotels at that point and there were seventeen people fighting for six bunks. Nobody really got any sleep until the day after that tour when we lay down an ultimatum: Hotels or take us home.

DANI FILTH
Cradle of Filth

We used to fight a lot with each other and it inhibited our productivity. As with anybody in the studio, arguments can sit and brood for weeks with the jilted party just spitting dark daggers from the corner.

So we came up with a novel way of ending arguments. We invested in air pistols with plastic ammunition and the whole studio turned into this gun battle war zone. It was like Beirut.

We wore glasses to be fair, but people were shot in the face and that fucking hurt. When you got hit it felt you'd been stung by a wasp. I've still got scars on my back from where I was shot when somebody bought an Uzi that discharged plastic bullets one hundred at a time.

KEITH BUCKLEY

There was a night in Germany when we all started yelling at each other and wound up drunkenly fighting in a parking lot after a show. I got knocked out by one of my own band members.

Afterwards, I thought, "Man, if I'm getting so bad that I'm offending the people I'm spending my entire life with and I'm making them so upset that they don't feel they can talk to me anymore and they feel they need to actually hit me, something's fucking wrong."

Even though it was never talked about again and not really a big deal, it led me on a path where I went, "I need to do some self-help here."

I started doing transcendental meditation more often and got more in control of my life. I was still drinking, but it was about finding a nice balance between meditating and being more present and grateful for the things that I have and not putting so many toxins into my body.

REX BROWN

We were some very tough individuals. You had to be to survive on the road. We would scream and fight and yell, but we never threw punches at each other. There were many times Philip wanted to strangle Dime and I'd have to pull him off: "Dime, fuckin' shut up, man!"

It was crazy, but it was fun. I wouldn't trade any of it for the world. Dime was the best, man.

JOHN GALLAGHER

Raven was touring in the American South with Metallica opening for us in 1983. The guitar tech was a black guy, Bill Case, and he said, "Oh, I'm scared. I've never been south before. You guys are gonna have to protect me in case I get any shit."

"Yeah, we got you covered, no problem," I said.

We went to a diner somewhere in Texas. And we were just sitting there when this redneck came over and sat down at the table.

"You rock and roll types. I bet you think you're real hot with your long hair!?!" he began. "You know what? I don't give a shit. I could break your arms and legs right in front of you right now."

As he spoke, he got more agitated and louder and angrier.

"You fuckin' dipshits. I need to smash you around! I could take you apart. Man, I'm a black belt in karate!!!"

"You're a black belt?" I said.

"Yeahh!" he snarled.

"Wow! Where did you study?" I asked.

He told us who his teacher was and I kept talking with him and he kept talking and he calmed down. We became best friends. He came to the show and everything!

MORGAN LANDER

One time we were in Houston at a club called Fitzgeralds and a guy jumped up onstage and punched me in the face. Immediately, I turned around and took my guitar and smashed him very hard with it.

And my guitar kind of went, "Nnnneeeeoooowwwww" out of tune.

It was a fantastic moment.

Some of our friends, who were big dudes, went after this guy and we didn't even stop playing.

SATYR
Satyricon

We played Saarbrucken, Germany, and there was a big, big bald guy who looked really mean. As I was standing by my microphone stand singing, I saw in the corner of my left eye this guy was running past the guards, getting behind the barriers, and running towards me. He looked like he was going to attack me. The guards saw him and started chasing him and as he was inches away from me they reached out and tackled him, then put him in a headlock. They dragged him out and he was furious and raging and screaming at me.

He wasn't angry and I could actually hear what he was saying even though we were in the middle of a song. He was screaming over and over, "Satyr, you have to play in Luxembourg!"

I was like, "Okay, I'll think about it."

It's funny because Luxembourg is considered like a Disneyland nation in Europe. There are only one hundred thousand people who live there and it's one of the smallest countries in the world. You can drive through it in fifteen minutes. And to have someone who looks like a badass Navy seal yelling that was really strange.

ERIK DANIELSSON

We are the fucking enemy and if people have a problem with that they should stay away. We toured for two months with [the Dutch death metal band] Legion of the Damned and it was pure hell. They came from a background where metal was about barbecuing with the guys from Cannibal Corpse. We came from a background where metal is about tearing things up and setting things on fire. They complained about us and it came to a point where we agreed that it's better that we don't say anything to each other for the rest of the tour because otherwise, somebody will get really hurt.

But I don't want to complain. If we would not be in situations like that now and then, something would be wrong. We are wolves, we are not sheep. Fuck the world. It's the enemy. We are not here to be friends with people.

But it's a matter of taking yourself seriously or not. If you're singing about certain things and then when you get off the stage, you just laugh about it, then, of course, you will get in trouble when you're with bands like us.

These bands are a bunch of funny clowns who like to play around and then go, "Yay, the concert is over. Let's go suck each other's dicks."

CHAPTER 16: WHEN THE GOING GETS TOUGH

Staring Down Hostile Crowds & Dodging Projectiles

Raven—lifers of the English New Wave of British Heavy Metal—landed a major label deal after almost nine years in the business. Fortunately, it only lasted three albums. Like many other groups cherry-picked from the independent scene in the '80s, Raven were asked by their new label to polish up their songs and write more commercial material. The results were mixed. Old-school fans far preferred the raw, urgent, NWOBHM style of their first three albums. An exception is the infectious "When the Going Gets Tough," from Raven's fourth full-length *Stay Hard*, which came out in 1985. Propelled by chugging, trebly guitars and chant-along vocal harmonies, the tune is a radio hit that never was, one that's just as enthralling as Accept's "Balls to the Wall," Scorpions' "Rock You Like a Hurricane" and Ratt's "Round and Round." Rather than accept defeat, Raven rolled with the crunches after escaping the stranglehold of corporate rock, bouncing between various independent labels over the last thirty-two-plus years, playing thousands of high-energy, acrobatic concerts in clubs around the globe.

The best bands occasionally have bad shows. Bad bands sometimes have great shows. In some cases, the audience's reaction to the best and worst performances has nothing to do with the quality of the show. This is especially true for opening bands that tour with veteran groups whose audiences shows up to see only one band and has to endure whoever takes the stage before the headliner. Sometimes the diversity of the bill itself will affect the reaction of the crowd. A death metal band opening for a melodic thrash band doesn't have good odds of winning over the audiences. European Festivals and events like Coachella are probably the worst environments for anyone but marquee caliber groups to succeed— especially since so many of today's festivals feature extremely diverse bills that include hip-hop, electronic dance, alternative and mainstream rock acts. Even established metal bands have been chased off the stage on the Warped punk-based tour, and new-school hardcore-influenced metal bands have fled to their buses on past Ozzfest and Rockstar Energy Mayhem tours.

If unhappy crowds held in the discontent, then metal bands wouldn't have so many stories about how they won over audiences that had been throwing coins and bottles at them. . . or didn't win them over and shuffled off the stage after short sets. It's hard enough for bands to endure long road trips, cramped quarters and semi-regular hassles, such as vehicle breakdowns, internal squabbling, and trying to cope with an unhappy spouse who is at home with the kids hundreds of miles away. The last thing any artist needs is to be heckled, booed, flipped off or given the silent treatment by an unhappy metal crowd. Maybe that's what separates the men in studded leather from the whiny mommy's boys. Perhaps surviving the metal game requires developing a thick skin, an even-keeled temperament or a give a fuck attitude. Or maybe the best coping mechanism is loads of offstage distractions. 'Cause as someone once said long before there were electric guitars, the show must go on—unless it grinds to a halt.

GARY HOLT
Exodus, Slayer

In my entire career in Exodus I've had one heckler and that's because we did a Bay Area show supporting the Red Hot Chili Peppers. There were eight thousand people or so and the show was killer. But there was one guy in the crowd and his girlfriend that didn't like me. They were just all about the Chili Peppers and didn't want to hear any heavy metal. I just flipped him off and launched a nice lunger at him that hit him because he was right up front.

What's funny is I've only had that one heckler in Exodus and I actually had four hecklers in Slayer over nearly six years. But one guy can fuck shit up if you let him. That's all it takes.

SCOTT IAN
Anthrax, S.O.D., The Damned Things

We were at the Olympic Auditorium in L.A. in April 1986. The show was No Mercy, Possessed, Corrosion of Conformity, D.R.I., and Anthrax. At the time, The Olympic was known as the worst, most violent place to go see shows—whether it was punk, hardcore or metal. But being from the East Coast, we didn't know how bad it could get. I don't even know what downtown L.A. was at that time. It was a really, really shitty area and we were warned not to venture too far off the premises.

There were thirty-five hundred people at the show and it was all different factions—punks, skinheads, metalheads. And The Suicidals, the gang member dudes, were working security. These weren't Suicidal Tendencies fans in T-shirts. They were forty-year-old guys that were in prison the week before and real Mexican Mafia-looking dudes. So our stage was lined with these dudes in the Crandall's shirts buttoned up to the neck and black wraparound shades and bandanas, and they weren't dressed like that because they like the music. They were actual gang people and they were all over the stage working quote-unquote security.

Immediately, the skinheads wanted to fight them and the gangsters wanted to fight the skinheads because they all hated each other. We got onstage and almost immediately there was a giant circle pit in the middle of the floor and all around that were people fighting. These skinheads were roaming around and punching anyone they could hit. Dudes were getting up on stage, not to stage dive but to fight the Suicidal security dudes.

At some point, a giant biker dude got on the stage and someone came running up from the side and cracked this guy in the head with a mic stand. The biker was lying unconscious on the stage with his head bleeding while we're standing there playing. I had never been a part of anything like that.

"What the fuck is going on?" I thought.

But we were still playing. We'd finish one song and we'd all look at each other and shrug our shoulders and start playing another song.

We were supposed to play a little over an hour and I think we did about forty minutes before a guy ran around the back of the stage and right through Charlie's drum kit and knocked part of it to the floor.

"That's it. We're fuckin' out of here," we all thought at the same time.

We walked off the stage and the lights came on. I think there was more of a sense of relief from the audience that the show was done rather than people being upset we weren't playing anymore.

We got back to our dressing room. Everything had been trashed or stolen. So we went straight from there to our bus and said, "Okay, let's get the gear off the stage as soon as possible and get the fuck out of here."

About fifteen minutes after we got on our bus, [S.O.D. vocalist] Billy Milano (Method of Destruction), who had come out to L.A. for the show comes walking in on the bus in a shirt but he looked like the Hulk. His shirt was all torn and there was blood all over it. There was blood on his hands.

"What the fuck, dude?" I said.

"Hey, don't worry it's not my blood," He responded.

He told us that every fucking skinhead in L.A. thought they were tough and wanted to fight the New Yorker so he let them try.

Apparently, he beat up ten people or something—just fucking hilarious. We left and never played the Olympic again.

DEE SNIDER
Twisted Sister, ex-Widowmaker

At the Wrexham Festival in North Wales, we would have gotten bottled off the stage. We were dodging these things left and right. Then [Motörhead frontman] Lemmy [Kilmister], who everyone in the crowd loved, stepped out and said, "Here are some friends of mine from America. Give them a listen."

I believe that was the quote, but I didn't speak Lemmy at the time. It just sounded like a bunch of garbled words. But the crowd seemed to understand. The audience literally gave us a reprieve for a minute and that was all we needed to win them over.

DEZ FAFARA
DevilDriver, ex-Coal Chamber

We opened for Opeth in 2003 and it was the roughest crowd I think I've ever faced. It was right at the beginning of DevilDriver's career. We had just done our first album and people still associated me with Coal Chamber, which a lot of dudes hated by that time because the nu-metal scene had died an ugly death. And these people didn't care that DevilDriver had nothing to do with nu-metal.

I was cursed by the past.

At the very first show with Opeth, there were a thousand people there when we went on and about three hundred turned their backs to us for the whole show. For the first week and a half of the tour, there was no applause whatsoever when we took the stage, between songs or when we were done.

Then, much to [Opeth frontman] Mikael Åkerfeldt's credit, he walked out and said, "I heard you are being dicks to our opening band. Please stop this."

Some fans in the crowd had cell phones and filmed Mikael saying that and it went viral. After that, the shows were incredible. In no time everyone was cheering and moshing and our merch had doubled. It was like, "Oh, Mikael loves this band. I guess we should love them, too."

KEITH BUCKLEY
Every Time I Die, The Damned Things

We played Ozzfest in Denver in 2004. We had a show to play in Syracuse right before the Denver show, so we played it, flew to Denver, landed and went right to the show and straight to the stage. We were over-tired and cranky. I was wearing a Michael Jackson shirt. And people straight-up started flipping us off and turned their backs to us. By the end of the set, nobody was looking at us. I was like, fuck this place. I started talking shit and everyone was throwing beers.

"Fuck you, Denver! We're never coming back here!" I said before we left the stage.

And now Denver shows are the fucking best. I couldn't ask for a better city to play in.

MICHAEL SWEET
Stryper

We played a death metal festival in Holland in 1986 and when we went on, the crowd hated us. They were throwing big, thick heavy chains at us and bottles and we were dodging all this stuff. If we had been hit by any of it, we would have been seriously injured. We had even taken precautions with the music. We shortened the set. We took out all the ballads and just did the most metal stuff like "The Rock That Makes Me Roll" and "Soldiers Under Command."

For three or four songs they were trying to kill us and booing and shouting, "Fuck Stryper!"

Then there was a sudden transformation. After four songs, they loved us! We won them over and after the show, one death metal fan after another came up and said, "Man, we had no idea. We love you now."

BURTON C. BELL
Fear Factory, Ascension of the Watchers

In 2004 we did a big radio show in Huntington, West Virginia, that Godsmack was playing. We were on after them because they were just breaking out when the show was booked but they were all over the radio by the time of the show. We had a tech who was a total New Jersey dude and he was a stickler for time.

Godsmack was running over so he cut their power.

That was a bad move 'cause the crowd was really there to see them and after Godsmack played, everybody left. It was a horrible night. Everything went wrong. I started throwing Heineken bottles everywhere. I was smashing one after another because I was so pissed off.

JOHN GALLAGHER
Raven

Some girl at the front of the stage was flipping off [our drummer] Joe Hasselvander. The girl was surrounded and couldn't move and Joe had a really bad cold so at the end of the show he walked up to where she was standing and blew his nose all over her hair. I dropped my pants and mooned the audience. And my brother [and guitarist Mark] screamed, "Fuck you lot. You don't know fuck-all! We were doing this back when you were still shittin' yellow."

ROB CAVESTANY
Death Angel, ex-The Organization

We played a show in Wales for a bunch of skinheads and punk rockers in the early '80s and they were totally spitting on us. I was covered in spit and [vocalist] Mark [Osegueda] was trying to get in between me and the people spitting. That wasn't working so he jumped in the crowd to fight some dude. He couldn't really get to him and the crowd wasn't having it so we stopped the show early and ran to our van and got the fuck out of there before all these punk rockers kicked our fucking ass.

MORGAN LANDER
Kittie

Once, we played in England and these people in the crowd were spitting at us. We were all covered with spit. To me, that's totally disrespectful and gross. But strangely enough, we found out later that when they do that it means they really like you.

DAVID DRAIMAN
Disturbed

Our very first European run was with Marilyn Manson and before we took the stage the crowd was chanting, "Manson, Manson, Manson!" They didn't even give us a chance. From the minute we walked up there, the entire fucking crowd was spitting. It was raining spit everywhere. You couldn't avoid it. I'd open up my mouth to sing and I'd feel a drop of someone's saliva. That's how fucking bad it was.

I know some English audiences have historically spit when they've liked a band, but these people were spitting at us out of sheer hatred. It went on non-stop for the first three songs. We kept going after the third song and they either ran out of spit or we fucking won them over.

REX BROWN
Pantera, ex-Down, ex-Crowbar, Kill Devil Hill

You go play up in Glasgow, Scotland, it's nothing but a gob fest. You get that in your fuckin' mouth, dude, it's the worst. You've gotta keep your mouth shut the whole time. And if you tell them to stop you get it more.

We could hold our own. I've taken my bass down on quite a few motherfuckers' heads, but when they're spitting like that, there's nothing you can do but keep playing.

PHILIP ANSELMO
Pantera, Down, Superjoint Ritual, Scour

In Ireland, if they love you they spit at you. That was a sign of success. As a lead vocalist that was always interesting to me. I hated it, but I liked that they loved us. Today it would be rude as fuck though. That's grounds for a left hook, Jack.

JOHN GALLAGHER

In Denver, some guy spit at me so I walked right up to him. I had my headset mic on so I made a great noise of sloshing phlegm around in my mouth.

"You wanna spit?" I said.

And then I just unloaded this big loogie on him to everyone's mirth.

PAGE HAMILTON
Helmet

We were on the Guns N' Roses tour in 2006 and their fans were just not diggin' us. Ames, Iowa, was one of the worst shows. It was the first time I saw mullets in years. They were throwing little plastic Jack Daniels bottles and some cans. No one got hurt.

But we have a song called "Trick" from *Betty,* which has an improvised feedback outro. So I just started that song and said, "Let's just play this for eight minutes."

I figured since they hated us anyway, we might as well give them a big fuck you.

CHRIS VRENNA
ex-Nine Inch Nails, ex-Marilyn Manson

On the tour for *The Downward Spiral,* we had the Melvins open a four-week run for us. They were supporting *Stoner Witch.* I'm a huge Melvins fans and we loved those guys. But that band got booed off the stage every night.

There was one night in Dallas that was in an ice arena and they had that press cardboard flooring they used to cover the ice during concerts. Fans were ripping that stuff up into Frisbee-sized chunks and whipping it at the Melvins. That stuff is heavy and it can cause some real damage.

So the Melvins got the biggest roar of feedback that they could generate and they walked behind all their guitar cabinets and sat there on the stage and let the noise go for thirty minutes before they left the stage. We felt so bad for the Melvins. Our fans freaking hated them, which I didn't understand.

BUZZ OSBORNE
Melvins

A whiskey bottle exploded on our drum set before we even played a note. The audience was so rabid to have our heads. We were opening for Nine Inch Nails in Dallas and the audience hated us so much they went berserk and were ripping the flooring up and throwing it at as. It was about three feet deep onstage and we would not stop no matter what.

Finally, I was just hiding behind my amp making the most noise possible. And the funny thing was Nine Inch Nails were going to film a long-form video that night. They had all the cameras and everything there for this live DVD.

We played and got done. Before we get offstage Trent [Reznor] walked out over all this garbage and said over the microphone, "I want you guys to stop this fucking shit right now or we're not going to fucking play. This is bullshit."

I thought the Nine Inch Nails show was going to be so energetic and amazing. But by the time they played the audience was totally dead and lifeless. So Nine Inch Nails shitcanned the entire thing. We literally took the life out of them and ruined the entire DVD.

REX BROWN

When *Cowboys From Hell* first came out we did a tour with Exodus and Suicidal Tendencies and people were like, "What the fuck is this?"

But we were so intense and tight as a band that instantly word started going around: This is the band to check out. And we took advantage of it.

We were on the road for 338 days that year. We even went to Europe with Judas Priest. They handpicked us because their singer Rob Halford really liked us. We thought it was gonna be great, but the fans fucking hated us. They didn't know us from shit. They were just there to see Judas Priest and I think we were a little too loud and heavy for them at the time.

MIKE IX WILLIAMS
Eyehategod

When we toured with White Zombie and Pantera, we went on first, and people had no clue what we were doing. Whoever was there was just looking at us stunned. They were either standing with their mouths open like, "What the fuck is going on?" Or they'd be screaming, telling us to fuck off and throwing quarters at us and trying to hurt us. We didn't care. We weren't like, "Oh, we gotta win them over," we were like: "Fuck these people. Let's play slower and add more feedback."

We knew that we were outcasts on that tour. They were there to see fuckin' White Zombie and Pantera. And we came out and were noisy, loud, and totally weird to them. For total redneck White Zombie folks from down South, it must have been shocking to see something that extreme. So, we never expected to emerge victorious. But some nights, there were fans there that knew the words to our songs.

But Pantera was legendary for bringing out these bands that were totally unknown by the mainstream. They took out Anal Cunt, Soilent Green, Neurosis, and Satyricon. That was totally cool. How else were we ever going to play a big stadium every night?

MATT BACHAND
ex-Shadows Fall, Times of Grace

We played with Judas Priest at the Mohegan Sun Arena in Connecticut in about 2009. It was a one-off and that was a hard crowd to sell. It was all seats.

Everyone was sitting down waiting for Priest. They didn't want to see us so they didn't stand up. They didn't even bother to boo or throw things. They just acted like we weren't there. There was total silence between songs.

I think we were a little aggressive for that crowd. Near the end of the set we sort of won them over and some of them started clapping for us but it was a tough one.

MARK SLAUGHTER
Slaughter, ex-Vinnie Vincent Invasion

The Vinnie Vincent Invasion opened for Iron Maiden in full glam metal gear and the crowd started throwing shit right away. They weren't even stopping at beer bottles. People were taking their shoes off and throwing them at us.

How do you go home after a show with just one shoe or without shoes?

[Guitarist] Vinnie [Vincent] was completely glammed out and people did not take well to that. But facing a lot of adversity is a great lesson in how to go downtown and get beat up and come back stronger.

MATT HEAFY
Trivium

I was so excited when we were invited to open for Iron Maiden. Unfortunately, not all of Iron Maiden's fans were as excited to see us. We were playing a show in Birmingham, and I kept getting hit with coins. It's bad enough to get smacked in the arm with a U.S. quarter that someone has whipped at you, but some of these people were throwing British pounds, which are about as heavy as a small rock. Most of the crowd was digging us but some fucker or fuckers were whipping these fucking coins. I kept getting pelted and it fuckin' hurt!

"Fuck, who would throw all these pounds?" I thought.

Seriously, each one is worth, like, $1.50 or something. So you've got to really hate a band or have a ton of money to keep whipping pounds at them.

I glanced around while I was playing and I finally saw the kid that was throwing the pounds. I got on the mic and pointed him out and said, "Hey you! The dude who's throwing change in my face. You've got two options. Either you come backstage with me right now and we sort this out or you get the fuck out of here."

The kid flipped me off, turned around, and started running the other direction. Thankfully, the crowd stopped him and I told security to kick him out. They did and the rest of the show was great.

The moral of the story is, if you don't like a band and you've gotta do something, just flip them off, don't fucking throw change at them.

ERIK TURNER
Warrant

We had three shows booked with Queensrÿche in 1989 on the West Coast. We played San Diego and that was fine. We played Irvine Meadows and that was great. Then we played San Jose, which is the home of lots of thrash metal.

We got onstage and they started chucking quarters. We lasted about three songs. That's the only time I can remember being pelted so hard that we actually quit playing and said, "Fuck this."

Nothing was hurt other than our feelings.

DINO CAZARES
Fear Factory, Divine Heresy, Brujeria, Asesino

We were at the beginning of the *Demanufacture* cycle and we were out with Ozzy Osbourne on the Retirement Sucks tour. It was a much older crowd that didn't want to hear anything except "War Pigs" and "Paranoid." In the U.S. they didn't even give us a chance. They threw beer at as. They pelted us with coins. I got hit in the forehead and I've still got a scar from one of the coins. And if we stopped between songs they'd chant, "Ozzy, Ozzy, Ozzy."

We learned not to stop between songs.

No matter what we did, we got shit thrown at us every night. At the end of our set every night, [vocalist] Burt [C. Bell] would walk around the stage and pick up all the coins. I thought that was kinda funny.

Then we got to Europe for the second leg of the tour and it was right when *Demanufacture* was hitting big. BOOM! We played huge arenas with Ozzy and twenty-five percent of the crowd was there for us. All the kids in the front were wearing *Demanufacture* shirts and we sold a shitload of merch. So it was kind of like vindication.

DEZ FAFARA

We were in Ohio and the buses were all in a big parking lot. We had sold twelve hundred tickets. We took a shitload of mushrooms. All of us ate mushrooms two hours before the show. And when it came time to do the show we went onstage, I grabbed the microphone and looked at [guitarist] Meegs [Rascón], and he started laughing at me hysterically.

I told the sold-out crowd, "Look, we're all on mushrooms. There's no possible way we're going to be able to do the show. But what we're going to do is we're going to hang out with you all night long at this bar and we're gonna talk to every single one of you. Feel free to return your tickets if you want."

There was only one refund. We hung out all night at that bar, we bought shots for everyone and we talked to them just like I said we would.

Our bar tab was $1,800, which in 1999 was a lot of money.

SAM RIVERS
Limp Bizkit

In the very beginning of our career we did a short tour with Soulfly. It was our first time in Europe. We were so grateful to be out there but their crowds just didn't like us whatsoever. They were booing and yelling that sucked and since we were playing really small venues, it was almost more personal. It was a hard tour to finish.

Then again, when you're a beginner band you have to take anything that's given to you. So we did everything we could and we always played as well as we could and sometimes we won over the crowd and sometimes we didn't.

RICHARD CHRISTY
Charred Walls of the Damned, ex-Death, ex-Iced Earth, ex-Public Assassin

When I was in the band Public Assassin, we used to play at this old venue in Lawrence, Kansas, called The Outhouse, which literally had an outhouse for their bathroom. The whole place was an old concession stand for a drive-in movie theater in the middle of corn fields.

Before one of our shows there we noticed chicken feathers all over the stage and the floor.

"What's going on here?" I asked.

"We just had a band here that killed a chicken onstage," one of the guys there told me.

We all thought, okay, that's fucked. Why didn't anyone clean it up?

Then our singer went up to the microphone and he said, "Ewww, this fucking microphone stinks!"

"Oh, G.G. Allin played here last week and he stuck the microphone up his ass," said the same guy who told us about the chicken.

Our singer went, "You know what? From now on I'm bringing my own microphone."

AL JOURGENSEN
Ministry, Revolting Cocks

In Detroit, in 1993 we came onstage for Lollapalooza and as soon as we hit our first chord the audience ripped out the seats, the benches, and all the turf and threw it onstage at us. These kids ripped up the entire outside field at Lollapalooza and did three hundred thousand dollars in damage just to the field itself.

Later, the venue tried to sue us. If anything, I should have sued the venue because we were under abuse for forty minutes of getting twelve-foot benches hurled at us. It was a coordinated effort, too. There were twelve to fifteen people carrying a bench the twenty feet between the gates and the stage and then nailing us with sod the whole time. You couldn't even see the sky. There was that much grass being thrown at us.

At one point my roadie became a sod roadie. He collected the sod off my guitar neck so I could actually play because my entire guitar and body was covered with these twelve-inch by twelve-inch chunks of sod.

And then of course, everyone phoned up their friends in the next town and said, "Man, that was cool. You gotta do that."

So we got that shit for three or four shows in a row.

SAM RIVERS

We were the band people loved to hate. There was never a case of everyone turning against us like some people think. Not everybody liked us to begin with. We'd say, "Hey, we're the most hated band in the world" and we played with it.

Some people really mean it when they say they hate you, but some people just go along with whatever everyone else is saying. If you listen to every hateful thing people say about you it doesn't change anything. You hear horrible things about every band out there. We just happened to be that band everyone hated [laughs].

And regardless, we still sold out shows and they were great shows. And even a lot of the haters bought tickets and showed up. Either they didn't hate us that much or they hated us enough to pay to go to a show and then be angry the whole time.

KIRK WINDSTEIN
Crowbar, ex-Down

If there was a shady club that didn't want to pay us and we weren't getting our guarantee we wouldn't take that lying down. We didn't do much
brawling but we made sure we got them back. You might say it's pussified,
but it's a lot better than getting stabbed or having the fucking cops called
on you.

We used to keep these heavy duty-type sewing needles for whenever
we got fucked over. So when we were screwed by a club we we'd take a
needle and stick it in the snake [wire] that runs all the channels in the PA
system. Then we'd break it off so you couldn't see it. The snake is fifty to
one hundred feet long and the needle's this little bitty dot. But it breaks
up all the channels on the board so Channel 2 will pop up on, like, Channel 16, Channel 3 will be on Channel 12, or whatever. It fucks it all up.

MARK SLAUGHTER

Once in around 1995, we walked into a truck stop and these people were
looking at us like, "Who the hell are these guys and why are they here?"

We were getting that whole, "Are those guys or girls?" vibe.

It was starting to feel weird, like something might go down. And then
in walked Marilyn Manson. He was just starting at the time and I didn't
even know who he was. So Manson and his entourage came in, I think we
didn't look so strange anymore and no one looked at us anymore.

COREY TAYLOR
Slipknot, Stone Sour

In 2005, we played Fury Fest in Lamont, France, where they've had this
heavy metal fest for years. The race track where it takes place decided
to raise its rent so the promoters had to raise the ticket prices and they
figured we were a big enough band that they could get away with it.

One of the local radio stations decided it was our fault that the ticket
prices were jacked up and figured that we had asked for too much money.
This caused a lot of problems and it started coming to a head. People
were talking shit about us at the radio station and no one warned us that
this radio station had really worked up their listeners and generated a
lot of hatred towards us. By the time we got to Fury Fest, thousands of
people there felt really hostile about Slipknot causing this ticket gauging,
which wasn't even the case.

When we went on there were glass bottles raining down on us. People were throwing everything: whiskey bottles, wrenches, dead animals, gigantic Evian bottles filled with dirt. It was insane because it was all the people in the back of the crowd that were throwing shit. Everyone up front was stoked to see us and everyone behind them was really ready to fight.

We realized that we were in some kind of shit, but we played our set while all these objects flew all over the stage. We didn't cut one song.

"Thank you so much for being with us," I said at the end of the night. "To those of you who thought you were going to stop us, you didn't win. So fuck you."

We stood right in the spotlights, which was dangerous because we weren't moving around anymore and we were easy targets. I got hit in the head with a nine-volt battery. I almost got hit right in the mouth with a fistful of coins and a glass bottle exploded just inches from my head.

It was one of the toughest shows we've ever had to play. But we did it, you know, because we believe in what we do and we will stand up for what we do no matter what.

MATT HEAFY

We were in Cardiff and for some reason everyone was throwing bottles at us. It wasn't everyone in the crowd, but a large portion of the audience was doing it. They weren't glass bottles, they were mostly plastic and it didn't really hurt to be hit by them. But I didn't want this to go on the whole set so I tried to figure out a way to get them to stop.

"It's good to be back home, I said. "We consider the UK our first home because this is where it all started for us so thank you all very much for that."

By shifting gears a little and not acting angry or afraid, that made a lot of people stop and actually listen to the music. I've seen a lot of bands lose their cool and that just makes most of these kinds of situations worse. The key for me is not freaking out or throwing a tantrum and just trying to encourage them to listen to the music and give you a shot. Sometimes that works and by the end of the show, you've got the crowd on your side.

BEN WEINMAN
The Dillinger Escape Plan

We were on tour with Megadeth, which seemed like a pretty big deal. We were playing either first or second on the main stage so it was early in the day. And the show was essentially put together for older metal guys because it was Megadeth and Dream Theater.

And then there was Dillinger playing in a big stadium for, maybe, twenty people. And they weren't necessarily our fans. These guys were throwing beer and cups and bottles at us for the whole set. I move around a lot so I didn't get hit, but it was pretty clear that the people in the audience wouldn't be buying our shirts at the merch tents after the show.

KIRK WINDSTEIN

In 2012, Crowbar were playing a show in Poland. Then we left to play the Brutal Assault Festival in the Czech Republic. They run those festival shows like clockwork. They don't wait for any of the bands to show up. If they're late, they don't play.

There was a lot of road construction, and the Czech Republic doesn't have the best highways. We left in enough time to be there three hours early. We got there and our driver and tour manager Rolf, a German Guy, screamed at security, "My guys are onstage in five minutes!"

We jumped out of the van and we didn't have passes, wrist bands, credentials, anything. Rolf was ready to kill the guys at security.

"I'm telling you! It's fuckin' Crowbar and we're onstage in five fucking minutes!"

By the time we got up there, I looked at the guys in Corrosion of Conformity, who were scheduled to go on right after us. I asked their guitarist Woody [Weatherman], "Dude, do you have any beer?"

He threw me a couple of Budweisers. I pounded one real quick. And we took our guitars and pedals and plugged in. Instead of having a forty-minute set, by the time we got up there we only got to play five tunes so it was a twenty-minute set. But it was the most stressful thing. It was the quickest throw and go situation I've ever been a part of and probably the most nerve-racking, but the show did go on.

It might not have been the longest or the best but at least we were all sober.

SAM RIVERS

A lot of people blamed us for ruining Woodstock '99. I don't know how that happened. We weren't the ones that did anything bad. I don't remember much from back then because I was drinking so heavily, but I remember Woodstock clearly. There wasn't anything that crazy about it.

By the end of the set, a couple of people tore up some plywood [from the stage] and they were dancing on it. But the next day they allowed another band to hand out ten thousand candles. And they blamed us for burning down Woodstock.

I was back in my house in Florida then watching it on TV. I was like, "Uhh, what the fuck is happening?" I think the Chili Peppers were on when all hell broke loose. It was just kind of a bummer that we somehow became the scapegoat when we were weren't there when everything went down. Woodstock tried to sue us and they lost. That says everything right there.

ZOLTAN BATHORY
Five Finger Death Punch

[Our singer Ivan Moody] has this pirate mentality. He has pulled disappearing acts and I've had to send Coast Guard helicopter to get him because he missed flights. That caused everyone a lot of stress.

The thing is, Ivan has never missed a show no matter what sort of crazy stuff has happened.

Once, they announced us on the PA, the intro was running and I saw the car bringing him pulling into the parking lot. He ran right out and made it onto the stage for the first fucking verse. Being in those kinds of situations brings on his anger. But that anger is real, wherever it is coming from—his relationships, his family, his daily shit. I'd rather have that than have him sing about dragons and Vikings and not have any real investment in his singing.

DEE SNIDER

There was one time the show did *not* go on, and it's a regret I have to this day. It was in San Francisco in 1984. We were touring with Y&T and we were opening for them.

Somebody was throwing large metal bolts at the band. They had a quantity of them and they were throwing them overhand, I assume, because they were coming at such velocity and they were an incredible danger. I got hit in the ribs, bruised a rib. [Drummer] A.J. [Pero] had a cymbal dented. I cut the set short and we left the stage.

I regret it to this day because one of my oldest tricks in the books is to turn the lights on the crowd and I don't know why I didn't do it. When I turned the lights on, we could see the crowd and they would be outed.

BURTON C. BELL

We were invited to The Gathering of the Juggalos at Cave-In-Rock, Illinois, in 2012. I had never seen anything like that ever in my life. I wouldn't call it a festival. It was a mass exodus of these Juggalos from across the country and it was kind of scary. I was walking around to check it out and I stood out like a sore thumb because I had all my teeth.

There was a guy standing with a bullhorn in the middle of the crowd shouting, "I got GBH, I got acid, I got ecstasy."

People were literally barking out the drugs they had to sell. People were walking around naked that you didn't want to see naked. There was a school bus with the top cut off dropping people off and picking others up. There were people having sex on it in the middle of the day. It was like, what the fuck?

We went onstage and they were just looking at us like we had shown a dog a card trick. As soon as we start playing a full plate of nachos came flying onstage. We got hit from some of the cheese. It was raining shit the whole show. We finished our set and got the fuck out. I don't think we won them over.

MARK MORTON
Lamb of God

We toured for about a year and a half with Metallica starting in 2009 when they were doing their show in the round. The actual stage was set up in the middle of the arena and the crowd was all around the stage. The tour was sold out before support acts were even announced. I was told Metallica were bringing bands out that they liked and they asked for Lamb of God, which we were totally flattered and honored by. And I don't want to seem ungrateful because it was the greatest tour we ever did. It established Lamb of God at a level that we hadn't reached prior to that point.

But there were a lot of nights on that tour when nobody gave a fuck. We couldn't buy a fuck. There were a few Lamb of God fans there but they were few and far between.

For me, the big joke of the tour was "Nachos."

It's one thing to play a festival and someone's eating a hot dog on the barricade watching you play. Obviously, they don't care. They're waiting for the band they want to see. But I remember seeing people eating nachos in the front row.

"Man, it takes two hands to eat nachos," I thought. "You really don't give a fuck. You've got both hands full and you're eating nachos while we play."

There's a couple ways you can handle it. You can get mad about it or you can choose to see the humor in it. And I chose to see it as funny.

SAM RIVERS

We toured with Faith No More in America in the late '90s, and, man, their crowd only likes them. We got booed off and people threw shit at us every night. We were like, "Damn, dude. We love Faith No More and their fans fuckin' hate us."

But it's one of those things you have to do. You have to earn your shit.

ERIK RUTAN
Hate Eternal, ex-Morbid Angel, ex-Ripping Corpse

Ripping Corpse was playing Long Island in 1990 with The Crumbsuckers reunion show. They were a hardcore band from New York that we loved, so we were really excited to play with them. And it was only their fans—about a thousand of them. There were a thousand people there and it was all Crumbsuckers fans.

We played one song and guys were yelling all this shit.

"Yeah, Satan! Fuck you, motherfuckers!"

I've never had a show like that.

Then, out of nowhere, this one guy yells, "Your drummer has no fucking timing."

And Brandon [Thomas] is one of the best drummers I've ever played with. I remember [vocalist] Scott [Ruth] saying, "Listen, dude, let's play all the songs straight through and get the fuck off the stage."

It's the only show I can remember playing where the crowd was yelling every fucking obscenity at us and booing us. We got offstage and we were sitting at the merch table and these guys came up to us.

"You guys fucking suck, man," one of them said. "What the fuck are you doing on this show? We're gonna beat your fuckin' ass."

It was harsh and they seemed to be looking for a fight so we fuckin' took off.

ALEX HELLID
Entombed

When we played in Mexico for the first time, we were booked at some small boxing venue that couldn't take the amount of people that showed up. When we started to play, people started getting onstage and it got really chaotic.

People weren't going on the stage and then jumping off. They were tearing everything apart and taking the equipment. There were so many of them on the stage that it caved in. That's when we said, "Okay, we need to leave now."

That was one of the only times we were scared and had to be rescued from a venue. We had flown in for the show so we rented all the gear. Nothing major belonged to us, so we didn't lose any of our instruments. But [guitarist] Uffe [Cederlund] lost his pedals, which sucked for him.

MORGAN LANDER

The support that we got in our hometown, London, Ontario, early on was almost non-existent. Everybody thought we didn't deserve what we had. Since we were young, a lot of our peers were very jealous and did a lot of hurtful things. We'd even get death threats.

For the very first show we did there after our first album *Spit* came out, we opened for Slipknot and people were throwing everything they could get their hands on at us all night. At one point, someone threw a bottle of piss at us. We dodged it. Nobody got hit, but I was really upset about it.

MATT HEAFY

In 2006 we played the Download Festival. The first time we played it years earlier was a legendary show for us so I was excited to be playing there again. I was behind a backdrop getting ready, doing jumping jacks and stretching. I was all nervous before the show.

Suddenly, this open water bottle hit me and I was all wet. It was this super-warm liquid. I smelled the air and I realized it was piss. Someone had thrown an open water bottle full of piss at me and I'm not sure it came from the crowd.

Anyway, I was doused, so I freaked out a little at first. I called out to the higher up bands and crew.

"Does anybody have a towel? Give me a towel. I'm covered in piss!"

No response. I had to go out and play the show covered in hot piss.

MYLES KENNEDY
Alter Bridge, Slash

I feel like whenever you play a festival and you're not the headliner the artist onstage becomes some sort of moving target. I've had coins thrown at me and bottles and cups full of beer or piss. Somebody once chewed a bunch of chaw and spit it into a cup and threw it at me. Fortunately, it missed my head and landed on my amp, but my amp still had a stream of Copenhagen dripping down the front of it.

BEN WEINMAN

When we opened for System of a Down in Europe, that was interesting because at that time they were the biggest band in the world. *Toxicity* had come out and we still hadn't had much diversity in our catalog. We just had these really intense, crazy, fucked up songs that no little mall kid who liked System of a Down would ever understand or like. And we were playing these ten-thousand-seaters.

The boos were so loud I couldn't even hear my music. Sometimes I'd put my ear up to my speaker because the boos were drowning out what I was doing on the guitar.

We always felt like we never had enough food in Europe. We'd sleep late and then we'd get up and by the time we were done with the show, everything was closed. There were no diners or Denny's there. So we were always hungry.

One time, someone threw a whole chicken sandwich at [vocalist] Greg [Puciato] and without even blinking he caught it in one hand, stopped singing and started eating it.

He was like, "Damn, thank you."

GENE HOGLAN
Dark Angel, Testament, Dethklok, ex-Death, ex-Strapping Young Lad

Strapping Young Lad toured with Testament when they did their *Demonic* album. That kind of music was not super popular at that time. We were playing a lot of bars and clubs and [vocalist] Devin [Townsend] had no filter. He was berating people practically every show.

And stuff would rain down on us.

My feeling was, if we were inciting it, cool. You kind of asked for it. And that happened a lot.

DEVIN TOWNSEND
Strapping Young Lad, ex-Steve Vai, ex-Wildhearts, Devin Townsend Band

I was really embarrassed after I left the Steve Vai project—not of the band, not of the music, not of Steve—I was a young kid and I was impressionable. My role in that band was not one that Steve Vai fans were particularly looking for. They didn't want to hear a singer. They wanted Steve to continue with his batch of work and be the ripping guitar player that he is.

So, I was damned from the start and I hadn't anticipated that.

The reaction was really negative and ugly and I was a scared fucking kid facing all this adversity. And there was just no way I was going to win them over because they didn't want to be won over by me.

The deflowering of my music industry idealism really came to a head once I left that band. I joined the UK band The Wildhearts and they had much more of a punk edge to them. There was a lot of drugs and a lot of violence. And I think between the embarrassment that I felt from my experience with Vai and the "fuck it all" attitude that came with The Wildhearts I decided I would use my talents to make the most obnoxious sound I could and frame that sound with the sentiment of "fuck everything." It was cathartic at the time for me and it was something I needed to explore and go through.

So, the whole point of Strapping was to be as confrontational as possible. But towards the end of Strapping I recognized that I was drawing all that negative energy towards me and when I began to feel like I had said everything I wanted to say and everything had run its course, it became clear to me that I needed to change things really quickly.

And, of course, a lot of Strapping fans weren't exactly pleased with the new direction I decided to go in, so I took a lot of shit for that.

NADJA PEULEN
Coal Chamber

Somewhere in Kansas, Coal Chamber was playing a show. And we got ambushed by a couple of people who sprayed the stage with fire extinguishers.

When that happens, you can't breathe or see through the fog so we had to stop the show.

Another time, someone cut our bus's alternator belt so we were stuck there for a while. If we knew who it was we would have killed him.

ERIK RUTAN

I was playing a show with Morbid Angel and somebody in the crowd whipped out tear gas. It hurt like hell and I wasn't even sprayed directly, there was just mist or something floating up onstage, but it was bad. People were rolling around the floor in agony.

BUZZ OSBORNE

We've been fucked with by bands before and not in a funny way. When we were the opening band we wouldn't get a sound check for no reason at all since there was plenty of time. We've been told we couldn't use the lights. We've been denied any room onstage to the point where I've almost had to get in a fistfight with another support band because they wouldn't move their shit.

When we've headlined, we've never pulled any of that crap. These other bands are musicians just like us and they're just trying to do their job. Why would we have the nerve to mess with them?

The worst band to us was White Zombie, without question. Rob Zombie, in particular, was the worst musician I've had to deal with when we were on the same bill. They hired this troupe of mullet-headed asshole fucking bastards to pull every dirty rock-and-roll trick in the book on us, and that's just how they were.

Here's a good example of how miserable it was: A few times when we were allowed a soundcheck we had to stop early. Their sound guy turned off the PA because Rob was eating and didn't like the noise.

"Oh my gosh. We're so sorry."

I mean, fuck. It's a fucking rock show, not quiet time at the goddamn public library. We were trying to do the best we could and these guys were standing in our way to trip us up. I would never do that. I can't even imagine what kind of an asshole you have to be to pull shit like that.

KING FOWLEY
Deceased, October 31

There was a point when these underground bands were acting like assholes. We'd to go to shows and all these groups had rules like, "You can't use all the lights, you can't use the stage, you can't stand here, you can't do that."

At one point we had it out with Six Feet Under. We went and played a show with them. This guy called me and said, "Hey, they're not selling enough tickets."

This was in the Frederick, Maryland, area in Hagerstown closer to where we were from.

"Could you guys come up here and play and help bring in some more people, "said the promoter.

We were recording *Fearless Undead Machines* at the time so we took some time off and went over there.

"Okay, what do we do with our gear?" we asked when we arrived.

"Well, you're not allowed in the room right now. They're soundcheck-ing," said a guy at the club.

So we went and ate dinner, came back, and now all of Six Feet Under's shit was on stage and there was nowhere to put anything. At the time I was the singing drummer so we had to at least get the drums up there so I could sing.

I went looking for anybody in Six Feet Under. Nobody wanted to say a word to me.

"Oh, talk to our management. Speak to our agent," they said.

I kind of knew [vocalist] Chris [Barnes] from the Cannibal Corpse days and even he gave me this total rock star behavior. We couldn't get all our gear onstage. It was literally the size of a bed and we had to cram all our shit there.

We played and had a great crowd. And the first thing I said was, "No thanks to Six Feet of Stage for having us play in this little corner."

"Hey, man. Thanks a lot," the promoter said to me when we finished our set. "You bought an extra hundred people to this thing and saved me because I was in pretty deep on the guarantee."

"Well, cool. Hey, we're gonna head back to the studio now," I said.

"Okay, good," he said. "Because Chris Barnes said he's not coming off the bus until you're out of the building."

WILL CARROLL
Death Angel, ex-Machine Head

We were in Poland playing this festival with Megadeth, W.A.S.P., Dark Tranquility, and other bands. We were there for a few hours and we started catching wind that Megadeth wanted to switch the timeslots around.

I don't know why, but [Megadeth frontman] Dave Mustaine told every-one he couldn't headline. He wanted W.A.S.P. to headline.

"You're fucking out of your mind," said W.A.S.P. frontman Blackie Lawless.

They weren't coming to terms.

Next thing you know, we saw all of W.A.S.P.'s tour buses roll away. This was hours before they were supposed to play. The crowd was furious. There were hella-W.A.S.P. fans there. People even had W.A.S.P. flags.

The next band on the chopping block was Dark Tranquility.

"You guys have to play after us," Dave Mustaine told them.

They canceled and left, too.

So, who was next in line? Death Angel. We had to play after Megadeth. When Megadeth went onstage, the crowd booed them. These people paid a bunch of money to see a full festival and two of the bigger names on the festival backed out because Dave Mustaine didn't want to headline. Dudes in the crowd were throwing rocks. You could hear them bouncing off the side of Megadeth's drums.

Then, this guy standing next to me on the side of the stage, who played in one of the opening bands, was pissed that W.A.S.P. canceled so he chucked a full beer at Dave Mustaine and hit him right in the chest. That was it. The show was over.

The guy got the shit beat out of him. Security grabbed him and dragged him off the stage and they roughed him up. Megadeth had only played seven or eight songs and they left the stage. The crowd was flipping out and we're looking at each other thinking, "Now we have to go on and make this crowd happy? Oh my fuckin' God!"

We were all nervous as shit going onstage. They were chucking shit at the stage. Then they got into us and they stopped throwing things. We did almost a two-hour set and it was one of the best shows we've ever had in our life. The crowd went ballistic for us because they wanted to see a band and hear music. It totally worked in our favor but we thought it was going to be a disaster.

ERIK TURNER

We played the last day of a festival in Puerto Rico. We were the headlining act Sunday night and we had to fly in by helicopter. There were fifty thousand people there. You couldn't even drive in.

We get onstage and start playing, thinking this is gonna be so cool. All of a sudden people are throwing bottles filled with sand. At one point someone threw a lugnut from a diesel tire and it tagged one of our security guards. He went down. The rest of us avoided any serious injuries.

And I don't even think they meant to throw things at us 'cause they hated us. They didn't boo. I think they were just wild, crazy fucked up drunks who had been partying for five days straight so they just started throwing stuff. There were fifty thousand people in the crowd and forty-nine thousand nine hundred fifty people were having a good time. But the fifty people that are left who are throwing stuff could have really screwed up the night.

TONY FORESTA
Municipal Waste

In about 2011 we were playing in Richmond and the crowd was going crazy throwing things, and not just at us. They were throwing bottles and cups all over the place and there was beer flying everywhere. A beer landed on the mixing board and spilled into the wires and stuff and blew up the entire PA.

I was like, "Okay, cool. I guess I don't have to keep singing. Thanks for giving me the rest of the night off."

PAGE HAMILTON

Marilyn Manson was a big Helmet fan and he wanted us out on tour. They had just sold a million records on *Antichrist Superstar,* so they were playing these massive places.

I said, "Of course we'll do that."

We got up there and there were just seas of blank stares. I looked up once and a guy in full makeup and a leather trench coat looking like Beetlejuice was flipping me off and pointing at his head. I think he was trying to tell me that I was small-minded because I was probably wearing a T-shirt and my garbage man pants because they're baggy and comfortable.

We played our hardest every night, but that tour wasn't the greatest success for us.

GENE HOGLAN

Testament played Indonesia in 2016. The crowd hated us and it wasn't even our fault. The band that went on right before us was the most popular Indonesian metal band. They were like their version of Judas Priest and they were playing way too long.

So [Testament vocalist] Chuck [Billy] went onstage.

"Look man," he said. "We need you to go. You have to get off the stage right now because the airport is six hours away and we have to get there to catch our flights later tonight, and we're supposed to be playing now."

In protest, the crowd sat down during our set. They didn't rock out. They didn't clap. They just stared at us the whole show. It's a good thing they didn't have spears to throw at us.

DINO CAZARES

I did a show with Brujeria in 2004 in the capital of Baja, California, in a place called Mexicali. It was a big show and while we were playing, I saw people in the pit gather up all the chairs in the venue and they started a fire and started piling things up on top of it. The crowd was slamming around it.

"Holy fuck!," I thought. "Should we stop playing and get offstage because nobody's putting the fire out and it and it smells like burning plastic?"

The flames were almost up to the ceiling. I was looking at everybody in the band and they were looking at me and we were all figuring out what to do. While I was playing, I crossed to the other side of the stage, which was closer to the side door just in case we had to make an urgent exit.

"Why are there no fire alarms going off?' I wondered. "Why are there no sprinklers spraying water over the fire?"

We kept playing and before the whole place went up in flames someone was able to put the fire out with his jacket and bunch of water.

BEN FALGOUST
Goatwhore, ex-Soilent Green

Soilent was touring with Dethklok and Chimaira and we played the Filmore in San Francisco in about 2008. An electrical fire broke out in the back part of the building near the soundboard. We were in the middle of our set and this guy at the side of the stage was trying to get my attention with all these hand gestures. I didn't know what he was doing.

Finally, he came up to me after we finished a song.

"There's a fire! You have to tell people they need to get out!"

I handed him the mic and said, "You need to tell people this. We have a full crowd and we're in the middle of a show. I'm not the one to do this."

He took the mic and explained the situation to the crowd. They got everyone out in single file and no one panicked. Then the fire department came and put out the fire and canceled the show.

RICHARD CHRISTY

Death played Santiago, Chile, and it was one of the most amazing gigs ever. It was in a huge arena and everyone was throwing these lit road flares at the stage. It looked like a fireworks display, but I'm sure it wasn't at all safe.

Me and Shannon [Hamm], our guitar player, walked over and stamped out one of these road flares so the stage wouldn't catch on fire. It looked pretty cool, but the last thing we wanted was the whole place to go up in flames.

That must have been the thing to do at the time. We did a gig in Greece and people lit these road flares and they also threw them onstage I don't think it would fly these days.

PAGE HAMILTON

We've played festivals with everyone from Mötley Crüe, Kiss, Sabbath, System of a Down, Slayer and I always feel like I should be honest and do what we do. I don't like the "rah-rah" thing.

We did an Arkansas festival and all these bands were saying, "Make some fucking noise."

I was like, "Dude, Ozzy Osbourne can say that. You cannot."

Sebastian Bach told me, "Man, you just gotta say, 'Hey, support our troops.'"

And I said, "Yeah man, I just don't do rah-rah. We'll play the music. If they like it, great. If I feel like I've played and sang well and the band was good that's all I can do. I'm not gonna try to win them over by telling them how much they rock or how good we are or asking them to start a pit."

ERIK RUTAN

A woman came up to the front row during a show and threw a full beer on me a couple of years ago. I think she was on drugs and I don't know what she was saying because we were in Germany. I was very composed because I think I was in shock. I couldn't believe I had just watched this beer splash all over my beautiful guitar. So we just kept playing.

MARK MORTON

Opening for Slayer, I had a full cup of beer come from the wings of the audience. It was a Solo cup and I watched it in the air coming towards me from twenty yards out. I knew it was gonna come close but I didn't figure it was gonna hit me. It rolled in the air but it held its contents somehow. Then it came in and hit me square in the chest and exploded. I had beer all over me and I just remember thinking, "I'm just glad that was only beer."

WILL CARROLL

In Germany, I got hit in the head once with a hard plastic cup full of beer. We were at the end of our set and we were playing "Bored." In the middle of the song, I felt something really hard bounce off my head and my first thought was that one of my cymbals fell over and hit me. I felt a bunch of liquid dribbling down and I thought it might be blood.

But I could smell it was beer. Then, I saw a beer cup on my snare drum. I was dazed for a minute so I stopped playing and we stopped the song. I took a second to dry off and get my bearings. Then we went into our last song and said goodnight.

I was fucking furious. I walked offstage and went into the dressing room. At that time, me and [bassist] Damien [Sisson] weren't getting along so great. He took that as an opportunity to lay into me. He came into the dressing room and he wanted to fight. Damien was furious that I stopped and I was furious that he didn't have any sympathy for the fact that I got hit with a beer. The other guys came in and stopped us. That's the only time I've almost gotten into a fist fight with a bandmate. And everything blew over after that.

MARK SLAUGHTER

We were playing with Ozzy in Red Rocks, [in Colorado]. The band is real close to the crowd there so you can see everything. There was a guy who kept throwing oranges at me. I don't know what his deal was. A couple came up and I ignored it.

And then he threw another orange and nailed me right in the crotch.

I was pissed so I jumped into the crowd. It wasn't like going into a mosh pit. It was like Moses had put the staff down and the crowd parted. And I could see the guy standing there with oranges. I ran through that little opening and grabbed the guy by the hair, singing the whole time. I dragged this guy to the stage by the hair. I pulled him to the side.

I stopped singing because there was a guitar solo and I turned to the security guy and said, "Either you deal with him or I'll deal with him."

So they escorted him off.

I don't usually snap like that and the promoter was really pissed.

But I said, "All's fair in love and war, man. This guy nailed me, I got him back."

KEITH BUCKLEY

We did a whole tour with Gwar. Those fans are like Slayer fans. They go to see Gwar and that's all they want. We were playing and their crowd hated us so much.

It was [guitarist] Jordan [Buckley's] birthday when we were in Albuquerque, New Mexico. We asked the crowd to wish him a happy birthday and everyone booed him. As much as we love the guys in Gwar I couldn't get offstage fast enough.

JERRY DIXON
Warrant

Towards the end of our stint with [vocalist] Jani [Lane], we did a show in Las Vegas in 2008 when we got back together with all the original members. Jani had been drinking since about eight in the morning. During the show, he completely forgot the lyrics. I think we played about nine songs but we sounded so horrible we got booed offstage.

It was bad.

First of all, it's scary to see someone like that. But when you're onstage and it's live, what do you do? We had to try to play the show and it was the worst feeling I've ever had.

We apologized and refunded everyone their money.

We only played about three shows with Jani after that.

MARK SLAUGHTER

In the '90s it was very difficult for us to go from playing big arenas to smaller clubs. We asked ourselves, "Do you want to keep doing this?" And the answer was, if that's what you do, you do that.

Those who do, do and those who don't bitch. We've never been bitchers. We've been doers so you just get out there, shut the fuck up and rock. You get by however you can. That's what happens, man. It's not always this amazing environment of fame and adoration.

There's a very difficult side of the music business and [to paraphrase Hunter S. Thompson], it's full of pimps and whores down a shallow hallway where people lose themselves and their lives, and that's the bright side of the business. You just gotta look at it for what it really is and realize we're selling art and that's the hardest part of this industry. So you just do what you do and you do your best.

PAUL LEDNEY
Profanatica, Havohej

Black metal crowds are the lamest. They just stand there with zero emotion. I don't antagonize the audience or anything, but when I'm putting on a show and I'm getting nothing back, I end up calling them "pale fucks" or "statues" in between pretty much every song.

But they don't do anything. They don't even move.

Afterwards, I've talked to people that were in the crowd.

"What the hell is wrong with you?" I've said.

"What do you mean?" they commented, acting surprised.

"Well, you were just standing there."

"Oh, we loved it! We were just standing there enjoying it."

That's just bullshit. I come from a punk, metal, and death metal background. I saw the whole thing unfold from 1980 on and I've never seen shit like this. When you like something, you move!

CHAPTER 17: METAL ON METAL

Influences & Inspirations

The title track for Anvil's 1982 sophomore effort, "Metal on Metal" is a stomping precursor to thrash from an influential Canadian band that never really got their due, even after the acclaimed 2009 documentary *Anvil: The Story of Anvil.*

Now that you've been regaled with tales of Satan, violence, drugs, arrests, puking, vehicle crashes, and various forms of assault, you're either ready to head into a mosh pit and kick some ass or you need a break from the barrage of chaos and dysfunction. We can't offer you a guided meditation to the strains of Prostitute Disfigurement, but we can ease off from the trauma and drama and conclude with an easier to digest chapter about how all these artists got started with this shit.

There's plenty of hero worship in this chapter, as well there should be. Led Zeppelin, Black Sabbath, Judas Priest, and Iron Maiden get plenty of play, sure. There are also some surprises. Who would have expected Sepultura co-founder Max Cavalera to cite Queen as one of the main bands that led him on a path of discovery, or for Exodus and Slayer guitarist Gary Holt to praise Nils Lofgren as a vital inspiration?

"Metal on Metal" may be the closest *Raising Hell* veers toward being any sort of chronological account of metal history. And if that's not something you give a shit about go back to the "That Was Spinal Tap" chapter and re-read about how ridiculous the world of metal can be.

DEE SNIDER
Twisted Sister, ex-Widowmaker

As far as metal goes, for me there is Black Sabbath, AC/DC, Judas Priest, and Dio. But that's not where my original influences came from or why I decided to join a band.

As a kid, I loved Paul Revere and the Raiders. They were always direct competition with the Monkees. It was kinda like the Monkees had a TV show, Paul Revere were the house band on *Where the Action Is* on TV. But Paul Revere was a little bit more dangerous than the Monkees. There was sexuality to it. The riffs had a tougher edge. Mark Lindsay, the lead singer, who had a long ponytail way before anyone had long ponytails, flirted with being dangerous. It wasn't metal but it pushed the envelope a little.

The Stones were a little better—a little tougher, greasier, and slimier.

I got into Twisted Sister by auditioning with Zeppelin songs. I could sing like Robert Plant. And that was money. If you could do Zeppelin, you could work. But I burned out my voice pretty quickly and I soon had to resort to the more growly singing, and Alice Cooper was hugely influential on that vocal styling. Bon Scott would be the finishing touches. Lyrically, I could never really connect with Zeppelin, anyway. They were so mythical and I was looking for the straight talk of Alice Cooper. "I'm 18. I'm a boy and I'm a man." Those words were like something you couldn't imagine your way around. It was very obvious, very clever, very straightforward. And I copped not only a lot of my vocal styling and my attitude from Alice Cooper and the original Alice Cooper band, but his lyrics as well and the way he approached lyrics and his theatricality were inspirational as well.

But the funny thing was I never saw Alice Cooper when I was a kid so I only had pictures to work from. So my act is what I thought Alice Cooper must be doing. There were all these great still photos. There was no video, you just had pictures, so that's what I had to work with. I was guessing that to get from photo A to photo B, he must be running around, so that's what I did. It turned out he was just slinking around.

When I finally saw him in 2000, when we got to tour together I watched him and went, "Oh, shit. He's nothing like I thought he was. Man, I've been doing it all wrong."

BUZZ OSBORNE
Melvins

Alice Cooper is extreme even for today's time. He has an amazing track record. To me, his early records are some of the most amazing rock records ever made. In some circles, he's considered absolutely incredible. In others, he's a joke.

Weirdly, I saw something where Bob Dylan said he thought Alice Cooper was a great lyricist and wrote great songs and was really underappreciated.

I agree completely. You had five guys that were ugly hippies and were not into peace and love. Count me in. I don't know what you'd have to do to be as weird and out there as he was then.

CRIK TURNCR
Warrant

When I was eleven years old my mom took me to a local music store, I think it was Pier One, and she told me I could buy two records. It came out to eight dollars. I was going through all the different album covers and I saw Alice Cooper's *Welcome to My Nightmare*. I thought, "Wow, what is this?"

So I grabbed that one and I kept looking and came across a record cover with a bunch of scary looking guys to an eleven-year-old kid. And it was Aerosmith's first album. So, based on the artwork alone, I went home and listened to them and I was a little scared of some of the Alice Cooper record but it was great. And the Aerosmith record got me really loving hard rock. I became an instant Aerosmith fan. Then later, one of my friends in junior high was playing Queen's *News of the World*, which was just amazing. And then when I was 13, I saw some records at another friend's house and one of them looked totally crazy. It was Kiss's *Alive!* He let me borrow it and take it home and I became a huge Kiss fan. From there I just became obsessed with collecting and buying hard rock records.

JESSE JAMES DUPREE
Jackyl

The music that had the most impact on me growing up were from black artists like Joe Tex, James Brown, Otis Redding, and Wilson Pickett. Those guys had the power. There's never been a metal record recorded that has the same kind of power as the voice of a Joe Tex or a James Brown when they were pumped up.

To me, that's the most metal thing there is.

Joe Tex had a scream that was just unreal. It was untouchable.

The first time I transitioned over into saying, "Okay, maybe I can do something like this, too" was when I realized that Steve Marriott from Humble Pie and Ian Gillan from Deep Purple were influenced by the same power as those soul singers had and were in bands making great music. And AC/DC. What can you say besides AC/DC, AC/DC, AC/DC? That was huge for me, and when I became friends with [vocalist] Brian

Johnson and he joined us on the track "Locked and Loaded" it was such an incredible honor 'cause AC/DC were probably the band that inspired me the most into becoming a rock vocalist.

REX BROWN
Pantera, ex-Down, ex-Crowbar, Kill Devil Hill

I lived in a little peanut town [of Graham, Texas]. All we had was AM radio. You didn't hear metal on the AM radio. The closest I got to any kind of rock and roll that really turned me on was ZZ Top. That Texas stomp was deeply instilled in me and that has influenced me to this day. Of course, I knew all the Stones and Beatles records. My sister was 17 and I heard all her albums.

MARK SLAUGHTER
Slaughter, ex-Vinnie Vincent Invasion

When I was a kid, the first time I heard Queen I was blown away. "Killer Queen" was the hit on AM radio when I was living in Las Vegas. I would drive around on my bike with a radio gaff-tapped to my handlebars. When I was riding and that song came on, it took me to another place.

MAX CAVALERA
Soulfly, Cavalera Conspiracy, ex-Sepultura

Oddly enough, it was Queen that first put me on the path to metal. They made me and my brother, [ex-Sepultura drummer Igor] in love with rock and that led to metal. We saw Queen in 1981 at a soccer stadium. They were touring for *The Game* and Freddie Mercury was incredible onstage. He had the crowd in the palm of his hand for the whole show and watching that was mesmerizing.

They were inventive and they were not afraid to take risks. They did crazy stuff with a song like "Bohemian Rhapsody" and then they'd do something really heavy like "Sheer Heart Attack" or "Stone Cold Crazy." They went different places, which always inspired me.

After I heard Queen, I wanted to learn guitar so I entered this guitar class called AMAA and it was full of hippies and rockers—people with long hair. We had never seen that kind of people before and they were all wearing Black Sabbath T-shirts and AC/DC T-shirts. It was crazy and that was my first exposure to all that shit: AC/DC, Black Sabbath, Deep Purple, Jimi Hendrix, and Led Zeppelin.

But, it was crazy. My dad died when I was nine and he had a huge record collection that was mostly Italian opera. He'd come home every day from his job and listen to opera for two hours. One day when I was snooping through his opera collection I found frickin' *Black Sabbath* and *Led Zeppelin IV.*

So I can say it was my dad that really led me to these bands.

Those are such great albums. Also, they were showing the AC/DC movie *Let There Be Rock* at a theater near my house. I think me and Igor went to see that movie thirty times. We'd buy a ticket and just stay in the movie theater all day. And we did that for, like, a whole week.

Then I bought AC/DC's *Dirty Deeds Done Dirt Cheap.* I looked at the images on the sleeve, and the pictures of the guys in tattoos who look like renegades and real rebels. I got attracted to that imagery.

It was the same with Motörhead. They were so scary looking that you liked them. You wanted them to be on your side. Lemmy was the scariest looking guy ever. And he was one of the coolest, nicest guys ever.

FRANKIE BANALI
Quiet Riot, ex-W.A.S.P.

I had the unique opportunity to see Led Zeppelin live in 1969 on the last two shows that they performed in the United States for the first leg of the U.S. tour. They were amazing and the key to their performance was energy and improvisation. I saw both shows and they were essentially the same sets, but there was so much improvisation they were played completely different. The level of musical communication and diversity between all of them, but particularly between John Bonham and Jimmy Page, was unbelievable. I'd never seen anything like that and I had seen the Jeff Beck Group shortly before that. And they had the right idea but Led Zeppelin took it to a completely different level.

PHILIP ANSELMO
Pantera, Down, Superjoint Ritual, Scour

I have very vivid memories of my early childhood. I must have been a tot stumbling around like a fool. I was living in the French Quarter of New Orleans in an apartment with my mother, my aunt, her boyfriend and the floors were rumbling with the tones of Jimmy Page and the riff for "Black Dog." Many will point to the band's blues roots, many will point to the classic rock era. Well, I must still say that's one of the more deceptive riffs you'll ever hear in your life. When that groove and that riff kick in, the feel of that thing is very upbeat. It's an energetic thriving thing. Yet, when you investigate it as a musician you find the drums are slow as a motherfucker but you still have this hyper riff ripping in the background. The innovation right there, to me, is heavy metal.

PAGE HAMILTON
Helmet

I was listening to the album *Led Zeppelin IV* and when I first heard the song "Black Dog" I was done. I just started fantasizing about being a musician, being a guitar player, and being Jimmy Page. When I was 10, I loved the Beatles and the Monkees and Jim Croce and the Eagles. Then I heard Kiss and I thought, "This is crazy." As far as straight up metal, *Rolling Stone* had a cool extra-large coffee table book about the history of rock. And they had heavy metal in there. They included Led Zeppelin, so back when I was 16, we did think of them as heavy metal. You wouldn't think of Led Zeppelin as a metal band now, but that was the start for me. I loved them and Aerosmith and the first two Ted Nugent albums.

A lot of people in metal liked Helmet. We'd see guys like Nikki Sixx and Tommy Lee coming to our shows. The thing is, Helmet came out of the New York indie rock scene. I was really into bands like Sonic Youth and Live Skull. A friend in college really liked Judas Priest and I wasn't into them at the time. I really like them now. But I also got introduced to Black Sabbath in college and that ended up being a huge influence for me. When we did the *Jerky Boys* movie, we met Ozzy Osbourne and he told me he was driving in his car in L.A. and he heard our song "Unsung" on the radio and he said, "I don't remember recording that." And then the DJ came on and said it was Helmet. And he said, "Helmet. Hmmmm? Them boys done their homework."

ZAKK WYLDE
Black Label Society, Ozzy Osbourne

Jimmy Page is the pope of rock and roll. Pontiff Page is a religion unto himself. He's transcended just being a guitar player, songwriter, and producer. He's basically a whole school of theology. Then, you have Lord Iommi and Lord Blackmore. That's the Bach, Beethoven, and Mozart of modern-day riffs. Their faces should be on Mount Rushmore.

AL JOURGENSEN
Ministry, Revolting Cocks

I was totally duped by Robert Plant, man. Growing up, I thought Led Zeppelin were the greatest, but I wanted to be Jimmy Page, not Robert Plant. I didn't want to sing about hobbits and shit. I just wanted to play guitar. But I still loved Led Zeppelin.

Fast-forward to 1983. John Bonham is dead, Zeppelin's done. And Robert Plant's playing Chicago. I had just started to work at Wax Trax. I was the rookie. They said I had to keep the store open because this "real famous person" was gonna come in after hours. They wouldn't tell me who it was. All they said was, "He won't shop during the day."

I had a date that night with a girl that loved ass fucking. And it was gonna be my first ass fuck. So I was like, "Goddammit! I got stuck running the counter and missed my date."

Eventually, Robert Plant comes in and he keeps me there for almost five hours. I was looking at my watch the whole time going, "Can I still meet this chick?" No, Robert Plant's there and he's got me playing records before he buys 'em. It was all this shit about dwarves and dragons. So I'm there for five hours. I'd blown my date and now I'm pissed.

So, he comes up with a two-foot stack of vinyl and he wants it for free. It was my second day on the job and I'm like, "I don't know if I can do that, man. Let me call the owner."

I called Jim Nash and put him on the phone with Robert. I had to go through another hour of, "This record's twenty percent off for Robert. This record's ten percent off. This record's five percent off." I had to figure out all this math shit. I'd blown my date. I'm with this wanker in these bell bottoms with his shirt tied off at the navel. He was a fucking asshole.

MIKE BORDIN
Faith No More

A lot of people overlook Deep Purple but, man, between *Machine Head* and *Burn*, Ritchie Blackmore was one of the baddest motherfuckers on the planet. He pissed on everybody. And that's the role of a great lead guitarist. It's like they're raised to be bullfighters and ballet dancers. Mick Jagger once said that, but it's so true. The solos he plays on the first side of the live album *Made in Japan* alone are full of mindblowing passion, arrogance, and skill. Blackmore was calm, but he could explode. I got to see him in Rainbow, the band he formed with Ronnie James Dio and [bassist] Bob Daisley. They played San Francisco at The Winterland

and they literally destroyed the place. Even when the show was supposed to be over they wouldn't stop. Blackmore snatched up this dummy guitar, threw it over the lighting truss and pulled it up and down over the audience. He was going insane and the crowd was completely losing its mind. He kept going and going. And then the stage manager guys drop the curtain while Blackmore was still doing his thing. We were right up in the front of the stage watching. There was no barrier so we were touching the stage. And we could see Blackmore's white boots underneath the curtain. He was rolling around fighting with the stage manager because he was angry that they dropped the curtain on him.

GARY HOLT
Exodus, Slayer

The first thing I heard as a kid that kicked my ass was classic hard rock stuff because I'm the youngest of six kids, four of them brothers. They were rockers. So I grew up hearing the first Montrose album and Frank Marino and Mahogany Rush and Nazareth. Bands like AC/DC meant a lot to me and I still have a vinyl copy of Nils Lofgren's *Crying Tough*. I also liked stuff like Robin Trower and Roy Buchanan. The list goes on and on. I had my brother's record collections to thumb through and that had a really huge influence on me as a guitar player. But they had the Black Sabbath records and that was a really big inspiration to me.

As I got a little older and started getting into some serious drug experimentation, mainly LSD, I was still years away from actually playing guitar. Everybody else was listening to Parliament and Ohio Players and fuckin' loved that shit, too. But we were kinda isolated in our own little thing. At the time, underground music was Judas Priest. There was a large contingent of the rocker crowd at high school who looked at Judas Priest and didn't like the clothes. AC/DC ruled and those guys were wearing shiny pants. Iron Maiden was the first really underground band that had a big effect on me because Exodus started doing Iron Maiden covers. No one knew the songs in our whole area outside of Exodus. A friend of ours had bought the album in an import section solely based on the front and back covers of the record. Listening to it, it felt like I was hearing music for the first time in my life. It was unbelievable. And obviously, Motörhead and the big extra puzzle piece for Exodus was Discharge. My next oldest brother was a full-on punk rocker at the time. He had safety pins in his ears and he turned me on to all that old British hardcore punk. You listen to anything off of Discharge's *Hear Nothing See Nothing Say Nothing* and the energy is unbelievable. The guitar sound is so huge and the power just blew me away. He also turned me onto GBH, Exploited, Sham 69 and all this other stuff that was huge to me. And that's where the thrash element really came from for me. It was a combination of the hard rock I grew up on, the New Wave of British Heavy Metal—Angel Witch pretty much still have the greatest debut album ever made; it's not the only album they ever made—and the punk stuff. That all pretty much shaped who I am. Mix it all in a pot and you have Exodus.

DINO CAZARES
Fear Factory, Divine Heresy, Brujeria, Asesino

I was nine years old the first time I saw AC/DC guitarist Angus Young play. It was on *Don Kirshner's Rock Concert* and the band was doing "If You Want Blood." That really got me going, not because he was such a great player. It had more to do with his stage antics. His energy was amazing and it just looked fun. I was like, "Wow, I want to do that. I want to headbang and play guitar and run around the stage." That's when I made my decision to play guitar in a band.

REX BROWN

When I moved to [Arlington, Texas] in '75, I was 10 years old and there was a kid across the street that had all this Deep Purple. And Black Sabbath's *Master of Reality* had just come out and I walked around with the eight-track in my back pocket. This was even before cassettes became the thing. It's funny 'cause "Sweet Leaf," which starts with that echoing cough, blew my mind in such a big way. And that was before I knew the connotations of what it was about. I didn't start smoking pot until seventh grade. That's when I begged my mom for a stereo so we went to Sears and got this piece of shit and I blew one of the speakers out so I bridged up mono, where I could hear both sides in one speaker and then stashed my weed in the other side. But Sabbath are the ones that definitely took hold and it got me into all kinds of stuff. In seventh grade, I got *Alive!* It was probably a year old, but that's what fuckin' turned it all around for me. Seeing the cover and going, "What the fuck is this?" Then I listened to the music and I realized, take away the greasepaint and there were some really great riffs there. And then I went and saw them live and that was even more larger than life bombastic shit.

JOHN GALLAGHER
Raven

When me and my brother, [bassist] Mark were kids in Newcastle and we started the band with the guy down the street, Paul Bowden, we'd be playing the records we heard on *Top of the Pops* in England. We were very limited. There was that one half hour show once a week. Luckily for us in the early '70s, there was a lot of hard rock and the glam stuff was basically hard rock dressed up. So we were big fans of Status Quo, The Sweet, and Slade and we're cranking up and jumping around with our tennis rackets, saying let's eventually form a band.

Then in '73, we went to see our first ever concert, which was Slade and the opening act was The Sensational Alex Harvey Band. That basically changed our lives. Everything was there. We had never heard of the Alex Harvey band, being little teeny boppers that we were, and Alex Harvey was the consummate frontman and won over an entire crowd who had no interest in him whatsoever at first. It was fascinating to watch him get everyone in the palm of his hand. And then Slade came off and blew the doors off. They were incredible, too. And that was it, really.

After that, we were determined to play music. Newcastle had a small hall with a 2,000-people capacity and there was the Mayfair Night Club, which had a similar capacity and you could get up and close and personal. And that was our education, watching every band come through.

WILL CARROLL
Death Angel, ex-Machine Head

When I saw the gatefold picture in *Alive II*, that's when I decided what I wanted to do with my life. I was only five or six years old, and I had actually heard Kiss before. But when I saw that image, everything solidified in my mind. I was like, "Holy shit. Things and blowing up and it's madness. I wanna be involved with this!"

JIMMY BOWER
Eyehategod, Superjoint Ritual, Down, ex-Crowbar

I was 12 years old and me and a guy I knew got into Kiss together and we lost our fucking minds. I got *Alive!* and *Alive II* for Easter. And then I went back and got the rest of their records. Me and him would totally try to imitate Kiss and we had fake concerts with lightsabers we held as guitars. We'd charge a nickel. It's funny 'cause I had a drum kit at the time and my neighbor was trying to turn me on to Sex Pistols so I'd go and play drums with him. But I was more interested in Kiss.

KING FOWLEY
Deceased, October 31

I was at The Grand Union grocery store with my mom and my grandmother and I was looking through these rock magazines like *Circus* and *Creem* and discovering Kiss. The visuals got me, which, obviously, Kiss was famous for. And the pictures of Gene Simmons spitting blood really made me realize that I like the "extreme" side of the music. I'm not looking at the pictures of Cheap Trick, who are probably better musicians and songwriters. I'm looking at Kiss because they caught my eye and I thought they were just vicious. So then I'm eight years old, looking at the cover of Kiss's *Destroyer* album and it's all coming out as morbid. They're standing there in hell and I'm thinking, "What am I getting myself into?" And at that point, I haven't even heard the music. Then I listen to the first track, "Detroit Rock City," which has the intro about a guy dying at a concert. It was more extreme than a lot of the other mainstream stuff that was out there and I loved it. That theme repeated itself through my life. I always loved the bands that were left of center. When I was older, my friends said, "I love metal," and they were listening to Rush and Ted Nugent in the earliest of the '80s. And I was like, "No, no. You gotta hear Exciter, Saxon, and Anvil."

DAVID DRAIMAN
Disturbed

I was at a buddy's house. We were playing Dungeons and Dragons and his brother had a great record collection. So we listened to all this stuff, then we put on *Black Sabbath*. The vibe felt like nothing else. Even those three notes of the song "Black Sabbath," you know that tritone progression. No one else made that choice before that and it was extremely effective. I loved it. What is it, that frequency that's supposed to summon Satan or something? It was this deep, thunderous low and rhythmic wave of music. And if you combine it with a bit of herbage, it hit you like nothing else ever before.

OZZY OSBOURNE
Black Sabbath, Ozzy Osbourne

We just decided to write scary music—horror music. We were flirting with the dark side. We always want to get the bogeyman out of the covers. It's like when you go and see one of them stupid fucking *Friday the 13th* films. You know the next door that opens, an axe is gonna come through the guy's head. And you go, "I can't watch, I can't watch." When's it's happening you might put your hand over your eyes, then you look through your fingers. So you still watch it. A lot of people are interested in that darkness and that's where we started.

FRANKIE BANALI

Sabbath were instrumental in bringing heavy riffs together with darkness and Tony Iommi is the king of the scary riff. He's just the best at it. The diminished notes they used were so perfect and Ozzy was always left of center and a great frontman. So they definitely are the high priests of the holy church of metal. And they lay a wonderful foundation for everybody else to build on.

GEEZER BUTLER
Black Sabbath, Heaven & Hell

I'm most proud of the fact that we went in and recorded the first album against all the odds when nobody gave us a chance. I think that made it our greatest accomplishment. Back then, nobody wanted to manage us. Nobody wanted to sign us. Our families didn't believe in us. Our friends said we'd never make it. But that just brought us closer together and more determined to make it happen. We literally went in and played the songs as if it was a live gig. We didn't know anything about studios or production or engineering. We just went in, set up and played and Roger Bain and Tom Allom recorded us. It sounds easy, but it's actually a really hard thing to do—to record a band live in the studio and get the whole feeling across. A lot of producers tried that but dismally failed. But Roger and Tom just had the knack of doing it. When it was done, we had something physically in our hands to show our parents and friends: "See! Look what we've done." And slowly, people started believing in us.

MARK SLAUGHTER

A friend of my mom's heard "Iron Man" on the radio and bought the *Paranoid* record on eight-track. But he didn't like the rest of the record, so he gave it to me 'cause he knew I liked guitar and I thought, "Man, what a cool riff, but is it okay to like this?" It was just so dark and different. It wasn't your common, happy-go-lucky pop that was on '70s radio at the time. It was something that made you go, "I don't know. I think this is wrong." But I couldn't help myself. So my parents would fall asleep, I'd put the headphones in and listen to Sabbath.

RICHARD CHRISTY
Charred Walls of the Damned, ex-Death, ex-Iced Earth, ex-Public Assassin

I got to meet Ozzy when I worked with Howard Stern. Then, I got to meet the rest of the guys when they played at Radio City Music Hall as Heaven & Hell. When I was shaking Tony Iommi's hand I thought to myself, "Man, I'm shaking the hand that invented heavy metal. I'm shaking this hand with the tips of the fingers that were cut off in a factory accident when he was young, causing Tony to make fake tips for his fingers. That influenced his playing style and also influenced the sound of heavy metal." I felt like a Christian getting to shake the hand of Jesus. It was definitely a spiritual moment for me.

JIMMY BOWER

For me, it all started with Sabbath and then it was a matter of finding other bands that sounded like them. So there was Pentagram and Saint Vitus and shit. And then [Graveyard Rodeo guitarist] Pepper [Keenan] gave me a copy of the Melvins' *Gluey Porch Treatments* on cassette and I lost my fuckin' mind. That was the band I was hearing in my head. I thought, "Dude, this is the shit we want to do!" That record fuckin' raped me for years because around then everyone was playing thrash. So there was that, Carnivore, Witchfinder General, Trouble, The Obsessed, and everything that led to our sound. When we did our second record, *Take as Needed for Pain*, we were really into Soundgarden and we were learning how to play a little better. I was starting to bend strings like Lynyrd Skynyrd, Allman Brothers and these bluesy bands that were heavy to me.

DEE SNIDER

I was a fan of a band in Junior High School called Armadillo. I even roadied for them. I was so proud to do that. At a battle of the bands, they played the song "Black Sabbath." That's the first time I ever heard that song. They played it on a totally black stage in the dark and only thing I remember was the red lights of their amps on. It was terrifying. The note progression, there was nothing like it. Nothing had ever been heard before like it. And the screams of, "Oh no please God help me." It was the shot heard round the world with that riff. The tritone, the progression. It was terrifying. I was literally scared by a band of my friends playing in the Battle of the Bands. I was like, "What the fuck was that?" And then I got to hear the real thing and it was 100 times more mind-blowing.

ZAKK WYLDE

The first time I got into Sabbath I hadn't even heard them yet. I was in sixth-grade art class and my buddy was drawing a skull with a lightning bolt through and it said "Black Sabbath 666." I said, "What is that?" And he said, "Oh, it's this band my brother listens to." It looked cool. I went to the store with my mom and she said I could get a record but I could only buy one so I got *We Sold Our Soul for Rock and Roll* because it's a double album. I put on the record and from the start, I was terrified listening to it. The funny thing is that jawless skull from the album *Sabbath Bloody Sabbath* basically became Skully [the mascot] for Black Label Society.

SCOTT IAN
Anthrax, S.O.D., The Damned Things

I heard Sabbath the first time as a kid in my uncle's room. I put the record on and just sat there scared, listening to the rain and the wind and the bell. And then the riff started and it just blew my mind. So I was into Sabbath from an early age. They wrote the playbook for heavy metal. Any metal riff any band has ever written is just some type of rephrasing of what Tony [Iommi] did on those first five Sabbath records. I truly believe that he's the guy responsible for all of this. Fast-forward to 1986 and Anthrax was asked to open shows for Black Sabbath. It wasn't the Sabbath I grew up loving. It was this weird lineup for their album *Seventh Star* that featured Glenn Hughes on vocals. But getting to meet Tony for the first time backstage was a complete mind fuck. You know? How do you even handle that as a young musician? How do you stand in the room with him and not lose your mind? I felt like I was standing there with some-one who's almost not even human. Of course, he is, but when you're 22 it's hard to fathom. And he was very polite and cool. He thanked us for being on the tour with him. *He* actually thanked *us.*

GARY HOLT

Me and my friends used to listen to *Master of Reality* at night with the win-dows all blacked out in the dark, just high as fuck on tons of LSD. It was a life-changing experience. If you turned the lights on, you expected Satan to be two inches from your face and you didn't even know he was there the whole time. It felt like the end of the world and I loved it. It was rad.

COREY TAYLOR
Slipknot, Stone Sour

Discovering metal all kind of happened all at once for me and I'd have to say it all started with Sabbath. I can remember the day that I put two and two together and realized that Ozzy Osbourne—who was doing solo stuff —was also the singer for Black Sabbath. And that's a unique perspective because when I was growing up it wasn't readily apparent to someone of my age. To somebody my mom's age that just made sense, but to me it was a bombshell. It didn't seem like it was common knowledge. I was like, "Are you telling me Ozzy Osbourne also sang for Black Sabbath?!?" It was a monstrous moment for me to find that out. I was like, "Holy shit, that is fucking amazing." So, right out of the gate Ozzy was obviously a huge favorite for me. But then moving forward from that I listened to tons of stuff and discovered bands like Mötley Crüe, Metallica, and Judas Priest. I began to pick my favorite bands, which were always the ones that stood out and had a distinct vocal style.

GEEZER BUTLER

Tony [Iommi] used to manage the first lineup of Judas Priest. He took them into the studio and co-produced the first album. They were more about singles in England, whereas we were more concerned with albums. And they really came with the second wave of metal. They were the ones who brought out all the leather and studs and whatnot. And they were great.

GLENN TIPTON
Judas Priest

We came from Birmingham which has spawned many a heavy metal band and rock band. Members of Zeppelin of course, and then there's Sabbath and Priest. There's a legacy there that's engendered by, I think, the area. The city was very industrial and when we were young you could always hear steam hammers, which used to pound the metal into shape and it was used everywhere. It was the industrial center of England. The area where we grew up was very hard, really. There was a lot of poverty. And that desperation and that determination to escape came out in the music that all these bands were making. I used to work for British Steel, actually—which, of course is the name of a Priest album—and the most poignant thing about that is that being in that situation and in that environment gave me the determination to say, "There's a better world out there somewhere than working in a factory for eight hours a day and I'm going to find it. And maybe I'll find it through music like these other bands did." I've known Robert Plant for years. We had the same manager for 20 years. So Rob's a great guy. He's a Midlander like me but we support different football teams. I remember at school he was a big, tall, blond guy with a great voice and even then he was loved by beautiful women and everyone around him was rather jealous in those days.

GENE HOGLAN
Dark Angel, Testament, Dethklok, ex-Death, ex-Strapping Young Lad

I was very fortunate to meet [Black Sabbath] drummer Bill Ward at a really young age. I was in Dark Angel and he lived not too far from me and we were at a rehearsal studio called DC Sparks in Orange County. And Bill Ward was there. I think he was doing the *Ward One* album at the time. He was in the lobby at the end of the night and I was done jamming with Dark Angel. All the boys had split. I would usually sit on the couch in the lobby for a few minutes before I drove home. So, Bill Ward's on the phone and I could tell he was a little frustrated by the way he was talking with this manager or record label person who was on the other end of the line.

When he got off the phone he turned to me and said, "Hey, you're obviously in a band. What's your band called?" I said, "Well, we're called Dark Angel." He's like, "You got an album out?" And I said, "Yeah, we've got a couple albums out. We've done some touring." And he said, "Does your record label tell you what to do or who to play with or what songs to write?" We were on Combat at the time and they didn't tell anyone anything except maybe, "Play faster." I said, "I'm on a small label, but nobody tells us anything. They just wait for us to write a whole batch of new songs and we record a new album."

And I couldn't believe it. The legendary drummer of Black Sabbath said, "You are so fortunate. I'm so envious of you."

He told me he was in the process of doing a solo album and just wanted to get a few friends together and put out an album. And he said, "Now I've got my record label telling me I've got to use this hotshot singer and I need to hook up with this other hotshot guitarist. All I wanted to do was write a little record and put it out and now I'm being told what to do by my management and my label and envy you because you don't have to go through any of the shit I'm going through." I was eighteen or nineteen and that was super cool and it was also kind of a wake-up call about the music industry.

ROB HALFORD
Judas Priest

I have a very vague memory of seeing Sabbath at a club called Mothers in Erdington, which was a little place within the bombing zones and there was still damage there from the German bombings in World War II. There were lots of subdivisions in Birmingham, and Erdington was near the city center. At the time, they were somewhat like Priest as far as having a progressive, bluesy kind of sound. It wasn't totally metal as we know it, but it was loud and very in your face and you could sense that was something magical about to happen.

Then, of course, when Geezer [Butler] saw the Boris Karloff poster with "Black Sabbath" on it, that seemed to be a catalyst that brought the band to the next musical step.

So yeah, we've kind of been joined at the hip from the way both bands lived their lives in metal. Some people think there was a rivalry, but that couldn't be further from the truth. Sabbath really relieved a lot of us by starting the heavy metal movement and it's just it's an extraordinary feeling to have been there at the beginning.

K.K. DOWNING
ex-Judas Priest

When I was growing up in England, the whole world was still reeling from the war. And when I think about it now, it really was the dark ages.

And then we moved into the '60s and it was still kind of early days. Everybody was still trying to find a pedestal to perch on. And then the '70s hit and you had Priest and Sabbath and so many great bands. But the '70s was the breeding, nurturing grounds for what was to come. We were getting going like so many other bands, pushing forward and forward.

DEVIN TOWNSEND
Strapping Young Lad, ex-Steve Vai, ex-Wildhearts, Devin Townsend Band

I loved Judas Priest. I think it was K.K. Downing more than anything else. His guitar playing was such an influence on me as a kid. I felt like the whole aesthetic of heavy music was summarized by that band. They had long hair and the Flying V guitars and the leather. It was such a cool thing to look at and how it translated into music was an echoing force.

PHILIP ANSELMO

Only a fucking hypocritical weakling would deny the power, the voice, the fucking distinct, absolute director, the curator of all, Rob Halford of Judas Priest. His cadence, his ability, his stage presence, his command of the audience is untouchable. He may be one of the greatest voices in the history of this shit called voice and that transcends all genres of music. When my best friend played me "Delivering the Goods" from 1978's *Hell Bent for Leather*, that was a complete ass-whooping and I immediately had to go out and get all the rest of the band's albums.

FRANKIE BANALI

In 1983, when Quiet Riot first went to the UK to open a tour for Judas Priest, I got to see them every night and that was eye-opening because they were a complete finely tuned well-oiled machine. They went onstage and then they meant business. They sounded unbelievable. The two guitar players and the harmonies they played—everything was just perfect. [Vocalist] Rob Halford was the consummate professional. I mean he is the epitome of the studded God.

GLENN TIPTON

We started with Jimi Hendrix and Cream and Led Zeppelin. It was a great time for music. The songs that people were writing were blues-based, but they were very progressive. It was an era where the songs were just classics. They were very unique for the time and it was nice to be brought up on that style of music. It was so diverse yet it was all in the same league.

I've always listened to a great selection of music. I listen to all sorts of music. I think that helps as a writer. I take my inspiration from such a wide area it makes it a little bit unique in a sense. Rory Gallagher from Taste was the person who really got me to pick the guitar up and play. I used to watch him at a club called Mothers. He was just phenomenal. He was an Irishman with an old battered Stratocaster. He used to come out onstage and throw out so much energy, my jaw just dropped when I first saw him. It was then that I knew what I wanted to do. He had the most effect on me of any musician.

Honestly, Black Sabbath weren't hugely influential to me. I liked Sabbath, but I didn't particularly listen to them at that time. I don't know why that was. I probably listened to Sabbath more in later years. But they certainly were there in the beginning. They were a great band and influenced a lot of people.

K.K. DOWNING

Heavy metal was put to bands like ourselves who had moved away from not just the progressive blues, but also from the rock era and the hard rock and heavy rock. Because I think it's fair to say that quite a few bands had become rock bands or even heavy rock. And then bands that took it a step further in one way or another, were basically labeled as heavy metal bands.

GLENN TIPTON

We did, I think, three months alone in Texas in little bars like Bill's Bamboo Bar and places like that. But the crowds were enthusiastic and we enjoyed playing and they liked the metal—it wasn't called metal in those days, it was rock, really. They found an interest in Priest.

We bound the book everywhere in America and some bands only break the West Coast, some bands only break the East Coast or the Midwest. But we broke everywhere except the West Coast. And we were ready to come home after this tour. We were so ready to get back on that couch and pet the dog and be with our loved ones. And then we had the chance to play Oakland Coliseum supporting Zeppelin for two days. We couldn't believe it. Part of us really was desperate to get home. Part of us wanted to stick around for two weeks and do the shows.

We decided we couldn't afford to turn it down.

We got no money or very little for playing and we had to stay in one of the worst motels you can imagine. The air conditioner rattled and moaned but didn't give out any cool air. And you had a 50/50 chance of getting through the night without having the door kicked in. It was an awful hellhole. And we stayed there for two weeks and then we played this gig which, for us, was really like jumping off of the deep end. We were used to playing small places and there were tens of thousands of people there. It was a coliseum and it was full. We had to go on at 10 o'clock in the morning. It was very difficult to get out of bed and go and play for that many people, but we did it and it really broke us on the West Coast.

So without realizing it, on our first couple of tours we worked hard and got the breaks and suddenly metal fans just took to Priest and we struck a chord with America.

TOMAS LINDBERG
At the Gates

Judas Priest is my favorite heavy metal band and they sum up what metal is to me—the look, the music. I like them best when they were more progressive and had a really intricate, weird way of playing rock with a little blues touch that still had an edge, like on *Sad Wings of Destiny*. But then, *Stained Class* is also a great record because it mixes the broad styles of *Sad Wings of Destiny* with a really full, crunchy production and it has those more intricate guitar lines. And then there are all the albums with the hits, like *British Steel* and *Screaming for Vengeance*, which are also great. *Stained Class* is the logical bridge between the early Priest, which I'm actually more into, and the Priest with all the hits, like *British Steel* and *Screaming for Vengeance*. That's all really good, too, but in a different way.

BUZZ OSBORNE

I love Judas Priest. I think *Unleashed in the East* is the best metal record ever made. Seriously. I don't think you could do better than that—not in that genre of metal. They improved on the songs they did in the studio. And I don't know how much of that is actually because of tweaking they did on the live recordings. But, man, the songs are not even close to the way they sound on the record. They improved them tenfold. I like the originals, but you listen to those two versions and it's like there's no comparison with the live versions.

MICHAEL SWEET
Stryper

Eddie Van Halen is one of my biggest influences and I don't think there will ever be anyone like him again. He changed guitar playing and rock. I heard some demos in 1977 before their first album came out in 1978. A friend of mine had a bootleg of the demo. It was a copy of a copy and it was a live recording because they played the L.A. club scene often. Not long after that, the album came out and it exploded. The first song I heard from that album was "Runnin' With the Devil." That was before I got the album but I knew instantly who it was.

SCOTT IAN

1980 was the best year for hard rock and heavy metal in history and I was the perfect age for it. I was 16 years old, hanging out with a bunch of like-minded kids and we all thought we were the smartest, coolest people in town, because nobody knew the shit we knew, and all these bands at the time were still underground, so really it felt like it was our thing. What a year for records, from Maiden to Motörhead to Ozzy to Black Sabbath's *Heaven and Hell* to Priest's *British Steel*. After I heard all that stuff there was no going back for me. There was no way I was going to do anything else with my life than play in a band.

ERIK TURNER

When the Ozzy solo albums *Blizzard of Ozz* and *Diary of a Madman* came out, oh my God, my life was changed forever. I worshipped the ground that Randy Rhoads walked on and played on. The best thing that ever happened to Black Sabbath was Ozzy leaving and getting together with Randy and then Ronnie James Dio hooked up with Sabbath and it was, like, twice as much great music.

PHILIP ANSELMO

When Ozzy Osbourne came out with *Speak of the Devil* at the same time as Black Sabbath with Ronnie James Dio came out with that live album *Live Evil*, Oh my God. Dio was unparalleled. I've shared the stage with many a vocalist and I've seen what certain vocalists do and how they do their thing and operate whether they use in-ear monitors or whatever. Ronnie James Dio never used an in-ear monitor in his life and he was the loudest motherfucking instrument on that stage. He was *booming* every night.

FRANKIE BANALI

Randy Rhoads had that special quality. I have known and seen an amazing number of guitarists that are ridiculously talented. Randy was an amazing musician. There was nothing he couldn't play and he was always constantly learning and constantly improving. So he never really relaxed what he was doing. He was also an incredible showman on stage and he just looked great. He even had just the right hair.

The thing that is truly amazing about him is that he never let his talent go to his head. When someone looks that good and plays that great, more often than not you find out he's not a very nice person. Randy could not have been any sweeter. As great of a talent as he was, he was an even greater person, which is what makes [his accidental death in a plane wreck at age twenty-five] so tragic. He was so young and we're never really going to know the heights that he would have gone to because what he did with us and Ozzy was just the tip of the iceberg.

K.K. DOWNING

Suddenly, 1980 hits and Priest comes out with *British Steel* and then everything seemed to kick off. Then you had Def Leppard, Iron Maiden, and Saxon. But I think the '70s was really just kicking to the '80s and the golden years of the '80s kicked off where everything was just unreal.

Then you had the Van Halens moving on and the Golden '80s as we say. Everything was established in the '80s. Everything that was important musically was there, it was accessible, it was accepted, whereas in the '70s it was all a big question mark of what would survive and what wouldn't, bearing in mind that we were all hit hard with the new wave movement and the punk movement. There was the question of who would stay the course. And for bands like Priest, UFO, Scorpions, really cool bands like that, there was the question of whether they would actually make it to great heights. And then when the '80s came about it was just such a magical time for all those bands.

DEVIN TOWNSEND

There was a moment there after Rob Halford left Judas Priest when I got sent a letter from Judas Priest asking me to audition. I actually declined that because I liked the band so much and I didn't want it to be sullied with my presence.

PHILIP ANSELMO

The first time Pantera were even on Judas Priest's radar was when me and Dimebag were rooming together and we just got to Canada, somehow made it through customs. We had just gotten into our rooms and we were going to play a small club. It was in 1990 in the *Cowboys from Hell* days. The phone rang, which was kind of weird. I figured it must be our tour manager, so I picked it up. On the other end is this strange voice in a British accent and I completely denied it at first. I was like, "C'mon, who is fucking with me here?"

But sure enough, it was Robert Halford calling the hotel room at 10 a.m. I looked at Dimebag like I had seen a ghost. I almost dropped the phone. Then I realized it was Rob because I could tell it from his voice.

I acted all straight and tried to be cool and said, "What's going on, man?"

He said, "I hear you're playing a club. I'd like to come out and see you."

Dude, do you understand how much that meant? We could do an entire Judas Priest set at the time.

So I said, "Hell, yeah. And pick a fucking Judas Priest song so you can come up and fucking jam with us."

And he took us up on it. I think we did "Grinder" and a couple other songs. He sounded great and was an awesome gentleman. And sure enough, he championed us for the European tour for *Painkiller* in 1991 and that was our first trip to Europe.

ALEX HELLID
Entombed

Kiss and Iron Maiden were the bands that turned me on to hard rock. At eight or nine years old I was taking a few acoustic guitar lessons and then I met Nicke Andersson (Entombed, The Hellacopters) at age 10. He was already playing drums and doing it well, but he could also play guitar and he had an electric guitar and an amp. The first time I went to his house he actually played along to a Maiden album and I remember being amazed. I had no idea anyone could actually do that—that it was even allowed. To play along with something that great without having a sheet of paper was mindblowing to me because I was playing guitar with sheet music. That's when I first understood I could listen to something and try to figure it out myself. That was a revelation and I swiftly forgot how to read music after that. That was a big year for me. I saw my first concert when I was 10 and it was Iron Maiden.

KING FOWLEY

On December 3, 1981, I went to see Black Sabbath's the *Mob Rules* tour. It was the second birth of the band. Ozzy was out, Ronnie James was singing. My friend's dad got us tickets. We wanted to go to AC/DC, but by the time he went to get the tickets, there weren't any good seats left. So he bought Black Sabbath tickets.

I was actually bummed 'cause when I was younger I went through my brother's record collection and saw *Paranoid* in the pile. And when I put it on, I started with the song "Planet Caravan" and I was like, "What is this hippie shit?" I totally missed on the greatness of the record.

So when my friend made me watch them onstage, Dio is talking about the devil, there's a red light shining on his face and a cross. It's brutally dark-edged and it's not hard rock, it's heavy fucking metal! And I went, "Yes!! This is what I want to fucking do! I don't want to play some bullshit. I don't want to be happy like the Beatles. I don't want to be whatever else. I want to do this dark shit."

ZAKK WYLDE

I was talking to Ozzy once about how all these bands take their influence from other bands and throw them together into a cocktail and that's how they get their sound. I was telling Ozzy he would really like Crowded House because they've got tons of Beatles floating around. We were talking about this singer and that singer. Then he said with surprise, "Zakk, no one's ever sounded like me in any of these bands," which, of course, it totally untrue. But then he kinda sounded sad and said, "Well, maybe they don't want to. Maybe there's a reason why."

MAX CAVALERA

My wife Gloria and I were invited to go to dinner with Ozzy and Sharon at this really fancy restaurant in L.A. in 1992. It was the first time I met him, and he was a legend to me. I was already nervous, so I ordered a drink called Cucaracha. I had never heard of this drink before, but it said on the menu, "This drink comes with fire."

So I thought, "Fuck yeah, I want to impress Ozzy with this fire drink."

The waiter brings the drink and the motherfucking cup's on fire. You're supposed to drink it real fast with a straw and keep your face away from the fire. I didn't know any of that so I grabbed the straw and started sucking really slow. The next thing I know, my hair is on fire. I see Ozzy blowing and lifting a napkin from his side of the table to put the fire out. That's how the dinner started. I made an ass out of myself.

Before we left, I wanted to take a picture with him. I had a shitty camera and I asked the waiter to take the picture and the guy tried to use the camera again and again but it wasn't working. I could tell Ozzy was getting irritated.

I said, "Try one more time, man. I really need this picture."

Ozzy said, "Gimme the camera."

He grabbed the camera from the guy's hand and took a selfie-style photo. He clicked it once and the photo came out.

I thought, "Yeah, he is the son of the devil. He even made the broken camera work."

But, man, Ozzy and Sharon have been so good to me and Gloria and they're such good friends. They're like family.

LZZY HALE
Halestorm

My introduction to metal was Black Sabbath. But it wasn't the Ozzy stuff, it was the Dio years. I heard *Mob Rules* and *Heaven and Hell* and I totally adored those albums. After I got those, I worked my way back into the Ozzy years. And I love both but for some reason the years that Sabbath had Dio as a singer really resonated with me.

It's funny because I remember when I was first starting to write songs—before we even decided to start the band—I would write small songs and I remember thinking, "Well, if Dio can write about slaying a dragon I can write about anything."

And so I remember writing these songs and we put a couple of them on our first ever Halestorm demo cassette. I would write these songs about mythical time travelers that would try to tell you what to do. It was ridiculous, but it was a very freeing time. When you're a kid, you're writing these small songs just to show your parents or your relatives. And with Dio I remember thinking, "Well, I don't even know what he's talking about here and it doesn't matter. As long as I feel good about it and it sounds good I can just do it."

My dad was a mechanic and he ended up opening this small space in his garage. It was a little side room. And he got me this four-track Tascam recorder. I would sit there for hours while my dad worked on whatever and made these songs.

JERRY DIXON
Warrant

The record *Heaven and Hell* got many hours of jumping up and down on the bed playing air guitar with the tennis racket when I was 13. I didn't know shit at the time. I picked it up at the record store at random and right away I went, "This is badass." The playing on that is so great and the rhythm section is so up in the mix. You can really hear the great melodic bass lines and that made me want to play bass even more. That was my first exposure to Sabbath.

The town I lived in was pretty small, La Crescenta, California. I only had a few records. I had the Sabbath, Aerosmith's *Toys in the Attic*, something by Iron Maiden and I had heard some Judas Priest. Four records were really all I needed. I started playing bass and I knew I was never putting that bass down. Three years later I was in Warrant.

BRENDON SMALL
Dethklok, Galaktikon

The animated movie *Heavy Metal* was a big part of my life and it included the Dio-Black Sabbath song "The Mob Rules." I drew a connection between the aggressive music and the wild sci-fi imagery. One of the first times I smoked pot I was listening to Black Sabbath "Sign of the Southern Cross" and I couldn't believe something like that existed. Dio's vocals were so commanding and they told this *story*. And the band played these big, building tunes that were huge and driving and epic. I love stuff like that.

DAVID DRAIMAN

Dio was *the* voice of metal, even as far back as his days in Rainbow with Ritchie Blackmore. His control, his power, his resonance, his delivery, his range, his effortless slip into vibrato at all the right times. Dio was a legend and there was nobody then and nobody now that could touch him, I don't care who we're talking about and anybody that disagrees is doing so on a level of personal preference, not technical ability. That man was the most gifted physical individual as a vocalist I've ever seen in my life.

I went to see him in Chicago. It was the first time I got to meet him and I was nervous as fuck. I went up to him. He's got a cigarette in one hand he's got a glass of wine in the other and it's maybe fifteen minutes before the show.

I said, "Hey you know it's a pleasure to meet you. You're one of my idols. Listen, can I pick your brain?"

And he said, "Sure."

I was like, "What do you do to warm up?"

And he says to me, "Warm up?"

And I'm like, "Yeah, how do you warm up? Do you do vocal exercises or something?"

And he says to me, "Brother, if you have to warm up, you don't have it."

That's what he says to me. And all of a sudden, I felt like I was shorter than Ronnie James Dio. He was joking with me, of course, but the truth was, he never had to warm up. He literally had a drag from his cigarette and swallowed the last bit of his glass of wine and he went onstage and was invincible. Unbelievable.

DAVE WYNDORF
Monster Magnet

I saw Hawkwind's Space Ritual tour when I was a kid, and it completely blew me away. I snuck out of the house and went to a venue on 14th Street in New York to see it. But just the spectacle of it was outrageous. It was more punk rock than punk rock.

Hawkwind with Lemmy [Kilmister (Motörhead)] in it was unrelenting. You could tell they didn't even know what they had. The total sum was a lot more powerful than the parts. It was vibey, cool, and spacey and pulpy. They were drawn from 1920 pulp magazine covers and all this retro-future stuff. And the show was an absolute assault. I mean, what band faces the strobe lights directly at the audience? And they had movies of old science fiction stuff. And there was a dancer. I swear to God, she was six feet tall. And she was naked. A naked babe with giant boobs dancing in my face.

Right away I went, "This is what I like!" They were rock gods to me.

Cut to a few years later, and I saw the Ramones at CBGB and that was the moment. I went, "I can do this!"

I was looking at Joey Ramone and thinking, "If that guy can do it, I can do it," which was really inspiring.

DAVE NAVARRO
Jane's Addiction

If it wasn't for Jimi Hendrix I wouldn't have ever picked up a guitar. He's my all-time hero. Hendrix got me invested in the instrument and then I really became a metal head.

Jane's Addiction is not a typical metal band, but if you listen to the guitar there's lots of metal in there. [Drummer] Stephen Perkins and I met in high school and we were metalheads. But for some reason, we weren't into Judas Priest. They weren't heavy enough for me. I needed Iron Maiden. I needed more evil and more devil.

I was buying Slayer records in high school. So Perkins and I were speed metal kids and we were also prog-metal kids. We were super into Rush and all that nerdy prog-rock. But we were also super into the punk scene. We loved anything that was off the beaten path. We didn't identify with a culture in L.A. so we just liked what we liked. And then we came into Jane's Addiction and those guys were so against metal and so against anything current or that remotely sounded like Sunset Strip. And me and Perkins were all about that, so we would sneak as much metal riffing and tricks into the music as we could get away with. But [vocalist] Perry [Farrell] and [bassist] Eric [Avery] wouldn't pick up on it because it would be techniques from metal that, since they never listened to metal, they wouldn't recognize. That's how we did it and that's what made it work. If you listen to "Three Days" it's fuckin' "Xanadu" by Rush.

MAX CAVALERA

The things we would listen to got heavier as we went along. We were looking for the heaviest thing we could find. There was Judas Priest and Iron Maiden, of course, and then we discovered Motörhead and that was another world. And then we found Venom.

DEZ FAFARA
DevilDriver, ex-Coal Chamber

Hearing Motörhead for the first time made my brain explode. I was like, "Holy shit I can't even believe this kind of sound exists." Lemmy's voice was so low and raspy, he played a distorted bass and everything was fast. There was no thrash metal yet and I didn't know much about punk rock other than the Pistols and The Ramones. So that was a revelation to me.

And of course, the first time I heard Metallica I thought it was a step from what Motörhead was doing without ripping them off. I was in awe.

JEFF BECERRA
Possessed

A lot of people think [Motörhead's] Lemmy [Kilmister] influenced my vocals and Cronos inspired my lyrics. But mostly, my greatest influences were monsters. I wanted my voice to sound like a ferocious movie monster. I still love monsters and I still have *The Complete Tales of Edgar Allan Poe* on my nightstand. It's like the Bible to me.

AL JOURGENSEN

[Motörhead's] Lemmy Kilmister was the living embodiment of metal. A religion should have been started around him. He was very hedonistic and I loved him. It amazes me that people who are that primal and hedonistic survive in this world and everybody still loves them. It takes a certain character to pull that off. It's almost God-like. If some average Joe tried to pull that off, everyone would go, "That guy's a fucking maniac cunt. I hate him." But with Lemmy, everyone went, "Oh yeah that's fuckin' great. It's Lemmy. What else would he be doing?" The slack that you cut for his behavior is almost religious. We cut our gods slack when they decide to make a giant flood and destroy humanity. "Well, he had a reason."

MATT HEAFY
Trivium

My dad was a guitar player and it seemed like the cool thing to do. I thought that if I play guitar, maybe girls would think I was interesting. I was in eighth grade and at this point, I had never heard metal before and these kids were starting a pop-punk band that I wanted to join. My tryout song was "Dammit" by Blink-182. I never got the callback and I was super depressed.

Then, a couple months later, a kid lent me this thing called *The Black Album* by Metallica. I'd never heard it before, but as soon as I put it on and felt the power of the songs, I thought, "This is the kind of music that's meant for me. This is what I should be listening to and what I should be playing." I tried to emulate what I heard on the record. I practiced countless hours a day to try to get to the level of what I heard on the

CD. Eventually, I could play the songs pretty decent. Then, at a school talent show this local high school band asked me to try out for their band, which was called Trivium. I auditioned with the Metallica song "For Whom the Bell Tolls" and I made it in. And I've been in the band ever since, thanks to Metallica.

MATT BACHAND
ex-Shadows Fall, Times of Grace

When I was 13, I saw Metallica on the . . . *And Justice for All* tour in 1989. I knew their music, but it was my first real concert. You can love a band all day long and see them on TV and it's just not the same. You're in the room with the energy and when I saw that show I went, "Yeah, this looks like fun!"

MARK MORTON
Lamb of God

I had a brother who was eight years older than me so at a pretty young age I was hearing from my teenage brother the hard rock of the late '70s and early '80s. So I was hearing Aerosmith, AC/DC, Van Halen, Lynyrd Skynyrd, Molly Hatchet, Blackfoot. That kind of stuff was coming out of his room and later his car.

For me, those first few Van Halen albums sounded otherworldly and really captivated me. I didn't even associate Eddie Van Halen's sound as being created with an actual guitar. It was just an indescribable sound that was coming from him.

That started it and then in seventh and eighth grade some of my friends were getting into Sex Pistols and earlier Metallica and Megadeth. And that's the stuff that switched it on for me. When I heard *Ride the Lightning* and *Peace Sells* there was something about the way it brought together all the elements I loved and I had a really visceral reaction to it. The thrash metal of the '80s solidified for me that I wanted to be a part of this somehow even if it's just with my own little band in a garage somehow.

MIKE IX WILLIAMS
Eyehategod

I had two older brothers. One of them was totally into Alice Cooper, Black Sabbath, and The Who. That was the first time I heard music that

I liked and thought I would want to do something like that. Then later on when punk rock happened, Black Flag was the one band that really made me want to tour as much as possible and put out records like they did. I used to write letters to Black Flag's [bassist] Chuck Dukowski, and he would write me back encouraging me to keep playing my guitar and trying to create something. He said it didn't matter if I had shitty equipment or if I didn't think I could sing. His main message was don't give up.

I was staying at this boy's home when I saw Black Flag on *The Today Show*, so I ran away and went to this club where they were playing. I didn't have a ticket to get in, so I stood by the club and every time someone opened the door I could see the band playing.

ERIK RUTAN
Hate Eternal, ex-Morbid Angel, ex-Ripping Corpse

The first record I ever bought was the first Iron Maiden record, and from that moment on I became an official metalhead. Iron Maiden inspired so much of what I do. Prior to that my uncle listened to Black Sabbath, Ozzy Osbourne, AC/DC, Van Halen, Kiss, and Alice Cooper, so that was my first introduction to heavy music. But after I discovered Iron Maiden I was always looking for the heavier thing and I got into Judas Priest and Metallica. *Ride the Lightning* and *Master of Puppets* are two of my favorite albums of all time. And that led me to the thrash movement and I started listening to Anthrax, Exodus, and the German bands like Kreator, Destruction, and Sodom. But Slayer was the thrash band that really made me want to write even darker and more evil kind of music. That was the gateway from thrash to death metal for me. I had just started playing guitar at that point and I always wanted to push the limits even further and do something faster and heavier.

BRENDON SMALL

When I first started the cartoon *Metalocalypse* the idea was to take people from the heavy metal world and let them be funny. We thought, "Let's cast them as characters. Let's cast them completely against type and have them do stuff people might not expect." Somehow, I weaseled my way into the world of Metallica. I had heard that Kirk and James were interested in doing voiceover so I asked them and they said yes. And meeting James Hetfield, first of all, is a big fuckin' deal. He's the frontman of Metallica! I was nervous, but I thought, "Okay, I've got to direct this guy and make sure he feels really comfortable acting like an idiot in front of me on this microphone."

It turned out great, but he's an intimidating guy. Whether or not he wants to be, I think he just kind of walked around all day and one night he realized that he's the frontman of Metallica, the biggest metal band in the world.

The way I look at it, there are people that are totally nice dudes and have pretty down to earth lives because they're living in their skin, but outside their front door, they're viewed by fans as deities, basically. I felt like that a little bit, but I kept calm and before long that fizzles a bit because I've got James playing a troll and just screaming and bellowing into a microphone. And I had Kirk Hammett playing a nice old lady. So the ridiculousness of it all just kind of overtook the situation and we ended up having fun. But put those guys onstage and they're total rock royalty.

MATT HEAFY

We were in the dressing room getting ready to play a show and all of sudden the door opens up and it's Lars [Ulrich]. For us, having to actually get to meet these dudes that got all of us into this kind of music we make and inspired us to do what we do, it was extremely intimidating meeting him at first. But he was one of the most welcoming, humble, amazing people we've ever met in our entire life. Lars was really funny, he knew about our band and we just talked about music and had conversations as normal people. And soon after that, we met James, Kirk, and Robert and they were all just as cool to us.

MARK MORTON

Getting to know the guys in Metallica as human beings and realize that they're really good, normal dudes was kinda cool to me. It's a lesson I guess I should have already learned, but Metallica is such a huge machine. They're a giant brand. They're the biggest metal band ever. But at the core of it are four really, really genuine nice guys who love playing music and really care about their fans. They're really cool, humble guys that I had real conversations with and got to know as people. That was a good experience for me because they're people that I grew up listening to that I viewed as heroes. And to see them on a human, personal level and to learn from them and talk to them and get their insight was really special.

TREVOR STRNAD
The Black Dahlia Murder

The face in the clouds for me is Dave Mustaine. Megadeth were my first love in metal and the ones that made me want to jump off the cliff of getting into metal culture, finding other people that liked it, and totally associating myself with it. Megadeth made me realize I didn't have to go down the same path as everyone else and do sports and things like that. It was a big revelation for me.

I used to draw pictures of the guys' face. I'd painstakingly sketch Dave Mustaine. And there was a time in seventh grade that we printed [Megadeth's mascot] Vic Rattlehead on the dollar bill. And Megadeth is still my favorite band to this day.

The first day I got home from sixth grade I saw Megadeth's "Symphony of Destruction" music video and it blew my head off. I had seen Megadeth's name around and the artwork, but that moment was so huge. All I cared about from then on was getting that album and getting behind the band. It led down a whole path of figuring out my place in the universe, the path that I'm still on today.

SAM RIVERS
Limp Bizkit

I loved Megadeth when I was a kid, but the second time I saw them, Stone Temple Pilots opened up the show. They were supporting their first record [*Core*] and they blew my mind. That was when I went, "I want to do music for the rest of my life."

DAVE PETERS
Throwdown, ex-Eighteen Visions, ex-Bleeding Through

I was 12 and I was just starting to play metal when I heard Sepultura's "Dead Embryonic Cells." This drummer guy I knew played me songs off Sepultura's *Arise* record and then I went and bought the tablature book. I learned some of those and after a few months, we were starting to hack our way through "Dead Embryonic Cells" minus the solo. That and the *Chaos A.D.* record were such big musical influences on me. I saw Sepultura for the first time at the first Ozzfest before it was even a tour. They played out in San Bernardino and I got to meet Max, which was such a trip. Max, for example, was awesome. And I ended up doing a song with Soulfly. It was such a weird feeling to go from looking at this guy as someone I idolized for so long and then finding out he's just a cool, down to earth guy.

DAVID VINCENT
ex-Morbid Angel, Vltimas

I was fortunate to grow up in a household that enjoyed music. It wasn't metal but my mother listened to a lot of music. I was always drawn to music. I listened to whatever was playing whether it was radio or my mother's album collection. I was six years old and I recall my best friend who lived right behind me he was a couple years older than me and he had an older brother who was five years older than I was. I would go over to his house to listen to music and the first time I heard the Black Sabbath *Paranoid* record was very, very life-changing to me. The feeling I got from that was entirely different than the feeling I got from anything heretofore. And that probably cinched it for me to go in the direction I ended up going.

When I got a little older and I started playing music I would go back and forth between so-called heavy metal or hard rock and punk because I liked the energy of punk but they couldn't play and I liked the playing ability of the hard rock/metal musicians but they didn't have the same attitude. Meandering back and forth between the two I thought, "Boy, wouldn't it be great if these two music styles could be a little closer?" Getting people from one scene to give the other a chance was very difficult, at least in Charlotte, North Carolina. But that was always the thing I wanted with a band, the energy of one and the proficiency of the other. Some other people had the same idea and things started to creep in that direction anyway. You had Iron Maiden and Motörhead. And some of these other things were starting to bridge the gap naturally. I was into a lot of the D.C. stuff, Minor Threat, Void, Iron Cross. And there was a scene of sorts in North Carolina. Obviously, all of this stuff was bubbling underground for a period of time and many of the bands didn't have any kind of mainstream following. It was all tape trading at first. There were virtually no record labels. Cultivating my sound was just a matter of sticking to my guns and constantly searching for newer and heavier bands. And one way I did that was from going to a local record store that had imported *Kerrang!* magazine and looking for stuff that wasn't generally known stateside.

MAX CAVALERA

We were in Belo Horizonte, Brazil, so we were so far away from the metal underground and there were no good record stores for metal, but we were dying to hear this stuff. The only way to find albums was to go to Sao Paulo and go to Woodstock. We had a group of 20 friends and every weekend one of the friends got chosen and had to go to Sao Palo. Everybody would chip in a little bit of money and the guy would go to Woodstock and bring the records back. Then they would get back and we'd divide the records. One of those times was my turn and I went and that's when I first saw Venom's *Welcome to Hell* and *Black Metal.* I got Slayer's *Show No Mercy* and the *Haunting the Chapel* EP, Exodus' *Bonded by Blood* and the first Voivod record. I brought them all home. We kept *Welcome to Hell* and *Haunting the Chapel.* We put it on and *Haunting the Chapel* is in 45 RPM and we played it at 33 RPM and it was sludgy and heavy as fuck; it sounded like Venom! We fuckin' loved it. And then one of our buddies said, "Hold on, you guys are playing this wrong." And he put it on 45 and it kicked in faster than fuck. We went, "Whoa, shit. This is even better than it was." It was already good.

BEN FALGOUST
Goatwhore, ex-Soilent Green

I saw Corrosion of Conformity on the *Technocracy* tour in 1987. It was at a little VFW hall and Confessor opened the show. I had some friends that were in a band. It wasn't like seeing someone on a huge stage. They were on a little intimate place where the stage was probably put up on cinderblocks with plywood and they had a little PA. The impact of seeing a band in a place like that where everyone was having a good time was monumental to me. I thought, "I wanna be a part of this. I want to have some kind of relevance in what's going on in this kind of scene."

TONY FORESTA
Municipal Waste

I liked metal and some punk but the first time I heard Stormtroopers of Death (S.O.D.), [the crossover band featuring members of Anthrax, Nuclear Assault, and hardcore vocalist Billy Milano] it really made me want to play music like that. I was like, "Yes!! This fuckin' speaks to me." It was fast and funny but at the same time, a lot of the music was catchy. That led me to bands like early Agnostic Front, Corrosion of Conformity,

Gang Green, and D.R.I. I wasn't into super-death metal at the time. I liked being able to understand what the vocalist was saying, but I got into the death stuff, too, later.

MORGAN LANDER
Kittie

Super early on in my life, I listened to a lot of stuff my parents were listening to before I was able to develop my own interests. So way back in the day, I heard Rush, Blue Öyster Cult, Kiss, Van Halen, and other stuff they liked. That was my introduction to guitar-driven rock and also that was when I understood what a metal god was. With Van Halen, you look at David Lee Roth and Eddie Van Halen and those are larger than life people. You couldn't even imagine what they would be like in real life. I'd look at them and think, "Whoa, that's what it's like to be a star."

Then, as I got a little older I started developing my personal influences. I came of age in the '90s around the grunge era so I was really into a lot of '90s metal. We started off listening to stuff like Marilyn Manson, Helmet, Faith No More, Deftones, and some of the grunge stuff like Alice in Chains, Soundgarden, and Nirvana. It's strange because that era was not the era of the larger than life metal god. It was more about wanting to be looked at as normal dudes. Then I was introduced to Pantera and they were the first band of my era that made me think, "Wow, there are still metal gods around. It isn't just a title for the older classic bands."

When we did Ozzfest in 2000, Pantera were one of the headlining acts and that was a completely different experience altogether because all these people that you have idolized and looked up toward, they're right there and you're talking with them and drinking with them. And they're lighting off fireworks in the parking lot and you're having a great time. It totally changed my perspective on things. [Guitarist] Dimebag [Darrell] and [drummer] Vinnie [Paul] were the nicest people. They were so welcoming. They just wanted to party, have a good time, drink, and live that lifestyle. And it was really cool to be able to say I was a part of it for that short period. I got to see Pantera almost every night for two months on Ozzfest, which I'll always cherish.

GENE HOGLAN

I saw Slayer when I was 15 and they looked kind of like the Scorpions and did a bunch of covers. They were just one of the bands on the bills and I literally thought they were called Slaver because there was a flyer posted up at all the clubs. They were playing at a high school, Southgate High, and they had lots of zebra stripes, spandex, and bandanas. I remember seeing them and not even giving them a second look.

Then, on Valentine's Day of 1983, my sister and I went to see a friend's band at the Troubadour and Slayer were on the bill. It was the greatest show I had ever seen. They were wearing leather and they had a little tiny bit of eye makeup. I started going to all of their shows and they were literally drawing twenty-five to thirty people at their shows. And I loved that because all these other bands I had discovered early like Iron Maiden and Judas Priest were getting big and all these people who didn't have a clue were suddenly getting into them. I thought, "Slayer are awesome. This band is so fucking heavy that nobody is going to like them. They're going to be my band forever. I don't know if they'll even ever get out of the clubs." Metallica hadn't even released *Kill 'Em All* yet.

COREY TAYLOR

I had heard Metallica, but I came across Slayer a little later when my buddy, Chas Schmidt, who I discovered a lot of music through, played me *Reign in Blood*. We were over at his house and he put the record on. At the beginning of "Angel of Death," that riff kicks in and you're like, "Holy fuck, what is this?" And then Tom [Araya's] scream is bloodcurdling and it comes out of nowhere. I was sitting on Chas's couch while he was standing on the couch screaming the lyrics at our friend Corey Helgerson.

It was this fucking bizarre, nuts moment in my life where not only was I hearing a band that would become very, very monumental to me, but two of my friends were losing their shit and screaming the fucking lyrics, which I had never heard. It was a very bizarre moment and I was hooked from the second I heard "Angel of Death."

BRENDON SMALL

I played football in high school, believe it or not. I don't know why. I wasn't exactly a fan. One of my buddies said, "Let's play football." And I was like, "Okay, all right." I needed direction so I followed my friend. I found myself on the football field in these terrible practices.

Then, before games, we would listen to "Angel of Death" to get pumped up. "Yeah, now I can go and kill people!!" It was some of the most perfect music for going into battle. The truth is, there's a reason this shit resonates because there's no other music that does what metal does, which is to provide this weird, empowering encapsulation of rage.

And if you're a teenager, you know, you're like a crazy person. You don't even know how you feel from moment to moment. The stakes are so fucking high and you feel like a weird outcast even if you're not an outcast. And I wasn't an outcast. No one fucked with me or anything. I just felt weird and self-conscious and for some reason, metal served, and continues to serve, as this conduit for weird feelings and rage, anger, and frustration. It's really cathartic.

DALLAS TOLER-WADE
ex-Nile, Narcotic Wasteland

I started out as a drummer and then when I picked up the guitar I was kind of a rock guy and then kind of got more into thrash and speed metal and then I discovered punk music. Then, of course, I started discovering death metal and by the time I started playing in a band I was already writing songs. It just felt right and I did it my own way. Some of the discordant stuff in the music we did was just me exploring different chord positions and trying to find things that sounded different from everything else that was out there. Compositionally, one of my favorite death metal bands from back in the day was Gorguts. There was just something about the way they did their twin-guitar composition that was unique.

BEN WEINMAN
The Dillinger Escape Plan

It's kind of funny because I pretty much went straight from Mötley Crüe and Guns N' Roses to very underground extreme death metal, which are polar opposites. I had a friend whose older brother had all these CDs from underground record labels, so two of the bands I was listening to in my formative years were Obituary and Deicide. We got some death metal stuff from the CD clubs where you could order 10 CDs for $1. I gradually got into more and more underground stuff like Disharmonic Orchestra.

But I was just obsessed with Obituary and Deicide. I thought of these groups as being giant bands back then. And then the other extreme metal band I got into was Mayhem. I knew about all the murders and church burnings and everything that surrounded them and other Norwegian black metal bands so I was like, "Okay, I probably shouldn't have that one."

Mayhem and Obituary were probably the scariest things to me. Obituary could play fast, but they also played slow and they were so noisy. The vocalist sounded so evil. When he opened his mouth, he was like some monster from a deep cave. I went to see them many, many times, many, many years later. Then Dillinger Escape Plan played with Obituary at this weird festival in Finland. They put us all on a private jet to get over there because it was out in the middle of nowhere. So we ended up sharing this jet with Obituary and it totally ruined my vision of them as the spawn of Satan.

When we get to the airport, the guys in Obituary are sitting there wearing flip-flops and giggling. Their hair is in ponytails, they're talking about *Star Wars*. And one of them is wearing a Loony Tunes T-shirt. It was fucking Obituary and I was like, "Oh, no, no, no!"

BRETT CAMPBELL
Pallbearer

I heard nu-metal stuff when I was in middle school but I never got super into that. Once I started learning guitar and learning music more, as stereotypical as it may be, it was Metallica for me. My friend got me into *Ride the Lightning*. That was in the early 2000s, but my search really exploded after that. You could still buy CDs in the store. I'd spend hours at record stores trying to find elusive metal stuff that was a little weirder than mainstream stuff like Slipknot and Limp Bizkit. I found *Blackwater Park* by Opeth. I got obsessed with that.

What I liked about Metallica so much was they had these unusual classical song structures. Opeth had something similar, but they were more extreme and took it further than Metallica. Through Opeth, I discovered a lot of more extreme death metal and prog, so from the age of 16 through my early to mid-20s I spent a good portion of my time searching for every piece of weird music I could find. It was like my gateway drug into all the weirdo stuff that I later graciously sought out.

Also, early on, after I had been obsessing over thrash and death metal for a little while, my buddy gave me a burned CD that had Black Sabbath's *Master of Reality* and *Sabbath Bloody Sabbath* on it. I had never heard either of those albums. I knew songs like "Iron Man" and "Paranoid," so that was a pretty big game changer for me. I had always thought of Black Sabbath as this radio band. But *Sabbath Bloody Sabbath* has a bunch of weird stuff, "A National Acrobat" features a pretty unusual riff and I thought, "Damn, there's a lot more to this band than I ever realized." That made me interested in exploring more metal from the past.

That's when I discovered Judas Priest. People forget how early they started. They were putting out amazing stuff that was unlike anything else in the mid-'70s. Priest took Sabbath and other proto-metal stuff so much further than anyone else was doing at the time. And Rob Halford, who is like the true metal god, flying the flag for this kind of music. He calls himself that but I don't think anyone can rightfully argue that. He still rides a motorcycle onstage. That's pretty metal.

ALEX WADE
Whitechapel

I'm a huge Deftones fan. They're one of my top three bands of all time. And one time when we were on Mayhem, we were backstage walking around. I had just gotten out of the shower and was walking back to the bus. And their guitarist Stephen Carpenter, who's one of my hugest influences ever, was just standing there talking to somebody. Our drummer came up behind me and went, "Dude, is that Stephen?" We were all freakin' out like lame-ass schoolgirls. I was too much of a pussy to go up and talk to him or ask for a picture. I had seen them play, but I had never seen him in person before so it was almost like seeing a unicorn.

ACKNOWLEDGMENTS

Thanks to:

Elizabeth Kaplan, Joshua Wiederhorn, Chloe Wiederhorn, Sheldon Wiederhorn, Miriam and Hap Rust, Frank and Carole Kaplan, Gary Holt, David Dunton, Keith Wallman, Scott Waxman and the whole Diversion team, Lissa Warren, Gino DePinto, Matt Oppenheim, Hannah Wigandt, Brian Ives, Ian McFarland, Ken Micallef, Jeff Perlah, Erin Amar, and Phil Raskin. And a special thanks to the outlets in which some of the quotes in *Raising Hell* originally appeared: *Revolver, Guitar World, Metal Hammer, Penthouse,* Loudwire.com, AOL Noisecreep, *Stuff,* Obelisk.com, *Louder Than Hell: The Definitive Oral History of Metal, Ministry: The Lost Gospels According to Al Jourgensen,* and *I'm the Man: The Story of That Guy from Anthrax.*

INDEX

ABOUT JON WIEDERHORN

Jon Wiederhorn is the co-author of *Louder Than Hell: The Definitive Oral History of Metal* (with Katherine Turman) and the co-author of *My Riot: Agnostic Front, Grit, Guts & Glory* (with Roger Miret), *Ministry: The Lost Gospels According to Al Jourgensen* (with Al Jourgensen) and *I'm the Man: The Story of That Guy from Anthrax* (with Scott Ian). He has written for *Rolling Stone, SPIN,* MTV, *Guitar World, Revolver, Penthouse, Entertainment Weekly, The Village Voice,* Loudwire.com, Kerrang.com, Emusic.com, and Bandcamp Daily. He also hosts the Gimme Radio podcast *Metallography.* He lives in Montclair, New Jersey.